# THE
# CYPRUS EMERGENCY

This book is dedicated to all those members of
the Armed Forces and their families who
have served in Cyprus

To David Carter 1939–2009

*Also by Nick van der Bijl*

Pen & Sword Military Books
*Nine Battles to Stanley*
*5th Infantry Brigade in the Falklands*
*Victory in the Falklands*
*Confrontation; the War with Indonesia 1962-1966*
*Commandos in Exile; The Story of 10 (Inter-Allied) Commando 1942-45*
*Operation Banner; The British Army in Northern Ireland 1969-2007*
*The Brunei Revolt 1962-1963*
*Sharing the Secret; The History of the Intelligence Corps 1940-2010*

Osprey
*Argentine Forces in the Falklands*
*Royal Marines 1939-1993*
*No. 10 (Inter-Allied) Commando 1942-1945*

Hawk Editions
*Brean Down Fort and the Defence of the Bristol Channel*

# THE CYPRUS EMERGENCY

## The Divided Island 1955–1974

Nick van der Bijl BEM

Pen & Sword
**MILITARY**

First published in Great Britain in 2010 and reprinted in this format in 2014, 2018, 2020, 2021 and 2025 by
**Pen & Sword MILITARY**
An imprint of Pen & Sword Books Ltd
Yorkshire – Philadelphia

Copyright © Nick van der Bijl, 2010, 2014, 2018, 2020, 2021, 2025

ISBN: 978 1 78346 216 2

The right of Nick van der Bijl to be identified as the Author of this work has been asserted by in accordance with the Copyright, Designs and Patents Act 1988.

A CIP catalogue record for this book is available from the British Library

All rights reserved. No part of this book may be reproduced, transmitted, downloaded, decompiled or reverse engineered in any form or by any means, electronic or mechanical including photocopying, recording or by any information storage and retrieval system, without permission from the Publisher in writing. No part of this book may be used or reproduced in any manner for the purpose of training artificial intelligence technologies or systems.

Typeset in Palatino by S L Menzies-Earl P

Printed and bound in the UK by CPI Group (UK) Ltd, Croydon, CR0 4YY

The Publisher's authorised representative in the EU for product safety is Authorised Rep Compliance Ltd., Ground Floor, 71 Lower Baggot Street, Dublin D02 P593, Ireland.

www.arccompliance.com

For a complete list of Pen & Sword titles please contact PEN & SWORD BOOKS LIMITED 47 Church Street, Barnsley, South Yorkshire, S70 2AS, England E-mail: enquiries@pen-and-sword.co.ok • Website: www.pen-and-sword.co.uk
Or
PEN AND SWORD BOOKS
1950 Lawrence Rd, Havertown, PA 19083, USA E-mail: Uspen-and-sword@casematepublishers.com Website: www.penandswordbooks.com

# Contents

*Acknowledgements* . . . . . . . . . . . . . . . . . . . . . . . . . . . . . . . . . . . . . . . . 6
*Glossary* . . . . . . . . . . . . . . . . . . . . . . . . . . . . . . . . . . . . . . . . . . . . . . . . . 8

Chapter 1 – Historical Background . . . . . . . . . . . . . . . . . . . . . . . . . 13
Chapter 2 – The Emergence of EOKA . . . . . . . . . . . . . . . . . . . . . . . 25
Chapter 3 – Build Up of British Forces . . . . . . . . . . . . . . . . . . . . . . 40
Chapter 4 – The Outbreak of the EOKA Campaign . . . . . . . . . . 49
Chapter 5 – Cyprus in Turmoil . . . . . . . . . . . . . . . . . . . . . . . . . . . . 62
Chapter 6 – The Emergency Declared . . . . . . . . . . . . . . . . . . . . . . 75
Chapter 7 – The Long, Hot Summer . . . . . . . . . . . . . . . . . . . . . . . 91
Chapter 8 – The Suez Crisis . . . . . . . . . . . . . . . . . . . . . . . . . . . . . . 109
Chapter 9 – The Destruction of the Mountain Gangs . . . . . . . . 123
Chapter 10 – A Glimmer of Hope . . . . . . . . . . . . . . . . . . . . . . . . . 136
Chapter 11 – EOKA at Bay . . . . . . . . . . . . . . . . . . . . . . . . . . . . . . . 150
Chapter 12 – The Defeat of EOKA . . . . . . . . . . . . . . . . . . . . . . . . 168
Chapter 13 – Independence . . . . . . . . . . . . . . . . . . . . . . . . . . . . . . 177
Chapter 14 – The Turkish Intervention . . . . . . . . . . . . . . . . . . . . 195
Chapter 15 – Conclusions . . . . . . . . . . . . . . . . . . . . . . . . . . . . . . . . 211

*Bibliography* . . . . . . . . . . . . . . . . . . . . . . . . . . . . . . . . . . . . . . . . . . 216
*Index* . . . . . . . . . . . . . . . . . . . . . . . . . . . . . . . . . . . . . . . . . . . . . . . . 219

Maps
  Cyprus . . . . . . . . . . . . . . . . . . . . . . . . . . . . . . . . . . . . . . . . . . . . 10
  The Troodos Mountains . . . . . . . . . . . . . . . . . . . . . . . . . . . . . 11
  1974 – The Turkish Invasion. . . . . . . . . . . . . . . . . . . . . . . . . . 12
  Nicosia Airport . . . . . . . . . . . . . . . . . . . . . . . . . . . . . . . . . . . 204

# Acknowledgements

On 20 July 1974, Cyprus was an island with a single government. Three weeks later, it had been divided into two. This books sets out to tell the story of how this tranquil and idyllic island in the Eastern Mediterranean was torn apart by a nationalist rebellion and then suffered sixteen years of uncertainty and instability until Turkish intervention in 1974 led to it being split into two republics. Few tourists know why or that 371 British Armed Forces died during the Cyprus Emergency between 1955 and 1959, most of them National Servicemen aged twenty-one years and under, and now buried in a military cemetery that international politics makes largely inaccessible.

I am beholden to Pen & Sword Books, who for the third time have given me the opportunity to tell some of the story of one of the United Kingdom's forgotten post-1945 campaigns. I am indebted to several people who helped me with information: to Captain Tony Dunn and Commodore Michael Clapp for supplying me with detailed accounts of the seizure of the caique Ayois Georghias in Janaury 1955; to the former journalist and BBC producer, the late David Carter, who passed away almost on the day that I finished this project. He permitted me to use his research and the accounts of the campaign that he has collected which he posted on the Cyprus segment on the www.britains-smallwars website. I must also thank those contributors. This unfettered and invaluable website allows Service veterans and dependants to lodge their recollections and reminiscences for historians and researchers. Robert D Egby, who worked for British Forces Broadcasting in Egypt and Cyprus in the 1950s before becoming an award-winning news photographer, very kindly donated his collection of *Cyprus News* photos. I should also like to thank the librarians of Bridgwater Library in Somerset who patiently tracked down some obscure books and pamphlets.

I must thank two stalwarts who have helped me in the past. Peter Wood, of GWR Ltd and a former Royal Engineer surveyor and cartographer, created the maps for this book. The former Royal Navy John Noble compiled the index. He sailed home from Malta on a troopship with the 2 Royal Inniskilling Fusiliers after their tour in Cyprus in 1955 and remembers the soldiers playing endless card games

# ACKNOWLEDGEMENTS

on the decks. Brigadier Henry Wilson, Commissioning Editor, Pen & Sword Books, was again invaluable in championing this project.

My wife, Penny, has again been invaluable in proofreading and asking searching and awkward questions about the draft, as was a former colleague, Roy Millard, who used his considerable experience in proofreading to ferret out inconsistencies. I must also thank George Chamier for his patient and meticulous editing of this book.

Nick van der Bijl<br>
Somerset

# Glossary

| | |
|---|---|
| AGRA | Artillery Group, Royal Artillery |
| AKEL | *Anorthotkon Komma Ergazomenou Laou*: Reform Party of the Working People |
| APC | Armoured Personnel Carriers |
| CIA | US Central Intelligence Agency |
| CIGS | Chief of the Imperial General Staff |
| DLI | The Durham Light Infantry |
| ESBA | Eastern Sovereign Base Area |
| ELAS | *Ethnikos Laikos Apeleltherotikas Stratos*: People's National Liberation Army |
| ELDYK | *Elleniki Dynami Kyprou* – Hellenic Forces Regiment Contingent in Cyprus |
| EOKA | *Ethniki Organosis Kyprion Agoniston:* the National Organization of Cypriot Fighters |
| GHQ | General Headquarters |
| GOC | General Officer Commanding |
| HF | High Frequency |
| HMC | Higher Military Command |
| HMT | Her Majesty's Troopship |
| HQ | Headquarters |
| KEM | *Kypriakon Enotikon Metapon:* Cyprus Enosis Front |
| KOYLI | King's Own Yorkshire Light Infantry |
| LAC | Leading Aircraftsman |
| MILPOL | Military/Police committees |
| MV | Motor Vessel |
| OHEN | *Orthodoxos Chistianiki Enosis Neon*: Orthodox Christian Union of Youth |
| PEK | *Panagrotiki Enosis Kypro*: Panagrarian Union of Cyprus |

# GLOSSARY

| | |
|---|---|
| RAF | Royal Air Force |
| RAOC | Royal Army Ordnance Corps |
| RAPC | Royal Army Pay Corps |
| RASC | Royal Army Service Corps |
| REME | Royal Electrical and Mechanical Engineers |
| RFU | Raiding Force Unit |
| RGJ | Royal Green Jackets |
| RMP | Royal Military Police |
| RAOC | Royal Army Ordnance Corps |
| RUC | Royal Ulster Constabulary |
| RWF | Royal Welch Fusiliers |
| RWK | The Queen's Own Royal West Kent Regiment |
| | |
| SAC | Senior Aircraftsman |
| SBA | Sovereign Base Area |
| SIS | British Security Intelligence Service also known as MI 6 (Military Intelligence Department 6). |
| SLR | 7.62mm Self Loading Rifle |
| SOE | Specialist Operations Executive |
| | |
| TMT | *Turk Mukavemet Teshkilati*: Turkish Resistance Organization |
| | |
| UK | United Kingdom |
| UN | United Nations |
| UNFICYP | United Nations Force in Cyprus |
| US | United States |
| | |
| VHF | Very High Frequency |
| | |
| WRAC | Women's Royal Army Corps |
| WSBA | Western Sovereign Base Area |

# MAP 1 - CYPRUS

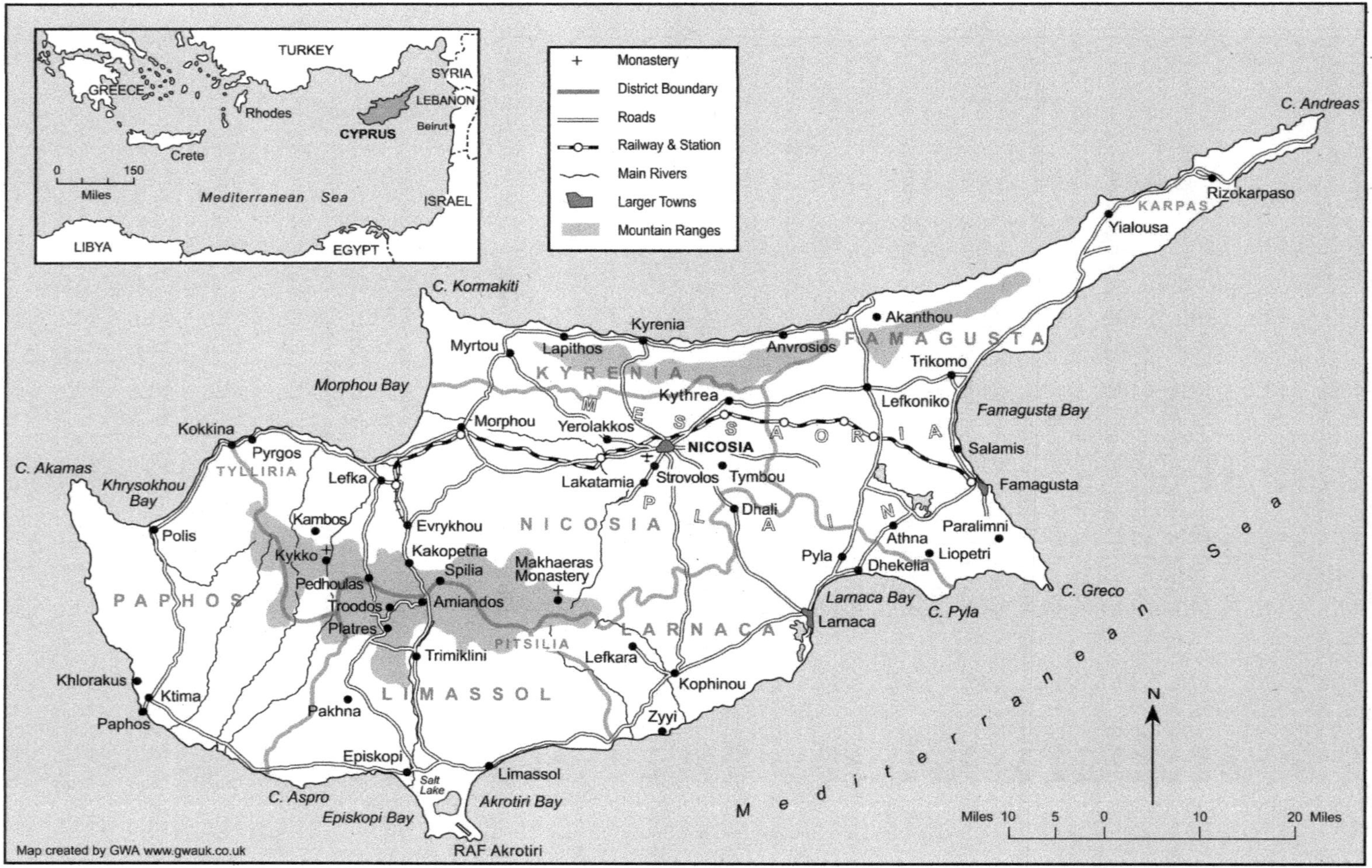

TURKEY
SYRIA
GREECE
LEBANON
Rhodes
CYPRUS
Beirut
Crete
0
150
Miles
Mediterranean Sea
ISRAEL
LIBYA
EGYPT
Monastery
District Boundary
Roads
Railway & Station
Main Rivers
Larger Towns
Mountain Ranges
C. Andreas
Rizokarpaso
KARPAS
Yialousa
C. Kormakiti
Akanthou
Kyrenia
Myrtou
Lapithos
Anvrosios
FAMAGUSTA
Trikomo
KYRENIA
Morphou Bay
Kythrea
Lefkoniko
Famagusta Bay
MESAORIA
Morphou
Yerolakkos
Kokkina
NICOSIA
Salamis
Pyrgos
C. Akamas
TYLLIRIA
Lefka
Lakatamia
Strovolos
Tymbou
Famagusta
Khrysokhou Bay
Dhali
Kambos
Evrykhou
NICOSIA
PLAIN
Paralimni
Polis
Athna
Kykko
Kakopetria
Liopetri
Spilia
Makhaeras Monastery
Pyla
Dhekelia
Pedhoulas
PAPHOS
Amiandos
Larnaca Bay
C. Greco
Troodos
C. Pyla
LARNACA
Larnaca
Platres
PITSILIA
Lefkara
Trimiklini
Khlorakus
Kophinou
LIMASSOL
Ktima
Pakhna
Paphos
Zyyi
Episkopi
Limassol
Salt Lake
C. Aspro
Akrotiri Bay
Episkopi Bay
Mediterranean Sea
N
Miles 10
5
0
10
20 Miles
RAF Akrotiri
Map created by GWA www.gwauk.co.uk

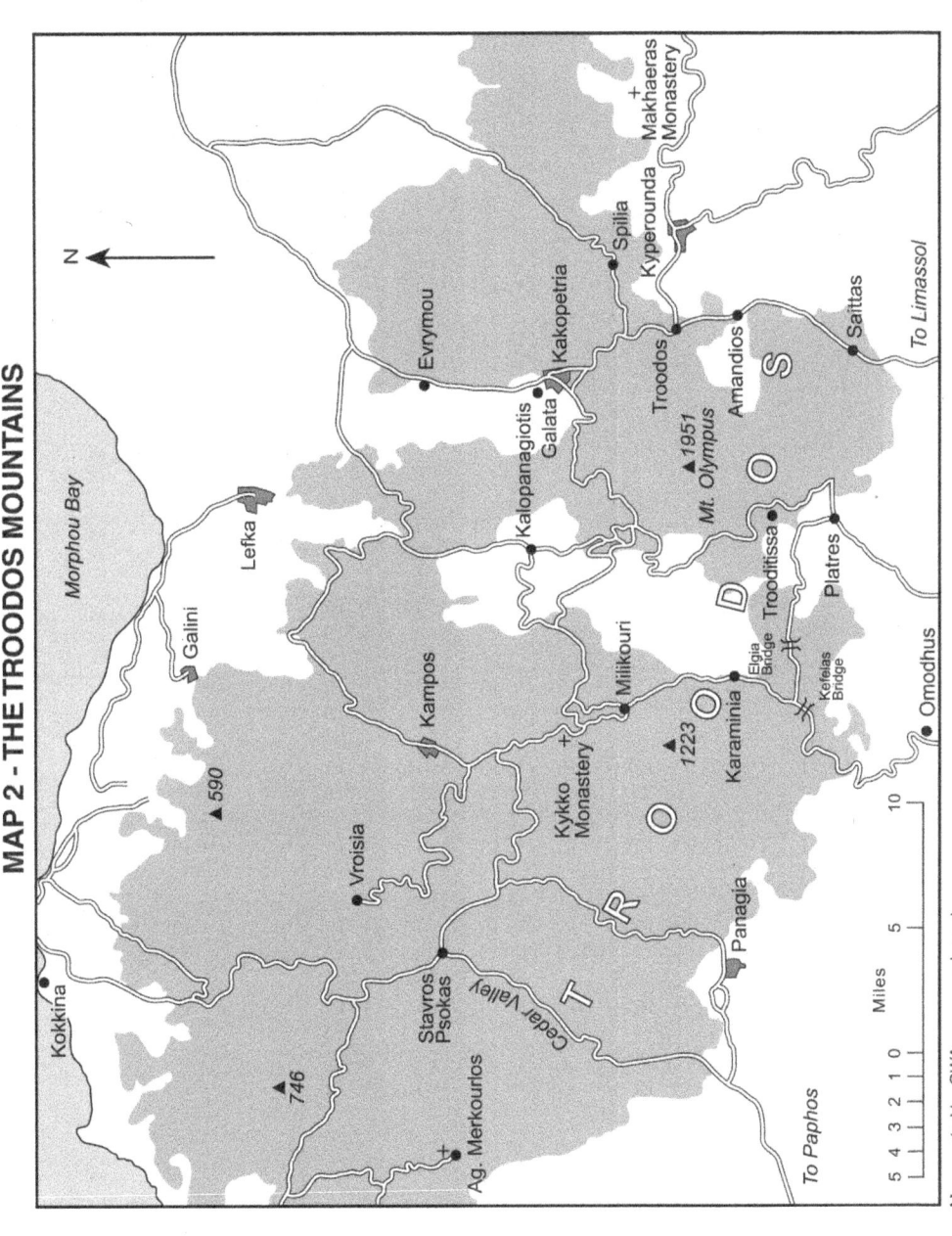

## MAP 3 - CYPRUS 1974: THE TURKISH INVASION

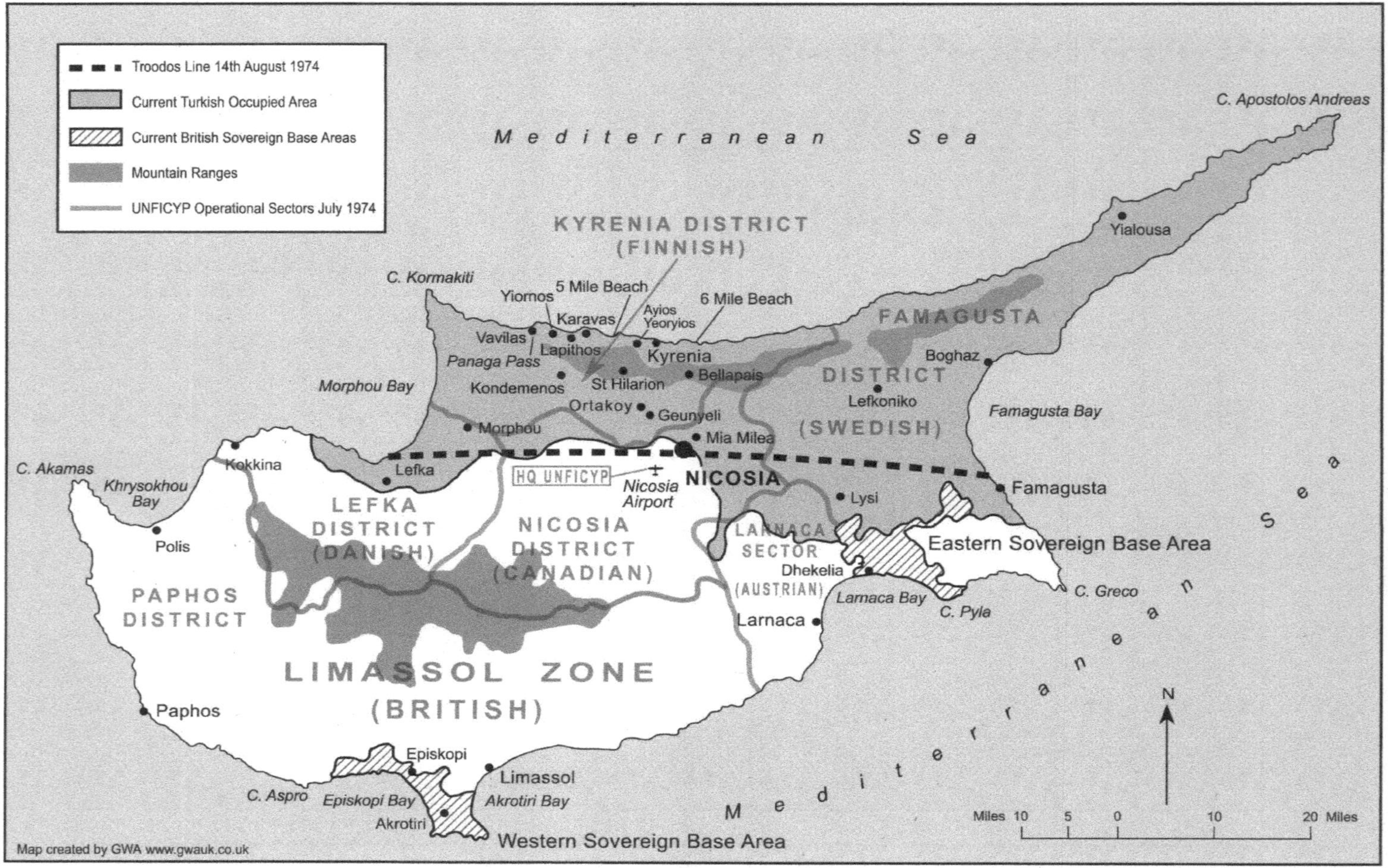

**Legend:**
- ---- Troodos Line 14th August 1974
- Current Turkish Occupied Area
- Current British Sovereign Base Areas
- Mountain Ranges
- UNFICYP Operational Sectors July 1974

**Locations and Features:**

- C. Apostolos Andreas
- Yialousa
- FAMAGUSTA DISTRICT (SWEDISH)
- Boghaz
- Lefkoniko
- Famagusta Bay
- Famagusta
- C. Greco
- Eastern Sovereign Base Area
- C. Pyle
- Lysi
- Larnaca Bay
- LARNACA SECTOR (AUSTRIAN)
- Dhekelia
- Larnaca
- KYRENIA DISTRICT (FINNISH)
- 6 Mile Beach
- Bellapais
- Kyrenia
- Ayios Yeoryios
- St Hilarion
- Ortakoy
- Geunyeli
- Mia Milea
- NICOSIA
- Nicosia Airport
- HQ UNFICYP
- NICOSIA DISTRICT (CANADIAN)
- C. Kormakiti
- Yiornos
- Karavas
- 5 Mile Beach
- Vavilas
- Lapithos
- Panaga Pass
- Kondemenos
- Morphou
- Morphou Bay
- Lefka
- LEFKA DISTRICT (DANISH)
- Kokkina
- LIMASSOL ZONE (BRITISH)
- Episkopi
- Episkopi Bay
- Akrotiri
- Limassol
- Akrotiri Bay
- Western Sovereign Base Area
- C. Aspro
- PAPHOS DISTRICT
- Paphos
- Polis
- Khrysokhou Bay
- C. Akamas
- Mediterranean Sea

Scale: 0, 5, 10, 20 Miles

Map created by GWA www.gwauk.co.uk

CHAPTER ONE

# Historical Background

*I have seen old ships sail like swans asleep*
*Beyond the village which men still call Tyre,*
*With leaden age o'ercargoes, dipping deep*
*For Famagusta and the hidden sun*
*That rings black Cyprus with a lake of fire*

So wrote the English poet James Flecker, a minor diplomat in Turkey and Lebanon who wrote the poem *Old Ships* a few months before he died in 1915. Lying sixty-three miles west of Lebanon in the Eastern basin of the Mediterranean Sea is a beautiful island that claims to be the mythical birthplace of the Greek goddess Aphrodite. Opinions about the origins of its name range from the Greek descriptions of the Mediterranean cypress tree (*Cupressus sempervirens*) to the Greek for copper – *kypros*.

Measuring 140 miles east to west, sixty miles north to south and covering 3,584 square miles, Cyprus is smaller than Sicily and Sardinia to the west. Fifty miles to the north is Turkey, 500 miles to the west is Greece, sixty-four miles to the east is Syria and 320 miles to the south is Egypt where, in 1954, the British had 10,000 troops managing growing nationalist unrest, particularly around the Suez Canal. Dominating the island are the Troodos Mountains with, in the centre, Mount Olympus at 6,400 feet, draped with conifers, cedar, cypress and the tall shrubs of strawberry trees and surrounded by rugged lava, rich in copper, and slopes of scrub. Its peaks overlook the fertile Messaoria central plain that blows hot in summer and cold in winter, stretching from Morphou Bay east to Famagusta Bay. To the north of the brooding mountain are the lower Pentadactylos Mountains stretching 140 miles from Lapithos to the western fringes of the panhandle-shaped Karpas Peninsula. This high ground is also known as the Kyrenia Range. Dotted among the churches and minarets of the towns and villages and their surrounding fields, orchards, vineyards and groves are derelict Crusader castles. The climate in summer is hot and dry but it is chilly and wet between November and March. The summer's light to moderate breezes are ideal for sailing. Winter storms are spectacular. Variable autumn and winter rainfall flowing from the mountains through a series of dams is held in reservoirs. Deep winter snow on the upper slopes of the Troodos provides the challenge of ski-ing in the morning and water ski-ing off a southern beach in the afternoon.

The earliest human activity is thought to be that of hunter-gathers at Aetokremos on the southern coast from about BC 10,000. Scattered communities developing from about BC 1,800 traded copper with Greek and Mycenaean merchants. Several Phoenician colonies were founded in the eighth century BC near Larnaca and Salamis. Cyprus suffered several conquests, including by Assyria in BC 709 and Persia in BC 545. In BC 499 the Cypriots joined Greek cities rebelling against the Persian Empire and were brought under Macedonian governorship by Alexander the Great and his successors based in Egypt. During this period, Greek art and literature flourished. Annexed by Rome in BC 58, Cyprus figured in St Paul's missionary journey to Rome in 45 AD. Since the island was in the Byzantine region of the Roman Empire, it escaped the savage overthrow of the Western region by the hordes from the East. In 395 the island was absorbed into the benign Byzantine Empire until it was lost to Arabs in 643 and then reclaimed in 966. During the Third Crusade, Richard the Lionheart of England seized the island in 1191 and used it as a base safe from Saracen intervention. The imposing Kolossi Castle near Limassol had significant strategic importance. After the easy-going Cypriots had rebelled against stringent English Catholicism, Richard sold Cyprus to the deposed French Lusignan dynasty until the last in line sold it to the Venetian Republic. The Venetians converted Cyprus into an important commercial hub and fortified Nicosia with impressive walls against Ottoman raids from the north. In 1539, the sacking of Limassol by the Ottomans led to the Venetians fortifying Famagusta and Kyrenia; however, spirited Venetian and Cypriot resistance in Nicosia and Famagusta collapsed in the face of overwhelming odds in 1570. Although the conquerors encouraged emigration from Turkey and permitted the Orthodox Church to act as mediators in the administration of the island and encouraged community religious, political and economic participation, heavy taxation led to twenty-eight risings between 1572 and 1668. The first census of the Ottoman Empire in 1831 showed Cyprus to have 14,900 Muslim men looking toward Turkey and its Asian culture and 29,200 Christian men looking to Greece and its Orthodox Church. By 1872, the population had risen to 44,000 Muslims and 100,000 Christians.

Four years later, resistance to the Turkish occupation of southern Central Europe broke out in the Balkans. When, a year later, Russia attacked Turkey and reached the gates of the former capital of the Holy Roman Empire, Constantinople, Western European sympathy, remembering the enmity with Russia during the Crimean War in the mid-1850s, swung in favour of the plucky Turks. As the British music hall song went, 'We don't want to fight, but by jingo if we do, we've got the ships, we've got the men, we've got the money too!' After the Turks, in the Treaty of Stefano, handed Russia control of the Balkans, the Great Powers, including Great Britain, at the 1878 Congress of Berlin undermined the agreement. However, Turkey had secretly ceded the administration of Cyprus, but not its sovereignty, to Great Britain in return for guaranteeing its territorial integrity, in particular its vulnerable southern coast. Early Greek-Cypriot resentment of the agreement was embodied in the annual Turkish Tribute paid by Cyprus. Widely regarded as a gem by Imperial Britain, the island had a romance that attracted the Victorians – Greek mythology, the Romans, Richard the Lionheart and a climate and scenery that matched its history. The more practical Foreign Secretary Lord Salisbury saw Cyprus as a strategic military base guarding the route to India through the Suez Canal and a protector of British interests in the Near East. But as Cyprus developed, the Greek-Cypriot majority yearned for union with Greece – *enosis*. The origins of *enosis* are rooted in the concept of Hellenism in which the Greeks were conditioned by their priests and teachers to believe that all Greek-speaking peoples should live within the frontiers of the Motherland. This included the communities in Cyprus and Anatolia in Turkey. Thus when General Sir Garnet Wolseley, the first British High Commissioner, arrived at Limassol in 1882 with an infantry brigade, he was greeted by the Bishop of Kitium with, 'We accept the change in government inasmuch as we trust that Great Britain will help Cyprus, as it did in the Ionian islands to be united with Mother Greece, with which it is nationally connected'. The Bishop was referring to British support of the Greeks when they rebelled against the Turks in 1821. The Bishopric of Kitium became well known for its militancy and the Bishops' plea became a regular welcome to new High Commissioners.

Cyprus slid into decline when the British garrisoned the Suez Canal and Alexandria in Egypt became an important Mediterranean base alongside Malta and Gibraltar. When Turkey allied itself with Germany in 1914, Great Britain annexed Cyprus and next year offered the island to Greece if she would help Serbia fight Turkey and her Central European allies; however, Athens rejected the offer until 1917. Inexperience in amphibious warfare and the presence of the Royal Navy had deterred Turkey from invading. By 1918, Great Britain realized

Cyprus was of some strategic value and quietly forgot its wartime offer to Greece. In 1920, Turkey and the Allies signed the Treaty of Sèvres by which Turkey agreed to return several islands in the Aegean Sea and the port of Smyrna in Anatolia to Greece. But the Treaty was widely resented in Turkey and when hostilities broke out in 1921 Turkey inflicted a massive defeat on Greece in Smyrna. Great Britain offered Cyprus as a sanctuary to the indigenous Greeks in Anatolia fleeing Turkish reprisals. Hostile and resentful against Turkey, the refugees swelled the Greek-Cypriot population at odds with the authorities over the Turkish Tribute and raised support for militant bishops demanding *enosis* and encouraging non-participation in the administration of Cyprus. Under the Treaty of Lausanne, Turkey surrendered her claim to Cyprus and two years later the island became a British Crown Colony with a colonial administration overseen by a Governor. Although the hated Turkish Tribute ceased in 1927, four years later the combination of its legacy and the global depression led to the pro-Greek Governor Sir Ronald Storrs presenting a stringent budget to the Legislative Council. This led to the representatives walking out and serious civil disturbances fanning out throughout Cyprus. Government House was burnt and for the first time British troops enforced internal security by patrolling the streets and helping the Cyprus Police to round up 2,000 Cypriots, some of whom were deported to Greece. They included the Bishop of Kitium, seven bishops and others who formed the hard core of the drive for *enosis*. A consequence of the deportations was continual ideological clashes between the colonial authorities and the Ethnarchy. The Ethnarchy was essentially the council who represented the people and since it was Greek-Cypriot, this meant the majority. It was led by the Archbishop of Cyprus, who was known as the Ethnarch. Safe from German invasion because of the distance from Occupied Greece and undisturbed by the neutrality of Turkey, the Second World War brought prosperity. Cypriot mule transport companies supported the 8th Army in Italy and the Cyprus Regiment defended the island. Many other Cypriots served as individuals in the Armed Forces or with the Greeks. Political parties were permitted, with the communist AKEL *(Anorthotkon Komma Ergazomenou Laou*: Reform Party of the Working People) and right wing pro-*enosis* KEM *(Kypriakon Enotikon Metapon*: Cyprus Enosis Front) following political opinion in Greece.

Meanwhile, in Occupied Athens, two former secondary school pupils of the Nicosia Pan Cyprian Secondary Gymnasium, Michael Mouskos and George Grivas met in 1942. They had similar views on the future of Cyprus and *enosis*. Michael Christodoulou Mouskos was born in 1913 in Panayia in Paphos District to a farmer and a mother who died soon after his birth. Educated first at Kykko Monastery, his father supported his secondary education in Nicosia Secondary Gymnasium, which was then staffed by teachers preaching Hellenism. In 1936 Michael won a place at Athens University to read theology and law but was trapped in 1941 by the German invasion.

George Theodhorous Grivas was one of six children born to a devout, wealthy Greek-Cypriot cereal merchant living in Trikomo, a town that overlooks Famagusta Bay. At school, he had been fascinated by Digenes Akritas, the half-mythical defender of Alexander the Great's eastern empire. Near the family home was a huge rock said to have been thrown by Digenes. Although his father wanted him to be a doctor, in 1916 Grivas won a place at the elite Military Academy in Athens and met Cypriot students agitating for *enosis*. In 1919 he was posted to Asia Minor where, while mopping up Turkish guerrillas, he was particularly impressed by a band equipped with rifles holding up his division for a day, but was wounded when the Greeks were driven from Smyrna. In 1929, while visiting his widowed mother, Grivas noted the undercurrent stirring for *enosis*. Captain Grivas then attended the French Staff College where an instructor was Captain Arthur Wintle, an eccentric British officer of the Royal Dragoons with an inclination for unorthodox warfare. After joining the French 8th Infantry Division for an advanced staff course, he returned to Greece. When Italy attacked Greece in October 1940, Lieutenant Colonel Grivas trekked and rode a mule through deep winter snow and joined the 2nd (Athens) Division in the mountains, as a senior Operations Officer, as it drove the invading Italians back into Albania. Noted for his meticulous staff work, he regularly visited the front line. In April 1941 Germany invaded Greece, and as the Allies fell back the 2nd Division fought hard against the Italians advancing from Albania. When Greece surrendered, Grivas escaped into the mountains for several weeks before returning to Athens and a ruthless German occupation. Living in the affluent suburb of Thyssion nestling below the Acropolis, he spent the next two years reeling from the humiliating interruption to his career. Watching Greek resistance, he noted that only the Communist Party was well organized and that its military wing, ELAS (*Ethnikos Laikos Apeleltherotikas Stratos*: People's National Liberation Army), was being supported by Allied officers. Grivas had maintained his links with Greek Army officers but when this led to an arrest warrant being issued in March 1943, he went underground and formed a resistance group from 2nd Division officers living in Athens and named it 'Xhi' – symbolizing 'The Unknown'. Generally shortened to X, noticeably right-wing and equipped with a few weapons acquired from the Italians after Italy had surrendered to the Allies, the quality of its resistance is debatable. Running X from Thyssion, Grivas regularly moved between safe houses. Highlighting the Allied support given to ELAS, Grivas accused the British of starving loyalist resistance groups of arms and failing to appreciate that ELAS was preparing to govern Greece after liberation. Refusing an offer by Allied officers to affiliate X with ELAS, he claimed that he was gathering intelligence for General Headquarters, Middle East in Cairo. When Cairo rejected his proposal to prepare a beachhead in the Peloponnese to facilitate a landing, he became embittered towards the British; nevertheless, he joined ten nationalist groups assembled by a New Zealand Special Operations Executive captain to assist in liberation. The exiled Greek Government then rejected his offer to protect Athens from a communist takeover; true to form, this embittered Grivas against Greek politicians. Meanwhile, skirmishes had broken between the loyalists and communists, and when he led men to receive a consignment of weapons, Grivas became embroiled in a stiff battle with communists. When several officers he sent into the mountains were murdered, his hatred turned on the Communist Party.

In preparation for an ELAS coup after liberation, Grivas divided Athens into fifteen sectors and organized X into cells of about twenty men. But when the Germans began withdrawing from the city on 8 October 1944, X was too weak to compete with the communists and vicious fighting broke out in Thyssion. Grivas was lucky to survive an ambush. A week later the British III Corps landed in the Peloponnese and, accompanied by the Greek Mountain Brigade, liberated Athens. Two days later, the Greek provisional government of national unity arrived. Although the British placed ELAS under its military control, the Mountain Brigade demanded that it be disarmed; this would have left the communists at the mercy of the Royalists and right-wingers. ELAS agreed to disarm if the Brigade was removed from the city. Matters deteriorated on 2 October when the provisional government banned a communist demonstration planned for the next day to be followed by a general strike. But next morning, police opened fire on a large crowd, killing twenty-five people and wounding about 150. Gun battles and fierce hand-to-hand fighting broke out in the narrow streets as rival factions settled scores incurred during the Occupation. The British, largely confined to the city centre, were not entirely successful in negotiating truces; nevertheless British infantry and a tank troop rescued Grivas and several X fighters on 3 December after they had enthusiastically joined in the fighting and then faced near annihilation when ELAS attacked Thyssion. When Prime Minister Winston Churchill ordered that Athens be treated 'as a captured city where a local rebellion is in progress', British troops, supported by aircraft, cleared the suburbs of extremists. Ironically, the city which had not been bombed during the war because of its ancient treasures came under fire from those who liberated it. By 6 January 1945, ELAS had been driven into the countryside, where they were hunted down in the so-called White Terror. Faced by a government determined to impose its authority, Grivas disbanded X but renegades joined in the Terror and promoted its presence by daubing the letter X on buildings. Once seen as a future commander-in-chief, his association with the extreme right led to Lieutenant Colonel Grivas being placed on the Greek Army Reserve list with a small pension in March 1945. He was still living in Thyssion, when two events then shaped his future.

The first occurred after Grivas had unsuccessfully dabbled in right-wing politics and had then learnt from his dentist brother in Nicosia, Michael, that a prominent Cypriot contemporary was promoting communism through AKEL. Knowing that the United Nations (UN) was insisting on decolonization and believing that the British would procrastinate in leaving Cyprus and that when they did AKEL would step into the void, for the next five years he studied the methods used by the Communist Party and ELAS to convert Greece into a communist state. He probably did not realize that he was one of several insurgency leaders promoting guerrilla warfare to overthrow colonial governments. In Indonesia, Colonel Nasution was developing strategies to drive the Dutch from the Dutch East Indies, which he would use in the Confrontation with Malaysia between 1962 and 1966; and Ho Chi Minh had begun his ultimately successful campaign to convert French Indo-China (Vietnam) into a communist state.

After the liberation of Athens, Michael Mouskos studied at Boston University in Massachusetts until in 1948, while still in the US and now an active supporter of *enosis*, he was elected Bishop of Kitium and adopted the title Makarios III. He had met several Cypriots living in Occupied Greece intent on *enosis*, with one faction favouring passive resistance and the other military action. These contacts included the Cypriot brothers, Savvas and Socrates Loizides, both lawyers, who had been exiled in 1931. Socrates had been a Greek Army officer, as was another Cypriot, Notis Petropouleas. Makarios had known about X during the German occupation and when in 1949 he invited Grivas to present his ideas to the exiles and then launched the Greek-Cypriot drive for *enosis*. In January 1950 the Turkish-Cypriot minority boycotted a referendum on *enosis* organized by the Cyprus Orthodox Church that was conducted only among Greek speakers. It was hardly surprising that with the Greek-Cypriots making up eighty-seven per cent of the population, 95.7 per cent of them agreed. Later in the year, Makarios was appointed Archbishop of Cyprus, the Ethnarch, and, now the political and spiritual leader of the Greek-Cypriots, he declared, 'We want *enosis*. We shall carry on the struggle uncompromisingly.' Although he had taken up Greek citizenship when he was seventeen years old and was regarded as a security risk by the British, in July Grivas obtained a visa to visit Cyprus. Accompanied by his wife, he spent a month in Cyprus carrying out his first recce and although he concluded that Cyprus as an island was unsuitable for armed resistance, he sensed the commitment to *enosis* was strong. Although good roads linked Nicosia to the main towns, passed through the Troodos and Pentadactylos Mountains and threaded across the Messaoria plain to Famagusta Bay and the Panhandle, guerrillas could dominate the mountains with ambushes and mines. He recognized that the nature of Cyprus as an island meant that a naval and air blockade would restrict the delivery of arms and war stores. Although he believed that a considerable disadvantage was the characteristics of the Cypriots as a tranquil people inexperienced in war, in August he briefed an unconvinced Makarios that a campaign could be fought on two fronts – rural guerrillas and urban and village saboteurs. Returning to Athens, Grivas established a revolutionary committee under the reluctant chairmanship of Makarios.

When Athens suggested in 1951 that if Cyprus became part of the Hellenic Motherland, the British would be given land for military bases, London rejected the offer, in spite of the UN's promotion of self-determination. Many Greeks hoped that since their country had sided with the Allies, they would be rewarded with Cyprus. Although the Greek Government believed it could provide a base on the island, and even though Cyprus was not critical to NATO, London and Washington agreed that the island could not be allowed to pass into the hands of an unstable government still recovering from occupation. The rejection of the UN proposal led to a deterioration of relations between London and Athens.

In June 1952 Grivas returned to Cyprus but Makarios refused to meet him and told him to return to Greece until further notice. Impatient, Grivas turned to Archbishop Spyridon of Athens, who was junior to Makarios, in the Eastern Orthodox Church, and he overruled the instructions of Makarios. Spyridon had formed a Cyprus support group in Athens. For the first time a Greek politician had bypassed Makarios. Again obtaining a visa as Nicos Petrou, an electrician aged fifty-seven with a Limassol address, Grivas returned to Cyprus in October and spent the next five months drawing up a strategy to liberate Cyprus from the British using a combination of guerrilla forces and urban

## HISTORICAL BACKGROUND

sabotage groups. He carried out a very detailed recce ambush sites, identifying bases in the mountains and developing a network of contacts. A sandy bay with good exits from the beach near Khlorakas, a few miles north-west of Paphos, was ideal for smuggling. The village strongly supported the nationalist Pan Agrarian Union of Cyprus (*Panagrotiki Enosis Kyrpou or PEK*). The Azinas family lived in the village, including Andreas, a Reading University graduate and now the PEK General Secretary, who had met Grivas in Nicosia. The area west of the village and north to Polis was sparsely populated and not far from the sombre, lonely Kykko Monastery in the Troodos Mountains. A caique loaded with pottery made a trial run, and although investigated by a Cyprus Police patrol, its significance and the personalities on the beach were missed because of Special Branch's oversight. Originally from the Turkish *kaik* to describe a light boat propelled by one or two oars used primarily in the Bosporus and as the Sultan's ceremonial barge, the term also applied to small schooners with lateen rigs used for Levantine island trade. Grivas also met with the militant Bishop of Kitium.

In spite of the diplomatic and political manoeuvres surrounding the future of Cyprus on the island and in Greece, the Cyprus Police were complacent, demoralized and poorly led by the long serving Commissioner of Police Ashmore from the Central Police Station in Nicosia. Armed and paramilitary by nature, the force had lost the confidence of the community to such an extent that information was difficult to acquire during investigations, and the intimidation of witnesses with threats and bribes was rife. Some isolated village police stations lacked telephones. The consequence was that in some areas anarchy prevailed, the authorities were dissuaded from investigating and vendettas were common. While the Commissioner and several senior officers were drawn from the Colonial Police, the quality of the local police officers meant that there was little incentive for anyone with decent qualifications to enlist. A labourer could earn twice the pay of a constable. This meant that Turkish-Cypriots, whose educational opportunities were fewer than the Greek-Cypriots and were demographically in the minority, made up just thirty-seven per cent of the force.

Grivas and Makarios believed that youth was fundamental to the campaign. During the visit, Grivas helped establish the militant PEON (*Pankyprios Ethniki Organosis Neolaias*: Pancyprian Youth Organisation) by forming clubs governed by secret rules that appealed to youthful fantasies. Priests and teachers contributed by indoctrinating the young with anti-British and anti-communist propaganda and then sent them on tasks, such as daubing *enosis* slogans on the walls of public buildings. During the Coronation celebrations of Queen Elizabeth II in 1953, the first stirrings of the violence that would rip Cyprus apart emerged when PEON was banned after instigating several riots. Makarios retaliated by forming OHEN (*Orthodoxos Chistianiki Enosis Neon:* Orthodox Christian Union of Youth) and placed it under the control of Papa Stavros Aganthangeolou, a militant priest in Nicosia closely allied to Makarios and also the equally fanatical Bishop Kyprianos Kyriakides of Kyrenia. When Grivas returned to Greece, he had become something of an expert on Cyprus but was quietly sidelined by the Greek Government and threatened with arrest if he continued with his plans. However, he ignored the threat and began talent-spotting Cypriots supportive of *enosis*. But his subversive activities reached inquisitive ears in the British Embassy, in particular those of MI 6, who, with the Central Intelligence Agency (CIA), had recruited senior members of the Greek administration and Greek Army officers on to their payrolls.

For several years, Athens had been reluctant to support *enosis*, however when political heavyweight, Field Marshal Alexandros Papagos, was elected Prime Minister in 1952 and undertook to keep Cyprus on the UN agenda, Makarios felt more confident of success. By 1954, the plans were well advanced. On 2 March with the help of the Greek Navy, the first shipment of mostly X Group weapons – three Brens and two Italian light machine guns, four Thompsons, seventeen Stens, forty-seven assorted rifles, seven pistols, 32,000 rounds of ammunition, 290 grenades and 20lbs of explosive and fuses – were loaded on the caique *Ayios Nikolaos* in Attica and safely delivered to Andreas Azinas, who concealed the consignment in caches in fields around Khlorakas.

The second event that inspired Grivas was the overthrow in Egypt of King Farouk by the nationalist Free Officers movement, which included Colonel Gamal Nasser and the subsequent announcement by Field Marshal Sir John Harding, then Chief of the Imperial General Staff (CIGS), that under the terms of the 1936 Anglo-Egyptian Treaty, British troops would leave Egypt by 1956, quicker than expected, and that HQ Middle East Command and HQ Middle East Air Force would jointly deploy to Cyprus as the Middle East Defence Organization. Much to the irritation of Athens and the Greek-Cypriots, because the announcement was made in spite of the drive for *enosis* and intelligence suggesting a resurgent AKEL, the tranquil island had suddenly become strategically important to the British because it became a pivot of its foreign policy of maintaining a strong garrison in the Near East to guard passage through the Suez Canal to the Middle East and Far East.

Fours years after the end of the Second World War, General Headquarters, Middle East Land Forces decided to install a permanent garrison in Cyprus. Largely constrained by the only convenient port facilities being at Famagusta, a War Office planning team selected a windy plateau in St George's Cantonment, four miles west of the town for the administration units. This became known as Four Mile Point. A second site, one of several camps that had housed Jewish refugees struggling to reach Israel between 1945 and 1947, was selected as a barracks, using stocks of prefabricated material from Egypt. It would take until 1959 to complete and would contain a barracks, a military hospital, space for two major units, married quarters, schools and extensive sporting facilities with a dramatic view over Larnaca Bay. The Cyprus Government wanted to develop land west of Limassol and agreed to the development of Akrotiri Peninsula for an airfield and a site near Episkopi for a second barracks, this one selected to be the new GHQ. The buildings would be constructed from precast concrete blocks. In 1953, 30 Squadron, 35 Engineer Regiment arrived from Maidstone to supervise the army of local contractors. One of their first tasks was to build an eighteen-mile gravity-fed water pipe from the village of Kissousa at 1,800 feet in the Troodos Mountains across broken country to Episkopi. Work was interrupted by two earthquakes, one in Paphos and the other in Greece. Water from deep boreholes in the low ground that became known as Happy Valley was lifted 700 feet through fourteen pumps to Episkopi. Happy Valley became a notable sports arena and was known for its green grass the year round. Tunnelling Troop, 32 Fortress Squadron from Gibraltar drove a tunnel to an enclosed beach. Temporary married quarters built near Limassol were known as Berengaria Village.

Field Marshal Harding's announcement prompted Makarios to preach in Athens that he had gained the support of the Greek Government to promote *enosis* and he promised a hostile reception for Middle East Command. The 419,000 Greek-Cypriots increased their agitation, much to the anxiety of the 105,000 Turkish-Cypriots. When the British Minister of Colonial Affairs Henry Hopkinson then firmly suggested that Cyprus would never achieve full independence, because of British defence obligations in the Middle East, Aneurin Bevan, the prominent Labour left-winger, commented that it was folly to establish Middle East Command 'in the midst of a hostile population'. Next month, thousands of Greek-Cypriots defying new legislation against sedition by parading in Nicosia were assured by Makarios that, 'We shall remain faithful to our national claim'. An alarming factor was the hostility displayed by youths. When the nationalists then refused to co-operate in a proposal to establish a Legislative Council of non-elected members, the British dropped the idea because it would have led to an AKEL-led government.

In June, Grivas applied for a visa from the British Embassy in Athens to visit Cyprus; however, his reputation as an agitator this time led to the Colonial security authorities refusing it. In hindsight, it was a fatal error because his activities could have been investigated and the *enosis* movement undermined. In July, Archbishop Makarios invited Colonel Grivas to send more arms to Cyprus; nevertheless, with Cypriot self-determination listed on the UN agenda, Athens resisted supporting a second boatload pending diplomatic progress. Grivas, who strongly believed that diplomacy should be backed up by direct action, then instructed Azinas to prepare for his arrival at Khlorakas. At the end of August, when the UN deferred the debate on Cyprus, Athens relented and incited civil disturbance with vitriolic broadcasts against the British. In the first week of October, Grivas despatched a second arms consignment, which included 350 kilos of dynamite, 100 mines, 300 hand grenades and bomb making material to Khlorakas, on the caique *Ayios Eleftherios*. He also began training for living as a guerrilla in the mountains of Cyprus, where the supply of food would be precarious, and, pleading a stomach ulcer, restricted his diet to fruit every hour and a plate of cold meat twice a week. In November, Commissioner of Police Ashmore was replaced by George Robbins, who had been transferred from Tanganyika (now Tanzania). But even though MI 6 sources in Greece were reporting evidence of weapon smuggling to Cyprus, such was the inefficiency of the information collation system that the police remained largely ignorant of the drive for *enosis*. To address this and other issues, Robbins brought in a former MI 5 officer, Mr P B Ray, to invigorate the slumbering Special Branch, which he did by introducing energetic and bright young officers. Among them was PC Pavlos Stokkos, an enthusiastic nationalist whose father had been deeply involved in the 1931 uprising.

CHAPTER TWO

# The Emergence of EOKA

(November 1954 to March 1955)

On 26 October 1954, Colonel Grivas put on his faithful military boots, and telling her that he was going to Salonika for a few days, bade farewell to his long-suffering wife, Kiki. He would not see her again for over three years. Instead, he met Socrates Loizides and Notis Petropouleas at Piraeus where they boarded the SS *Aegean* bound for Rhodes. Loizides had recently married. In Rhodes, the trio went to Kallithea Bay expecting to meet the caique *Siren* hired to take them to Cyprus; however, an autumn storm brewed up during the voyage from Rhodes and Grivas's intended one day in Rhodes stretched out to twelve. The group spent the first night in a guest house, but fearful of arrest, wary of government agents and frustrated, because Grivas wanted the imminent UN debate on Cyprus to be backed up by a display of force, they moved to a former Masonic lodge in the old part of town. When the anchorage of the *Siren* was reported to be empty and it was feared that she had foundered, Grivas asked Azinas to hire another caique. But Azinas was unable to find one for several days. Meanwhile Grivas finalized his lines of communications between Cyprus, Rhodes and Athens and listened for favourable meteorological reports. To everyone's relief, on 7 November, the *Siren* chugged into Kallithea Bay, her skipper having sheltered in Lindos Bay during the storm. The harbourmaster arranged for her to be refuelled and then at about midnight on 8 November, the caique slipped out of the bay and headed east into rising seas and another gale. Although Grivas had no love of the sea, he feared arrest by the Turks and instructed the reluctant skipper to avoid hugging the picturesque Turkish coast and to set a course south-east to Cyprus. Two days later at dusk, a miserable, seasick Grivas was rowed onto the beach at Khlorakas and answered the challenge with, 'Digenes is here!' Hustled by the shore party, the trio were led to the isolated farmhouse of Nicolas Azinas, father of Andreas and a future leader in Paphos. Next day, the weather cleared and the group cleaned the consignment of weapons buried by Azinas in March. Grivas was expecting the pink-hulled caique *Ayios Georghios* with a large consignment of arms and twenty-seven boxes containing 10,000 sticks of dynamite acquired from an explosives manufacturer in Athens; however, when its skipper, Evanghelos Koutalianos, saw flares as he approached Cyprus and believed that he was about to be intercepted by the Royal Navy, he jettisoned the cargo and returned to Rhodes. He had previously distinguished himself in clandestine operations collecting Allied personnel from Occupied Greece.

Using the farmhouse living room as a night-school, Grivas set about creating the nationalist organization that would bring turmoil to Cyprus from members of PEON and OHEN. OHEN had been toying with forming a national resistance group, however factional disagreements, which included the right wing and the communist AKEL failing to agree a common strategy, led to stalemate. Among the first recruits was Evghenios Cotsapas, a PEON district leader, and Gregoris Afxentiou. Born in 1928 in the village of Lysi and educated at the Famagusta Hellenic Gymnasium, Afxentiou failed entry into the Hellenic Military Academy as an officer cadet and had enlisted in the Greek Army in 1949 as a private. Selected for reserve officer training, he was posted to the Greek border with communist Bulgaria before returning to Cyprus in 1952 to help run the family farm by driving a lorry. Living in the village of Kakopetria in the prosperous Marathassa Valley and teaching in nearby Evrykhou was the Greek Army reservist, Ioannis Katsoullis. He agreed to instruct weapon training and explosives handling. By mid-November, Grivas had formed sabotage groups in five towns and seven villages. Grivas appointed Afxentiou to command the Famagusta Town Group. Later in the month, Grivas had just been driven through the British garrison on his way to a safe house found by Petropouleas in Nicosia in a car with a boot full of weapons when it skidded into a ditch and was towed out by a British Army lorry full of cheerful soldiers. In Limassol, the weapons were cached in a secret cellar. Grivas selected men for the mountain Guerrilla Groups but noted that some candidates were below standard in terms of loyalty and enthusiasm.

With religion playing a dominant role in Greek-Cypriot society, many Cypriot Orthodox priests were active supporters of *enosis* and not only recruited activists and indoctrinated youths with anti-British propaganda, but also took full advantage of the respect for churches to secrete war stores in cemeteries, prepare weapons for use, provide printing presses and give sanctuary to terrorists on the run. The *Pankyprios Ethniki Organosis Neolaias* (PEON: Pancyprian National Organization of Youths) also supplied activists. Although the relationship between Grivas and Papa Aganthangeolou was rocky, the priest was a useful conduit to Makarios and those clerics actively prepared to support *enosis*. It was to him that Grivas turned for houses that could be used to secrete arms. In December, he sent Loizides to Limassol to recruit Sabotage Groups while Petropouleas remained in Nicosia to help with training.

As the British withdrawal from Egypt gathered pace, on 1 December General Sir Charles Keighley transferred General Headquarters, Middle East Command to Wolseley Barracks, Nicosia pending the completion of the headquarters in Episkopi. HQ Cyprus District moved into temporary buildings. As the Army began thinning out its brigades in Egypt, 2nd Battalion, Green Howards (2 Green Howards) arrived by practising a landing near Larnaca, followed three weeks later by the 2nd Battalion, Royal Inniskilling Fusilier Regiment (2 Royal Inniskilling Fusiliers) joining their detached company at Wayne's Keep Camp. Neither encountered hostility, indeed, a ceremonial parade by the Inniskillings proved 'very popular'. In January 1955, 40 Field Regiment RA arrived in Karalaos Camp, Famagusta with their 25-pounders and sent a detachment to support the radar detachment at Coral Bay, about ten miles north-west of Paphos. But when the US objected to Cypriot self-determination at the UN in December, rioting gangs of youths shattered the tranquillity of Cyprus. The Cyprus Police subdued disturbances in Nicosia with baton charges and tear gas. On 19 December in Limassol, when a squadron of 35 Engineer Regiment was instructed by the District Commissioner to intervene and their warnings to disperse were ignored, the sappers were ordered to open fire by the police and wounded a student. The crowd rapidly scattered but as they returned to taunt the soldiers, the Commissioner returned authority to the police until at 9 pm a rainstorm broke up the crowd.

Grivas found the first week of the New Year frustrating as he battled to convince the easy-going Cypriots of the necessity for discipline and secrecy. He then realized that the lack of training grounds meant that his men would have to gain battle experience in action. More frustrations followed when the manifest list of a small consignment of arms and explosives did not match his inventory and of nine boxes of dynamite delivered just one was usable. On 3 January, Grivas was advised that an informer had reported his presence in Cyprus to the police. Although throughout the next three years he personally managed and controlled virtually every aspect of the development of his organization, haemorrhaging information remained a serious blight. It also became clear that the newly-wed Mrs Loizides was fed up with the revolutionary zeal of her husband and that he was missing her. Grivas decided that he should return to Greece as soon as possible. He also noted that Petropouleas was putting pleasure before duty.

On 10 January, Makarios returned from New York and the next day he and the Bishop of Kitium met Grivas and several of his officers in the Larnaca Bishopric and told them that as a result of the UN impasse Field Marshal Papagos fully supported the drive for *enosis*. Grivas believed that advantage should be taken of the long dark evenings and ineffectiveness of the Cyprus Police to start immediately, but Makarios favoured Greek Independence Day on 25 March. The delegates then agreed to name the underground movement *Ethniki Organosis Kyprion Agoniston* (EOKA – National Organization of Cypriot Fighters). Ironically, the meeting ended abruptly when a police car unexpectedly arrived outside the Bishopric and the conspirators left, the date of opening the uprising undecided and the solution of the shortage of weapons and explosives reliant on Azinas.

Makarios then financed a delivery of arms by Captain Koutalianos. On 13 January, when Azinas showed Grivas a telegram indicating that the *Ayios Georghios* had left Greece, they drove to Khlorakas and selected seven members of PEK to help unload it. Grivas returned to Nicosia and was told two days later by Azinas that Archbishop Makarios had learnt from an informant inside Special Branch that British intelligence agents in Greece were looking for a caique scheduled to deliver arms to Israel or Cyprus. When it then emerged that Cypriot authorities were expecting a caique to make landfall at Khlorakas, either on 19 or 20 January, Makarios vetoed a suggestion by Grivas that men be sent north to Xeros as a diversion. Furious, and anxious that EOKA had been penetrated, Grivas learnt later in the day that the departure of the caique was well known in Athens. It later emerged that a former British SOE officer had reported to MI6 that his maid had blurted out in tears that her boyfriend was involved in smuggling arms to Cyprus. When the reports reached Sir Robert Armitage in Government House in Nicosia and he activated Operation *Purse Net* to intercept it, Shackleton maritime aircraft flying from RAF Luqa in Malta patrolled the approaches from Rhodes and Crete, while HMS *Charity*, with a Mr Lakin from the British Middle East Office in Nicosia and a Special Branch sergeant on board, loitered below the horizon during the day. The destroyer was one of six warships that made up the 6th Destroyer Squadron of the Mediterranean Fleet, based in Malta. When the ship closed on the coast at night, watch keepers had noted several green and red lights being regularly flashed out to sea from near Khlorakas Bay at about 7.30 pm each evening. When the caique had not arrived by the 19th, an anxious Grivas was so concerned that the operation had been compromised that he sent Azinas to Athens to find out what was happening. He was then to fly to Rhodes, prevent Captain Koutalianos from sailing and find another caique. A commercial airline pilot agreed to smuggle new sealed sailing orders for the new skipper through Customs at Athens. But when Azinas arrived in Rhodes and learnt that Koutalianos had sailed, he advised Grivas to expect the *Ayios Georghios* with several cases of arms and ammunition and 10,000 sticks of dynamite concealed under general cargo in the hold. Although Grivas had little confidence in the Khlorakas PEK's ability to organize the reception of arms without drawing the attention of the police, in one of very few such occasions, he decided not take direct control of the unloading. Instead, he sent Loizides to command the shore party with instructions to return to his wife on the caique. Grivas then learnt from his Special Branch contacts that Azinas was known to be mixed up in the conspiracy and told him to remain in Athens as his principal logistics and support agent.

In Malta, Commander Tom Burton and his ship's company on the destroyer HMS *Comet* were looking forward to the weekend when, on 22 January, he received orders to take over from HMS *Charity*, which was low on fuel. The two warships were friendly rivals and it was thus with a sense of anticipation and excitement that two days later in the early morning they met about forty-five miles south of Paphos. Mr Lakin and the Special Branch sergeant cross-decked to HMS *Comet*, and then at 10 am HMS *Charity* departed, leaving Burton to loiter below the horizon for the rest of the day. On board *Ayios Georghias*, Koutalianos and his four crew made good time in calm seas. He had orders to wait for a signal from Khlorakas but if that failed, he was to make landfall off Trikomo, Grivas's home town. As they neared Cyprus from the northwest, at about 5 pm, the caique was spotted by a Shackleton about six miles off Cape Akamas and given the identification key, *MT Able*.

When at about 6.10 pm the sighting was received on HMS *Comet*, the sense of anticipation of some sort of action increased, especially among the boarding party. This was led by the recently promoted Lieutenant Michael Clapp, who was normally the Correspondence Officer with responsibility for drafting official letters and papers for the Captain. He was also the Torpedo Anti-Submarine Officer. Burton selected him because his other officers were fully occupied at their action stations and, as a rugger player and boxer, Clapp was fit and strong. The party consisted of eleven seamen, including the Chief Engineer, a signalman and an engine room artificer. Burton lent Clapp a pair of stout boots and suggested that since Jewish women in Palestine had used needles to stab soldiers and sailors in the crotch during boardings, he should wear a box as used by cricket batsmen to protect their groins. Lieutenant Tony Dunn, the Navigating and Operations Officer, plotted a course to intercept the caique outside Khlorakas Bay. Ten minutes later, the Coral Bay radar detachment reported the darkened caique steaming at six knots on a south-easterly track.

In the gathering gloom, the darkened destroyer steamed at speed toward Khlorakas until she was about five miles offshore, but the green light which had regularly been seen at 7.30 pm did not appear. A gentle sea was stirred by a cool breeze and bathed by the moon. Her radar then picked up the caique stopped about a mile from Khlorakas Bay. HMS *Comet* loitered bow on to the coast to reduce her profile, and waited. After twenty tense minutes, the green light flickered and the destroyer tracked the caique until at 9.15 pm it merged with the coast. Burton immediately alerted Assistant Superintendent Alexis Ioannou who was commanding the combined police and 40 Field Regiment cordon sealing the landward approaches to Khlorakas. Burton edged inshore and for the next fifty minutes those on HMS *Comet* waited. Nothing was heard from the police cordon.

Koutalianos was unloading the consignment into rowing boats when at 10.10 pm twelve Very flares burst above the bay, followed by police officers arresting two men near some low dunes, one holding a torch with red and green glass. He was the bespectacled Loizides and beside him was a briefcase. Crossing over a sandy shelf, other police arrested four farmers and two sailors beside a beached rowing boat loaded with boxes. Seeing the commotion ashore, Koutalianos cut the warps, steered the darkened caique through the neck of the bay and accelerated north-east to Cape Akamas, the two surviving crew on board jettisoning the consignment. The flares had been seen by Burton, and as the caique broke into open sea her radar signature was picked up. Determined that she should not reach the 3-mile limit, Burton closed in and when she was 400 yards off his starboard quarter, he instructed a yeoman to illuminate the caique with the 20-inch signal projector. The Special Branch sergeant used a loudhailer to order the caique to heave-to immediately. Although she was caught in the powerful beam and the crew were seen jettisoning boxes, Koutalianos ignored the order until Burton instructed his Chief Bosun's Mate to use his rifle and 'Fire a shot through the rigging'. By now it was about 10.30 pm. Realizing that it would be essential to recover the jettisoned cargo from the seabed, Dunn had been plotting the course of the caique.

Burton ordered Lieutenant Clapp to muster his boarding party at the 25ft Motor Cutter and as soon as the destroyer stopped and the boat was lowered, encumbered with helmets, lifejackets, 18-inch bayonets, .38-inch revolvers and a sailor carrying a Lanchester sub machine gun, the boarding party climbed down scrambling nets into the cutter. Guided by the projector, Leading Seaman Robbins, the coxswain, approached the caique, which was drifting at about four knots in the current, from dead ahead. As the two hulls passed, Clapp's aspirations of a dramatic leap onto its deck dissolved when he became tangled up in its rigging. Alone and suspended over the glistening wash, he was grateful when 'a nice smuggler grabbed me by the collar and pants and lifted me onboard. I was then unkind enough to wave a loaded revolver in their direction and they duly behaved'. Meanwhile, followed by the searchlight, Robbins went about and, bringing the cutter alongside the caique, delivered the remainder of the boarding party.

With the beam lighting up the caique, Clapp instructed Robbins to transfer the handcuffed Greeks to HMS *Comet* where they remained under guard on the upper deck for the rest of the night. Among them was Anargyros Melos, the owner of the caique, acting as the mechanic. Lieutenant Commander Bruce-Lockhart, an engineering officer, joined the boarders with a steaming lights crew to help out during the night after it had been decided overnight not to shut down her sizeable diesel engine. A search revealed a Union flag, a Turkish flag, the ship's log, an expensive pair of Zeiss binoculars in the wheelhouse and two suitcases and the steaming lights in the crew's quarters forward. In the lobby by the engine room, Able Seaman McLean found several suspicious sticks of explosive wrapped in paper inscribed in Greek in a small black case. The two suitcases were sent to HMS *Comet*, as was the case of explosives, which was stored in the demolition locker, much to the irritation of Commander Burton. On the deck aft was a torch with a red and green alternating glass and a sounding line. Although nothing incriminating was found in the hold, Clapp believed that it had recently been emptied of cargo.

At about 6.30 am next morning, the District Commissioner and a pilot boarded HMS *Comet* and then, with a White Ensign flying from its masthead, the caique was escorted by a police launch to a berth in Paphos where it was impounded by the Cyprus Police. The explosive was later found to be potassium chloride, a substance frequently used to help engines start. During a search of the beach next day, a note signed by Azinas acknowledging the receipt of gold coins and money from Loizides towards financing the liberation struggle was found in a cave. Documents in the briefcase provided details of a well-organized armed secret organization in Cyprus led by someone called 'Digenes' inciting *enosis* and rejecting colonial rule. Radio Athens suggested that the boarding was a travesty as the caique was carrying dynamite for fishing until, in April, Royal Navy divers, working about half a mile offshore in rough winter seas that crashed onto the nearby rocks, used Lieutenant

Dunn's charts to recover eight cases of dynamite, a Bren gun, two rifles, pistols, ammunition and scraps of Greek newspapers. Today, the caique is preserved in a special building at Khlorakas. Colonel Grivas was at Palouriotissa inducting Gregoris Afxentiou into becoming his second-in-command and instructing him on sabotage techniques when he heard about the disaster. Angry and fearful that the arrested men would compromise his plans, he moved to the village of Kakopetria in the Troodos foothills for several days until, in early February, his host asked him to leave. He returned to the safe house in Nicosia.

When interviewed by the police, the arrested men made little effort to defend themselves and suggested, 'We played heads and tails. We lost, you won'. Nevertheless, the Colonial security authorities failed to identify the link between EOKA, Athens and Makarios; instead they collectively believed that armed insurrection had been neutralized. For EOKA, the loss of arms was serious. Grivas persuaded Makarios to release funds to buy arms and smuggle explosives from the mines while Afxentiou recruited divers to recover explosives and grenades from Italian ships sunk off Cyprus. The arrests unsettled Grivas but he seems not to have appreciated that he had been outwitted by the improved performance of Special Branch. Although there was no evidence that Koutalianos and his crew knew that he was in Cyprus, he warned the mountain Guerrilla Groups to expect attacks and adopted his principle of staying in one place as long as possible and only leaving when there was a suspicion of compromise.

As the winter wore on and the US continued to object to a UN debate on Cyprus, Grivas's determination to back up the Greek negotiating position with violence was rejected by Makarios. His strategic aim in his Preparatory General Plan for military operations was:

> To arouse international public opinion, especially among the allies of Greece, by deeds and heroism and self sacrifice which will focus attention on Cyprus until our aims are achieved. The British must be continuously harried and beset until they are obliged by international diplomacy exercised through the United Nations to examine the Cyprus problem and settle in accordance with the desires of the Cypriot people and the whole Greek nation. (*Memoirs of Colonel Grivas*, p204)

This would be a campaign based on Hellenic ideologies. The Turkish-Cypriots were not included in the equation. Recognizing that the British could not be defeated militarily and believing that *enosis* could be achieved by keeping their cause on the international political and diplomatic agenda, he left the diplomacy to Makarios and the Greek

Government. EOKA would contribute by dislocating the government machinery, by attacking the financial resources needed to defeat a military insurrection and, in so doing, would aim to incite public anger in England and force the Cyprus authorities to increase taxation to enforce internal security. This, in turn, would lead to public unrest.

Using his study of ELAS, Grivas appointed himself the Field Commander and initially divided EOKA into three independent Guerrilla Groups based in the mountains and ten Sabotage Groups in eight towns and at Episkopi and Dhekelia.

Grivas regarded EOKA as an insurgency organization, with the Guerilla Groups forming the overt military aspect of his campaign. Technically, insurgency is organized resistance that uses espionage, sabotage, subversion and armed confrontation to achieve its aims of:

- Creating conditions to force the occupying power to withdraw.
- Establishing a self-governing territory within the borders of an existing territory.
- Extracting political conditions unachievable through less violent means.
- Overthrowing an established authority but not the social establishment.
- Replace the existing authority.

Grivas welded the Guerrilla Groups into bands of about ten men dispersed throughout the Troodos and Pentadactylos Mountains. The elite of EOKA, they were to ambush patrols and attack vehicles with mines but avoid pitched battles. The groups each lived in a permanent lair supported by several secondary hideouts. Caves were not favoured because their locations were well known to shepherds, forestry workers and walkers and were therefore likely to be searched. Use was made of local builders and artisans to construct them. Most were hacked from rock runs, with expertly camouflaged entrances and were as a solid as possible so that a person could walk over them without the ground giving way. Most were cramped and airless, particularly in the heat of summer. A quartermaster was expected to support each group by managing a logistic cache located some distance from the hideout. The bands were expected to be self-sufficient in water, food and equipment so as to remain underground for weeks, and to have emergency supplies of tinned food in case they needed to abandon a hideout. A problem was the disposal of human waste and rubbish. Other hides excavated in houses, churches, farm outbuildings and monasteries provided places of safety for guerrillas en route to a mission or were 'priest holes' for guerrillas on the run, in danger of arrest or trapped in villages during

## GUERRILLA GROUPS

### Olympus Group

| Area | Sector of activity | Force | Weapons |
|---|---|---|---|
| Kykko/Stavros | Road from Lefka, Pedhoulas, Kykko Monastery to Stavros. | 8 men | Bren gun<br>2 x Stens<br>8 x rifles |
| Chrysoroyiatissa Monastery | Khrysokhou to Kykko Monastery, Prodromos and Platres. | 8 men | Bren gun<br>2 x Stens<br>6 x rifles<br>1 x automatic pistol |
| Troodos Village | Kakopetria, Ayios Ephiphanios, Makheras Monastery, Lefka and west of mountain occupied by the Chrysoroyiatissa Group | 6 men | 2 x Stens<br>6 x rifles<br>1 x automatic pistol |

### Pentadactylos Group

| Area | Sector of activity | Force | Weapons |
|---|---|---|---|
| Kyrenia Mountains | Apostolos Andreas, Myrtou to Lapithos | 23 men divided into 3 groups | 2 x Brens<br>1 x Thompson<br>10 x rifles |

### Reserves

| | | | |
|---|---|---|---|
| | | | 1 x HMG<br>8 x Stens<br>22 x rifles |

security forces' operations. By April, EOKA had a line of hideouts from Kykko Monastery to Limassol. Some monasteries exchanged their tradition as places of study and worship to become arsenals, logistic caches and communication centres. Some hides reached remarkable degrees of unexpected sophistication. One in the Panhandle was entered from above the high-water mark in a well and had a passage wide enough for two men to walk side by side along a 60ft passage to an emergency exit underneath some foliage overhanging a nondescript bank of earth. A second subterranean passage led to a house.

Located in the vicinity of the village of Lyso, about eight miles east of Polis, was a thirteen-man group recruited by George Raftis. The main hide was about 80ft below the summit of Mount Proferti and had a panoramic view of the Merkourios region. One secondary hideout was about 350ft above the church at Ayios Pantes, its entrance accessed by removing a bush. The father of Raftis provided the second, hidden in some dense brambles in an orchard about 1,000 yards from the church. The third was dug into a field and accessed through an oil drum covered by a lid. The fourth was in a house and provided shelter for Demitrakis Constantinides, an illiterate waiter employed at the Paphos Palace Hotel, which was also a well known brothel. Although deemed to be a Group Leader, he was more valued as a 'Mr Fixit'. Feeding the group were a monk and three families, and a man living in the village was the courier to Paphos.

Using the government Districts' boundaries as a basis for organizing Sabotage Groups, Grivas appointed a District Leader and small HQ in the main town to run operations and gave them some autonomy to select and dismiss recruits. He also supplied them with target lists of Government installations, military posts and individuals and encouraged them to carry out special operations in the towns and villages in which they lived. This could mean the execution of Greek-Cypriots suspected of being police informers. If the identity of reliable EOKA became known, they were usually transferred to a Guerrilla Group. Sabotage Group weapons were largely confined to pistols and revolvers, grenades, time bombs, mines and dynamite. District Leaders had direct access to the Field Commander and were to submit weekly situation reports. Short of competent leaders and to reinforce the necessity for unity, he mixed opposing factions and political persuasions in the cells. The Districts were expected to recruit committed activists, grow slowly and gain experience by holding demonstrations, distributing leaflets, providing couriers, carrying out attacks and providing shelters.

Initially, targets were identified by Grivas from the list that he had compiled in his 1952 recce. Grivas, using his military experience, wrote in his Memoirs that:

> intelligence is a pilot which guides one to the right course of action and brings one to one's objective; it is also a scout which spots traps and rocks which the enemy sets in one's path in the hope of tricking and finally crushing his opponent. No fight can be carried on without intelligence. (*Memoirs of George Grivas*)

Members of the Cyprus Police and employees of the British Forces were recruited to provide information, and youths were encouraged to listen to conversations and observe police and military activities. To preserve the operational security of EOKA, Grivas strictly applied the 'need to know principle' that 'each fighter should only know what concerned him personally, nothing more. Every member of the public should keep his ears and eyes open but his mouth shut'. He insisted that each cell be independent and members of EOKA select a codename. For instance, the guerrilla leader Markos Drakos was known as 'Lykourgos'. Born in Kalopanayiotis and employed in the Hellenic Mining Company, he was a former member of PEON and always carried an English copy of the Greek New Testament with him. A fund was established to help the families of those killed. As had become habitual with resistance groups, every member was expected to sign to the EOKA oath thus:

I swear in the name of the Holy Trinity that:

1. I shall work with all my power for the liberation of Cyprus from the British yoke sacrificing for this even with my life.
2. I shall perform without objection all the instructions of the organisation which may be entrusted to me and I shall not bring any objection, however difficult and dangerous this may be.
3. I shall not abandon the struggle unless I receive instruction from the leader of the organisation and after our aim has been accomplished.
4. I shall never reveal to anyone any secret of our organisation neither the names of my chiefs nor those of other members of the organisation even if they are caught.
5. I shall not reveal any of the instruction which may be given even to my fellow combatants.
6. If I disobey my oath, I shall be worthy of every punishment as a traitor and may eternal contempt cover me.

(Source: *Memoirs of George Grivas*)

For command and control Grivas relied upon an extensive network of couriers, with only a few trusted ones knowing his location. This solved the problem of radio transmissions being intercepted, but as the campaign progressed and security force intelligence improved, couriers were at increased risk of betrayal, interception during searches and being pressurized into allowing their messages to be seen. Fake links inserted into the chain disrupted networks. As far as possible, the couriers were not aware for whom the correspondence was intended, just the next destination. The system of cut-outs made it very difficult for military intelligence to penetrate EOKA because trails ran out; consequently, surveillance became an important intelligence asset. Until her arrest in September 1957, Miss Nikki Artemiou, aged eighteen years and part of the Nicosia Group, was Grivas's main courier in Cyprus.

Andreas Yiangou was most trusted because he audited the Groups' budgets and their suppliers and was used by Grivas to take messages to and from Greece. The network was also used to transfer small packages, for instance a pistol. In Larnaca, a bookshop was part of the network based in the port.

Since dropping consignments by parachute was out of the question and smuggling onto beaches had already proved to be risky, the supply and distribution of weapons remained a major problem throughout the EOKA campaign. Greece was the prime source, with most weapons initially smuggled to Cyprus from those originally delivered to wartime resistance groups in Greece or supplied after liberation to re-equip the Greek Army, and mostly stolen from armouries. Some were brought in by couriers, however delivery was piecemeal and always the risk of interception at the ports and airports. A Limassol doctor issued false medical notes that allowed students to travel to Athens for treatment and return with packages containing weapons and ammunition. A Post Office sorting clerk arranged for parcels to be addressed to distinctive remote addresses and ensured that they were provided with a Customs voucher and were therefore less likely to be searched. Early importation was considerably eased by the ports of Famagusta and Limassol having particularly effective smuggling operations that included Customs officials who arranged for consignments to be addressed to distribution points and shipping clerks who watched for consignments that could be intercepted. Opportunities increased as the British transferred stores and supplies to Cyprus from Egypt. Grivas used women to charm their way through roadblocks, and the Greek Consulate in Nicosia abused its diplomatic status.

Grivas appreciated the value of propaganda and aimed to arouse national and international public opinion in favour of Cypriot self-determination. One concern he had was that EOKA might be compelled to operate outside the Geneva Conventions because it could not necessarily conform to the laws and traditions of armed conflict. This he believed he could counter by accusing the authorities of activities that could be deemed controversial, in the knowledge that there would be occasions when deeds committed by EOKA would need to be deniable. But he had a formidable opponent, then with an enviable international reputation for impartiality – the BBC. From his time in Occupied Greece he knew that subversion was effective but that all conversations were at risk of being overheard and reported. Knowing that the fight for independence would hinge on whoever held the 'hearts and minds' of the general public, Grivas emphasized the need for a united front in the pursuit of liberation; political faction fighting was counter productive.

He later claimed that he never lied to the Cypriot people.

Underpinning the military activity, Grivas expected the entire Greek-Cypriot population to engage in passive resistance, take part in strikes, boycotts and demonstrations and to distribute leaflets and newspapers from illegal printing presses. Youths would be major contributors. Total popular participation, particularly from mayors and village elders, was expected in civil disobedience and in supporting EOKA sabotage, attacks on police stations and guerrilla operations. He expected that 'Committees of Arbitration' would hear criminal allegations and settle civil disputes between Greek-Cypriots, thereby reducing the authority of Colonial jurisdiction.

Colonel Grivas expected quick results and hard work; however, much of the spring was taken up with addressing disciplinary matters among EOKA recruits whose romantic views of resistance did not match his Teutonic approach to life. While some EOKA had been toughened by employment in the mines where explosive was used to expose copper and magnesium, most were young men and women with sedentary occupations, such as clerks, shopkeepers and civil servants. A few had served in the Cyprus Regiment, the Cyprus Volunteer Force, the British Armed Forces and the Greek Army. Most were unfamiliar with the rigours of outdoor life and the physical fitness needed to live in the field for months, let alone survive in a town or village under the constant threat of sudden arrest.

At a meeting on the last day of February at the Kykko Monastery annexe in Nicosia to discuss funding the campaign, Makarios agreed with Grivas that sabotage attacks could be carried out only against military and government targets, but that casualties were to be avoided. The Monastery was the richest in Cyprus and was known by EOKA as 'The School'. Not yet based in the mountains where he could defy the Archbishop, Grivas had no alternative but to agree, however he feared a communist reaction, similar to the events that had led to the Greek Civil War, and suggested that arrangements be made to buy or acquire all the weapons on the island. On 2 March, another consignment of weapons and explosives arrived by caique, including three Bren light machine guns and 300 grenades. Three weeks later, in a letter to Makarios, Grivas envisaged a five-phase operation, stage one being to arouse national and international public support for an independent Cyprus. By 21 March Grivas had re-checked the plans to attack the twenty targets he had selected; when he then made a final inspection of EOKA, he found the sabotage groups in Famagusta, Larnaca and Limassol were confident but the Nicosia Group lacked drive. Each had been supplied with explosives and fuses, hand grenades and bombs fitted with time pencils. He also visited the Guerrilla Groups in the mountains. While EOKA waited nervously, the Colonial security authorities, blinded by a demoralized and inefficient police force concentrating on the communist AKEL, were blissfully unaware of the subversive threat that had buried itself in Cyprus. Everything appeared normal.

At a final briefing on 29 March, Grivas, accompanied by Markos Drakos and Christakis Eleftheriou, won the blessing from Makarios to begin the liberation struggle early on 1 April, which was April Fool's Day in the Cypriot calendar. Summoning the Town Sabotage Group leaders, Grivas gave them final orders and, rejecting their pleas to secrete himself in Kyrenia, moved his command post to the Nicosia suburb of Strovolos, where he would be able to hear the outbreak of the rebellion and intervene if necessary. He had prepared a revolutionary proclamation that he later claimed equalled that of Leonidas inspiring his 300 Spartans, of the Greek independence fighters in 1821 and the Greek Army going to war in October 1940, and appealed to the Cypriots to help EOKA throw off 'the English yoke'. To the international community, he pleaded how shameful it was in the twentieth century that people should have to fight for their freedom, as he had done against the Nazis.

CHAPTER THREE

# The Build Up of British Forces

In 1954, Cyprus District was commanded by Brigadier Abdy Ricketts from his HQ at Wolseley Barracks on the outskirts of Nicosia. Late of the Durham Light Infantry, he had commanded 3 West African Brigade during Major General Orde Wingate's second Chindit campaign in Burma in 1944 and then led 29 Infantry Brigade during bitter fighting in Korea.

The garrison numbered about 1,500 men and included a 2 Royal Inniskilling Fusiliers company detached from Egypt providing an infantry presence and the Governor's Guard at Government House. The Royal Army Service Corps (RASC) provided transport; distributed fuel, ammunition, war stores, rations by air, sea and land; managed Barracks Services and married-quarter accommodation; and provided clerical services to Brigade HQs upwards. Units in Cyprus included 17 Transport Company, 74 Supply Depot, 252 Command Petroleum Depot providing bulk petrol, oil and lubricants, and were supported by the mixed military and civilian 42 Army Fire Brigade at Four Mile Point, 539 Field Bakery at Wayne's Keep Camp and 136 Supply Platoon in Wolseley Barracks. The Royal Army Ordnance Corps (RAOC) was represented by 625 Ordnance Depot at Four Mile Point and the military police by 227 Provost Company.

A fundamental principle of military withdrawal is to ensure that rear-area logistics are in a suitable condition to support the front line. Within weeks of Field Marshal Harding's announcement, sheds were built at Larnaca for stores shipped from Egypt. Cyprus Signal Troop had relied on civilian-manned military telephone exchanges, the Cable and Wireless and the Forestry Telephone system used for forest fire emergencies. When Major General Morrison, the Command Signals Officer, planned for the transfer of Middle East Command, he enlarged the Troop into the Cyprus Signal Regiment. Needing to support the two HQs in Cyprus and Egypt, he convinced the War Office to send him the Marconi Relay System used by the disbanded Anti-Aircraft Command

## THE BUILD UP OF BRITISH FORCES

and placed it on Mount Olympus in three Nissen huts that would eventually house about fifty radios linking Army, RAF and naval command nets and the Cyprus Police. The antennae were mounted on two 60-foot towers that gave a wonderful panoramic view in summer, threatened to topple in gales and were too cold to touch in the four months of deep winter snow.

As the force levels rose from about 1,100 in April 1955 to about 27,500 within a few months, Deputy-Director Supplies and Transport formed 1 (Transport) and 65 (Motor Transport) Companies at the Golden Sands Leave Camp, Famagusta and 40 and 41 (Motor Transport) Companies at Dhekelia and Limassol respectively. Ten-ton Leyland Hippo and AEC Mammoth lorries of 65 Company moved ammunition from Army Landing Ship Tanks at Famagusta and Limassol ports and on to beaches elsewhere. 45 (Independent) Transport Company at Episkopi supplied drivers for the growing fleet of Humber Super Snipe staff cars. Although Land Rovers were first introduced to the Army in 1948, it was not until 1956 that they became widely issued. As an intermediary to reduce reliance on US vehicles, the British-designed Austin Champ had replaced the ubiquitous Jeep. Air portable, able to tow a quarter-ton trailer and adaptable to carry stretchers, compared to the Jeep it was heavy and difficult to extract from sand and mud. For years, the Armed Forces relied on variations of 3-ton trucks, in particular the Austin K3 and Bedford QL, for general-purpose transport until they began to be replaced by the Bedford RL in 1953, a lorry that saw service until the mid-1970s. First-line repair of weapons, radios, vehicles and equipment was provided by REME-manned unit Light Aid Detachments supported by second-line services from the Cyprus District Workshop REME and later by 8 Infantry Workshops in October 1955 and 9 Infantry Workshop in 1957. When vehicles broke down or were damaged in crashes and ambushes, it required military operations to prevent interference by EOKA or local sympathizers during the recovery. The ingenuity of the REME in rigging ropes and pulleys to recover damaged vehicles jammed in ravines was fully tested. The REME also provided infantry attachments, as did other Corps.

RAMC 2 Field Ambulance at Four Mile Point had several detachments across Cyprus supporting Regimental Medical Officers. As for ambulances, the Austin K2 RAF crash vehicle had been adapted to carry four stretchers but lacked sufficient room for medical staff. The seriously injured were treated at the British Military Hospital, Nicosia, which was serviced by 37 Medical Company, and later at Dhekelia and Akrotiri. The hospitals were supported by the Command Medical Equipment Depot and the Command Medical Laboratory. Queen

Alexandra's Royal Army Nursing Corps nurses were also posted to the military hospitals, as were Princess Mary's Royal Air Force Nursing Service nurses to Akrotiri. Those casualties with life-threatening wounds, injuries and illnesses were stabilized in Cyprus and then flown to a naval or military hospital in the UK for specialist treatment and rehabilitation.

Royal Air Force (RAF) Nicosia was established in 1940 when the existing runway was expanded to include dispersal areas. As the fighting in North Africa ebbed and flowed, 272 Squadron Beaufighters escorted Allied convoys and patrolled the Eastern Mediterranean, while 162 Squadron electronic warfare Wellingtons jammed enemy communications and the Spitfires of 680 Squadron photographed enemy activity. After the Allies landed in Italy, 79 Operational Training Unit dominated the region. When a civil airport was built alongside RAF Nicosia in 1945, squadrons rotated through No. 26 Armament Practice Camp and its live firing range at Morphou. In 1953, Transport Command flew in supplies when an earthquake hit Paphos. Helicopters had first been used in the Burma campaign and then in Korea for casualty evacuation and liaison. On 1 April 1955, the Joint Experimental Helicopter Unit was formed at RAF Middle Wallop as a joint RAF/Army venture to develop the operational uses of helicopters, particularly in assaults from aircraft carriers and the delivery of small numbers of troops in counter-insurgency operations. The only helicopters in Cyprus were several Bristol Sycamore HC 14s of the RAF Search and Rescue Flight, which had been based at RAF Nicosia since May 1954. This aircraft had been introduced into service in 1953 to support Fighter Command pilot search-and-rescue and also for coastal anti-submarine warfare. With a crew of two, a Sycamore could carry up to four lightly-equipped soldiers with an endurance of three hours.

One of the most crippling restrictions suffered by Grivas was the naval blockade. The controversial submariner Rear Admiral Anthony Myers, who was nicknamed 'Gamp' and had been awarded the Victoria Cross in 1942, was Flag Officer, Middle East and directed naval operations from Maritime HQ alongside HQ Middle East Command. His principal objective was to prevent the smuggling of weapons and thus any ship entering Cypriot waters was liable to be boarded. In mid-September 1955, the minesweeper HMS *Appleton* fired a shot across the bows of the Italian liner *Enotria* and then boarded her. Although the ship was within Cypriot territorial waters, the Italian Government lodged a complaint. Boarding could be hazardous. On 26 February 1958, a boarding party in a cutter returned to the destroyer HMS *Alamein* after boarding a Cypriot fishing boat; but as the cutter was being hoisted on board, a fall shredded and the sailors were tipped into the sea. It took

## THE BUILD UP OF BRITISH FORCES

several minutes for the the destroyer to go about and search for survivors. One body was recovered but two others were lost. Over the horizon, patrols were provided by the 1st Destroyer and the 6th Frigate Squadrons. They were often guided to suspect vessels by the 38 Squadron Shackletons Maritime Reconnaisance aircraft flying from Malta. Ton-Class minesweepers of 104 and 108 Squadrons from the Inshore Flotilla of the Mediterranean Fleet provided coastal patrols from the naval base at Famagusta until 104 Squadron was sent to Aden. The sailors sometimes exchanged places with soldiers and not only went on patrol but were also subjected to Army cooking, which most rated as poor. Not surprisingly, the soldiers welcomed the traditional tot of Navy rum. Four former torpedo recovery boats were formed into a patrol boat squadron at Famagusta until it was decommissioned in September 1956. Also involved in coastal defence were seven sections, consisting of an officer and about twenty soldiers of 188 Search Light and Radar Battery, covering the entire Cyprus coastline. It lost a major and two gunners killed in attacks on posts. For a year from January 1958, 847 Squadron Fleet Air Arm provided Gannet anti-submarine aircraft.

Many of those who served in Cyprus were National Servicemen. The Labour Government that ousted Winston Churchill in 1945 had not been convinced of the need for post-war conscription; however, the need to discharge Hostilities – Only servicemen called up during the war, the loss of the Indian Army in 1947, the requirement to provide forces to support UK's global strategic commitment and provide sizeable garrisons in West Germany, the Far East and the Mediterranean all led to conscription under the 1947 National Service Act. By 1954, National Servicemen were fighting Communist terrorists in the Malayan jungles, Arab nationalists in Egypt and the Mau Mau in the forests of Kenya. Some had survived brutal prison camps as prisoners of North Koreans and Chinese determined to subvert them to communism. Others were involved in nuclear weapon testing in the South Pacific. Women joining the Armed Forces did so as volunteers. The National Servicemen were backed up by a hard core of Regulars and Reservists, many of whom had fought in the Second World War. Almost all had survived the rigours of the Second World War as children, some experiencing the death of close family members in action and in air raids, and most had interrupted educations.

By 1954, the post-war austerity was drawing to a close and most National Servicemen were reluctant to exchange the excitement of Elvis Presley and Bill Haley, winkle-picker shoes and the Teddy Boy fashion for a drab uniform. Men aged up to twenty-six years and usually resident in UK were committed to two years' full time service followed by three and a half years in the Reserve. Exemptions included the clergy, trawlermen and merchant seamen, some agricultural workers and those in government positions overseas. Deferments were granted to apprentices, university undergraduates and those undertaking professional articles. Northern Ireland was excluded, because of the fear of Catholic dissent, as were the Channel Islands, still recovering from German occupation. After a medical, interviewing officers allocated the recruits, with the Army taking about seventy-two per cent and the Royal Navy about two per cent. The remainder entered the RAF. Those with existing skills increased their chances of entering either the RAF or Royal Navy or a relevant Corps in the Army; for instance, a bank clerk could probably be sent to the Royal Army Pay Corps (RAPC). Army basic training usually took place in dilapidated camps or stone barracks built to house soldiers of the eighteenth and nineteenth centuries. Although some had been evacuated to Canada, the USA and the British shires during the war, joining up for most was their first time away from home and suddenly they found themselves sleeping in a large cold dormitory with a bunch of strangers from all over UK and eating food that lacked the quality produced by Mother – 'Take it or leave it, son!' Royal Navy and RAF accommodation was usually more adequate, and haircuts were less brutal than in the Army. As the basic training progressed and the recruits adapted to Service life, they moulded into units and left for trade and advanced training. Few regarded the rantings by corporals, sergeants and sergeant majors, the insistence on traditions and compliance with restrictions as bullying or an attack on their human rights; these were simply a necessity of life in uniform.

Most officers had gained military experience in public and grammar school Combined Cadet Forces. The Royal Navy and RAF sought experience in the Reserve Forces. Those Other Ranks talent-spotted as Army officers were assembled into potential officer platoons at training depots where they prepared for the three day commissioning War Office Selection Board – 'WOSBee'. Not all made the grade. Lord Willoughby de Eresby, heir to the Earl of Ancaster, served as a trooper with the Royal Horse Guards in Cyprus. Those selected for three-year Army Short Service Commissions (SSC) attended either Eaton Hall or Mons Officer Cadet Training Units (OCTU) near Chester and Aldershot respectively and could apply to convert their SSC into Regular commissions. Regular Army officers graduated from the Royal Military College at Sandhurst after two years.

Some of those posted overseas flew in RAF Transport Command aircraft such as the Hastings, others on civilian aircraft contracted by the Ministry of Transport, sometimes with a stopover in Gibraltar or the heavily bomb-damaged Malta where they may have sampled its lazy beaches, the delights of Valetta and its infamous 'Gut' of bars, tattoo rooms and prostitutes. Most knew the island for the award of the George Cross for its heroic stand during 1941 and 1942. The vast majority sailed in crowded troopships contracted from shipping companies by the Ministry of Trade. Some had led adventurous lives, for instance, the 9,523-ton German East Africa Line *Ubena* had spent the Second World War as a U-Boat depot ship until she was converted to a hospital ship in 1945. After being captured at Travemunde, she was renamed Her Majesty's Troopship *Empire Ken*. She was scrapped twelve years later. Part of the joining instructions presented to a soldier on embarkation was the Army Form 5218D Bedding Card which gave the name of the ship and the man's deck, section and berth in one of the tiers of retractable steel bunks in crowded large spaces below decks. The ship's Regimental Sergeant Major managed the Other Ranks. Officers led an altogether more comfortable life in the equivalent of first class accommodation. Dependants had cabins in a third sector. The departures from and returns to such ports as Southampton were often nostalgic occasions of military bands, flag waving and tears from families and girlfriends. The voyage to Cyprus usually took about eleven days with a run ashore in uniform either in Gibraltar, where it was not unknown for some to go absent without leave into Spain, and or in Malta where most hit the Gut until turfed out by the naval and military police. Although those originating from Glasgow and the Tyne had seen ships being built and those in Liverpool had witnessed the arrivals and departures of Atlantic convoys, few had experienced ocean-going ships and the heaving waves of the Bay of Biscay. The voyage through the Mediterranean in summer was pleasant and gave the Servicemen time to develop tans. Sunburn and sunstroke, in environments where air conditioning rarely existed, were disciplinary offences.

The summer uniform was Khaki Drill shorts and a shirt with either a helmet or beret. In winter, Battledress was worn. Boots were leather and fitted with hobnails that signalled the presence of patrolling soldiers. Webbing consisted of two 1938 Bren gun pouches, water bottle and a 6-inch spike bayonet in a scabbard attached to a belt supported by braces, until the 1958 webbing pattern and its yoke appeared. Accommodation spaces were inspected daily and expected to be spotless. Duties and fatigues included the provision of fire picquets at watertight doors with orders to slam shut and lock when instructed, and helping the cooks prepare meals by peeling potatoes and vegetables and washing up pots and pans. Training ranged from drill parades and weapon training to physical fitness, games and lectures. Off-duty activities included reading, betting and gambling, and lounging on the rails, interrupted by queuing for food. There was also the inevitable 'sod's opera' – entertainment put on by crew and passengers in the Ship's Own Dramatic Society. This is very much part of Service life on ships, in a Mess, in a prison camp or even a jungle clearing. Performers are drawn from all ranks, either real talent or those who think they have it. Officers usually come in for extensive ribbing. Meeting another troopship was usually an occasion for shouting and waving and envy at those returning to England and discharge. Little did those on the returning ship realize that on reaching port, kitbags would be unceremoniously searched by HM Customs and Excise, who very rarely granted any leeway to servicemen returning from active service. Weekly 'free from infection' inspections were undignified affairs in which the men dropped their PT shorts so that their genital areas could be inspected by doctors and medical orderlies looking for evidence of sexually transmitted diseases and infections. Some canny soldiers retained their issue Durex to protect the muzzle of their rifles from dirt, rust and dirt. After the sinking of a troopship off Algeria in 1954, life boat drills were taken seriously.

On arriving off Famagusta or Limassol, troopships anchored offshore while military port operations, such as that run by 51 Port Squadron, Royal Engineers, organized the transfer of men in lighters and Z-Craft to port assembly area where they were allocated lorries or coaches and taken to their units. Some were unlucky enough to be allocated to the holding unit at Wayne's Keep and the dreaded parade square. Wayne's Keep hosted, as it still does, the military cemetery. In 1955, the War Graves Commission was responsible for the upkeep of the graves of those killed in the First and Second World Wars and the two memorials to the men of the Cyprus Regiment and Cyprus Volunteer Force, as well as the Cremation Memorial to those Hindu soldiers cremated in Cyprus.

Also at Wayne's Keep, for those who fell foul of naval and military legislation and were convicted by commanding officers and courts martial anywhere in Middle East Command, was the forbidding 52 Military Corrective Training Centre, in which discipline was strict and the training regime hard. In July 1955, 2 Green Howards suffered public embarrassment when three of their men were convicted for attempting to sell a pistol to a Greek-Cypriot. Three other soldiers were the first to be convicted at a court martial for stealing a fishing boat in order to desert to Turkey. Some soldiers were sent home with dishonourable discharges while others emerged better sailors, soldiers and airmen. At the height of the Emergency there were about 350 prisoners under sentence, with convictions ranging from persistent ill-discipline and refusal to obey a legitimate order to desertion. About 150 Turkish prisoners were also held in order to avoid them mixing with Greek-Cypriot offenders.

The majority of the new arrivals moved into one of the ninety-two camps spread across Cyprus. From 1954 to 1956, Royal Engineers surveyors of No. 1 Radar Air Survey Liaison Section, which consisted of about seven soldiers commanded by a major, and 42 Survey Regiment, were kept busy carrying out topographical surveys of sites before the field engineer squadrons built the camps. Three types emerged. Cyprus Scale 'A' were suitable for a stay of a few months and came in two stages of tented 'get you in', supported by the basics of ablutions, cookhouse shelters and assistance in pitching tents, followed by piped water, hard standing and soakaways. Most units lived in Scale 'B' tented camps with a few communal buildings, electricity and hot water. The men lived six to eight men to a 160lb canvas tent, each commanded by a corporal or lance corporal, surrounded by a low sandbag wall that helped drainage and gave some shelter. The sides could be rolled up to let in the summer breeze. Water for washing and shaving was usually collected from several taps early in the morning. By midday in summer the water was almost boiling, while in the chill of winter it could freeze. Most camps were equipped with a water tower, which fed primitive showers. It was not unknown in the summer for drinking water to be rationed to one water bottle per day. Ablutions were generally rudimentary affairs, with a range of lavatory seats perched over cesspits. Urinals consisted of a half tube of corrugated iron feeding into a hole. Hygiene was critical. Since Nissen and Romney huts were not available, locally designed, prefabricated Symmonds huts sufficed. Scale 'C' camps consisted of temporary huts.

Some camps such as that at Xeros, were located alongside one of the copper mines, which allowed the Royal Engineers to divert water, electricity and drainage, as opposed to having to bore for it. The camps on the Messaoria plain suffered from summer spirals of 'dust devils' that scurried through the tents several times a day. In the autumn and winter, some camps ran the risk of flooding. Polymedhia Camp close to Berengaria had been blasted from a rock face and the tents placed on concrete bases. It was first occupied by 35 Engineer Regiment, who also inhabited about thirty married quarters first used by Major (later Field Marshal) Herbert Kitchener in 1882. The camps were surrounded by barbed wire, with access through a barrier at the Guardroom that was controlled from 6 am to 6 pm by the Regimental Police and from 6 pm to 6 am by a Guard assembled from the incumbent unit. Tented life tended to be relaxed, although several grenade and shooting attacks meant the men were expected to carry their personal weapons. Initially, the standard rifle was the .303-inch Lee Enfield bolt action, although after the British Government had signed a contract for the 7.62mm Self Loading Rifle, this semi automatic weapon became common from 1957 onwards. The 9mm Sten sub machine gun was replaced by the 9mm Sterling. Officers usually carried a .38-inch Smith & Wesson revolver. This was also used as a personal protection weapon. Unlike in Northern Ireland, there was little if any pre-deployment training, and consequently the young and inexperienced National Servicemen were pitched straight into operations that they had only read about in newspapers or heard about on the wireless.

Each camp had separate Messes for officers and senior non commissioned officers, while the NAAFI provided for the remainder. Cigarettes were rationed. When 1st Battalion, Highland Light Infantry (1 HLI) moved into the camp at Dhavlos, beer glasses were not available because they had been used in a fight, so the Jocks resorted to using mess tins. Coca-Cola was freely available from a kiosk run by a Cypriot. When the Black Watch arrived in 1958, they were not too surprised when an entrepreneurial Indian trader they had used elsewhere set up shop. Contact with home was limited and usually confined to letters and parcels distributed by the Royal Engineers of 19 Command Postal Depot at Wayne's Keep, under the British Forces Post Office 53 nomenclature before it moved into the new camp at Dhekelia in 1958. It also distributed classified mail. Seven field post offices were provided by 275 Postal Unit, one at RAF Akrotiri. As the terrorism in Cyprus escalated and EOKA infiltrated camps, all outgoing letters were held for a day and parcels for two days to allow devices to detonate. When 19 Postal Command Depot installed an inspection machine, it was not then known the damaging effect X-rays had on undeveloped rolls of photographic film. The machine also vetted incoming parcels for weapons.

A few applicants were mentioned on the regular BBC Light Programme *Two Way Family Favourites,* broadcast at midday as families in UK sat down for Sunday lunch. The Forces Broadcasting Service supplied entertainment, and *Soldier* magazine was one Service periodical that ran regular articles from Cyprus. Leave was usually taken at one of the rest camps near the beaches. Some soldiers who elected to be discharged in Cyprus used rail warrants to return to UK through Europe.

CHAPTER FOUR

# The Outbreak of the EOKA Campaign

(April to October 1955)

At midnight on 1 April 1955, Colonel Grivas was in his room listening for the explosions to open the EOKA drive for *enosis* and expecting to see the lights go out. The Markos Drakos group broke into the newly refurbished Cyprus Broadcasting Service compound at Athalassa near Nicosia Airport where they gagged the unsuspecting night watchmen and planted bombs that badly damaged the transmitters. The Forces Broadcasting Service was not attacked because, it seems, young Greek- and Turkish-Cypriots liked its pop music. The Nicosia group led by Christakis Eleftheriou, a senior EOKA who had been with Grivas when Makarios gave permission for the campaign to begin, threw hand grenades at the Colonial Secretariat. The plumber Stylianos Lenas, who had become a formidable bomb-maker, threw a device over the Wolseley Barracks perimeter fence at the Communication Centre. In spite of the belief the explosions might be an April Fool's Day joke, 2 Royal Inniskilling Fusiliers immediately stood to, and Lieutenant Colonel Ian Freeland sent the Internal Security Platoon to guard the HQ Middle East Command compound. 2 Green Howards were on exercise. In the Famagusta Group area, several bombs failed to explode, but 2 Wireless Regiment installation at Ayios Nikolaos came under fire. An attack on Dhekelia Power Station led by Andreas Karios failed when Modestos Pantelis was electrocuted as he threw a rope damp with dew over live electricity cables. Had he succeeded, he would have blacked out much of Cyprus. His body was found next day.

The success that the police enjoyed was largely a combination of good luck and EOKA incompetence. The brother of Pantelis, Christofis, was arrested at a roadblock near Akhna on his way to join the Troodos Guerrilla Group and was later sentenced to seven years. In Larnaca, the former PEON Secretary-General Stavros Poskottis, the Town Group leader, was arrested during the day after an explosive device was found outside his house. He was sentenced to nine years for possession. His

Group had damaged the Courthouse and Police Station. The Limassol Town Group, led by Evghenios Cotsapas, was largely deterred from completing their tasks by police patrols and incompetence. Cotsapas was arrested in November 1955 in possession of bombs in his car at a roadblock and sentenced to three years. A number of leaflets found throughout Cyprus read:

> With God's help, faith to our righteous struggle, the support of all Greeks, and the help of Cypriots, WE START OUR FIGHT AGAINST THE BRITISH RULERS, having as a dictum what our forefathers left as a holy testament, "COME BACK WITH YOUR SHIELD OR ON YOUR SHIELD"
>
> CYPRIOT BROTHERS
> From the depths of the centuries, they look upon us all those who glorified Greek history, the soldiers of Marathon and Salamis, Leonidas' 300, the fighters of the Albanian front. The fighters of 1821 have turned our eyes towards us and teach us that that freedom is only won with BLOOD. All of Hellenism is watching us as well, with anxiety and national pride. Let us show with our actions that we will surpass them.
>
> The time has come to show to the world that, even if international diplomacy is UNFAIR and COWARDLY, the Cypriot soul is nevertheless brave. If the conquerors do not want to give us our freedom, we will take it ourselves with our own HANDS and BLOOD.
>
> Let us show to the world that no modern Greeks can bear slavery. The struggle will be difficult. The tyrant has the means and numbers.
> We have the SOUL. We have RIGHT on our side. That is why we will WIN.
>
> INTERNATIONAL DIPLOMATS
> Look at the result of your work. It is a disgrace in the 20th century for people to shed their blood to win their FREEDOM, this holy present for which we fought on your side, while you claim that you have fought for against fascism and Nazism
>
> GREEKS
> Wherever you are, listen to our voice.
> FOLLOW US FOR THE FREEDOM OF CYPRUS
>
> EOKA                                                    CAPTAIN DIGENES

The call to arms to Greek-Cypriots was typically full of images of Ancient Greece, a feature that would surface several times over the next four years. 'Come back with your shield or on your shield' was the farewell of Spartan mothers when their sons left for war. 'Let us show with our actions that we will surpass them' was part of the Oath of the Athenian Warriors.

On 2 April, EOKA declared their intentions to attack the British when a grenade was thrown into a military bus taking Service wives shopping in Nicosia; fortunately, it failed to explode. Questioning of about twenty EOKA suspects by Special Branch soon produced results when the entire Limassol cache of 300lbs of explosive, twenty-seven smoke grenades, detonators and .303-inch ammunition was seized. The first arrest warrant against a member of EOKA, with the posting of a reward of £250, was issued against Gregoris Afxentiou on 4 April after nine grenades, two sticks of dynamite and three packets of commercial explosive were found in his abandoned car, not far from a roadblock. A police search of his house also revealed a Greek Army handbook on sabotage. Although Grivas had issued instructions to his second-in-command to stay at a safe house in Kyrenia and to communicate through a nominated courier, Afxentiou had disobeyed. Grivas had no alternative but to sack him and appoint Pavlos Pavlakis, a shipping clerk, to lead the Famagusta Group. Afxentiou was sent to lead the Pentadactylos Group. Among the new recruits attracted to EOKA was Michael Rossides, a mining clerk aged twenty-one years.

Although the incidents would prove an embarrassment to Sir Robert Armitage, and London would criticize him heavily for being caught on the hop and allowing nationalist subversion to bed into the Greek-Cypriot community, the fact was the intelligence and security authorities believed that in spite of the *enosis* disturbances in Limassol and Nicosia in December 1954 and the interception of the *Ayios Georghias* and arrest of the exiled Socrates Loizides, the struggle for *enosis* had been nipped in the bud before it had begun; consequently no precautions had been taken to protect sensitive buildings. Armitage acknowledged that while weapons and explosive had been smuggled to Cyprus, there was no indication that they were about to be used. The local authorities always expected trouble at events in the Greek calendar, in this instance April Fool's Day. In relation to the proclamations, Commissioner of Police Robbins admitted that little was known about EOKA or the meaning of the acronym. Everyone seemed to know that 'Digenes' was a twelfth century Byzantine warrior renowned in an epic poem. The Greek Communist Party's disclosure that it was the codename of the infamous Colonel Grivas of X in post-war Athens was largely rejected as nonsense and mischief.

Robbins placed the Cyprus Police on full alert and intensified the patrolling of urban areas. General Keightley, the experience of Palestine still fresh, doubled the military guard at key points and ordered that

Government buildings be protected against blast damage with sandbags and tape on windows. Armed sentries controlled access to Famagusta port and patrolled its perimeter fence. On the 21st, 40 Field Regiment exchanged places with 2 Royal Inniskilling Fusiliers at Wolseley Barracks. The incidents did not immediately harness the popular support expected by Grivas, indeed 'Voice of the Fatherland' broadcasting from Radio Athens supported passive resistance. Makarios was shocked by the bombings and insisted that Grivas should regroup. However, Grivas, recognizing that the passive resistance practised by Mahatma Gandhi in India had been effective, believed that the profile of Cyprus must be raised with the British public and that at the same time the effectiveness of the Cyprus Government should be undermined with violence.

A feature of all terrorist groups is to search for scapegoats, and when Petropouleas was blamed for failing to order the Troodos groups to explode their bombs and then was implicated in the arrest of Christofis Pantelis after being questioned by the police, Grivas, believing that he had been 'turned' to become an informer, wanted him eliminated. Having become something of a liability after exploiting his illegal presence in Cyprus to promote his reputation as a playboy, he was quietly transferred to Beirut. Since the expected difficulties in smuggling weapons from Greece had materialized, Grivas ordered EOKA to confiscate shotguns from farmers and sportsmen.

On 6 May the sentences for those involved with the *Ayios Georghios* were handed down at Paphos, with Socrates Loizides sentenced to twelve years to be served in England. Radio Athens was intemperate in praise of the Cypriot patriots. But Grivas had lost both his lieutenants and there was little to suggest that the Greek-Cypriots had the relentless desire for the pursuit of freedom so recently exhibited by the Greeks during the occupation of Greece. Perhaps he failed to recognize that after decades of relative tranquillity and a benign colonial government, while Greek-Cypriots supported *enosis*, engaging in armed rebellion was a gigantic step for very many.

Since the authorities had little intelligence on EOKA, they were forced on to the defensive. General Sir Gerald Templar, who was the Director of Military Intelligence and architect of successful intelligence operations against the Communist Terrorists in Malaya, arrived in Cyprus in mid-May and recommended that the relationships between government and the Cyprus Police be thoroughly overhauled. During the course of the year, the Colonial Office Police Adviser and a logistic expert assessed the likely needs of the police in the event that an internal security emergency developed.

## THE OUTBREAK OF THE EOKA CAMPAIGN

Grivas knew that he could rely upon youth and student groups to create civil disturbances, the first of which had culminated before Christmas. The next wave of unrest emerged on 8 April when pupils at the militant Nicosia Pan Cyprian Gymnasium boycotted lessons, and although the headmaster managed to persuade some to return, a hard core marched to Nicosia Prison and sang nationalist songs to the EOKA suspects held inside. Three days earlier, Sir Robert Armitage had warned teachers, after EOKA oaths of allegiance had been posted on notice boards, that the overlooking of EOKA activity evident so far would not be tolerated. The oath read:

> I swear by the Holy Trinity's name that I shall work with all my power for the liberation of Cyprus from the British yoke, sacrificing for this even with my life.

Although parents and teachers objected, on 23 May about 500 students, most from the Nicosia Pan Cyprian Gymnasium, insisted they be allowed to attend school, as opposed to enjoying the Empire Day bank holiday, and staged a demonstration in Metaxas Square in Nicosia. When the Cyprus Police attempted to disperse them, the students stoned Government House, smashed windows of local authority buildings, jeered a group of Service wives on a shopping trip and seriously injured the driver of an RAF lorry. But the momentum of youth unrest slackened when the annual summer examinations arrived. When it was announced that as part of the Empire Day celebrations Sir Robert Armitage would attend a special showing of the film *Forbidden Cargo* in aid of the British Legion at the Pallas Cinema in Nicosia, Grivas tasked Marcos Drakos to assassinate him. Drakos suggested to a municipal worker that he smuggle a time bomb into the theatre during an earlier showing and place it underneath the balcony to be occupied by the Governor and his party. However, the special showing started earlier than expected and when the device exploded the auditorium was empty; nevertheless, considerable damage was caused. The Greek Consulate delegation were conspicuous by their absence.

On 6 June, after Archbishop Makarios and Colonel Grivas agreed at Kykko Monastery to a campaign of intimidation against the Cyprus Police, Grivas met Renos Kyriakides, who had formed the Kyperounda Guerrilla Group, and charged him to attack police stations for weapons, ambush patrols, execute police officers working closely with the British and hinder police freedom of movement. Kyriakides had studied maths and physics at Athens University and was a brother of the militant Bishop Kyprianos of Kyrenia. He was one of several students allied to PEK who had been trained by the Greek Army in guerrilla warfare and had then been distributed among the EOKA mountain groups in Lefka, Kyrenia and Amiandos. EOKA was already being considerably helped by disloyal Greek-Cypriot police officers passing information and refusing to do their law enforcement duty. Grivas also talent-spotted a militant clerk employed at the Nicosia Chamber of Commerce named Polycarpos Georghadjis, who was in a position to recruit Cyprus Government officials and the police prepared to supply information on such activities as operations, investigations and details of informants. Georghadjis proved to be a talented conspirator. Initially, he met informants to transfer information, but when one was nearly caught with a written report, he arranged for meets through cut-out contacts. A prized informant was Special Branch Inspector George Lagoudontis, who throughout the campaign reported on the daily operational meetings held in Nicosia Police Station between senior Army officers and police representatives. Indeed, he claimed to be Grivas's Intelligence Officer and persuaded him to protect his cover as an anti-vice officer by placing him on a list of Greek-Cypriot traitors.

The first direct attack on a police station occurred in Limassol on 10 June when a bomb injured several people, including Able Seaman Alexander Thompson. It was the start of a sustained bombing and grenade campaign that would see over 4,000 devices delivered or thrown, causing death, severe injury and distress to those involved. In the first of fifteen attacks over the next six months, on 19 June, Kyriakides and his fifteen-man group attacked Amiandos Police Station and killed Station Sergeant Ioannis Demosthenous, the first Greek-Cypriot police officer to die in the campaign. Operational inexperience led to a gunman being arrested at a roadblock with a Sten gun concealed in a violin case. On 20 June EOKA attacked several British commercial interests in Nicosia with explosive devices and carried out its first direct attack on the Armed Forces when RAF Acting Corporal Myles O'Connor, of 264 Signals Unit, would be awarded the British Empire Medal for gallantry when he tossed out a grenade thrown into the Palms Bar through a window, at the same time shouting to nine friends to take cover. On the 21st, a bomb exploding outside Cyprus Police Headquarters in Nicosia killed the first Greek-Cypriot civilian, a bystander, and injured thirteen Turkish-Cypriots. This angered their leader, Dr Fazil Kutchuk. Not unexpectedly, the Cyprus Police were insufficiently equipped or trained to deal with unexploded devices, although they were fortunate to have Chief Inspector Bird, a ballistics expert who had served in Palestine before and after the war. RAOC bomb disposal officers removed devices from the home of Lieutenant General

## THE OUTBREAK OF THE EOKA CAMPAIGN

Keightley, Brigadier Ricketts and several other senior officers. A proposal by Grivas to ambush Keightley at Boghaz as he travelled between HQ Middle East Command and his house at Kyrenia was vetoed by Makarios in favour of a grenade attack on married quarters in Nicosia and Kyrenia two days later. These attacks highlighted the vulnerability of Service families, in particular those living in private hirings within the community, many of them unaccompanied dependants of servicemen serving in Egypt.

Early in July, Colonel Grivas, who had been travelling around Cyprus incognito for several months, joined the Troodos Guerrilla Groups and stayed with the Greek Army reservist and schoolmaster Ioannis Katsoullis in a house on the outskirts of Kakopetria, nine miles to the east of Kykko Monastery. Since police or Army patrols were rare, the guerrillas led a relaxed life, training by day and sleeping in villages near their hideouts, a lifestyle that suited their romantic notion of resistance fighters. Civilian clothes were worn, except when photos were taken, in which case British Battledress and berets added to the romance.

In mid-July, Field Marshal Harding visited Cyprus and in talks with Lieutenant General Keightley and Brigadier Ricketts agreed that if a State of Emergency was declared, Cyprus District would be reinforced by 50 and 51 (Independent) Brigades from 1st Infantry Division in Egypt and 3rd Division units sent from the UK and 3 Commando Brigade in Malta. Grivas and Athens both claimed that the transfer of troops from Egypt was because the Cyprus had become ungovernable.

Encouraged by sedition stoked up by Archbishop Makarios, a general strike at the end of July led to serious disturbances, with soldiers supporting the police by patrolling in Nicosia. Intelligence had identified the EOKA offensive against the police after several inept assassination attempts and then Special Constables Zavros, a postal worker with three brothers in the Police, was murdered on 11 August. A fortnight later, Special Branch Constables Kostopulous and Poullis were shot dead outside Alhambra Hall Market in Ledra Street, Nicosia while they were observing a PEON rally. When the three gunmen left the scene on bicycles, the crowd seized Charilaos Michael, a Revenue Department clerk, and handed him over to the police. On 8 September, EOKA scored a significant propaganda coup when twelve young men led by Dinos Charalanbous seized several weapons from Kyrenia Police Station and withdrew without loss, all within sight of a British Army detachment in the Castle, then being used as a detention centre. Among the detainees was Marcos Drakos, who had been arrested for terrorist offences. By the early autumn, the operational capability of the Cyprus

Police was near to collapse, particularly among those sidelined for duty because they were not Greek-Cypriots. Appeals at the end of June for 1,500 volunteers to join the new Cyprus Police Reserve had met with limited success.

Deteriorating internal security led to Cyprus being discussed at a tripartite conference at Lancaster Gate in London between the UK, Greece and Turkey, but the exclusion from the negotiations of anyone representing *enosis* led to Makarios threatening that if the talks failed, the 'liberation struggle would be continued by other means.' While the delegates agreed that Cyprus was important to the defence of the NATO southern flank and therefore the British military contribution was essential, Greece warned that tranquillity in Cyprus could not be guaranteed unless *enosis* was granted. Turkey insisted the island was critical to the strategic protection of her southern ports and coastline. Britain and Turkey doubted the stability of the Greek Government. A proposal by Prime Minister Sir Anthony Eden that the two communities be given self-government guaranteed by representatives in Nicosia reporting to a British governor responsible for defence and foreign affairs was rejected. The stalemate induced serious rioting against Greek interests in Turkey.

Grivas re-opened his liberation struggle with the second attack on the Cyprus Broadcasting Service and also Central Police HQ on 31 August. Several grenades and improvised devices were thrown at British married quarters, most of which failed to explode. Two days later, a time bomb in a lorry smuggled past the Guard Tent by a Greek-Cypriot employed at 264 Signals Unit RAF at Ayios Nikolaos exploded, badly wounding Pilot Officer Norman Harvey. The day before, a 2 Royal Inniskilling Fusiliers patrol was ambushed near Famagusta, and when Archbishop Makarios was stopped in his official car during follow-up operations, he registered a complaint. Masked gunmen seized rifles and shotguns from Paralimni Police Station and an attempt was made to assassinate the communist secretary-general of the Pan Cyprian Federation of Labour (The Old Trade Unions).

By the early autumn, the Cyprus Police was in dire straits. Although the force was compelled to work longer hours, at continual risk from EOKA, their pay not keeping up with the costs of living, Commissioner of Police Robbins was refusing to accept the growing list of Greek-Cypriots resignations. To relieve routine activities, the Auxiliary Police was formed almost entirely from Turkish-Cypriot farmers to guard government buildings and provide escorts during the slack periods of their agricultural calendar. The 1,084 officers recruited in 1955 had risen to 1,595 three years later. Local policing with crime reduction patrols in urban areas was increased with the recruitment of about 750 Ordinary Specials, mainly Turkish-Cypriots, rising to 1,475 in 1956, and Emergency Specials being recruited from the expatriate community and government officials. On 5 September, Foreign Secretary Harold Macmillan tabled proposals that government for Cyprus should be similar to the principles applied in Malta of appointed ministers and an elected assembly to manage internal affairs.

In early September, the first joint Army/Police cordon-and-search operation of Strovolos, a suburb near the Airport, by the Cyprus Police, the Royal Inniskillings and 5 Wing, RAF Regiment was opened by a police loudspeaker waking the residents at about 3 am. While the detailed searches unearthed material associated with EOKA, a picnic lunch was provided by the Army for the residents.

The Army developed three basic types of search. The 'whirlwind' involved the swooping of a small party of soldiers and police, often using a civilian lorry, to search a particular house or area, usually based on intelligence, or perhaps by setting up a snap roadblock. The 'village' search was usually speculative or based on information received and began with the dawn establishment of a cordon to prevent farmers leaving for their fields and to catch guerrillas making their way to their hideouts. The loudspeaker then announced a curfew after which the men and boys were assembled centrally, perhaps on the football field or in the village square for screening by intelligence officers, while police and soldiers carried out house-by-house searches. Sometimes a masked informer pointed out EOKA suspects or sympathizers. Women from 27 Independent Company (Women's Royal Army Corps) or 114 (Women's Royal Army Corps) Provost Company helped with the searches. 'Large scale' swoops usually involving several battalions or a brigade, applied the same principles but called for a high degree of co-ordination and security.

As the internal security situation worsened and the Cyprus Police became less effective, and when the Cyprus Government appealed for military assistance to aid the civil authorities, 50 Infantry Brigade began arriving by troopship from Egypt and took up positions in north Cyprus, including Nicosia in mid-August. The 1st Battalion, South Staffordshires (1 South Staffords) moved into Wolseley Barracks. Brigadier JAR Robertson's 51 Lorried Infantry Brigade, also landed and took over the south-east sector of Cyprus that included Larnaca and Famagusta. The Army were still in support of the civil authorities and largely confined to guarding government buildings, unless requested by a senior police officer to support police operations, such as riot control and search operations. The troops were restricted by strict rules of engagement.

After the MacMillan proposal was rejected in the first week of September, 3 Commando Brigade was instructed to deploy to Cyprus and to take over the south-west sector from 35 Engineer Regiment. The Royal Marines had taken control of the management of amphibious operations when the Army Commando brigades were disbanded in 1945 and had formed the Amphibious Warfare Squadron. It was capable of lifting 600 troops, their vehicles and equipment in two Landing Ships Tanks converted into assault ships, HMS *Striker* and *Reggio*, the two tank landing craft, HMS *Bastion* and *Redoubt*, with the HQ on HMS *Meon*. A shambolic Army landing exercise at Tobruk in 1952 had led to 3 Commando Brigade, then based in Malta, providing the Embarked Force to be ferried to trouble spots by the Squadron. The Brigade was about to depart for an exercise in Libya when it was warned to deploy to Cyprus and take over the southern sector that included Limassol. Within four days, 1,300 Royal Marines and their vehicles were at sea, with 45 Commando embarked on the assault ships and 40 Commando crammed into the light cruiser HMS *Birmingham*. After landing at Limassol on the 10th, 45 Commando took over operational responsibility for the Pentadactylos Mountains and the 'Panhandle', with Commando HQ based at Aghirda at the southern end of the Kyrenia Pass. Under command it had an Amphibious Warfare Troop with its light assault boats. Transferred by the Amphibious Warfare Squadron from Egypt and landing at Famagusta, 1st Battalion, Royal Scots (1 Royal Scots) gave the Royal Marines the three battalions expected in brigades. Moving to Coral Bay Leave Camp near Paphos, it covered 600 square miles that contained fifteen police stations. C Company was sent to the Limni Sulphur Mine near Polis on the north coast.

Within four days, four Troops launched Operation *Storm Sail*, a cordon-and-search of the village of Mandras, which included the first search of a church. Surgeon Lieutenant Guy Bradford held a surgery that lasted over two hours. At the same time, in a combined operation, Z Troop and Royal Engineers executed an amphibious raid at Xylophagen on the Panhandle while a land move by elements of 2 Royal Inniskilling Fusiliers, 2 Green Howards and 200 police officers led to the arrest of 200 EOKA suspects. On the 13th, amid escalating damage and vandalism to British businesses, including the NAAFI, 40 Commando landed at Limassol. Within two days, two Troops had quelled a disturbance. A week later, two other Troops were embroiled in an ugly riot in the mining village of Pano Amiandos in the Troodos when police officers tried to remove EOKA slogans from walls. Church bells

## THE OUTBREAK OF THE EOKA CAMPAIGN

summoned the mob.

In mid-September, when the Cyprus Government declared EOKA to be illegal, Makarios began to reflect Greek-Cypriot concerns that the United Kingdom was about to get tough. Henceforth, penalties for supporting EOKA included the imposition of curfews and the collective fining of communities that actively supported EOKA or failed to take measures supporting law and order. Measures were also introduced to hold EOKA suspects without trial at several detention camps. Kokkinotrimithia Camp, about eight miles west of Nicosia and usually known as 'Camp K', was a former isolation hospital surrounded by several Nissen huts with corrugated roofs and could house about 260 internees. It had a section for wealthy prisoners who could be supplied with expensive foods by their families. The camp was surrounded by a double perimeter fence that was patrolled by military patrols and dog handlers with their German Shepherds. 'Goon' towers overlooked the compounds. The Cypriot Prison Service managed the detainees and detention quarters.

In August the Mayor of Nicosia had refused to assist the Cyprus Police quell an ugly disturbance and claimed that all Greek-Cypriots were members of EOKA. The Mayors of Larnaca and Famagusta then declared that the Greek-Cypriots would continue 'their sacred struggle without fear of any repressive measures'. Since the loyalty of the Greek-Cypriot element of the Cyprus Police could not be guaranteed, Turkish-Cypriots were invited to join the 165-strong Police Mobile Reserve. A specialist unit led by Colonial Police officers with experience in Kenya, Malaya and Palestine, it was initially specifically trained to disperse urban demonstrations. By 1957, its role was widened to include cordon-and-search operations specifically against Greek-Cypriot villages and its establishment increased to 580. This role led to considerable resentment from Greek-Cypriot communities but at least the authorities could rely upon effective searching.

In much the same way as the Romans had introduced a planned road network in England, the roads built in Cyprus by the British since 1878 were the envy of the Near East. Of a total network of 3,300 miles, 800 asphalted miles connected the principal towns, the remaining miles being narrow secondary roads linking villages. Innumerable narrow tracks filtered alongside fields, orange groves and vineyards, to beaches and through mountain forests. The increased use of lorries in supplying the camps and barracks sprouting up throughout Cyprus and the ferrying of troops on operations fell onto the young shoulders of the RASC and regimental drivers, many of whom had never driven until they joined up and were now expected to acquire combat driving skills under active service conditions. When a 1st Battalion, Gordon Highlanders (1 Gordon Highlanders) convoy ran into an ambush, the drivers did not realize that the shooting was an attack and stopped too close to each other; consequently, the Highlanders suffered several casualties before they could counter-attack and drive the guerrillas from their positions. The mountain roads and tracks perched on the side of ravines and valleys had countless tight hairpin corners unsuited to lorries and were treacherous from dust in summer and rain and snow in autumn and winter. Of the estimated forty-seven men killed in road traffic crashes, about forty per cent died in the Troodos after lorries, armoured cars and light vehicles skidded into ravines; at least one Ferret Scout Car was blown into a deep valley by a mine and its crew killed. At the time, the only mule pack transport in the Army was used in Hong Kong to support observation posts overlooking the Chinese border. Although a column was not formed in Cyprus, some places were so inaccessible that donkeys were hired to carry awkward and heavy equipment over broken ground.

When a police officer apprehended youths daubing 'EOKA' on several buildings in Metaxas Square during the evening of 17 September, a major riot developed during which the British Institute and its historic library of 16,000 priceless books and documents was burnt. A Royal Military Police (RMP) Land Rover being used by a patrol to prevent British soldiers and families entering the seething square was wrecked. It was three hours before the Cyprus Police sought support from 1 South Staffords, and then shortly after 11 pm the lead platoon dispersed the mob by firing tear gas and several rifle shots.

Riot control centred on a Riot Platoon deployed into a disciplined box formation designed to be psychologically powerful in comparison to scruffy and undisciplined rioters. Wearing steel helmets, respirators at the ready and armed with batons and shields, which at first were dustbin lids, two sections led followed by the platoon commander, the megaphone-carrying bugler, two projectile firers armed with a tear-gas gun and dye sprayer and two carrying a banner on 10-foot poles which when unfurled, read, 'This is an unlawful assembly and you must disperse immediately.' When the warning failed to impress, as it usually did, the two soldiers crossed to display on the rear, 'If you do not disperse now, we will fire tear gas.' There were occasions when troops opened fire, for instance in Limassol on 27 September, when 40 Commando shot a ringleader. Bringing up the rear was the third section carrying barbed wire, stretchers and a wireless set.

In a raid on Akhna Police Station on 22 September, EOKA gunmen stole rifles and several radios, but several suspects fingered by Cypriots were detained in Kyrenia Castle. EOKA again achieved international recognition when Cyprus was discussed at the UN on 23 September but the simmering disagreements were once more aired between Greece and Turkey. The British suggested that the terrorism in Cyprus had nothing to do with colonialism but was a bid engineered by Greece for *enosis*. As Athens failed to convince the Assembly to place Cypriot self-determination on the General Assembly agenda, the island braced itself for further violence.

That night, seventeen EOKA detainees confined to two rooms in the north tower, among then Markos Drakos and Gregoris Afxentiou, began a noisy disturbance to cover the breaching of a bricked gun port, and then several bed sheets tied together were thrown out. Over the previous nights, the detainees had calculated the time that it took a sentry to patrol the parapet around the tower and, using this as a guide, Drakos controlled the abseiling of each escaper onto a platform overlooking the adjoining Country Club. The story goes that when a British officer reported a commotion on the beach to the prison authorities, he was advised that since it was part of the club, this was not entirely unexpected. Seven escapers were quickly recaptured, four by 45 Commando, but most of the remainder joined the EOKA groups in Nicosia and the mountains. One of those invited to review the security of the castle was Royal Marines Major Hugh Bruce, who had made an unsuccessful escape from Colditz Castle during the war. He assessed that it would be easy to escape from the tower within twenty minutes. It was remarks such as this that led to speculation that the authorities made no great effort to prevent the escape, so that the escapers could then be tracked to EOKA cells. The escape shattered public confidence, and leaflets distributed by a subversive Turkish-Cypriot group known as *Volkan* criticized security lapses. When a newspaper then exposed that several senior officials were at a dinner party held at Government House on the night of the Metaxas Square riot, London finally lost patience with Sir Robert Armitage and in the last week of September announced that he had been posted to Nyasaland (now Malawi) and would be replaced by Field Marshal Sir John Harding as Governor. The reasons given for the appointment of a Service officer were to satisfy the United Kingdom's NATO obligations and the need for a co-ordinated approach to address the problem of terrorism.

CHAPTER FIVE

# Cyprus in Turmoil

(October to November 1955)

A month before schedule, Field Marshal Harding relinquished his duties as CIGS to Field Marshal Templer, and on 3 October he and his wife Mary flew to Nicosia. During the Swearing-In Ceremony, he stated that he had three missions: restoring law and order with strong policing and military power, implementing social and economic reforms and developing the constitution using strong civil administration. Critically, his powers and financial resources were greater than those available to Sir Robert Armitage.

Born in 1896 and educated at Ilminster Grammar School in Somerset, Harding joined the Territorial Army in 1914 and was commissioned into the Somerset Light Infantry when war broke out in August, serving mainly in Palestine. During the Second World War, he commanded the 7th Armoured Division in North Africa and VIII and XIII Corps in Italy. In 1946, he commanded Middle East Command until in 1948 he was appointed Commander-in-Chief Land Forces, Far East. In 1951 he commanded the British Army of the Rhine before becoming CIGS.

Harding knew that he must negotiate, but with whom? Yannis Clerides was the Greek-Cypriot leader on the Legislative Council and recognized to be the elected representative by the British Government. His son, Glafkos, had been shot down while serving as an RAF bomber tail-gunner and had escaped three times from German prison camps. Or should it be Archbishop Makarios and his Ethnarchy Council of Cypriot Orthodox priests? Although he knew that he would risk undermining Clerides, the power of the Ethnarchy was significant and it was to Makarios that he turned. On 4 October, the same day that Field Marshal Papagos of Greece died, who had been a significant supporter of *enosis*, Harding and Makarios met in the Ledra Palace Hotel card room, where Harding suggested to Makarios that since communism was the main threat to regional stability, he could make a major contribution toward gradual self-determination since it was likely that the strategic importance of Cyprus would change. He also emphasized that with or without Makarios he would tackle EOKA. Over several meetings during the next week, Makarios insisted that once London recognized Cypriot self-determination, then he would draft a constitution to put to the electorate. When they discussed the content of the Lancaster Gate Agreement, Harding detected that although it was obvious that he was prepared to compromise, Makarios was under increasing pressure from Ethnarchy hardliners not prepared to budge from self-determination, in particular from Bishop Kyriakides of Kyrenia, whose brother, Renos, was the EOKA commander leading the attacks on police stations. Sending Makarios a draft constitution, Harding wrote, 'It is not therefore the position that the principle of self-determination can never be applicable to Cyprus' – a double negative leaving the door open because of the perceived importance of Cyprus to NATO. Makarios replied that while the demand for self-determination was non-negotiable, the timing was, and once agreed he would help the British Government frame a constitution. Harding referred the offer to London and was told the British position remained as at the Lancaster Gate Conference, in particular that guarantees were required for the minority Turkish-Cypriots. But Makarios was unable to give any, and a stalemate emerged. By 8 October the talks had collapsed and a £38 million development package announced by Harding to raise the prosperity of the island, on the proviso that the internal security situation improved, was rejected by the nationalists.

The failure of Greek diplomacy at the UN and the arrival of Harding led to Grivas opening his next offensive, his aim being to paralyse the police into inaction and thereby draw the Army into ground of his choosing. Lefkoniko Police Station was identified as a soft target and was recced by the son of a village mayor who was part of the EOKA Group led by Gregoris Afxentiou. On the same day that Harding first met Makarios, Afxentiou led six EOKA to the high school where they donned masks and then walked down the main street to the Police Station. The duty constable fled and the remaining police were locked in a cell without resistance. Afxentiou's men broke into the armoury and left carrying nine .303-inch rifles, two Greener shotguns, ammunition and a radio set. The raid replicated the attack on Akhana Police Station and again shattered the Cyprus Police's morale. Elsewhere, the Sabotage Groups in Nicosia, Famagusta, Larnaca and Limassol escalated their operations.

By the autumn, the pressure on the RAOC led to 625 Ordnance Depot, which had been in Cyprus since 1949, being expanded with the addition of 146 Vehicle and 238 Vehicle Depots. The specialist 4 Mobile Laundry and Bath Unit supported camps that lacked heavy duty laundries and showers and set up showers near rivers and reservoirs. When 9 Base Ammunition Depot transferred 11,000 tons of ammunition from Egypt to 310 Ammunition Depot at the former RAF Lakatamia, however, security was tested when light civil aircraft still used the runway. The Corps also provided local employment, which proved treacherous on several occasions with the result falling on the shoulders of soldiers. When the Famagusta EOKA Pavlos Pavlakis was tipped off by a shipping agent that weapons arriving from Egypt were being stored in a 625 Ordnance Depot warehouse at Four Mile Point, George Matsis and eight men raided the store, tied up the Turkish-Cypriot night watchman and loaded Sten guns, .303-inch rifles, ammunition and other war stores that had just been unloaded from the cargo ship, the *Halcyon Med*, into a lorry and left leaving a receipt signed by 'Digenes' and an undertaking that they would be paid for when Cyprus was freed. An investigation focused on the weakness of the security of the warehouse. Another group successfully raided the Mitsero mine for explosives and detonators.

As Harding reviewed his bailiwick, he found that so long as EOKA continued to operate unopposed, internal security was likely to deteriorate. Although intent on catching 'Digenes', he noted that the Cyprus Police morale was very low and bolstered their performance by instructing that all police stations were be reinforced with a permenent military presence. He replaced failing Colonial Police officers and obtained authority from the Colonial Office for Commissioner of Police Robbins to second British police officers into the self-contained UK Police Unit being raised to provide a model of modern policing to the Cyprus Police and also to target EOKA cells in towns. Despite manpower shortages in British constabularies, advertisements were circulated in the Constabularies of Kent, Lancashire, Staffordshire, Yorkshire West Riding and Scotland, seeking 150 officers for two-year secondments divided into twenty-one months' service in Cypus followed by three months' leave. Although young unmarried officers were needed, they did not come forward, and Robbins had no alternative but accept older men close to retirement seeking to enhance their pensions. But very few had been to Cyprus and they therefore had little knowledge of its history, culture and people. The advance guard of thirty policemen that arrived on 28 November was accompanied by RAF Police reinforcements and six police dog handlers and their German Shepherds. Although the Cypriot Judiciary largely resisted intimidation, EOKA raised the tension against them, resulting in additional judges being sent from the United Kingdom on three-month postings to hear cases in four new Courts.

Realizing that he was now facing a popular soldier with a formidable reputation already adopting a 'strong hand' by hardening the defences of government and military installations, police stations and key points, Grivas took the opportunity of the collapse of the talks between Harding and Makarios to order Operation *Forward to Victory*. Needing to prop up Greek-Cypriot morale, among his objectives was to create favourable conditions for the offensive by absorbing 'the enemy's blows' and retaliating with shootings, ambushes, bombings and unrest in quick succession. The demoralization of the Cyprus Police, dislocation of security forces' intelligence and drawing the Army into the open remained high on his target list. The execution of his plan depended on the youth provoking the security forces by displaying Greek flags and daubing EOKA slogans. At his disposal and largely intact after a summer of inactivity, were the motivated mountain Guerrilla Groups, the two strongest being the one based at Pitsillia commanded by Afxentiou and the one at Kykko formed from the Kyrenia Castle escapers by Markos Drakos. In November he instructed the twenty-strong Kyriakides Group to construct a network of seven hideouts on a massive ridge overlooking Spilia and Kourdhai in the Adelphi Forest about five miles south-east of Kakopetria in the Troodos. Collectively known as the Castle, the dugouts were burrowed into rocks and earth, reinforced by corrugated iron taken to the site by donkey and expertly camouflaged with earth, bushes and boulders. Each hideout was capable of accommodating about five men, and they were connected by passageways. Outside there was even a weapon training range. When Kyriakides had finished, Grivas moved to the Castle and assembled a force of about thirty guerrillas consisting of his headquarters and the groups led by Afxentiou, Kyriakides and Christos Chartas. Afxentiou was back in favour after stealing weapons from the Amiandos mine security guards. If there was one weakness of the Castle, indeed of the hideouts, it was that locals knew about them and not all were supporters of EOKA.

Deciding to take direct control of internal security, Harding created an operational HQ under his command and independent of Middle East Command and Cyprus District. To organize civil affairs as Deputy Governor, he appointed the experienced colonial administrator George Sinclair, fresh from several West African postings. In early November, Brigadier Geoffrey Baker arrived as Chief of Staff to Harding. Baker was a Royal Artillery officer who had recently instructed at the Imperial Defence College. Wounded fighting the Italians in the East African campaign and also while commanding 127 Field Regiment RA in Sicily, he had commanded 3 Royal Horse Artillery and had held a staff appointment at the War Office. Brigadier Ricketts was promoted to Major General and reverted to Cyprus District with administrative responsibility for the Brigades. He was also appointed Director of Security. Lieutenant General Keightley remained in command of Middle East Command but was not directly involved in the management of operations in Cyprus. Fortunately, the amicable relationship between Baker and Major General Benson, who was Keightley's Chief of Staff, soothed any difficulties. Harding formalized the existing brigades' areas of operations by forming 3 Commando Brigade District centred on Limassol, 50 Infantry Brigade District at Nicosia and 51 Infantry Brigade District at Famagusta, each supported by an infantry and armoured car reserve and under command of Baker, who was also Director of Operations.

Harding quickly found that the intelligence structure was weak and that the Cyprus Secretariat and District internal security organizations were inadequately structured to meet the crisis. Part of the problem was that the expatriate Colonial Service officials and Colonial Police officers were largely divorced from the indigenous community and therefore few spoke Greek or Turkish; indeed, the paucity of Greek speakers was a hindrance throughout the Emergency. Using internal security structures being developed in Malaya as templates, Harding divided Cyprus into eight operational sectors each supervised by a senior Army officer, with the Police superintendent and the District Commissioner providing the civil and political input. The hub of internal security centred on joint military and police HQs known as MILPOLs. To improve the understanding and co-ordination of counter-insurgency, army, navy and air force officers and police officers attended a joint staff academy; within the year this became known as the Internal Security Training School. Harding also invited Lieutenant Colonel Geoffrey White, who was the Chief Constable of Warwickshire and had been his Provost Marshal in XIII Corps in Trieste, to advise Robbins on policing.

After transferring from Egypt, Middle East Air Force reorganized in July 1955 to HQ Air Levant at RAF Nicosia, controlling operations in the Eastern Mediterranean region, including Cyprus; RAF Aden took care of the Persian Gulf and Indian Ocean operations. Complementing the Shackletons flying from Malta, in April 1956 Gannet anti-submarine aircraft from 847 Naval Air Squadron began coastal surveillance and anti-smuggling operations from RAF Nicosia and directed RAF Venom fighter bombers of No. 6 Squadron and 208 Squadron Hawker Hunters to suspect vessels. Although gliders were no longer used by the Army, the provision of air observation and co-ordination with the ground forces was retained by the officers and sergeants of the Glider Pilot

Regiment flying Austers. With an aircrew of a pilot and observer, the Austers had won an enviable reputation during the war as reliable communication platforms and spotters. In April 1956, 1915 Light Liaison Flight was formed at Middle Wallop and, moving to Cyprus as the Independent Light Liaison Flight, joined 1910 Flight from 651 Air Observation Post Squadron at RAF Lakatamia. However, its three Austers did not arrive for several months and the Flight shared the aircraft of 1910 Flight. The Austers operated from eight airstrips, including a golf course at Xeros, a soccer pitch at Famagusta and the road near Episkopi. At least one aircraft was designated as the Voice Aircraft and had loudspeakers fitted under each wing that enabled announcements and messages to be broadcast. The Austers could also be fitted with four 20lb bomb racks, and while the release mechanism inside the cockpit was simple, it was not always reliable. When the Army Air Corps was formed in 1957, the two Flights were renamed 10 and 15 Independent Flights respectively until in May 1958 they were amalgamated into 653 Squadron. In December 1958 the Army pilots suffered their only fatality when an Auster flown by Captain Terence Mulady struck overhead electricity cables near Nicosia. Two members of the Royal Horse Guards and a Lancashire Fusilier at a roadblock attempted unsuccessfully to save the pilot from the burning wreckage.

Each Brigade was supported by a Signals Troop of about thirty Royal Signals responsible for all aspects of communication. The Brigade Command was operated through the VHF Wireless Set B44 manpack transceivers, which had been introduced as part of the Larkspur range of military radios in about 1948 and, with a well-sited antenna, had a range of up to fifteen miles. The No 62 HF set and Canadian Wireless Set No 19, which incorporated High Frequency and Very High Frequency (VHF) frequencies in the same chassis, remained in service in Cyprus. A major advantage of the B44 was that its VHF function meant it did not suffer the increased 'mush' static and interference when the ionosphere descended earthwards at night. The Troop also maintained the field telephones lines laid to the units, which could number at least thirty sub-stations, and provided technicians to repair equipment. When 50 Infantry Brigade established a Brigade Tactical HQ at the Central Police Station, its 214 Signal Troop erected antennae on police stations and laid line to the extent that the headquarters could be operational within half an hour. Its fellow 215 Signal Troop supported 51 Infantry Brigade. The three brigades and those that arrived later in the campaign also brought their own RMP Provost Companies, Ordnance Field Parks to administer its logistic support, Medical Groups and REME Workshops.

In the third week of October, reinforcements sought by Field Marshal

Harding began flooding into Cyprus. The 1st Battalion, The Gordon Highlanders (1 Gordons) arrived in Transport Command Hastings aircraft from RAF Lyneham and, joining 3 Commando Brigade District, moved to the largely tented Aberdeen Camp, which had been built by 30 Field Squadron next to a mine near Xeros in the middle of an area of largely Turkish-owned citrus groves. D Company, 1st Battalion, The King's Own Yorkshire Light Infantry (1 KOYLI) deployed from Aden and, joining 1 Royal Scots at Paphos, first took over Limni Camp before moving to East End Camp near Ktima. Joining 50 Infantry Brigade from the United Kingdom was 1st Battalion, The Royal Norfolk Regiment (1 Norfolks), which moved into Britannia Camp near the Cyprus Broadcasting Service as the Island Reserve. It also provided platoons to guard Government House and Wolseley Barracks and a Guard Force for Camp K detention camp. Two more battalions were taken under command by 51 Infantry Brigade District to join 2 Royal Inniskillings at Famagusta and 40 Field Regiment RA at Larnaca. The 1st Battalion, The Royal Leicestershire Regiment (1 Leicesters) disembarked at Famagusta from the troopship HMT *Charlton Star*, having travelled from Sudan with their families, and moved into the Golden Sands Leave Camp. The 1st Battalion, The Middlesex Regiment (1 Middlesex) also disembarked at Famagusta on 28 October from HMT *Empire Clyde* and, replacing 2 Green Howards, moved into the tented Alma Camp at Dhekelia. Rioters had to be cleared from the streets of Larnaca before the families could move into married quarters. The Green Howards returned to Strensall and disbandment to meet reductions in defence spending, by which infantry regiments were to reduce their establishments to one Regular battalion.

Although the organization of battalions depended on their locations, commanding officers adapted their orders of battle to meet the requirements of their sector. Lieutenant Colonel Brinkley, who commanded the Norfolks, merged the heavy weapons platoons of Support Company into rifle platoons, giving him four companies. When the Battalion took over as the Duty Internal Security Battalion in Nicosia in December, it remained in its lines at the Cyprus Broadcasting Service Camp with Brinkley appointed Operational Commander, Nicosia reporting directly to Field Marshal Harding and frequently meeting with the District Officer and Police District Superintendent. An officer at Nicosia Central Police Station provided military/police liaison and was the interface should Battalion Tactical HQ be required. The Standby Company, which was accommodated in tents in Wolseley Barracks on immediate readiness, was plagued with call-outs to incidents and false alarms. The Reserve Company remained in the Battalion lines ready to move when required. Brinkley placed a 'troubleshooter' platoon in the old Post Office overlooking Metaxas Square opposite the gateway leading to Ledra Street in Old Nicosia. The remaining two companies guarded the camps, provided patrols and helped administer the running of the camp. The Signals Platoon found that the distances between detached sub-units meant that the signallers needed to learn Morse.

By 1956, the standard infantry section of eight soldiers had been grouped into two 'flat foot' patrols, the concept allowing a platoon to swamp an urban area with a large number of patrols. In Northern Ireland this formation became known as a 'brick'. The Royal Military Police in Nicosia, Famagusta and Limassol soon developed mobile Anti-Assassin Patrols consisting of three military police and one Cyprus Police in largely unprotected Land Rovers from early morning to midnight; however, these were targets for bombers and gunmen lurking in side streets, gardens and on balconies. Ambush Patrols were essentially counter-ambush operations in which military patrols lurked in or near places from which ambushes had previously been sprung. Although Harding insisted on courtesy and firmness, many troops found dealing with the youth of both sexes by removing Greek flags and EOKA slogans to be humiliating and frustrating, particularly in the knowledge that one false move would inevitably result in controversy.

In September 1955, 11 (Field) Squadron, RAF Regiment arrived to protect RAF assets. Having protected RAF stations in the deserts of the Middle East and North Africa for thirty-three years, it was initially tasked to lift minefields laid to defend Cyprus during the Second World War. In November the Squadron supported military operations and added to its vehicle pool by recovering several undamaged Humber armoured cars from a bombing range. It also trained RAF technicians in weapons and anti-ambush drills. One regular event was to escort a convoy ferrying stores from Famagusta to RAF Ayios Nikolaos, where a unit provided radar coverage from a hut and a few Bedford radio trucks in a tented camp at Cape Greco. In February 1957, the convoy, which usually included a Humber, was attacked several times. On the 5th a device seen 6ft up a tree was defused. Three days later a similar device damaged a lorry. Later, when a second convoy taking men from 751 Signals Unit to Cape Greco ran into an electonically controlled mine, the Unit commander, Squadron Leader R Street and the RAF Regiment escort captured a terrorist. Three weeks later, in a fourth ambush, three grenades that damaged a lorry also badly wounded an RAF officer. A search by 11 Field Squadron, again with a Humber, resulted in one EOKA being shot and another being captured.

As troops began arriving in Cyprus, camps and their associated employment opportunities sprung up all over the island. Since married quarters had originally been established to the requirements of Cyprus District, the increased need led to RASC Barracks Services being enlarged to manage the accommodation of long suffering families, some of whom had been posted overseas for several years. Since the building of the garrisons and the married quarter 'patches' at Episkopi and Dhekelia were months behind schedule, a large number of families were accommodated in hirings rented from local landlords. This proved unpopular, and when some families of the Middle East Command rearguard arrived from Egypt, screaming Greek-Cypriot mobs stoned their buses as they were being driven to their bungalows at Berengaria on the outskirts of Limassol. Such was the hostility in the town that families were largely confined inside the married quarter perimeter and could only shop when the streets were patrolled by soldiers. As the hostility gathered pace, there was clear evidence that the vetting of locally employed employees was weak. Some were terrorists willing to lob grenades into married quarters.

As part of his strategy to intimidate the Army, Grivas escalated attacks on soldiers and airmen – anywhere. On 21 October, Private Sidney Ingram of 1 South Staffords was the first soldier to be killed when he died from wounds after a grenade was thrown into a Nicosia bar. A teenage gunman shot an RAF officer in the face. A week later, the Royal Scots Lance Corporal Angus Milne was the first soldier to be killed in action when his convoy was ambushed at Kissonerga, a few miles north-west of Paphos. In the same incident, a young Greek-Cypriot was mortally wounded. The banning by Harding of the annual 28 October Oxi Day celebrating the refusal of Greece to surrender to Italy in 1940 and the confirmation of the death sentencing of Michael Karaolis, who, in spite of a clemency plea from the French author Albert Camus, had his appeal refused for the murder of the Special Branch Constable Poullis in August, led to the escalation of violence, much of it egged on by Colonel Grivas and Radio Athens, and led by hundreds of students. Several schools were closed. Karaolis had been educated in British schools in Cyprus but resented colonial rule. Three days of violent disturbances were experienced by 40 Commando in Limassol in which several military vehicles were destroyed and a NAAFI grocery burnt. Although the Royal Marines had imposed a curfew on the 28th, such was the disruption that they had difficulty imposing it. When a patrol armed with truncheons and commanded by Sergeant Harry James came under fire from two curfew-breakers in a hut, who also threw a grenade, Marines James Coughtney and Kenneth Goodey barged through the door and captured them. Coughtney received the British Empire Medal. Rioters in Famagusta were drenched in green dye from an Ack Pack spraying vehicle operated by Fusilier Swain of 2 Royal Inniskillings Fusiliers.

By mid-October, the internal security had deteriorated to such an extent that the Cyprus Police were unable to maintain law and order, even with the troops in support, and the Colonial Office agreed with Harding that the Army should formally aid the civil authorities. On 28 October Harding issued a Royal Instruction granting HM Forces the same legal status as police officers, meaning that soldiers could provide riot squads, patrol, search and mount operations with or without the police. To some extent, Harding had been convinced after Commissioner of Police Robbins had submitted a report on the same day expressing the opinion of several observers that the 1,838-strong Cyprus Police was ineffective. Field Marshal Harding knew that Cyprus would only return to stability after 'Digenes' had been neutralized. By November, MI5 and Special Branch had discovered from Greek communists that he was none other than Colonel George Grivas, the right-wing leader of X Group; however, the *enosis* leaders in Cyprus and Greece were reluctant to accept the fact and accused the British of malicious propaganda, a line they stuck to almost to the end in 1959.

Since most of the troops had been tied up in the endless drudgery of guarding barracks, courts and government buildings, patrolling the streets, enforcing curfews and providing cordons after an incident, manning roadblocks and escorting officials, the collection of intelligence on EOKA was limited. Indeed, not for the only time since 1945 had the Armed Forces been sent on operations by the British Government with little or no intelligence. The collection of intelligence was limited because of the EOKA cell structure and use of couriers, and consequently optimistic assessments were suggesting that EOKA was slow, demoralized, lacked discipline and its lines of communication had been disrupted by police activity after the April Fool's Day bombings. However, interrogations and informant information were producing results, as they would until 1959. Within days of his arrival, Brigadier Baker placed parts of the Troodos and Pentadactylos Mountains out of bounds and launched two cordon-and-search and intelligence collection operations against the EOKA Guerrilla Groups. They were supported by 214 Signals Troop detachments commanded by corporals providing radio detachments from box-body radio lorries and using Land Rovers to lay miles of line in the forest between the tactical HQs. The drivers found negotiating the roads and tracks of the Troodos decidedly more nerve-wracking than EOKA ambushes.

In Operation *Turkey Trot*, 45 Commando supported by companies from the Norfolks and Leicesters began searching for the Afxentiou Group in the Lefkoniko area of the Pentadactylos Mountains. When on 6 November, information was received that a shepherd turned butcher had grown tired of living as a guerrilla, Captain Derek Pounds, the Adjutant, and a patrol from Commando HQ removed him from his house in Lapithos. The butcher then guided patrols to several hideouts, including Afxentiou's lair near Kalogeria where several police weapons and uniforms were found, including some stolen from Lefkoniko Police Station. One hideout that produced forged coins could only be accessed by abseiling fifteen feet to its entrance on a small ledge. Afxentiou and his group escaped because disloyal police officers had compromised the operation; nevertheless, for the second time, a furious Grivas sacked him because he had recruited the butcher and appointed Tassos Sofocleus to command the Pitsillia Group. During the operation, Lance Corporal Gordon Hill of B Company, 1 Leicesters left camp armed with a Sten and two grenades claiming that he was going 'to sort out EOKA'. When he did not return, he was posted absent without leave.

Meanwhile, the longer term Operation *Fox Hunter* was underway in the Troodos. On 10 November, after handing over its sector to the Leicesters, 45 Commando joined the 800-strong battle group at Platres that included C and D Companies, 1 Gordon Highlanders, A Squadron, the Life Guards with their Second World War-era Daimler armoured cars that had been left in Cyprus in 1945, the remainder of 1st Leicesters, elements from 40 Field Regiment and 6 Army Dog Unit. The remaining two Gordon companies were guarding police stations, patrolling roads and carrying out searches along the coastal strip to the north. In support were Sycamore helicopters and Auster aircraft, and in Platres the formidable prison was being as an interrogation centre. Within three days the Commando won a trial of strength in a riot in Vouni, and after rounding up about 300 villagers, thirty men and nine women were charged with incitement to riot.

One major problem experienced throughout the Emergency was long convoys of vehicles heading toward a particular area and thus broadcasting to EOKA that an operation was imminent. This, combined with disloyal police officers supporting Grivas, led to Army commanders finding it difficult to prevent guerrillas slipping through cordons using the innumerable rural tracks. Searching wooded areas was also difficult. Nevertheless, both operations gave troops valuable experience, particularly when HQ RAF Levant agreed that since the Search and Rescue Flight was generally under-employed, it should be reformed as the Internal Security Flight and its Sycamores used to deploy troops on high ground. Patrolling helicopters also forced the guerrillas to go to ground while Army lorries were driven as fast as possible along roads and tracks to them cut off. Although Grivas dismissed such operations as nothing more than theatrical displays of military muscle designed to terrorize the population, he responded by taking the pressure off the Guerrilla Groups with a counter-attack in the towns against the Army. It became a predictable tactic.

On 18 November Cyprus reeled as a blitz of about thirty grenades and bombs were thrown at patrols and tossed into bars. RASC Staff Sergeant Gilbert Cripps, posted to HQ Cyprus District, was killed and a warrant officer was seriously wounded when a time bomb concealed in a bicycle blew the roof of the HQ 51 Infantry Brigade Sergeants Mess at Kykko Camp, about three miles east Nicosia at 3 am. This and a device exploding at the Golden Sands Leave Camp near Famagusta, injuring a soldier, underlined the vulnerability of barracks from disloyal Greek-Cypriots at a time when the Armed Forces were becoming a major employer in a period when investment to Cyprus was on the downward slope. A bomb dropped into a Nicosia Post Office post box destroyed most of the building. In Larnaca, a British police officer was knocked unconscious by young rioters firing stones from catapults and then as the phalanx of the Middlesex Riot Platoon advanced through the narrow street, a swarm of youths bolted into the sanctuary of St Lazarus Church. Anxious parents extracted the less defiant ones, but when food was delivered to the troops, it was too much for the sixty trapped diehards and they meekly surrendered. In an attempt to contain the unrest, and in spite of EOKA intimidation, some parents were persuaded by teachers to send their children back to school, but several schools were forced to close.

Next day in Famagusta, a 2 Royal Inniskilling Fusiliers patrol ambushed near the Cable and Wireless Building had an officer and soldier wounded as it fought a running battle with gunmen through the streets. On the same day, three soldiers were evacuated to hospital by a Sycamore following an ambush near Episkopi. On the 21st, Sergeant Andrew Steel, of 42 Company RASC, died in Limassol Hospital after being wounded in an ambush near Dhekelia. In one of several attempts by EOKA to acquire explosives, the Kyriakides Group ran into determined opposition while raiding Mitsero mine. Next day, when EOKA ambushed a 45 Commando convoy transferring explosive from the asbestos mine at Amiandos to Xeros near Morphou, they had not counted on the inspirational gallantry of Marine William Stevenson. Although badly wounded, he stopped his lorry, allowing Sergeant Hodges, also in the front, to give covering fire while the escorting Royal

Marines led by Lance Corporal Maghee leapt from the back and counter-attacked, during which Maghee was seriously wounded. Several more Royal Marines vehicles were ambushed over the next week, including a marked ambulance attacked by EOKA armed with automatic weapons, including a Bren gun. Next day, a Greek-Cypriot woman died from injuries when a bomb destroyed the Maple Leaf Bar, which was frequently used by soldiers, near Metaxos Square. In Famagusta, the homes of Lieutenant Colonel Cowan, who commanded 625 Ordnance Company RAOC, and Major Reverend Benyon, an Army chaplain, were attacked with grenades.

Grivas led the Kyriakides Group in two ambushes near Khandria on the road between Kyperounda and Agros. Early on 23 November, he posted two groups of five men on high ground astride a sharp bend while he remained with five others in positions overlooking the killing zone. In mid-afternoon, the group shot up a military police Land Rover, killing Lance Corporal Frederick Todd and wounding two others, one of whom would later die of his wounds. Two days later, a 45 Commando cordon guarding the scene of this attack shot dead an elderly Greek-Cypriot believed to be acting suspiciously and failing to halt when challenged. Next day at about 3 pm, it was getting dark and snow was falling when a Ferret Scout Car and Land Rover were spotted, and the guerrillas in the first blocking position opened fire without orders. The Ferret sped through the killing zone, missing mines laid in the road, but the Land Rover skidded into a deep ravine killing Sapper Robert Melson of 37 Field Squadron. The Squadron was part of 25 Engineer Regiment and had had arrived from Maidstone to improve the facilities in the tented camps springing up across Cyprus. The attacks continued with Royal Engineer Sergeant James Shipman of HQ Cyprus District murdered near his married quarter in Nicosia and Craftsman Kenneth Heyes dying in an ambush at Petra, both on the 25th. Next day, Sapper Peter Percivale, also of 37 Field Squadron, was killed and another soldier from Northern Ireland seriously wounded when a large boulder was rolled down an embankment into the path of his vehicle.

During the fortnight, Royal Engineers lost six killed. Among other deaths were Colonel Philip Hatch RE OBE, then posted to HQ Middle Eastern Command, who had died from a heart attack in early June, and three other non-battle deaths since 1 April. Royal Engineer casualties were heavy. Although the success of EOKA attacks was largely sporadic and often not pressed home, the overall intelligence assessment on their capability changed significantly to clear indicators that EOKA was well organized, well armed and widely supported. Of growing concern were the disloyalty of Greek-Cypriot employees in military bases and the network of gunmen and bombers in the urban areas.

CHAPTER SIX

# The Emergency Declared
(November 1955 to November 1956)

The internal security situation had reached such a dangerous level that Harding had no alternative but to declare a State of Emergency on 26 November. While Grivas regarded EOKA as an insurgency group, Harding regarded them as terrorists. Terrorism is variously defined but in principle it is violence used by a formed organization or loose grouping of individuals who have rejected negotiation and use violence, fear and intimidation in the pursuit of an ideological, political or religious goal.

Henceforth, the military campaign became known as the Cyprus Emergency. Service personnel in Cyprus were now officially on Active Service and qualified for the General Service Medal with the 'Cyprus' clasp awarded after a minimum aggregate served of 120 days, but the British Government did not regard the Emergency as a military campaign and consequently most awards for gallantry were of a non-combatant nature. Every man was issued with a pamphlet governing the Rules of Engagement and arrangements were made for off-duty military personnel to carry revolvers as personal protection weapons. Unfortunately, several Servicemen managed to lose their weapons, some by leaving them on the beach, and were court-martialled.

EOKA was outlawed, and henceforth, some church bells, which had sometimes been used as signals between communities that patrols were active, were silenced. Men in several troublesome suburbs and villages that flirted with terrorism were liable to be collectively fined, a measure that caused sectarian tension in mixed communities where Turkish-Cypriots were far from happy in being expected to fork out for disturbances strongly suspected to be the fault of Greek-Cypriots. There is no doubt that collective fines were sometimes counter-productive in terms of winning hearts and minds. Assembly without permission, except for religious congregations and trade union petitions, was already disallowed and the display of Greek flags and the wearing of paramilitary uniforms were banned. The existing death penalty was extended to those opening fire and throwing bombs and grenades. Possession of arms and explosive could mean life. Grivas would be condemned for encouraging young children to use weapons that they did not understand and then abandoned, usually because they were frightened. One child died and three others, all aged less than ten years, were maimed playing with a grenade near Lapithos. Youths aged under eighteen years arrested in disturbances were liable to a whipping with a bamboo cane. When Nicolas Demetrios, aged fifteen years, was sentenced to six strokes for taking part in an unlawful assembly, there was selective international outrage. From 1947 to 1974, the birching on the Isle of Man to punish boys aged fifteen years and over convicted of theft attracted little attention, mainly because the practice was considered just desserts and trivial, except to those on the receiving end. The tough measures had been predicted by Grivas and enabled Makarios to enhance international sympathy for Cypriot self-determination.

On the evening that Field Marshal Harding declared the State of Emergency, the great and good of colonial society and their guests ignored the internal security situation to attend the annual Caledonian Society's St Andrews charity ball at the Ledra Palace Hotel. Harding had been invited as Guest of Honour. For Grivas it was a tempting target, and when he ordered the Nicosia Town Group to attack, Yannis Pafitis, who was employed as a handyman at the hotel, smuggled two US fragmentation grenades concealed in a box of oranges into the hotel. It was then announced that Harding would not be attending because he was finalizing the Emergency measures with London. At about 11.10 pm, while the guests were dancing to the Royal Scots Band after dinner, Pafitis, dressed as a waiter, fused the lights in the ballroom and rolled the grenades towards the Governor's table, where one exploded, injuring five people, including the wife of Commissioner of Police Robbins, and caused some damage. Captain Peter Macdonald of the RAOC noted that the pin in the second grenade had not been pulled and, to the amazement of a police officer, he calmly picked it up, put it in the pocket of his Mess dress and took it outside. The explosion halted the dancing until the casualties had been evacuated, and then as the band played *Glasgow Belongs to Me*, the guests returned to a dance floor soaked by fire hoses and defiantly sang the National Anthem. Pafitis was interviewed during the investigation but was released. One of his colleagues was the former plumber turned bomb-maker, Stylianos Lenas, who was using the hotel basement workshop to develop a pipe bomb that was widely used by EOKA. Manufactured from a water pipe junction, filled with sharp metal fragments and fitted with a heavy base plate and screw cap, the fuse was lit by a burning cigarette.

Next day, Mr Sydney Taylor, a British businessman thought by EOKA to be an intelligence officer, was walking along a Famagusta street when Andreas Demetriou fired three shots at him with a revolver but missed. A foot patrol from B Company, 2 Royal Inniskillings commanded by Corporal Smith heard the shots and were racing to the scene when they encountered Demetriou running towards them still carrying his revolver. Fusilier Hobley dropped to one knee and fired a single shot which wounded him in the elbow. In mitigation, Demetriou pleaded that when he attempted to kill Taylor, it was a Monday and he was unaware that the Emergency regulations, which included the death penalty for the possession of a weapon, had came into force the previous Saturday.

On 4 December, Limassol Customs officers scored a major success when they discovered a consignment of Thompson submachine guns and other weapons concealed in the hold of the Greek ship *Aelia*. This led to the skipper fingering the well-known bookshop owner and self-styled founder of EOKA in Limassol, Andreas Ionnides. In February 1956 he was brought from prison and, in the glare of Pathe News cameras, married his fiancée, who was also a well known EOKA supporter. Three weeks earlier, following reports from a 188 Search Light and Radar Battery coast detachment, a Middlesex patrol had boarded the Greek ship, the *Trias*, on intelligence received and escorted it to Dhekelia where it was impounded.

The tension throughout the island increased when four RASC off-duty soldiers were wounded in the back on 7 December by a gunman using a Sten gun firing from a car speeding along Ledra Street. Next day, Harding sent a clear message to Archbishop Makarios and the militant clerics by ordering the searching of twenty-four monasteries in Operation *Black Beard*, including the one at Ayios Spyridou. It had been named by a Greek-Cypriot forestry worker as the venue of a meeting called by Colonel Grivas to discuss using monasteries and churches to cache weapons. With military chaplains playing a key role as mediators, the troops searched the grounds and buildings and accepted several ancient shotguns handed in. Two new .38 Smith and Wesson revolvers were found hidden in a box in Ayia Varvara Monastery. The operation was not exactly a public relations success and, predictably, Makarios led outraged protest against the violation of the sanctity of holy places by 'British barbarians', even though a search of his house had unearthed several letters signed 'Digenes' indicating his approval of the 'execution' of EOKA who failed to carry out terrorist activities assigned to them. Grivas retaliated by sending gunmen to attack the home of the Major Reverend Benyon, for the second time, which resulted in Mrs Benyon and their small child being hospitalized with cuts. Although Grivas claimed in his Memoirs that EOKA only shot British soldiers, traitors and intelligence agents and that his organization did not strike at random, the reality was that EOKA not infrequently attacked Service dependants and married quarters with grenades and shootings.

During the second week of December, Grivas was suffering from a heavy cold and painful toothache made worse by the winter chill and living in the Castle. Since there had been little military activity in the Spilia area, he felt confident enough to summon the Nicosia dentist, Andreas Lambrou, to treat him. Lambrou was trusted because in January he had smuggled a small consignment of weapons concealed in dental gas cylinders to his house in Nicosia. Escorted by Kyriakos Matsis, Lambrou arrived in Spilia on 9 December and was told by Renos Kyriakides that since it was pouring with rain and Grivas was unwell with his cold, his patient would visit him for treatment next day. Born in 1926 in Lefkosia, Matsis had studied in Thessalonika where he advocated nationalism and 'the rags of the mother Greece to the stepmother of colonialism'. Returning to Cyprus as an agronomist, he defended the interests of farmers and had become Grivas' chief courier. Indeed, such was the confidence and expectation of those in the Castle that they would be forewarned of military activity by police informers and local villagers that Afxentiou had left on a combined recce and hunting trip to Kannavia while Christos Chartas was visiting his family in his home village of Polystipos nearby. The Chartas Group overlooked Spilia and the road below running from Kakopetria to Amandios.

Working on information from a forestry worker of EOKA activity near Spilia and Khandria, as part of Operation *Fox Hunter*, 45 Commando, elements of the Gordon Highlanders and two Metropolitan Police dog handlers, who had arrived in Cyprus three days previously, were instructed by Brigadier Baker to search the area. Details of military operations were now being distributed on a need-to-know basis, which now did not always include the Cyprus Police. At 6.15 am on the 10th, while it was dark, damp and cold, the troops quietly surrounded Spilia and then lorries roared into the villages, taking the inhabitants by surprise. When Grivas heard the commotion below, he was suspicious because, in his opinion, it was unusual for the Army to be on the move so early; nevertheless, he alerted those in the Castle to the military activity in Spilia. In fact, the Army regularly commenced operations at dawn.

Soon after the Gordons had arrested a man trying to dispose of documents relating to EOKA, Lieutenant Robert Otway-Ruthven wounded a man seen climbing a steep ridge behind the village. Quickly identified as Renos Kyriakides and high on the wanted list, he was rushed to Nicosia for interrogation, along with the documents to be analyzed. The Royal Marines Z Troop on the cordon then captured Georghiou Zavlis, who although armed with a .303 rifle and carrying lengths of Cordtex, made an unconvincing effort to appear unconcerned at the sudden appearance of the commandos as he tried to leave the village. Faced with the death penalty, under interrogation in Spilia he betrayed his oath to *enosis*, as most captured EOKA did, and admitted that there were fifteen EOKA in hideouts in the hills above the village. He agreed to guide the Royal Marines to them.

Meanwhile, Grivas instructed Afxentiou and his men to form the rearguard with the Chartas Group and to open fire should the British appear. Afxentiou reported increased activity in the village and that some lorries were leaving Spilia. At about 10.30 am, two lorries containing forty-four Royal Marines drawn from Headquarters and Support Troops and the two dog handlers led by Lieutenant Colonel Norman Tailyour, the 45 Commando Commanding Officer, stopped on the road below the Castle. Guided by Zavlis, the Royal Marines shook out into two columns and scrambled through thick mountain mist up the woody steep slopes made slippery and treacherous by rain-soaked moss, grass and shale. When a guerrilla opened fire and the Royal Marines deployed a 2-inch mortar, two were wounded when the first bomb burst in the trees. As the columns converged on the Castle, the guerrillas collected their emergency belongings and, covered by Afxentiou, began trekking through the mist north-west toward Kakopetria; however, in the confusion of an unrehearsed withdrawal and pursued by Royal Marines for the rest of the day, some EOKA were captured as they crossed a main road and ran into a patrol accompanied by a dog. Grivas sprained his ankle in a fall. After a long night march across high mountain peaks, during which Grivas and three men formed the rearguard, the surviving EOKA reached a ridge above Kakopetria. Soon after dawn Grivas sent a scout to fetch food, and then that evening, after they had crept into the village, he was sheltered in the house owned by Ioannis Katsoullis, the Greek Army reservist. Kyriakides was sentenced to life and served his sentence in Wakefield Prison where he became friendly with an IRA terrorist named Seamus Murphy. He later told Grivas that the Castle had been attacked by 700 men who had fired on each other, causing over fifty casualties from friendly fire and that the commanding officer had lost control. It was nonsense.

Grivas needed to regain command and control and during the evening of 15 December he collected a guide to take him to Galata, about three miles to the north, where he intended to form a Guerrilla Group south of the village. This information was soon leaked to the British. Grivas and five men reached Galata at midnight but soon after they had left at dawn troops surrounded Evrykhou, the next village north. The group immediately withdrew from the area and, in heavy rain, marched deep into the mountains where, after constructing a temporary lair, Grivas began to receive and despatch couriers. The informant was later executed by EOKA, as was the forestry worker who had betrayed the hideout near Spilia.

On the same day, Major Brian Coombe, who commanded 37 Field Squadron, visited Mount Troodos where Lieutenant Jimmy Knobbs's Troop was constructing a radar site. His Squadron had recently lost Sappers Percevale and Melson. Coombe left in a Champ and was driving with Lance Corporal Brian Morun, his driver, in the passenger seat. By about 12.15 pm, Coombe had passed through Kykko and was negotiating a bend on the road that led north to Prygos, when they were ambushed by the Markos Drakos group. The windscreen shattered and Morun was killed. Coombe stopped the Champ in a ditch underneath a rocky overhang and found cover as two grenades exploded nearby. Identifying the EOKA position, he scrambled up the hill and, outflanking four gunmen in a gully, opened fire with his Sten from above and behind them until he ran out of ammunition. He ran back to the Champ, collected Morun's Sten, clambered back up the gully and opened fire on the four as they emerged from some trees and invited them to surrender. Three did, but Kharalambus Mouskas, who was a cousin of Archbishop Makarios, opened fire with an automatic weapon. Coombe suspected trickery and returned fire, killing him and wounding Andreas Zakos and Harilaos Michael. The fourth man, Drakos, ran off but not before Coombe had wounded him with his revolver. Coombe rounded up the prisoners and waited for an hour near the Champ until a Gordon Highlanders patrol appeared. Mouskas had been acquitted of terrorist offences in July but had a £5,000 bounty on his head.

In a decision that caused some concern to the Nicosia authorities, Field Marshal Harding agreed that Mouskas could be buried publicly – on the proviso that the mourners did not exceed fifty. However, the Greek-Cypriots were in no mood to compromise and a large crowd followed the hearse into Metaxas Square. Despite heavy rain, Archbishop Makarios conducted the service at Nicosia's Phaneromeni Church. But after Mouskas had been buried the 1 South Staffords saw that the hearse was empty and, believing the procession to be unauthorized, they ordered the mourners to disperse. They refused and a confrontation developed during which soldiers fired several tear gas canisters until a thunderstorm dispersed the soaked crowd. The soldiers were unaware that in Cypriot funerals the pall-bearers and the coffin follow the hearse to the wake. Makarios protested that the action was 'sacrilege' and 'a dark stain on the history of the British occupation of Cyprus', a sentiment that was largely rejected.

Although Major Coombe had displayed extreme gallantry in a military setting, the recommendation for a Military Cross was converted to the George Medal. Unusually for the period, he attended a press conference and, emphasizing that he should not be celebrated as a hero for killing 'a frightened young Cypriot', said, 'Do not deepen the rift between the Cypriots and the British. Do not encourage the Cypriots to build up a hero by producing a British hero; do not force them to make a hero of a murderer. I ask that there should be no jubilation, no exulting over the affair.' His noble gesture helped reduce EOKA's lead in propaganda.

The day after the ambush, Lieutenant John Kelly of 40 Field Regiment was the first officer to be killed in action when he was shot dead as he threw a grenade at a group of EOKA attacking Yialousa Police Station in the Panhandle. The attackers left in several stolen cars. The Gunners pursued them and captured several EOKA within about six hours, after forcing their car off the road near Dhavlos at the eastern end of the Pentadactylos range. Ten days earlier, Marine David Walker of 45 Commando was driving a Land Rover escorting an ambulance when the convoy was ambushed near Amiandos and Marine Terrance Roberts was killed. Walker rescued two other wounded Royal Marines and took up defensive positions until a Gordons patrol arrived. The recommendation that he be awarded the George Medal was downgraded to the British Empire Medal for gallantry.

Although the communists had stood up to EOKA and were providing most of the workforce building the bases at Episkopi and Dhekelia, Harding, concerned at the deterioration of internal security, accused AKEL of promoting a 'consistently harmful role in Cypriot politics in order to silence opponents of Archbishop Makarios' and proscribed it. The Royal Scots arrested 128 leading members and took them to the 'Lobster Pot' detention compound at Alma Camp, Dhekelia. Several printing presses were confiscated. AKEL protested that they always acted within the law, and the arrests prompted widespread strikes across Cyprus, including at Dhekelia. Potentially, the security forces were now in danger of facing two major subversive threats.

The year 1955 had seen twelve members of the Armed Forces killed, all in the last three months of the year. Five police officers and seven Greek-Cypriots had also lost their lives and about 300 people had been injured, most in riots. Several seriously wounded Servicemen had been flown back to England for specialist treatment. A total of 1,260 buildings had been damaged during riots or by fire and the courts had sentenced 600 people. With EOKA riding high and the Army still adjusting its strategies, tactics and developing its intelligence collection, there was no respite from the violence. On 3 January 1956, EOKA attempted to assassinate a female patient who Grivas believed to be a Government informant in Nicosia General Hospital, the first of several terrorist incidents involving the hospital. Three days later, another Service family was attacked when a grenade thrown into a married quarter seriously wounded the infant child of a soldier. In mid-February in Larnaca, the wife of Sergeant Smith of the REME attached to 1 Middlesex, lost a foot when she threw herself across her two children after a schoolboy had thrown a grenade through the open window of their bedroom while she was putting them to bed.

The Troodos Mountains usually have about four months of winter snow that provides some fine ski-ing. When 45 Commando trained X Troop in cross-country military ski-ing to help deliver dynamite to Amiandos Mine, it was in many respects, a precursor to the 3 Commando Brigade's contribution to the winter defence of NATO's Northern Flank in Norway from the 1970s. The Royal Marines and 1 Gordon Highlanders celebrated Hogmanay in the usual manner and then a day later in Operation *Mangel Wurzel* raided several hideouts near Kakopetria, capturing three armed EOKA, and roused five suspects from their beds in Pano Amiandos, among them Kyriakos Matsis. When asked by Harding to divulge the location of the EOKA leader, he replied 'The struggle is not for money, but for virtue', a response that resulted him being sent to the Omorphita Interrogation Centre and then Camp K. In another operation at the same time, the Leicesters, South Staffords and Middlesexes supported by the Life Guards and frigates from the 6th Destroyer Squadron swept the coast region from Phlamoudhi to Dhavlos, found several caches and arrested a number of suspects.

Naval operations were preventing the smuggling of weapons to Cyprus, the Greek Government was being pressurized into taking measures to stop the supply of arms to Grivas and military operations were beginning to make inroads into the EOKA arsenal. So when a high-ranking priest learnt that Field Marshal Harding intended to end a firearms amnesty on 23 January and this was passed to Grivas by Gregoris Afxentiou, Grivas saw an opportunity to raid every village for firearms. However, his plan was leaked to the police and on the 22nd he instructed EOKA to seize as many weapons as possible. In one instance, gunmen seized guns from a queue outside a police station. Grivas claimed EOKA acquired over 800 shotguns and these he distributed among the mountain Guerrilla Groups and newly-created town and village Shotgun Commandos. His armourers worked on increasing their range to about 100 yards by manufacturing heavier calibre pellets.

The murder of Police Sergeant Abdullah Ali Riza outside his home near Paphos on 11 January by four EOKA gunmen led to sectarian disturbances escalating in Turkish-Cypriot enclaves. Their leader, Dr Fazil Kutchuk, played a key role in calming the tension, but Radio Athens was mischievous in claiming that British Intelligence had murdered Riza in an effort to stir up the minority. In fact, Riza had been an effective police officer responsible for the conviction of about six EOKA. He was also the first Turkish-Cypriot to be murdered during the Emergency.

Grivas continued to encourage youthful civil disturbances. The South Staffords endured a pelting in Nicosia when 300 rioters egged on by two priests protested at the conditions at Camp K. About thirty people were injured. Such was the deterioration in public order that Harding closed the Nicosia Pan Cyprian Gymnasium at the end of the month. Three weeks later, students throughout the island were whipped in to fresh rage after a Leicesters sniper had been ordered by police to shoot a ringleader refusing to respect a restricted zone near the Famagusta Pan Cyprian Gymnasium. Two days later, the Norfolks in Limassol were stoned by girls waving a Greek flag and protesting against the shooting. Although the troops found confronting schoolgirls disturbing, discipline held. When a mob of thirty youths persistently refused to disperse, a platoon advanced from behind them with fixed bayonets and shepherded them into an Army lorry, which was then driven to the foothills of the Troodos Mountains where it stopped and the captives were ordered out. Some imagined that the great moment of martyrdom was at hand until an officer then smiled, 'Don't look so anxious. It's a lovely afternoon for a walk. Cheerio', and left. This method of displacing rioters several miles from the scene of a disturbance was widely used as a measure to defuse tempers and give rioters an opportunity to cool down, particularly if police officers were reluctant to arrest for breach of the peace and lock rioters in cells. The Army recognized that it was probably unlawful to enforce these compulsory walks, however it was felt that they would make rioters tired and less willing to engage in disturbances. By mid-February, although the education authorities had done their best to maintain order in schools, intimidation and violence resulted in eighty being closed. The Teacher's Union was accused of supporting the violence.

Meanwhile, Grivas centralized his Guerrilla Groups around Kykko

Monastery and marched with his command group through pouring rain from Kakopetria to Kalopanagiotis in the middle of the Paphos Forest, whence he was taken by car to Vassiliki where he set up his headquarters. Nearby were Marcos Drakos and his Kyrenia Castle escapers in a hideout being supported with supplies and shelter by the Abbot. The area was wild, wooded and isolated. In spite of Operations *Turkey Trot* and *Fox Hunter* and the loss of several loyal EOKA, the Guerrilla Groups generally had not been particularly troubled by military operations. Grivas estimated that his front-line strength stood at 750 men and women divided thus:

**Troodos Mountains**
  **Kykko District**
  Vassiliki Marcos Drakos Group (12 men)
  Tyllira Solon Pittarides Group (8 men)
  Milikouri Antonis Georgiades Group (5 men)
  Stavros Posokas Christakis Eleftheriou Group (6 men)

  **Pitsillia District**
  Makheras Afxentiou Group (10 men)
  Pitsillia Area Eleven village Groups

  **Paphos District**
  Lysos Yannakis Droushiotis Group (5 men)
  Paphos Area Ten village Groups

**Pentadytclos Mountains**
Kalogrea/AmvrosiosTassos Sofocleus (10 men)

**Towns and Villages**
Nicosia District Fifteen groups (80 people)
Nicosia Area Eleven village Groups

Larnaca District Two groups (6 men)
Larnaca Area Seven village Groups

Famagusta District Fourteen groups (76 men)
Famagusta Area Twelve village and Dhekelia Base Groups

Limassol District Eleven Groups (34 people)
Limassol Area Thirteen village and Episkopi Base Groups
Paphos District Three Groups (34 men)

Paphos Area Ten village Groups
Kyrenia District Two groups (3 men)
Pentadactylos/Karpas Five village Groups

The crucial courier system remained largely intact. Only the Guerrilla Groups and town leaders were full-time and paid an allowance; the remainder were either in employment or subsidized locally. The shortage of weapons had been resolved to some extent by thefts from police stations, and a military depot, smuggling and the seizure during the amnesty. The biggest problem was that those who had been arrested tended to divulge information and thereby expose EOKA. Along with those identified by Grivas to be traitors from the list that he had brought with him in November 1955, arrestees were no longer totally trusted and were to be intimidated and marked for execution.

In spite of the necessity for Britain to maintain its contribution to BAOR and support operations in Malaya and Kenya, the Cyprus Emergency sucked in troops. On 13 January the British Government announced that in response to the growth of Arab nationalism engineered by Colonel Gamal Nasser of Egypt, and the increased tension between Israel and Egypt and the destabilization of British interests in Jordan, 16 Parachute Brigade was being deployed to Middle East Command as the embryonic Middle East Strategic Reserve. Consequently, 1st and 3rd Parachute Battalions, The Parachute Regiment (1 and 3 Paras), each made up of a third each Regulars, Reservists and National Servicemen, then began arriving in an assortment of aircraft, including Shackletons and Transport Command Hastings, and were driven by 17 Company RASC to the tented Camp Kykko near RAF Nicosia where moving into tents in the chill of a Cypriot winter was not entirely welcome. In order to keep the troops fit and effective, Lieutenant General Keightley made the Brigade available to Field Marshal Harding as the Island Reserve, thus freeing the Royal Norfolks to take over from 40 Commando in Limassol, on the proviso that it would not be under direct command of one of three Brigade Districts. Harding immediately placed the Brigade under the direct operational command of Brigadier Baker for special operations. To replace 2 Para left in England, the Brigade inherited the 1st Battalion, The Highland Light Infantry (1 HLI), which arrived by air from England ten days later. Within three weeks of arriving, a Para patrol unearthed a communist cell in a cave near Kykko Camp. On the same day that the Brigade arrived, the increase in motor transport was reflected by the transport elements of the RASC being assembled into the regimental-sized 1 Transport Column. Toward the end of January, the troopship

*Lancashire* disembarked 1st Battalion, The Wiltshire Regiment (1 Wiltshires) at Famagusta for a three-year accompanied tour. Previously the Demonstration Battalion at the School of Infantry, Warminster, the Battalion relieved 2 Royal Inniskillings in 51 Infantry Brigade District, who, like the departed 2 Green Howards, were due to be disbanded. The Royal Horse Guards (The Blues) landed from the same ship and immediately expressed concern that the Second World War-era Daimler armoured cars they inherited from the Life Guards were hardly roadworthy. In due course, the force would be re-equipped with Ferret Scout Cars. On the 24th, 1st Battalion, The Royal Warwickshire Regiment (1 Warwicks) arrived by troopship from Egypt and, joining 50 Infantry Brigade District, eventually moved into Normandy Camp after taking over from 1 Royal Norfolks in Nicosia. The Norfolks moved to Paphos and relieved the Royal Scots, who returned to Scotland. There were now about 20,000 troops and fourteen battalions in Cyprus. On 31 January RAF Akrotiri was declared operational and by the end of February the 13 Squadron air photo-recce Meteors had deployed, followed by 208 Squadron and its Hawker Hunter fighters. An increasing number of Valettas, Pembrokes and Hastings were bringing in general stores and personnel. No. 3 Light Anti-Aircraft Wing, RAF Regiment, which consisted of Nos 27 and 37 Squadrons equipped with L40/L60 Bofors guns, was responsible for Low Level Air Defence and base security.

At the end of January, very heavy snow engulfed the Troodos Mountains, resulting in elements of 749 (Air Despatch) Company RASC dropping supplies to isolated communities from Hastings aircraft; however, this expression of humanity did not stop EOKA gunmen murdering two airmen and seriously wounding SAC John Beresford. His father complained to journalists in England that while the RAF could spare aircraft to drop aid to villages sympathetic to EOKA in the mountains, no arrangements were in place for parents and families to visit wounded husbands and sons; consequently, he was financing a flight for him and his wife to Cyprus. On chilly night shortly after midnight, when several airmen had gone to RAF Episkopi for a film show and a visit to the NAAFI, the tented camp near Khato Khivides in the Troodos occupied by 751 Signals Unit, a radar unit, was raked by automatic fire from several points. Such was the intensity that the Bren Gun Group of the twelve-man RAF Regiment defence section was unable to reach its sangar near the Guard Tent and set up near the barrier. Meanwhile, a lorry containing the off-duty party negotiating the icy Troodos hairpins had stopped to pick up an airman who had fallen out of the back, but as it then approached the camp the firing stopped, probably because the EOKA guerrillas believed that it was bringing reinforcements. In fact, the lorry was unescorted and only one airman was armed.

When 45 Commando were searching Amiandos in the middle of a snowstorm they entertained the village men waiting to be screened with a performance by the 3 Commando Brigade band, but the inevitable accusation from Greek newspapers was that the music was to drown the cries of torture. Heavy snow brought tragedy in mid-February when a 3 Commando Brigade Light Air Detachment recovery lorry skidded into a deep snowdrift. When Marine Benet Blakeway injured his ankle, the patrol commander, Warrant Officer 1 Mark Wheeler, stayed with him and two others while two Royal Marines then walked to Platres to seek help. But when a rescue patrol arrived the next day, Blakeway and Wheeler had died in the sub-zero temperatures and the other two were suffering from extreme exposure.

On 7 February the Norfolks searched the village of Pakhna in Operation *Little Chicago* on the basis of Special Branch informant information that it had a bad reputation. More significantly, the village was near the Kissousa Reservoir pipeline to Episkopi. It already had been blown up. At about 2.30 am, thirty lorries delivered the Battalion to a point two miles from Pakna, and over the next two hours troops surrounded the village. At about 5.20 am in the gloom of dawn, three figures approached the B Company cordon stretched along a track and offered Lance Corporal Jay cash to let them through. Jay offered them a five yard start, and when he arrested them it turned out that one was wanted for attempted murder. A daylight search of the track revealed a pistol, a Breda carbine, two Sten guns, ammunition and parts of a uniform ditched by the three men. Meanwhile in the village, search teams that included WRAC attached to the RMP, tracker dogs and a Royal Engineer troop, found incriminating documents and equipment suitable for making ammunition. By 11.30 am the troops had left the area. At the end of the month, the village Police Station was attacked by EOKA and its records destroyed. The Battalion mounted four more operations in the area, with very little success.

By the New Year the situation had generated sufficient concern from the US and UN for the British Government to despatch MI6 agents to the island to counter the EOKA propaganda campaign. In Operation *Tea Party* its most experienced propagandists were assembled in Cyprus as the Information Research Department, with the aim of blackening the name of EOKA by accusing it of being in league with the communist AKEL and by feeding black propaganda to eager journalists, for instance that schoolgirls involved in civil disturbances had been forced into sexual relationships with the guerrillas. However, the plot was flawed because the AKEL link with EOKA was very weak at best and the Greek influence on the struggle for *enosis* was largely ignored.

Further negotiations on Cypriot self-determination and another meeting between Harding and Makarios on 24 February resulted in Grivas declaring a temporary truce, demanding an amnesty from prosecution for EOKA, Greek-Cypriot control of public security during the transition period and the reduction of the British garrison to the Cyprus District levels in early 1955 of about 1,800 all ranks, should there be agreement. Makarios was still being prodded by Athens and hardliners on the Ethnarchy Council, and although the talks remained a stalemate, London again emphasized that once internal security had stabilised, constitutional matters would be discussed, including self-determination – provided that it satisfied the entire Cypriot community. Although Makarios implied that he was not entirely happy with the violence and was critical of Grivas, the confirmation of the death sentences of Andreas Zakos and Charilaos Michael in late February for their part in the ambush that killed Lance Corporal Morun led to further violence, with the detonation of twenty-one bombs in Nicosia and more casualties among Service families; another mother was injured in the face while protecting her son from an explosion. The English School was severely damaged. Two EOKA transporting a bomb arrested by the South Staffords near the US Consulate was a significant development which showed the willingness of Grivas to widen his targets by attacking London's closest ally. On 4 March, in the second aviation security incident worldwide since 1945, Grivas ordered the Afxentiou Group to place a bomb on a Hermes airliner that had been chartered from Skyways to fly sixty-eight Servicemen and families from Nicosia to England; it would be timed to explode after take off. However, embarkation fell behind schedule and the device, which had been smuggled into a luggage rack by a police officer working in the Immigration Department, exploded as the passengers lined up to embark and badly damaged the aircraft. Eight weeks later on 27 April, EOKA carried out the third aviation attack by blowing up a Cyprus Airways DC-3 Dakota, also at Nicosia Airport.

The increased regional tension and the possibility of Cyprus being used as a strategic forward operating base and airhead for operations led to Harding advising London, on 3 March, that Makarios should be deported on the grounds that he was subverting influential Greek-Cypriot clerics and was involved in EOKA. He accepted that deportation would probably cause a deterioration of internal security, however Makarios' removal would isolate the EOKA leadership. London agreed and began navigating the legal arrangements to send

Makarios and several other clerics to the Seychelles Islands, which were thought to be sufficiently isolated to keep the exiles incommunicado. Although the Seychelles Legislature had enacted laws prohibiting the detention of political activitists during the Mau Mau uprising in Kenya, these were repealed and a detachment of Seychelles Police was formed to guard the exiles. Since it was important that delays be kept to a minimum, Harding appointed the one-eyed, Anglo-Irish Group Captain Norman de W Boult DFC AFC to organize the deportation in Operation *Airborne* and asked that a Transport Command Hasting be in Cyprus by 6 March. Boult had trained Greek pilots during World War Two and had been awarded the Royal Hellenic Air Force Cross.

Harding entrusted the moving of Makarios from his Palace to RAF Nicosia without attracting undue attention to Lieutenant Colonel John Commings, the Commanding Officer of 1 South Staffords. Commings ordered Major Jos Jones to develop a plan, codenamed Operation *Apollo*, and reinforced his C Company with 1 Platoon, B Company. He also placed 3 Para on readiness for an unspecified special operation. Commings and Jones juggled several options in the knowledge that the deportation would be a political hot potato. In the meantime, Squadron Leader Wilfred Pink, commanding a Hastings, arrived on 7 March. When Makarios then announced that he and the hardline Bishop of Kyrenia intended to fly to Athens on 9 March to meet Greek political leaders, the British saw this as a window of opportunity to intercept him; and during the evening of the 8th, a British official visited the Archbishop and suggested that, for his personal safety, only he and his driver-bodyguard should go to the airport. During the day, the violence had seen a police officer killed, several people injured and Mrs Plumb, the wife of a 1 Middlesex corporal, injured in the face protecting her son. Interestingly, the Bishop of Kyrenia and EOKA recruiter Father Papagantheiou, the fanatical leader of PEON had denounced EOKA as being senseless if it believed its objectives could be achieved by violence.

Major Jones planned to intercept Makarios as he arrived at Nicosia Airport, and by 2.30 pm on the 9th his three platoons, in apparently broken down Army lorries, were deployed covering the roads to the airport, waiting for a signal from a RAF policeman that the Archbishop's car was approaching. The fourth platoon he held in reserve. At 3 pm, as Makarios and his driver left his Palace, they were surrounded by crowds wishing him good fortune in Athens. Lieutenant Peter Lee, who commanded the B Company platoon, was peering into the engine of his lorry when he saw an RAF policeman salute a black car and intercepted it, only to find that it contained Air Vice Marshal Joseph Crisham, the Air Officer Commanding Levant, whose presence was unexpected. A few minutes later, Makarios was intercepted, the only hint of trouble coming from his driver declaring that he would protect Makarios with his life. Company Sergeant Major Martin raised his Sten and invited him to do so. Makarios was then escorted to the RAF Nicosia dispersal area where Brigadier Baker watched a British police officer read the Deportation Order issued under Regulation VII of the Emergency Powers (Public Safety and Order) Regulations. With Major Jones' men hovering in the background, Makarios was separated from his driver and marshalled to the Hastings. In spite of reports circulating in Athens suggesting the British intended to arrest Makarios, to what extent he predicted British subterfuge is unclear; however, it was noted that he had packed more clothes than necessary for a short trip, including extra ecclesiastical robes and a Greek-English dictionary. Meanwhile, 1 Wiltshires had detained the Bishop of Kyrenia and Polycarpos Ioannides, personal assistant to Makarios and propagandist, and conveyed them to the airbase. Papagantheiou had also been arrested. Makarios thought they had arrived to bid him farewell. At about 4.15 am, Squadron Leader Pink rolled along the runway, headed south-east to RAF Aden to refuel and then flew through the night to Nairobi. That night, Harding broadcast that Makarios had been deported because:

> '[He] has remained silent while policemen and soldiers have been murdered in cold blood, while women and children have been killed and maimed by bombs, while a Cypriot woman was shot and wounded for the second time as she lay in hospital, recovering from a previous terrorist attack, and even while he stood by the coffin of an Abbot in his own church who was brutally murdered in his own monastery. His silence has understandably been accepted among his community as not merely condoning but even as approving assassination and bomb-throwing.'

Since a hostile reaction was expected from the large Greek community in Kenya, a military convoy quickly transferred the deportees to Mombasa where they boarded the East African Naval Vessel *Rosalind* and were escorted by frigate HMS *Loch Fada* for the final leg to Mahe, the principal island of the Seychelles. A twist in the story was that Makarios enjoyed travel and knew that the British would not harm him. Two days later, 3 Para carried out an extensive search of the Archbishop's Palace but found little of value except documents implying connections between Grivas and Makarios – and a skeleton several hundred years old.

## CHAPTER SEVEN

# The Long Hot Summer
### (March to September 1956)

For several days after the deportation of Makarios Cyprus was tense, even after Michael Georghiou was shot dead by 40 Commando near Ktima after he had thrown a grenade at a patrol. He had often used his truck to ferry the Afxentiou Group around their Trikomo area of operations. Militarily, the troops were developing tactics to tackle terrorism in most urban areas, in spite of having lost twenty-three men in the seven months since September 1955. Two major problems were the EOKA groups known to exist among the workforce building the garrisons at Episkopi and Dhekelia and the risks to families living in Cypriot hirings. Even though he believed that key to the future of Cyprus was an international solution, probably with NATO taking the lead, Field Marshal Harding could now concentrate on defeating EOKA. To examine constitutional affairs and self-determination, Prime Minister Eden sent Lord Cyril Radcliffe, a career civil servant and jurist, as the Commissioner for Constitutional Reform.

The deportation of Makarios angered Colonel Grivas, because his intelligence sources had been kept in the dark, however he now had unrestricted control of operations, except for the influence exercised from Athens dictated through the Greek Consulate-General in Nicosia. Responsibility for mobilizing and promoting *enosis* also sat squarely on his shoulders and while he could count on the poorer Greek-Cypriots, because they were heavily influenced by their clerics and had strong family ties that focused on their children, over whom Grivas had close control, the middle class were not so convinced because the terrorism was affecting politics, business and their personal interests. However, without the influence of Makarios, they were inextricably drawn into the EOKA campaign, and as internal security restrictions bit they began to resent the infringements and limitations on civil liberties. Grivas opened the next phase of Operation *Forward to Victory* by ambushing a 45 Commando patrol of two Land Rovers and an interpreter in his car on a track between Khandria and Argos, wounding five Royal Marines, including Sergeant Arthur Robinson, who had been injured in the serious riot in Vouni in mid-November 1955. The patrol returned fire and claimed one EOKA killed.

Radio Athens took advantage of the vacuum to spout vicious propaganda likening Harding to Genghis Khan and Hitler and accusing him of being a 'bloodstained ogre whose hands drip with the blood of his victim'. When Harding asked Major General Morrison to use 2 Wireless Regiment to jam the broadcasts, Morrison declined because the jamming of civil broadcasts was not a military job. A former naval officer with the Cyprus Broadcasting Service had some success, even though he lacked equipment. When Grivas warned Harding in a leaflet that EOKA would kill him 'even in your bed', Harding retorted that if he attempted to do so, he would then have to deal with his soldiers. In looking for opportunities to assassinate the Governor, Grivas first considered placing a sniper on the roof of the Greek Consulate opposite the Anglican Church to shoot him as he left Sunday morning service until he warmed to a plan suggested by Neophytes Sofocleos.

Aged twenty years, Sofocleos had been employed by Sir Robert Armitage to look after his two cats, Benji and Poo. By the time he was appointed to be a valet to Field Marshal Harding, he had joined EOKA. His resentment against the British surfaced and when he believed that he was about to be dismissed for being slack, he suggested placing a bomb in Harding's bed. Grivas agreed, and Theodoulou Katelaris, a carpenter and one of EOKA's top bomb makers, constructed a sophisticated device filled with gelignite whose detonation relied on room temperature reaching 67F. This was the estimated temperature in Harding's bedroom at 2.30 am. Iakovos Patsatsos, a deeply religious printer and member of the Nicosia Town Group, gave Sofocleos the device in a package and showed him how to set the time pencil. On 20 March Sofocleus cycled past the Main Gate sentries to Government House carrying the parcel strapped inside his raincoat. The previous day sectarian violence had broken out in Visalia, near Kyrenia, after several drunken Greek-Cypriots had attacked a Turkish-Cypriot wedding. The disturbance spilled over into Nicosia and troops from 1 Warwicks had made several baton charges and fired tear gas at a large Turkish-Cypriot mob that had burned a church. At 2.30 am next morning, Sofocleos woke up and set the fuse. At lunchtime, he greeted guests invited for lunch by Lady Harding and then suggested to his Armenian female supervisor that he should hoover the bedroom of the Governor, a request that she later thought strange because he usually had to be told what to do. In the dining room, the lunch was well underway. A short time later, she saw Sofocleos sweeping the carpet in the hall and then heard him enter the twin-bedded bedroom. Sofocleos placed the device under the mattress on Harding's bed nearest the window. The supervisor became suspicious when she did not hear Sofocleos hoovering, and when she checked on him he was standing between the two beds declaring that he had finished. She noted that the hoover cable was coiled. Sofocleos left Government House at about the same time as the lunch guests were bidding Lady Harding farewell, and after cycling into Nicosia he was driven to the Troodos Mountains where he joined the Marathassa Guerrilla Group.

Next morning, Sofocleos and two other Greek-Cypriots failed to turn up for work at 11 am, and when the remainder refused to prepare the bedrooms for guests expected that afternoon, soldiers at Government House were instructed to carry out a detailed search of every bedroom and every piece of furniture. Lance Corporal Peter Welch of the King's Royal Rifles Corps, who was Harding's orderly, and Guardsman Ball of the Grenadier Guards were checking the Hardings' bedroom when they discovered the bomb. Lady Harding, who was writing in her boudoir, ignored their warning to leave. The Guard Commander, Second Lieutenant Michael Buckley of the Norfolks, then arrived and after carefully edging the device on to a dustpan, he deposited it in a sandbagged slit trench. About three seconds later, the bomb exploded with such force that it 'would have demolished half of Government House'. The explosion was heard five miles away. A bomb disposal officer later confirmed that the device was the same design as the one that had damaged the Hermes on 4 March and had probably been made by the same person. The attempted assassination was a well-planned operation that foundered because Sofocleos had not noticed that Harding invariably slept with his bedroom window open. Furthermore, the night of 21/22 March was also chillier than usual. It was another major breach of security attributable only to a Greek-Cypriot employee, so Harding had little alternative but dismiss the twelve Greek-Cypriot staff, some with decades of service at Government House behind them. Buckley was awarded the MBE 'for the calm and gallant way' in which he had disposed of the bomb.

Attacks on patrols continued. On 29 March a Leicesters vehicle patrol was ambushed in the village of Phrenaros and the driver of the leading vehicle, Private Ronald Bowman, killed instantly. Out of control, the Land Rover careered into a coffee shop where it burst into flames, killing Lieutenant Jim Walker. An intelligence operation in the area two days later unearthed six illegal shotguns, dozens of Molotov cocktail bombs and Italian 'Red Devil' grenades and artillery ammunition that had been recovered from sunken ships. Sixteen suspects were arrested and the village fined £1,500. Another intelligence operation targeting Kykko Monastery found subversive literature, memos signed by Grivas confirming the link between EOKA and the Cypriot Orthodox Church, a printing press and a quantity of explosives. On 16 April the Larnaca Town Group seized Private Ronnie Shilton of the Leicesters, although the circumstances remain something of a mystery. A week later on the 23rd, Turkey's National Independence Day celebrations descended into sectarian riots in which shops were set alight. In spite of 21 Army Fire Brigade RASC assisting civilian fire crews, a serious confrontation developed in a bonded tobacco warehouse and a Turkish-Cypriot employee was shot dead by a Turkish policeman. A few hours later, Iakovos Patsatsos was one of two gunmen who attempted to murder a Greek-Cypriot policeman outside Nicosia Central Police and then shot Constable Nihat Basif as he ran to help his colleague; but as the two gunmen were leaving the scene on their bicycles, several Turkish-Cypriot women pushed them off and seized Patsatsos. He was beaten up by an angry crowd before being handed over to the police. He had been involved in the plot to kill Harding. The situation deteriorated when angry Turkish-Cypriots marched to the Greek-Cypriot quarter of Goldsmith Street, and Assistant Superintendent Willis placed himself in front of the mob. A Royal Horse Guard troop then arrived and marshalled about 400 rioters into a temporary cage at Metaxas Square. A twelve-hour curfew in the area was maintained by 1 Warwicks. Over the next two days there were further sectarian clashes, and several bombs were thrown at the cage.

Still chased by the jamming, Radio Athens accused the British of beatings, whipping, administering drugs, rape and tearing out the finger nails of those selected for interrogation and implied that 'Field-Marshal Harding commits tyranny, vandalism, cowardice and incites treachery.' The accusations were potentially damaging because interrogation for military information had become critical, particularly as the Cypriot Police could not be trusted. Harding moved quickly, and of six allegations against the police, three were dismissed and one policeman was sentenced to three years for wounding two Cypriots with a gun. The one case against the Army resulted in two captains, one each from the Intelligence Corps and the Gordon Highlanders, being cashiered in April after being convicted of actual bodily harm and conspiracy to distract the course of justice. Although some felt that they were sacrificial lambs to political pressures, Lieutenant General Keightley rejected the sentence imposed on the Intelligence Corps captain; nevertheless, both officers were dismissed from the Army.

Throughout the Emergency, Grivas was ruthless with anyone who criticized EOKA and any Greek-Cypriot inclined to support the British. Of 238 Cypriots killed between April 1955 and March 1959, 203 were Greek-Cypriots, of whom at least twelve were EOKA. Some were killed by bombs, most of which were planted by EOKA. Solon Pittarides, a former member of the Markos Drakos Group and now in command of the Larnaca Town Group, specialized in hunting informers. One of the most brutal murders happened in Kythrea when four hooded gunmen burst into St George's Church during a service and ordered the forty worshippers, 'Stand up and face the wall!' A gunman then singled out the lay reader Manoli Pierides and shot him in front of two of his four children. During the evening of 15 April, Assistant Superintendent Kyriakos Aristotelous was visiting his wife and new baby son in a private maternity home in Nicosia when three hooded gunmen armed with two pistols and a Sten gun murdered him in the doctor's office and wounded the doctor, all within earshot of his wife.

Ever since the Privy Council had dismissed the appeals of Charilaos Michael against his conviction for the murder of Special Branch PC Poullis in August 1955 and Andreas Demetriou for his attack on Sydney Taylor, tension in Cyprus and Greece had increased and the resolve of the security forces was again tested with illegal strikes, Greek flags flown at half mast and attacks on the British. Demetriou had become something of a cult hero as part of the EOKA group that had raided the 625 Ordnance Depot warehouse. A bomb that exploded near a family medical clinic in Kyrenia severely wounded Captain Dulson RAMC, the Wiltshires Medical Officer. When the two men were executed on 10 May, four people died and over 200 people were injured in subsequent disturbances in Athens. Grivas retaliated by ordering that the two captured Leicesters, Lance Corporal Hill and Private Shilton, should be executed. The problem for Michael Rossides, the Larnaca District Leader, and his colleagues was that they liked the personable Irish/American Shilton and suggested that killing him would harm *enosis*, however, their pleas were rejected. Grivas blamed Harding for forcing him to execute the soldiers as a reprisal for the executions of Poullis and Demetriou, but the integrity of his first statement was doubted when it was found to have several inaccuracies, for instance stating that Hill was a corporal and that he had been captured in December 1955, whereas he had been reported missing in November. On 11 May Grivas issued a second statement correcting the errors and described the identity dog tags worn by Hill. In relation to Shilton, he corrected his rank to Private and suggested that the soldier had said he had been demoted. Grivas had executed communist hostages in the Greek Civil War, but the executions of the soldiers mimicked the strangulation and booby-trapping found on the bodies of two Intelligence Corps sergeants captured by the Jewish Stern Gang in Palestine in July 1947 in retaliation for the execution of three Jewish terrorists. The brutality of these murders caused such public outrage that it affected the British will to maintain the Palestine Mandate. The murders of the Leicesters were rejected as morally reprehensible by most Greek-Cypriots, showing they were not natural rebels and the British were not natural oppressors. There was disquiet in Great Britain. The rejection led to Grivas not repeating the tactic.

During the morning of 16 May, Corporal Patrick Hale and Leading Aircraftman (LAC) John Hollis were in the Homer Hut at RAF Nicosia manning ground-to-air Direction Finding navigational radar. Since the equipment needed to be isolated from metal objects, such as hangars and moving vehicles, the Hut was situated at the southern edge of the main runway and was adjacent to several corn fields and a track that ran east and west. It was customary for the Hut to share its drinking water with travellers, farm workers and shepherds tending flocks of goats, but in spite of the deteriorating internal security and the Hut's isolation, none of the RAF radar operators were armed. At about 8 am Hale supplied glasses of water to three youths scything corn. An hour later, they again asked for water and then sat in the shade of the Hut for about half an hour before returning to the fields. At about 10.45 am LAC Hollis returned from pay parade at the Flight offices and was in the Hut when, at about 11.30, two of the youths asked for more water. Corporal Hale gave them a glass each, but as he returned to the radar they shot him with a revolver and fired at Hollis who had taken cover behind the radar and was reporting the attack to the Control Tower. Several RAF signallers working about 100 yards from the Hut then arrived and a soldier chased three men he saw running away. Meanwhile, Flight Sergeant Tony Harrison and Master Pilot Jim McCorkle in a Sycamore were scrambled and followed the men along a track until they gave up through exhaustion. Harrison landed his helicopter while McCorkle arrested the third man hiding in an acacia tree and waited until an 11 Field Squadron, RAF Regiment patrol arrived. A search by soldiers, RAF and the police led to two .38-inch pistols used in the attack being found the following day. At the trial of the three youths, identified as Andreas Panaghides, Michael Koutsoftas and Paraskevas Hiropoulis, Mr Justice Shaw commented that the murder had been cold-blooded, since the airmen were unarmed and the youths had exploited their kindness in supplying water. Koutsoftas and Panaghides, who had shot Hale, were executed, along with Stelios Mavromatis who had been convicted of the attempted murders of a Service wife and her daughter and a RAF storeman in March. Hiropoulis, aged eighteen years, was sentenced to life because of his youth. Corporal Hale, who had served in the Second World War, was the father of a boy aged three and left a widow expecting their second child within the month. There was the usual retaliation, with three soldiers injured when three grenades were thrown at a convoy, and Leicesters Company Sergeant Major Roy Crisell murdered in front of his wife and two others wounded when his car was blown up.

At the end of April, a Gordon Highlander patrol commanded by Second Lieutenant Henderson was escorting Royal Signals technicians tapping local telephone lines in the Paphos Forest when they intercepted three men hiding in bushes. Patrols had discovered that EOKA were exploiting the ringing mechanism of the Forestry Telephone network to alert guerrillas groups to military activity. The Royal Signals had developed a counter measure of stripping the insulation from a length of cable and shorting the circuit; by throwing the cable over the wires and earthing to pins, the use of telephones could be restored easily. The stories of the three men differed, and when Henderson handed them to the Platres interrogation centre, they divulged the location of several EOKA hideouts and suggested that 'Digenes' was based in the Kykko area.

As a consequence of the intelligence gained over the past few weeks, Brigadier Baker launched Operations *Mustard Pot* and *Pepper Pot* in a co-ordinated box sweep of a 400 square mile area that stretched along the coast from Lefka to Polis and then branched inland toward Kambos, Kykko Monastery and the nearby village of Milikouri, in order to strangle the area where several EOKA Groups were reported to have hideouts, isolate them from their supplies and supporters in the villages and block escape routes to the coast. The general tactic was to advance to contact and swamp an area if something incriminating was found. The ground was difficult, with thick woods, deep ravines and steep cliffs. As usual, the area of operations was placed out of bounds and all routes controlled by the Royal Military Police and Cyprus Police. Units involved included the Norfolks, Gordon Highlanders and KOYLI, which had arrived from Aden and took over from 1 Warwicks in April. Warships patrolled the coast. The RAMC and Royal Engineers were tasked to hold surgeries and carry out repairs in the villages. Grivas learnt about the operations from his police contacts and, as usual, instructed the Town Groups to carry out diversionary attacks.

In Operation *Pepper Pot*, a 40 Commando convoy advanced from the south up the winding roads from Paphos until it arrived at the Kykko Bridge, only to find that it had been damaged by a bomb and there was some doubt that it would take the full weight of the Bedford lorries. The Royal Marines took up positions around the bridge and the lorries were gingerly guided over the damage. In the meantime, a lieutenant was reconnoitring the place where the troops would begin their advance, but a mine hurled his Champ upside down against a cliff on the final curve of several hairpins. It was fortunate that the explosion was misdirected otherwise the vehicle would have been thrown 600 feet into a valley. The wreck gave some shelter from guerrillas shooting across the valley until the lorries arrived. Kykko Monastery was isolated and its close association with EOKA confirmed when a detailed search revealed military equipment in the cell of one monk. The operations also undermined its use as a key hub in the Troodos courier network. Grivas was a compulsive recorder of events, and a hefty reward ensured that two coffee pots containing EOKA documents and his diaries that had been buried in nearby fields fell into the hands of Special Branch. These again undermined any suggestion that Archbishop Makarios was not involved in EOKA and proved that he controlled EOKA finances and the supply of equipment. Other influential figures in Cyprus and Greece were also named. A 45 Commando ambush then resulted in the capture of reels of film and a dossier of the Troodos mountain groups. Some of those named faced long prison sentences while others became informers. After a captured EOKA taken aloft in a Sycamore had indicated to his interrogators the location of several hideouts north of Kykko and patrols converged on the area, Grivas thinned the Guerrilla Groups by ordering Pittarides to join Eleftheriou at Stavros Psokas; but the group walked into a Royal Marines patrol and surrendered without a shot being fired. Another Group made it to Pyrgos on the north coast. Grivas rebuilt the courier network to Nicosia but when British patrols began searching the immediate area, Grivas abandoned his hideout and headed south, guided by Antonis Georgiades, who commanded the Milikouri group. The march turned to be a hazardous cross-country night trek, made more difficult because a member of his command group had earlier been wounded in the leg taking messages to a Guerrilla Group. After seventeen hours they reached safety in the area of the Mavron Kremas (Black Chasm), deep, lonely and high in the Cedar Valley, but Grivas was unable to find a suitable lair.

In the diversionary operations, sectarian violence in Nicosia led, at the end of May, to the Nicosia District Officer separating the two communities with the Mason-Dixon line of a 6-foot high barricade erected by Royal Engineers from Famagusta Gate to Paphos Gates in Old Nicosia. On 30 May two soldiers of the Leicesters were killed and eighteen others wounded when a grenade was lobbed into their lorry while they were travelling back to Golden Sands Leave Camp from Famagusta, where they had been rehearsing the Queen's Birthday Parade. Two days later, work was halted at the new garrison at Episkopi and at RAF Akrotiri when a dozen devices were found, and then a week later, Flight Lieutenant William Parker, of the RAF Regiment, saved several Meteor and Venom jets from destruction when he towed a bomb found in a hangar to a patch of grass. Five days later, Private George Garrett, of 625 Ordnance Park, survived torture and being shot in the back when the lorry in which he had been travelling ran over a mine between Dhekelia and Panayia. His colleague Private George Isbell was killed. Three Royal Engineers were killed by an electrically detonated mine on the road to Berengaria married quarters in mid-June.

With the reform of the Cyprus Police critical to restoring normality to the island, visits by several senior Colonial and British police officers resulted in the publication of a report by the Cyprus Police Commission, which included three British Chief Constables. The Commission recognized that the Cyprus Police could not be allowed to be defeated, and although instilling British constabulary traditions and culture was the ultimate goal, it was impractical during internal security instability. The establishment of better relations with the community was critical to success. Recommendations included improving employment terms and conditions, decent pay and training. By mid-1956 Harding had lost confidence in Commissioner of Police Robbins and invited Lieutenant Colonel Geoffrey White, who had been part of the Police Commission, to take his place. By now, a threefold strategy had developed.

Firstly, it was acknowledged that since the Greek-Cypriots could not be trusted, more reliance would fall on the Turkish-Cypriot police officers. This had already resulted in the establishment of the 569-strong Mobile Reserve Police and 1,417 Auxiliary Police.

Secondly, the need was to energize the UK Police Unit as a reliable and credible organization. Its original role as a 'hit squad' and 'a model force' independent of the Cyprus Police had proven unworkable, particularly as none of those seconded had any experience of the culture and people of Cyprus and some officers tended to be aloof and disinclined to set examples to local officers. The discipline of some officers was below that expected of British police and the force had thus acquired a reputation not dissimilar to the Royal Ulster Constabulary (RUC). The Unit had suffered its first casualty when Sergeant Gerald

Rooney (Kent Constabulary) was shot dead on 14 March, and a Turkish-Cypriot policeman was wounded while on patrol in Hippocrates Street, Nicosia. The reluctance of the Greek-Cypriot residents to share information about his murder and the twenty-one other murders and attempted murders that had happened in the district led a to four-day curfew in which the South Staffords and Warwicks controlled the access points of the barbed wire cordon while 3 Para helped police officers carry out a rigorous house-by-house search. As a further punishment, ten suspect families were evicted from their houses. Two days later there was another attack on a Service wife and her young son in Nicosia, however two airmen captured the gunman, Stelios Mavromatis, after he had shot another airman entering Wolseley Barracks.

In spite of the its shortcomings, the UK Police Unit had played a key role in filling the gap left by disloyal Greek-Cypriots and ensured that routine police patrols, criminal detection and Special Branch investigation survived during a period when the Cyprus Police was on its knees. The decision to reinforce it with a further 100 officers seconded from British constabularies led the way for fewer than ten non-Cypriot police officers listed in November 1955 to rise to 600 in 1958, most of the remainder being intelligence and communication specialists. By 1958 the Cyprus Police strength had rising from 1,397 in 1954 to 3,014, most taken up by the recruitment of 900 Turkish-Cypriots, with the UK Unit officers deployed in police stations throughout Cyprus and accommodated in requisitioned hotels. All were armed.

The third element of the new strategy was to mesh police intelligence with Army intelligence. The persistent leakage of information from within the Cyprus Police was resolved when Harding insisted that the Head of Special Branch, who was an Assistant Chief Constable, should report direct to the Chief of Intelligence at HQ Middle East Command, and not to the Commissioner of Police. The practice of allying Special Branch with military intelligence was being used successfully in Malaya and would be adopted in Aden and Northern Ireland. Known unreliable Greek-Cypriot officers were kept separate, as far as possible, from counter-terrorist operations. The nature of EOKA meant that its cell structure was difficult to penetrate, but it was informant information that had compromised the Castle and had led to seizure of Grivas's diaries, photographs and documents and had given the Police and Army a much-needed boost in understanding the culture, organization and structure of EOKA. Strenuous efforts were made to improve the collation of information and intelligence, with surveillance of known EOKA sympathizers and the exploitation of informants. To his credit, Harding did not shrink from the use of interrogation as a vital intelligence asset, as London would do in the early years of Operation *Banner* in Northern Ireland. Capturing Grivas remained Target Number One throughout.

When the intelligence from Operations *Mustard Pot* and *Pepper Pot* suggested that the Army was making inroads into EOKA, in early June, Brigadier Baker instructed 16 Parachute Brigade to plan Operation *Lucky Alphonse* to search the Troodos Mountains for guerrilla groups. As darkness fell on 7 June, the Royal Military Police and Cyprus Police set up control points on the main roads and selected minor roads, while the Royal Horse Guards patrolled roads and tracks. A naval gunfire support team landed from HMS *Diamond*, one of several ships patrolling the Cyprus coast. Meanwhile, 45 Commando, the Gordon Highlanders, 1st KOYLI, the South Staffords, Norfolks and C Company, 1 HLI and the RAF Regiment advanced to contact up and down the steep mountain slopes thick with forest and scrub and over rocky outcrops split by deep re-entrants and shallow gorges. Summer had arrived early, it was hot and the forest tinder dry.

At about 2 am on the 8th, Grivas was woken in his lair by a village dog barking and alerted his men. Suspicious that the Army had mounted another operation and not wishing to invite the near disaster of evacuating the Castle, in order to take the pressure off the guerrillas, he despatched orders to the Town Sabotage Groups to escalate civil disturbance, but most of the couriers had difficulty breaching the cordons. At dawn, his men watched as Army lorries full of troops moved up from Milikouri and noted that several captured EOKA were accompanying patrols. Again guided by Antonis Georgiades, Grivas and the three men of his command team headed south until at about 10 pm, after a long day in the mid-summer heat, they reached high ground overlooking a main road junction in a valley with forks leading to Limassol and Paphos. After two of his men reported there were troops to the east, Grivas led his men across the road and climbed to high ground. He later claimed that he knew there were troops nearby when he saw fresh boot prints and an empty English cigarette pack. Next day, Grivas moved east and slipped through the cordon between a military post and a helicopter landing site and laid up until dark. Padding along tracks through the dark woods, they headed north-east and continued marching through the morning, without seeing any troops, until at about 1.30 pm, after an exhausting seventeen hours, Grivas and his men reached a cool, wooded valley where they rested and ate the last of their food beside a stream that in winter was a torrent of fresh cold water bounding over rocks and large stones, but in summer was a trickle with a few clear pools. Controversy surrounds the question of whether his group were ambushed during the morning near a wayside chapel on the hairpin of a road at Ayios Ayia. Grivas denies the contact. At about 3 pm a C Company, 3 Para patrol, with a tracker dog, led by Sergeant Scott was following the stream when they saw Grivas and his men replenishing their water bottles. When one of the men slipped on some rocks, Scott attacked. The shocked guerrillas fled into the woods, abandoning most of their equipment, including spectacles, a camp bed, a small radio, binoculars, the Sam Browne belt and boots used by Grivas and, again, detailed diaries made up to 9 June. For the second time, Grivas, the man who executed traitors, compromised EOKA in a detailed manner and gave the British another intelligence coup. Grivas skips over the loss of his diaries in his autobiography and his embarrassment when, in September, they were sold to the public by Her Majesty's Stationery Office. Pinned down by Sycamores hovering overhead and 3 Para patrols beating the area, the EOKA hid in the dense undergrowth until dark and then made their way to the road that ran through the River Platres valley. Creeping across it, they climbed yet another peak until by about 3.30 am they were south-east of Kaminaria in the foothills of the Troodos Mountains, hungry, tired and thirsty. Two days later, using the information in the diaries, 1 Norfolks destroyed a District Group in the Paphos area and captured two EOKA with £5,000 bounties on their heads. The men guided troops to a cache containing a Bren gun, three shotguns, two rifles and two Sten guns.

Although it was hot, tiring and thirsty work, throughout the days the troops probed the ravines and climbed hills, forcing guerrillas to abandon hideouts and risk long marches along rough tracks in broad daylight. Each night before last light, the troops covered potential escape routes using Vickers machine guns and Bren guns on fixed lines of fire. The difficulties of command and control of inexperienced young soldiers patrolling in the confines of wooded, hilly terrain and forest inevitably led to 'friendly fire' incidents. During the evening of 10 June, 1 and 3 Paras were setting ambushes covering the boundary between their areas of tactical responsibility near Kykko Monastery when Sergeant Major Jimmy Foster of C Company, 1 Para was killed and two Paras seriously wounded when they were ambushed at the bend of a track in thickly wooded country. Only when an NCO of Foster's patrol returned to Company HQ to report the incident did it emerge that 3 Para had reported a contact at the same time and place as Foster's patrol had been ambushed, and the tragedy became apparent. Four days later another 3 Para patrol mistook a Norfolks' ambush for an EOKA hideout and killed Lance Corporal Peter Elliott. Next day, a 40 Commando patrol commanded by Corporal Robert Benbow, aged nineteen years, captured an entire EOKA group in their hideout without a shot being fired, along with weapons, equipment and 3,000 rounds of ammunition. The Lyso Group was attacked by Royal Marines and Demitrakis Constantinides was captured on 12 June. HQ and Support Companies, 1 KOYLI searching ruined buildings high in the Troodos found a bomb factory and logistic centre, and then Lieutenant Charlesworth and Private Richardson, of 2 Platoon, detained an EOKA suspect in possession of weapons, food, medical supplies and bomb-making equipment. His death sentence for possession was later commuted.

Grivas and his group remained above Kaminaria until sunset on 12 June and then crept to a stream on the outskirts to refill their water bottles. Meanwhile, Georgiades had entered the village to find food and reported that it and the immediate area was crawling with troops. For the next twenty-four hours Grivas remained near the stream, during which they were disturbed by a child and her goat and by an elderly woman cutting reeds. That night Georgiades and Pavlos Nikitas, one of the Kyrenia Castle escapers, entered the village but came under fire from soldiers. Hungry and exhausted, the group began walking the five miles to Trooditissa, but with every step risking an ambush, it took until 1 pm on the 13th for them to arrive and sit down to a meal in the nearby monastery. After sending a monk to deliver a message to the Nicosia Town Group that he was safe, Grivas and his four companions crossed the Troodos to Platres road after dark and next evening were overlooking Saittas in the southern foothills of the Troodos. When Grivas sent Georgiades and Lambros Kafkallides to contact the Limassol Town Group, its leader, Demos Hadjimiltis, said that preparations were underway to shelter Grivas in his house in the town but it would not be ready until the 18 June. Grivas decided to split up his group and he, Georgiades and a guide from Limassol, masquerading as farmers and keeping to tracks headed towards Yerasa, on one occasion exchanging pleasantries with an Army patrol that had left the main road to look for water. When the soldiers rejoined their main body and reported the exchange, 3 Commando Brigade District concluded that Grivas had left the mountains, and the search for him now focused on the general area between Paphos and Limassol. Meanwhile, tragedy blighted Operation *Lucky Alphonse*.

During the summer, the dry forest and scrub of Cyprus is prone to fires; indeed, Cypriots by law were expected to help the mostly Turkish-Cypriot foresters fight fires. During the afternoon of 16 June, a fire broke out on the slopes not far from the village of Vroisia, which lies at the end of a three-mile narrow, twisting road edged by cliffs and ravines that meets the secondary road to Galini and the main road from Kykko Monastery north to Kampos. There are no other roads or tracks suitable for vehicles. By the following morning, the embers had been whipped into full fires by a strong easterly wind funnelling up ravines, leaving exploding trees, burning charcoal and ash carpeting the ground a foot deep in places. Behind the wall of flames plodded the troops, but suddenly the wind changed to a westerly and the fire sped toward them. Captain Wallace, who was the HQ 3 Commando Brigade Administrative Officer in Limassol, had assembled a composite Troop of cooks, drivers and clerks and was under command of the Norfolks. As the flames spread, Wallace was instructed by a Gordon Highlander major commanding a fire-fighting party from his Battalion and from B and D Companies, 1 Norfolks to help several foresters while he sought reinforcements. When the reinforcements did not arrive, Wallace walked down the road hoping to meet the major and met a Gordons platoon and some foresters assembled by three Bedford lorries; he learnt from a lieutenant that the speed of the fire had cut him off from his rendezvous further down the hill. Wallace and his batman abandoned their Land Rover and, taking the advice of the foresters, climbed to the top of a hill. Below them, the soldiers had climbed into the trucks. Wallace was sheltering in a patch of burnt ground when he suddenly heard explosions, gunfire and screams and watched as two men supporting each other, one with his clothes burnt off, staggered up the road. Running down the hill to the road, Wallace saw that the lorries had been trapped by an abandoned Ferret blocking the road and then engulfed by a tunnel of flames. The smouldering bodies of the dead and injured lay where they had attempted to escape the inferno. It then dawned on him that the explosions were exploding fuel tanks and the firing was ammunition cooking off in the pouches of the soldiers. A Norfolks sergeant was organizing the collection of the dead and wounded and the Ferret was pushed off the road. When Wallace later rejoined his Troop having a smoke half a mile up the road, one of the Royal Marines casually remarked, 'We thought you were a goner, sir.' Second Lieutenant Bruce Kynoch and nine Gordon Highlanders died in the inferno. Three others would die of their injuries in hospital. Kynoch had arrived in Cyprus just three weeks earlier.

Lieutenant Stanley Sutton, the Norfolks Medical Officer, was driving towards Vroisia in his Land Rover when he was forced to shelter from the flames in a ditch; when he and his driver emerged, his right arm was badly burned and his vehicle a smoking wreck. Seeing that most of the casualties required greater medical care than he could provide and attempts to evacuate them was being thwarted by fickle winds, he made them as comfortable as he could. Sutton was awarded the MBE for his conduct. Lieutenant Shardlow of 23 Parachute Field Ambulance RAMC was lowered from a Sycamore to help the injured and was assisted by Private Ross RAMC attached to the Gordon Highlanders. For two days a military police section played a key role in regulating traffic and keeping the narrow road to Vroisia open by ensuring reliable communications.

At about midnight on the 19 June, Grivas and Georghiades arrived on the outskirts of Palodia but, hearing dogs, they believed the village to be occupied by troops and decided to walk the five miles back to Yerasa. Early next morning, Chief Inspector Costas Efstathiou, who was not aware of the identity of his passenger, drove the exhausted Grivas to the house in Limassol owned by Dafnis Panayides. Henceforth, Grivas would control EOKA from hideouts, occasionally travelling to Nicosia to receive medical treatment, usually from his brother, a doctor. He re-organized the EOKA Guerrilla Groups and instructed Markos Drakos to create a new group from his decimated Vassiliki Group and the disbanded Milikouri Group. Its leader, Antonis Georgiades, remained with Grivas as his personal assistant. Other surviving EOKA he sent to the Omodhus, Pakhna and Pitsillia Groups, the latter led by Afxentiou and still undamaged. Meanwhile, the terrorism continued.

In every campaign, an army has a low point. For the Army in Northern Ireland, it was probably Bloody Sunday. In Cyprus, it was probably Operation *Lucky Alphonse*, which concluded on 23 June. Strategically it had been a success, with several EOKA groups destroyed and seventeen guerrillas captured and handed over to 16 Parachute Brigade Provost Unit, but at the cost of twenty-five British soldiers dead, seven of them in road accidents. The operation had highlighted deficiencies in command and control and tactics, in particular that urban patrols, roadblocks and searches were not ideal preparations for operations against an enemy lodged in rugged mountains where physical fitness and stamina were essential. Unlike the Regular Army that emerged in the early 1960s of men with a minimum of six years service and several weeks training before deployment, the inexperienced National Servicemen in Cyprus were limited to a few weeks after basic training. Colonel Grivas commented that Operations *Pepper Pot* and *Lucky Alphonse* were the first time that EOKA Guerrilla Groups had faced the combination of infantry patrols supported by helicopters covering a large area. He was critical of the tactics, in particular the friendly fire incidents and the poor track discipline of discarded cigarette packets and rubbish from ration packs which left clues. When there were clashes, his view was that the responses were 'lamentable'. Nevertheless, the Operations had dealt EOKA a serious blow from which they never recovered.

# THE LONG HOT SUMMER

In addition to the thirteen mourned by the Gordon Highlanders, the Norfolks grieved for five. One RASC was killed. As the bodies of the two 3 Para trapped in their vehicle were being escorted to Wayne's Keep cemetery on 19 June, a bomb thrown at the cortege near the US Consulate narrowly missed Captain Horace McClelland, the Battalion Chaplain, but injured three Greek-Cypriots on bicycles. Escorting troops leapt from an armoured car, vaulted a wall and raced into a nearby garden, firing at the fleeing bomber. The area was immediately cordoned, houses searched and four suspects arrested.

Millions of pounds worth of vehicles and equipment were lost in the operations. A Norfolks officer noted that those who attempted to outrun the fire had perished while those who ran at an acute angle to its path and who had sheltered in fire breaks and patches of smouldering ground survived. While opinions about the origins of the fire differ, the consensus generally is that exploding mortar bombs were the cause. Between about 9 am and 10.20 am on 16 June, a sustained mortar barrage had bombarded the valleys near Vroisia while machine-gunners raked the high ground. Mortar Troop, 45 Commando were horrified when 3-inch bombs dropped short among A Troop, who were firing their 2-inch mortars, and wounded five Royal Marines. Checks on unused mortar bombs showed they were out of date. A member of the Parachute Regiment watching the barrages saw whirlwinds suck up flames from the explosions and rush at the speed of an express train at treetop height from one of side of the valley to the other. A claim by Elenitsa Seraphim, the EOKA Larnaca Area Commander, that the British had deliberately set the forest alight as part of the operation to capture Grivas is rejected, as were her claims that Greek-Cypriots had helped extinguish fires. At the inquiry, the Turkish-Cypriot foresters, who had been accused by Greek-Cypriots of deserting the troops and starting fires, were widely praised for their determination and commitment. The fact is that no one knows who started the fire but most agree that it was caused by mortar bomb detonations.

Meanwhile, the diversionary terrorism ordered by Grivas continued. In June, Mr Justice Bernard Shaw, a senior judge who had sentenced several EOKA to death and long terms of imprisonment, was seriously wounded by two gunmen in Nicosia. Limassol reeled after being collectively fined £35,000 for its complicity in supporting EOKA, the money being placed in a fund for victims and their families. When a bomb thrown into the stylish Little Soho restaurant killed US Vice-Consul William Botelor on 16 June in Nicosia, Grivas, while insisting it was a 'tragic mistake', warned foreigners not to frequent places used by British officials. On the 21st, Sergeant Reginald Tipple, a

Metropolitan Policeman attached to the Pyla Detention Camp, was murdered while shopping in Larnaca for a present for his young daughter. The camp was about ten miles north-east of the town. In July, eleven Greek-Cypriots were killed, including a young girl caught in an explosion in Yialousa targeting a Highland Light Infantry patrol. Five more Servicemen died, including RAF Sergeant Ernest Allen shot after being caught in a honeytrap.

When Andreas Zakos and Charilaos Michael had been sentenced to death for their part in the ambush that had killed Lance Corporal Morun in December 1955 and Iakovos Patsatsos had been convicted of the murder of the Turkish-Cypriot PC Nihat Basif, Grivas, while not wishing to affect their appeals, again ordered that hostages be taken against the lives of the three EOKA. In the first attempt, Nitsa Hadjigeorghiou, one of the more militant female EOKA, developed a plan to invite some soldiers to the Baths of Aphrodite near Polis and then seize them while they were helpless from drugged drinks at a café. However, the information haemorrhaged and the Polis area was placed under curfew. In her next attempt, she lured Sergeant Allen to her house at Ayios Demitos and shortly after she invited him into her bedroom, three masked gunmen rushed from the bathroom. Allen fought back but was shot dead. With the body in her house and his car outside, Georghiou coolly reported to the police that two gunmen had followed her and Allen home where they had murdered him. But her story was not believed, and because she was suspect EOKA and in case she associated with other soldiers, she was detained in Nicosia Prison for four months. Re-detained after being released and sent to the Omorphita Interrogation Centre, she admitted her association with Georghiou Afxentiou and Kyriakos Matsis and was again imprisoned. When Field Marshal Harding commuted the death sentence of her friend Nicos Xenophontos to life, as a measure of good will, Grivas believed, as he invariably did, that she had collaborated and ordered that she was to be ostracized. In spite of her commitment to EOKA, she died in poverty in 1958. Xenophontos had been captured during Operation *Lucky Alphonse* by a KOYLI patrol in an EOKA logistic base and bomb factory.

On 8 July, Mr Garth Karberry, a Customs and Excise officer, and his pregnant wife were ambushed in their car by a Group led by Tassos Sofocleus on the lonely Kantara Pass near Akanthou, north of Lefkoniko, and savagely murdered. On the same day, Sergeant Alan Smith, of the Gordon Highlanders was leading a patrol along a dried-up riverbed near Morphou Greek Elementary School when he challenged three armed men at a distance of about twenty-five yards.

They fired and, although mortally wounded, Smith emptied his Sten gun magazine and forced the men to abandon their shotguns as they fled. Morphou was thoroughly searched by the Battalion and a 1 Wiltshires company. Greek-Cypriot councillors refused to contribute to an inquiry into the clash. In mid-July, the arrival of 2 Para, the Guards Independent Parachute Company and its artillery, engineer and field ambulance brought 16 Parachute Brigade to near full strength. Although warned by EOKA not to return to the Troodos, the Brigade launched Operation *Golden Eagle* using 40 Commando, the Norfolks and Gordon Highlanders in another drive in 400 square miles of the western Troodos Mountains; within three days they had captured seventeen guerrillas and wounded several others trying to breach the cordons.

## CHAPTER EIGHT

# The Suez Crisis

## (September to December 1956)

The international crisis in the Near East had sharpened after Colonel Nasser officially assumed power as President of Egypt on 23 June 1956. He had then blockaded the Suez Canal with sunken ships and crippled the vital arterial trade route between Europe and the Middle East and Far East. Hostilities apparently imminent with Egypt, Lieutenant General Keightley was warned to prepare Cyprus and Malta as invasion assembly points for 80,000 troops. Since the RASC remained vital in ferrying men, equipment and supplies to and from the embarkation ports, 1 Transport Column was reformed into RASC Cyprus East and Cyprus West.

Determined to ensure that Cyprus remained in the international limelight, Grivas kept up the pressure on internal security with hit-and-run attacks and ambushes. Between 7 August and 15 September, which was the scheduled D-Day to land in Egypt, EOKA carried out fifty-six bombings of military targets including eighteen directed at Dhekelia, Akrotiri, Episkopi and the 625 Ordnance Depot in Larnaca and fourteen against camps in the Nicosia area. There were twenty attacks on military logistic facilities at Famagusta, Limassol and Paphos. An Army Field Security launch was also sunk. Most of the devices were delivered by employees. At least twenty were defused. There were twenty ambushes of military vehicles. In August, twelve loyalist Greek-Cypriots were murdered. As part of the plan to seize hostages in retaliation for the imminent execution, on 4 August, of the three EOKA who had killed Lance Corporal Morun, on the 3rd, Mr John Cremer, an elderly retired civil servant thought by EOKA to be an intelligence agent, was kidnapped as he walked to teach English in the Turkish hamlet of Temblos, west of Kyrenia. The authorities responded that the 'course of justice would not be affected' by the kidnapping, and Grivas's strategy backfired when Andreas Zakos appealed from his death cell that Cremer should be released, which he was three days later. When the three were hanged on the 9th, the expected retaliation did not materialize; instead, a week later, Grivas suspended operations to allow Archbishop Makarios to negotiate 'a free Cyprus'. The reality was that some communities fed up with the collective fines, roadblocks, cordon-and-searches, curfews and EOKA executions and punishment squads in the mid-summer heat, quite apart from the withdrawal of business investment, were challenging his orders for diversionary operations to deflect the pressure from the mountain Guerrilla Groups. The flow of informant information also increased.

On the 22 August Field Marshal Harding surprised diplomats by offering EOKA the option of either renouncing their British citizenship and being deported to Greece until the Emergency was resolved or taking their chances in court. To prevent the British claiming victory if EOKA accepted, the Greek Government offered safe passage to Grivas and his men. But Grivas, feeling that the struggle was by no means lost and judging the offer to his men to keep their British citizenship to be a touch arrogant, stuck to his principle of diplomacy through force by announcing next day, 'My reply to the Government is No! Come and take it' and that operations would resume on 27 August. Harding then revealed on 26 August that a week earlier a patrol had found diaries belonging to Grivas in jars near Lysi. For a few weeks after 1 April 1955, Grivas had stayed with a cousin of Afxentiou, who had become a bodyguard to Grivas. The bodyguard and his brother had undertaken to take the diaries to Lysi where they buried them in a field. In the same period, Grivas had also stayed with a man who knew where they were buried and had sold them to the British. They proved to be an intelligence coup of some significance because they described the organization, methods and personalities of EOKA during the run-up to the outbreak of the violence in April 1955. The extracts again undermined Makarios by proving that he was deeply involved in the insurrection and that it was he who had invited Grivas to form a clandestine army to liberate Cyprus. For the third time Grivas had compromised EOKA in ignoring his own principles by failing to destroy correspondence and documents. His claims that the diaries were forgeries were largely ignored.

The day of 27 August was tense, particularly in Ledra Street where businesses had enjoyed a week of welcome trading during the ceasefire, including from Service families, even though the street now had achieved international fame as Murder Mile. The street ran through Old Nicosia. At 57 Alexander Road, a few steps from Ledra Street, lived Dr Michael Grivas, elder brother to Colonel Grivas. The narrowness and hustle and bustle of the street in Old Nicosia allowed gunmen to identify their target, usually approach from behind, shoot at point blank range and then disappear, guns sometimes being handed to EOKA women who concealed them in shopping bags. Patrols were also easy targets. RASC Private Douglas Laventure was the first off-duty soldier to be murdered on Murder Mile, while he was purchasing a present eleven days before Christmas 1955. Private Raymond Banks, of 1 South Staffords was killed on 21 May 1956 when a grenade was dropped into his vehicle from an upper storey of a house. In mid-June 1956 a Warwicks patrol was ambushed, and although the radio operator, Private Ray Watkins, was badly wounded in both arms and legs, he maintained contact with Battalion HQ. It was not uncommon for Greek-Cypriot residents and shoppers to walk past victims lying in the road and pretend to know nothing about it. Patrols and families soon learnt that if shops were closed and there were few shoppers at times when it should be busy, then something was amiss.

Within hours of the ceasefire being lifted, a bomb exploded at an officer's house, a tank landing ship was damaged by a limpet mine, a fire destroyed the new Officers' and Sergeants' Messes at Episkopi and power lines near Paphos were sabotaged. A new dimension to Service life in Cyprus emerged when Greek-Cypriot NAAFI employees deposited bombs in Army married quarters. In another engagement in central Nicosia, two Service wives were caught in crossfire during a thirty-minute gun battle in which a patrol was ambushed.

When Polycarpos Georghadjis, the young hard-core guerrilla who had developed an intelligence network among the Cyprus Police, was detained in Nicosia Prison, Grivas considered him to be of such importance that he instructed the Nicosia EOKA murder group led by Nicos Sampson to rescue him. Born Nicos Georghiades in Famagusta, Sampson changed his name when he began working as a photo-journalist for the *Times of Cyprus* in order to distinguish himself from others with the same surname. The *Times of Cyprus*, was edited by Charles Foley and since it was pro-*enosis* was known by British soldiers as the *EOKA Times*. Also locked up in Nicosia Prison after her failed kidnap plan was Nitsa Hadjigeorghiou. She managed to contact Georghadjis and when she learnt on 30 August that he had convinced the prison authorities that he was unwell and was going for an X-Ray at Nicosia General Hospital on the next day, she persuaded a Greek-Cypriot warder to let Sampson know of Georghadjis' appointment. Next day, Georghadjis and two other detainees arrived at the hospital escorted by Sergeants Tony Eden and Leonard Demmon (both Metropolitan Police). One of the detainees was Argyrious Karadymas, the Greek owner of the caique *Ayios Georghias* boarded by the Royal Navy in January 1955, and he had been sentenced to six years as an agitator. As the prisoners and escorts came down the stairs from X-Ray, four gunmen who had been waiting in the main entrance hall opened up with revolvers that had been smuggled into the hospital by EOKA women. Demmon returned fire with his Sterling but he had been badly wounded and accidently shot two hospital orderlies as well as one of the terrorists. Eden shot a second terrorist and killed a third by clubbing him with his revolver when his ammunition ran out, but he was unable to prevent Georghadjis and Karadymas from escaping through the back entrance. Eden was awarded the George Medal and, although a marked man, he refused to return to the UK. In December he was killed when his cocked revolver fell from his shoulder holster while he was playing with his puppy. Demmon was later posthumously awarded the Queen's Police Medal for Gallantry. A week later, Pavlos Pavlakis and Antonios Papadopoulos of the Famagusta Group escaped from Pyla Detention Camp by crawling underneath the perimeter fence. Pavlakis assumed command of the Famagusta Town Group while his colleague joined Afxentiou.

As the Franco-British forces completed their final preparations for the landings in Egypt, Cyprus had become an enlarged aircraft carrier for the British and French army and air force units assembling in existing and hastily constructed camps. Among the French force was the 10th Airborne Division, which had three parachute regiments, one being Foreign Legion. It had recently been on operations in Algeria, where the French response to terrorism was considerably more robust than that of the British in Cyprus. Defending the anchorages and airfields was the 1st Artillery Group, Royal Artillery (1 AGRA) with 21 and 50 Medium Regiments RA replacing 40 Commando in Paphos and 2 Para in Limni Camp respectively, and the 16 and 43 Light and 57 Heavy Anti Aircraft Regiments RA. The naval elements were gathered in Malta where there were concerns that 3 Commando Brigade had been in Cyprus for nearly a year and had not exercised the complexities of an amphibious landing.

Much to his consternation, the influx of British and French troops forced Brigadier Baker to divert troops from some internal security operations to guard the camps springing up across the island, not only against EOKA but also the threat of Arab commando attacks. The inevitability of de-escalating internal security operations was also worrying, more so when industrial disputes and strikes led to troops being diverted to load ships at the embarkation ports. Privately, Field Marshal Harding was critical of the impact that the operation was having on his drive against EOKA, particularly as Operation *Fox Hunter* had dealt the Troodos Guerrilla Groups several severe blows. But EOKA would be given some respite when 16 Parachute Brigade was withdrawn from operations near Kambos and 1 and 3 Paras returned to Aldershot in several types of aircraft where, in rotation over ten days each, the soldiers carried out three training jumps and a battalion drop and had a couple of days leave before returning to Cyprus.

When in September the Limassol suburb in which he was hidden was subjected to an increasing numbers of searches, Grivas moved his hideout from the home owned by Dafnis Panayides to the house occupied by Marios Christodoules, his wife Elli and their baby daughter aged nine months, on the northern outskirts of Limassol. Ironically, Christodoules was a clerk at the Akrotiri branch of the Ottoman Bank. The hideout had been built by two members of Limassol Town Group, Andreas Papadopoulous and Manolis Savvides. Both were part of the syndicate successfully smuggling weapons with the connivance of Customs, indeed it was Savvides who had persuaded Christodoules to shelter Grivas. The hideout was accessed through a trapdoor under the kitchen sink and, dug under the garden, was topped by a concrete roof on which sat a poultry run. Behind the house was an escape route across fields. Inside there was sufficient room for two camp beds, a desk and a chair and an electric fan for ventilation. Grivas usually spent the day in the house; he rarely went out. As with other dynamic guerrilla leaders, Che Guevera being a classic example, some young women focused on Grivas, now aged fifty-eight years, among them Louella Kokkinou, whom he trusted highly as a courier. She claimed that her front teeth had been knocked out during an interrogation in May 1956 – until dental records proved they had been extracted in June. To help protect the bunker, Christodoules purchased a small black mongrel whose irritable, high-pitched barking warned of strangers approaching the property. Grivas' presence in the bunker was known only to Dafnis and Maroulla Panayides, who had sheltered him previously and brought his correspondence, Demos Hjimiltis, the Limassol Town commander and his fiancée, Nina Droushiotou, who became the principal courier for Grivas, and the two builders. Elli Christodoules also seems to have hosted Grivas.

Grivas stepped up the campaign of terror, with Greek-Cypriots again taking the brunt of civilian deaths. During the afternoon of 8 September, eight EOKA from the Tassos Sofocleus Group breaking into Kyrenia Police Station were interrupted when Captain de Klee, Scots Guards attached to the Guards Independent Parachute Company, and Cornet Gage of the Royal Horse Guards, walked into the police station and startled the terrorists. Thinking that the two men were part of an Army patrol, the raiders scuttled past the two officers, dropping weapons and ammunition in their wake. Ten soldiers were killed in the second half of

September, including during the morning of the 28th, Surgeon Captain Gordon Wilson, the Royal Horse Guards Medical Officer, shot by Nicos Sampson in his car at the junction of St Andrew and Queen Frederica Street in Nicosia soon after he had treated a seriously-ill Greek-Cypriot woman. Two shops suspected to have been involved in the murder were searched and closed. Next day, Sampson was one of three EOKA who shot Sergeant Cyril Thorogood (Leicester and Rutland Constabulary) and Sergeant Hugh Carter (Herefordshire County Constabulary) at point blank range and badly wounded Sergeant William Webb (Worcestershire County Constabulary) at the junction of Alexander the Great Street with Ledra Street while they were getting into a car after a shopping trip. Several British wives gave first aid to Thorogood and Carter while Webb, shot several times, attempted to engage the gunmen. Sampson found sanctuary in St Andrew's Monastery. On the same day, a 14/20th Hussars sergeant was shot dead and his wife wounded in front of their young daughter as they were returning from church in Larnaca. Two Greek-Cypriots were arrested, and another suspected to have been involved was Petrakis Kyprianou, the well-educated if rebellious son of a prosperous grocer. He had volunteered to attack a Royal Navy party ashore, but when this failed he had then led grenade attacks on Army vehicles and had been involved in the execution of Greek-Cypriots. He vowed never to be taken alive and was granted his wish in an engagement with troops in March 1957.

Losing patience with Greek-Cypriots' persistent reluctance to identify the killers and their unwillingness to help casualties, the authorities imposed a 7 am to 7 pm curfew on several Greek-Cypriot suburbs in the walled city, with a one-hour suspension at midday. Several thousand people evacuated their homes, leaving about 12,000 under curfew. Greek-Cypriot hotel bars, cabarets, cinemas and theatres and coffee shops were ordered to close, although hotels could cater for residents. On 1 October, when several hundred women intent on restocking empty larders attempted to access a Turkish vegetable market but found their way blocked by soldiers from 1 KOYLI, the District Commissioner agreed to a two-hour suspension either side of midday so that they could buy provisions from Greek-Cypriot markets. He also organized food centres along Ledra Street to ensure equitable distribution. After the Mayor of Paphos had complained that the curfew was causing excessive hardship because wage earners were unable to go to work, Harding raised the restrictions on 6 October.

Among the military casualties in late September were Corporal Paul Farley and Staff Sergeant Joe Culkin, both of 1 Ammunition Disposal Unit (Internal Security), killed within ten days of each other while dealing with devices in EOKA hideouts. From the earliest stages of its campaign, EOKA lacked explosives. After the seizures and non-arrival of explosive during the preparatory stages, EOKA divers had recovered landmines from captured Italian stocks dumped in the shallow waters off Famagusta, and although they were usually corroded, the TNT was sufficiently stable to be extracted and hammered into small lumps of explosive or crystals. Fishermen knew where the mines could be found because they sometimes dragged them in their nets and then used the explosive to stun fish. Local information enabled EOKA to map the locations of minefields used to defend Cyprus during the war and after lifting mines they then used the serviceable ones to ambush military vehicles. Detonators and dynamite were stolen or bought cheaply from the copper mines, quarries and road works. Potassium chlorate was widely used for agricultural purposes and mixed with sugar could be converted into improvised if unstable explosive. In spite of Army objections, it was not until late in the Emergency that the supply to farmers was strictly rationed.

Hand grenades smuggled to Cyprus included the British Mills 36, one of the three types of red-painted Italian Anti Personnel bombs known as 'Red Devils' and post-war US grenades supplied to the Greek Army. Improvised alternatives were nails, bits of metal and iron and stones packed into a covered tin can or perhaps a parcel surrounding a tube of improvised explosive into which was inserted a fuse detonated with a match or lighter. The 'pipe bomb' was popular. Manufactured from standard plumbing pipe filled with TNT and fitted at both ends with screw caps, grooves weakened the pipe so that it provided the shrapnel. The detonator was a short length of crimped safety fuse taped to usually two or more matches. Pipe bombs were difficult to identify and could be transported as part of a plumber's tool kit or a delivery to a shop or client. For devices left at targets, time delay fuses were built in. In the British L Delay detonator, a thin length of wire stretched under pressure until it snapped and dropped the striker to hit the detonator. In the Number 10 Time Pencil used by EOKA, a small glass capsule of crushed acid nibbled through the wire under tension.

Although Soviet pressure-switches were found in several devices, improvised versions were manufactured from two hinged pieces of wood fitted with a cheap bell push and a small battery kept open at one end by small springs placed on top of a tin of explosive buried under the surface of a road. When the wheel of a vehicle passed over the wood, the weight forced the two pieces together, which then pressed the bell push to complete the circuit to the battery and detonate the explosive. EOKA also developed a simple mortar from a length of plumber's pipe packed with explosive and shrapnel and either buried in a bank or fixed to a tree and detonated remotely from a battery at a concealed firing point. Alignment was usually pre-arranged at night using the lights of military vehicles to calculate distances. Some remotely controlled improvised devices were placed in culverts.

Initially, the Ammunition Wing, 625 Ordnance Depot had assisted the police with Ammunition Examiners attached to the Criminal Investigation Departments at Nicosia, Famagusta, Larnaca, Limassol and Paphos. Their role was to accompany detectives to incidents, disarm or dispose of devices and then be prepared to give expert evidence in the Courts. This required devices to be dismantled and then examined for the signature of the person who had constructed it. The senior Inspecting Officer was Major William Harrison, who in 1956 had been seconded to the Cyprus Government as the Government Explosives Officer based at Police HQ and who would be awarded the George Medal. He insisted on attending new devices wherever possible so that he could pass on his findings to his men. In terms of bomb disposal equipment, the Ammunition Examiners usually had an assortment of screwdrivers, pliers, spanners, masking tape, fishing hooks of various sizes and string kept in an ammunition box as their tools of the trade. Protective clothing was almost non-existent, yet only three Ammunition Examiners were killed in action. When Captain J W Greenwood formed 1 Ammunition Disposal Unit (Internal Security), it was an administrative move to formalize the deployment of the Ammunition Examiners, nevertheless it was the first unit established by the RAOC specifically for bomb disposal. The Examiners laid the groundwork for the collection of forensic evidence in bomb incidents for which the Corps has since gained deserved international recognition. Between 1 April 1955 and 17 March 1959, the Ammunition Examiners dealt with 4,688 devices, attended over 3,000 recoveries of arms, ammunition and explosives and investigated 4,300 incidents. Greenwood also commanded 17 Mobile Ammunition Inspection Unit, which was part of the Ammunition Depot at the former RAF Lakatamia airfield.

Since individual ownership of wirelesses was not widespread, particularly in rural areas, the British and EOKA indulged in sustained psychological warfare campaigns throughout the Emergency, with the distribution of leaflets frequently used in efforts to discredit each other. One provocative EOKA leaflet suggested, in the autumn of 1955, that the US and Great Britain were an unholy alliance and since the UN had denied Cyprus freedom, the Cypriots had no choice but to shed blood. A British leaflet depicting a Cypriot murdered by EOKA suggested that supporting Grivas would result in the sacrificing of children for a pointless cause in which freedom of speech and religion would be denied. Other British leaflets included wanted posters, safe conduct and surrender passes and offers of rewards for supplying information. Every soldier carried a small red pocket wallet entitled 'Wanted Men in Cyprus' issued by COSHEG (Chief of Staff to His Excellency the Governor) which listed the details and photographs of EOKA suspects. Much of the printing was done by the RAOC Printing Unit. While Grivas was reliant on youths to distribute leaflets, the British, in a standard psychological warfare tactic, generally used Austers to drop leaflets, with the aircraft flying at low level and relying upon the breeze to help distribution. Boxes of leaflets were also dropped for troops to distribute. When two apparently loyalist organizations appeared in 1958, 'Cromwell' and AKOE (EOKA spelt backwards), and distributed leaflets promising retribution against EOKA operations, a military counter-intelligence operation discovered that some printing had been done on duplicating machines in British bases and several Servicemen were quietly shipped back to the United Kingdom.

On 28 September the Tassos Sofocleus Group used a site identified by Grivas a year earlier to ambush two military vehicles negotiating a hairpin on the main road between Nicosia and Kyrenia below St Hilarion Castle with heavy automatic fire, including from a Bren and a home-made mortar, killing Mrs Mary Holton of the Women's Voluntary Service and her military driver, Private Colin Read of 1 Wiltshires, and wounding several others. Read was a professional Bristol City football player. This ambush led to HQ 16 Parachute Brigade launching Operation *Sparrow Hawk One* on 2 October with 2,000 troops from 1 HLI, 1 KOYLI and 40 Field Regiment searching an area of 200 square miles east of Kyrenia Pass for the Group. The Royal Navy sealed off villages along the coast. Among tactics developed to root out hideouts constructed in houses was pouring water on to the floor and watching its seepage. Next day, a C Company, 2 Para patrol commanded by Lieutenant John How was checking an isolated farmhouse about a mile from the Turkish-Cypriot village of Trapeza when Private Robert Taylor accidentally dislodged a rock to reveal a cave. Lance Corporal Staff entered and found a weapons cache buried in several oil drums, two wireless sets and clothing not normally associated with farmers. How then ordered a detailed search, and persistent patience profited for Privates O'Donnell and Pearce searching the fodder storage area in a barn. Removing a coat from a hook, they saw a hole in the wall and flashed a torch inside. On seeing a head, a shot was fired into the cavity and someone inside shouted 'Don't shoot! We surrender!' But no one emerged and it was only when How fired another shot though the wall that paras in another part of the barn saw straw moving and six partially-clad men emerge from a trap door, one bleeding from his ear. Among them were Tassos Sofocleos and Fotis Christofi, his deputy commander with a £5,000 bounty on his head. Forensics on a Bren gun proved that it had been used in the Kyrenia ambushes, including the murders of Read and Mrs Holton. Several of the terrorists were convicted of taking part in the St Hilarion ambush and sent to Dartmoor Prison. The hideout was ingenious and consisted of a 8ft by 3ft cavity between two rooms with ventilation supplied through the hole. Suspicion and luck on the part of an observant soldier proved its undoing. When several more hideouts were found in the vicinity of the farmhouse, the farmer had his house blown up as a punishment for harbouring terrorists.

The next day, acting on information, the grave of the missing Lance Corporal Gordon Hill was found nearby. He had been strangled. Forensic examination of a buried Sten showed that it was his and that it had been used in several murders. Operation *Sparrow Hawk One* essentially destroyed the EOKA groups in the eastern Kyrenia Mountains and removed a significant threat to the road that connected Nicosia to Kyrenia and the northern coastal fringe. Operation *Sparrow Hawk Two* followed in mid-October for five days and focused on the western fringes of the Pentadactylos Mountains; it was supported by six Sycamores of 284 Squadron, previously the Levant Communications Flight, under the direct operational command of Brigadier Baker. The remaining three helicopters were used to enhance communications and evacuate casualties. Even though the Sycamores sometimes struggled to reach sufficient height, their ability to hover and allow patrols to abseil through the trees restricted EOKA freedom of movement. Rubber-soled boots made an appearance and the semi automatic 7.62mm Self Loading Rifle (SLR) was replacing the .303 rifle, much to the disgust of some soldiers. With his Guerrilla Groups in the mountains still under intense pressure, the diversion of terrorism ordered by Grivas continued to ravage the rest of the island, with fourteen Greek-Cypriots, including one attending a wedding reception, and six servicemen killed during the month.

Wednesday afternoon in the Forces was, so far as was possible, a sports afternoon. EOKA had noted that the units stationed in Lefkoniko regularly used the High School football field. During the night of 20 October four students dug a 400-foot long trench from the communal fountain to an olive grove and then laid cable from a car battery to a bomb hidden near the tap. On the 22nd, a football game between two 1 HLI teams was watched by the students and their teachers, but after the final whistle, as the thirsty players strolled to the fountain, teachers discreetly marshalled the schoolchildren away from it. Two teenage girls watched the soldiers gather around the fountain and then waved their white handerchiefs to two students sat by the battery. As Private Matthew Neely was about to drink from the tap, they connected the wires to the terminals, disembowelling the soldier in an explosion that wrecked the fountain. Seven Highlanders were wounded, with Private John Beattie dying the following day and Private Benjamin Doherty after he had been flown back to England. When a company of Highlanders arrived, several vented their feelings while rounding up about 100 suspects by damaging some properties during searches. Some villagers later sought £3,000 compensation until Lieutenant Colonel Noble, the Commanding Officer, angrily retorted, 'The murders of Privates Neely and Beattie are probably one of the most dastardly acts that EOKA has committed. It was premeditated and aimed to catch soldiers when they were at play. If £3,000 are being claimed for alleged damage caused by troops, the amount is infinitesimal when compared with damage caused by EOKA to my soldiers.' Nothing more was said.

On 28 October 16 Parachute Brigade was withdrawn from Operation *Fox Hunter* and assembled in Kykko Camp outside Nicosia to finalize preparations for seizure of the Suez Canal, giving EOKA yet another valuable respite from sustained pressure. A suspect then claimed that the wife of a wanted terrorist living in Galini, named as mother-of-four Mrs Xapolitos, was strongly suspected of supplying two EOKA with food. Shortly before dawn on the 30th, troops surrounded the village and then Company Sergeant Major Dempster and Private Thomas of the 16 Independent Parachute Brigade Provost Group and two Provost WRAC, Sergeant Birbeck and Lance Corporal White, entered the house occupied by Mrs Xapolitos. When she was awoken and told by Dempster that she was being arrested on suspicion of supplying EOKA with food and would be taken to the Platres interrogation centre, Mrs Xapolitos explained that she had not seen her husband for several months and that she was penniless. But the military police had noted that her house was neat and showed no signs of destitution. Refusing the offer to take her children to Platres and declaring that their grandmother would look after them, Mrs Xapolitos was escorted from the bedroom by Birbeck and White to the room next door. As the two military police began a cursory search prior to a detailed one later, Dempster noted that a floorboard under the bed was loose. Silently attracting the attention of Thomas, they both carefully lifted the bed to one side and then Dempster covered Thomas as he gently prised up the floor board until a small, dark space was revealed. Two men then burst out and were arrested after a brief scuffle in the bedroom. When Mrs Xapolitos realized the commotion meant that her husband had been captured, she struggled to release him but was restrained by the two WRAC. Xapolitos and Thoma, the second terrorist, both had £5,000 bounties on their heads.

Operation *Musketeer* began on 31 October with British and French aircraft flying from RAF Akrotiri to attack Egyptian targets, followed a week later by airborne and amphibious landings. El Gamil airfield was seized by 3 Para while the remainder of 16 Parachute Brigade and 3 Commando Brigade disembarked from landing craft, followed by 45 Commando carrying out the first British helicopter assault in history. Even after the Greeks had presented the Greek-Cypriot cause to the UN Assembly, Grivas rejected an appeal from Athens to show restraint by declaring a truce, and on 2 November he used the scaled down internal security operations to blitz Cyprus by attacking Operation *Musketeer* assembly areas. Fifteen Servicemen, four British civilians, eleven Greek-Cypriots and one Turk were killed in the first three weeks of November, most in the Limassol area – where Grivas was hiding. A lorry carrying some 1 Norfolks was wrecked by a mine near Polymedhia, killing Corporal Richard Chittock and Private Cook and flinging fourteen other soldiers from the wreckage.

During the autumn fruit-picking season, the roads in some parts of Cyprus became sodden with juice squeezed from the squashed grapes and oranges loaded in carts and the backs of lorries. Near Paphos, a remotely activated mine placed underneath the liquid killed Warrant Officer Martin, whose unit, 6 Royal Tank Regiment, was in Cyprus as part of Operation *Musketeer*. The General Practitioner Dr Bevan was shot dead by the escort of a 'patient' after EOKA propaganda had accused him of administering 'truth drugs' at interrogation centres. A senior Colonial Police officer died and an Army captain was wounded when a bomb exploded in Gordon Highlanders Battalion Orderly Room in Platres. Staff Sergeant Donald Trowbridge, of 3 Signals Regiment at Episkopi, was killed and his wife narrowly escaped injury when gunmen ambushed his car. On 12 November, a Gordon Highlanders convoy of three lorries commanded by Lieutenant Bradshaw were about four miles from Lefka on their way to collect fire wood at a mine near Pedoulas when it was ambushed by the Markos Drakos Group. Sergeant Alexander Dow in the lead lorry brought a 2-inch mortar into action until he was killed by an EOKA Bren gunner. Meanwhile, Private Symon, who was badly wounded in the arm, had managed to turn around his damaged lorry and, in spite of a shredded front tyre, drove back to Lefka to summon help. Of the four wounded in the action,

Bradshaw and Symons were flown back to Great Britain for specialist treatment. The initial search of the ambush site yielded nothing, but the finding of a cache revealed arms, ammunition and explosive. Three gunners from 21 Medium Regiment were killed by a bomb placed in the NAAFI canteen juke box at Coral Bay Camp at Paphos by a Greek-Cypriot employee. An airman used his personal protection revolver to wound one of two terrorists who had just murdered a pro-British lawyer cycling to work. A Hawker Hunter blown up at RAF Nicosia was blamed on nationalists. At the end of the month, when RASC Sergeant Major Middleton was badly wounded by a gunman in the Nicosia married quarter estate, his furious wife Muriel chased the gunmen. Although she lost them, her description resulted in the arrest of two youths, one of whom, Christos Lambou aged seventeen years, was sentenced to death. This was later commuted to life because of his age. Mrs Middleton received the Queen's Commendation for Brave Conduct. In early December Charles Foley infuriated the authorities by writing an article in which he implied that the British expatriate community were blaming Field Marshal Harding for the increase in sectarian attacks on their community and he found himself prosecuted for breaching censorship legislation.

A week after the Suez landings, 16 Parachute Brigade returned to Cyprus by sea and immediately began handing over its special operations role to HQ 3 Infantry Brigade (Brigadier Hopwood), which had arrived on HMS *Ocean* at Limassol. The Brigade was part of 3rd Division and had been deployed to defend Malta during Operation *Musketeer*. One of its units, the 1st Battalion, The Somersetshire Light Infantry (1 Somersets) moved into Kermia Camp at Nicosia and relieved the Gordon Highlanders in 50 Infantry Brigade District, leaving the Scotsmen to embark on the troopship *Empire Ken* bound for England. The troopship *Dilwara* landed 1st Battalion, The Oxfordshires and Buckinghamshire Light Infantry (1 Ox and Bucks) who took over from the Norfolks in 51 Infantry Brigade District. 1 Suffolks took over from the two Gordon Highlanders companies in Platres. Then 3 Battalion, The Grenadier Guards (3rd Grenadier Guards) arrived a month later. In mid-December, 16 Parachute Brigade less 2 Para returned to Aldershot, followed by 1 Norfolks. Apart from the few days pre-Operation *Musketeer* training, 1 and 3 Para had been away from England for nearly a year.

In early December, 3 Infantry Brigade began the unfinished business left by the Parachute Brigade by launching Operation *Black Mak* in the south-west Troodos. By now, the troops had warmer winter clothing and sleeping bags, which if heavy and bulky, were better than blankets.

Although heavy snow and bitter winds again hampered movement, by the time the operation finished on 13 December after ten days, fifty-two guerrillas had been captured, their romantic notion of living an austere heroic life ambushing patrols dispelled by the rigours of surviving in cold hideouts in the wintry mountains, short of food, weapons and ammunition, and constantly at risk from Army patrols. Their interrogations led Brigadier Baker to conclude that the operations since Operation *Pepper Pot* had reduced the ability of the Troodos EOKA to take the offensive. There was also confirmation that teenage girls were supplying EOKA with information and that some were complicit in some murders and ambushes. In a sweep in the Paphos area, a 50 Medium Regiment RA and police patrol trapped the Lyso Group Leader George Raftis and two EOKA underneath a bridge near Kissonerga, not far from their hideout in an orchard. On the 23rd, a 21 Medium Regiment vehicle patrol stopped three civilians leading two donkeys staggering under heavy loads. Two of the men abandoned their colleague, leaving him to account to the gunners why a heavily-greased Bren gun and other military equipment had been found loaded on the donkeys. He turned out to be Evagoras Pallikarides, who was high on the wanted list. Aged eighteen years, he had been involved in *enosis* since 1953 and had been named as the murderer of two Greek-Cypriots, one an elderly man accused of collaborating with a Turkish-Cypriot policeman. When Grivas heard about the arrest, he essentially condemned Pallikarides to death by suggesting that he had been moving the Bren to a winter cache; however, it was for the murders that Pallikarides was executed in March 1957, the youngest and last member of EOKA to walk to the gallows.

Lord Radcliffe then published his *Proposals for Cyprus* in which he recommended a format by which the Governor would exercise executive authority over an elected ministerial assembly with a Greek-Cypriot majority. In spite of recognizing the cultural and linguistic differences between the two communities, he did not believe that the Turkish-Cypriot minority should be given equal representation because it was inconsistent with a democratic constitution and predicted that if the Turkish-Cypriots were given equal representation, it would most probably result in federal separation – a prophetic conclusion.

CHAPTER NINE

# The Destruction of the Mountain Gangs

(January to March 1957)

In December 1956, Major General Douglas Kendrew took over Cyprus District from Major General Ricketts and also Director of Operations from Brigadier Baker. Baker remained as Chief of Staff to Field Marshal Harding. Joe Kendrew, as he was better known, was born in 1910 and, as a lieutenant in the Leicesters, had represented England in the scrum at rugby union ten times, touring Australia and New Zealand in 1930 and captaining the team in 1935. During the Second World War, he had the distinction of being awarded the Distinguished Service Order (DSO) three times for leadership and courage in North Africa, Italy and Greece and was then won his fourth DSO while commanding the 29 Independent Infantry Brigade in Korea.

The year 1956 had been a tough one; sixty Service personnel had been killed in action, November being the worst month with sixteen fatalities. Nine UK Unit Police, six Greek-Cypriots and seven Turkish-Cypriots had also been killed as had twelve British civilians, 109 Greek-Cypriots, including several EOKA, and five Turkish-Cypriots. Total for the year was 213. Although the level of terrorism in the urban and rural areas was still high, the drive by Brigadier Baker against the mountain guerrillas was paying dividends, but EOKA was by no means finished, with the activists still willing to take orders from their invisible leader.

After the New Year, 1 HLI returned to Scotland on the troopship *Dilwara*, and then about a week later 1st Battalion, The Gloucestershire Regiment (1 Glosters) joined 3 Infantry Brigade from Bahrein and replaced the Somerset Light Infantry which departed on HMT *Empire Ken*. Unfortunately, the Somersets had not completed 120 days and therefore were not entitled to the Cyprus bar of the 1918 General Service Medal. Several of the Glosters had spent three years in North Korean prison camps, including Major Guy Temple, whose platoon had tackled the Chinese 63$^{rd}$ Army on the banks of the Imjin River before it had

## THE DESTRUCTION OF THE MOUNTAIN GANGS 125

overwhelmed the British position. He escaped three times and had his hands so tightly bound after one attempt that they were permamently injured.

In bitterly cold and wet weather in mid-January 1957, 3 Infantry Brigade launched seven battalions in Operation *Black Mak* on two search operations, the first near Milikouri, where it was still thought that Colonel Grivas was hiding, and the second in the general area of Omodhus in Adelphi Forest aimed at the Guerrilla Groups. As usual, both places were declared prohibited areas, which allowed troops to ignore the rules of engagement of giving a warning before opening fire. At the merest hint of guerrilla activity, Sycamore helicopters were ready to fly in patrols. The Army also knew where Afxentiou was, and in Operation *Cordon Bleu* the Ox and Bucks captured several important EOKA in the Pakhna area.

Sections of the 1 Suffolk operating in the general area of Evrykhou in the Adelphi Forest patrolled during the day and at night ambushed tracks leading from the pine forests in order to snare guerrillas visiting villages to shelter, collect food and gather intelligence of military operations. Since arriving, the Battalion had experienced a relatively quiet tour although in mid-November the Anti Tank Platoon was ambushed by gunmen firing from the upper floors of a house in Nikitari, not far from Morphou. The Platoon Commander, Lieutenant Trollope, immediately retaliated by leading a charge into the house and chased the gunmen into the back garden where a child was shot dead in the crossfire. One soldier was sufficiently badly wounded to be flown back to Great Britain. During the evening of 18 January, a section commanded by Corporal Brian King from D Company selected an ambush site based around a rocky outcrop overlooking the killing zone of a track that ran from a spur of trees into open ground. Establishing a patrol base 150 yards from the rocks inside the tree line, he divided his section in half and, following the standard tactic that night ambushes remained in position all night without relief, instructed Lance Corporal Henry Fowler and three men to occupy the patrol base while his half-section covered the track for the night. But as darkness fell, the combination of heavy, freezing rain, a biting wind and the danger of non-battle casualties from exposure led to King ignoring ambush drills and deciding that the two groups would change every two hours. At about 7 pm, Fowler was relieving King when there was an exchange of fire in the woods above. At about 11 pm, Fowler was taking over for the second time when Private Sydney Woods saw a figure about ten yards away walk into the killing zone. There being no reply to his challenge, Woods opened fire. The figure then returned fire, which led to the remainder of the section opening fire by shooting at muzzle flashes flickering in the darkness. A man was heard to shout in pain. Even though the ambush had been compromised, King stayed in position for the remainder of the night, and when next morning the section checked the killing zone they found the body of a man hit thirteen times and a Sten gun nearby. So far, Operation *Black Mak* had been relatively fruitless but when the dead man was identified as Markos Drakos, morale rose throughout the security forces at the news that a dangerous and committed guerrilla had been killed. It seemed the EOKA group were trying to breach the cordon. It later emerged that the engagement heard by King's section at 7 pm was the Drakos group searching for a route through the Suffolks' line of ambushes and colliding with a British patrol. They had avoided a second collision before being ambushed by King. The rest of the group, including a wounded man, escaped the ambush. A claim by the Greek-Cypriot historian Doros Alastos that Drakos had committed suicide is nonsense. King, Fowler and Woods were Mentioned in Despatches.

Next day, acting on information received, a 1st Battalion, The Duke of Wellington's Regiment (1 Duke of Wellington's) patrol was searching a remote farm owned by a senior Cyprus Police officer near Omodhus. Private John Davis was in the kitchen when he heard an unusual noise from the hearth. The patrol then noted that the hearth had unusual signs of wear and tear. When they moved a slab behind the fireplace, it exposed a chamber and five crouching guerrillas, including Polycarpos Georghadjis and Anargyros Karadymas. Both were high on the wanted list after their dramatic escape from Nicosia Hospital in which Police Sergeant Demmon had been killed. Three others had bounties of £5,000 on their heads. A total of 2,000 rounds of ammunition, a 3.5-inch Bazooka rocket launcher, six Thompson sub machine guns and several revolvers were found during the search of the house and surrounding property. During the night of 21 January, in the glare of parachute flares, a 2 Para company abseiled from Sycamores to several landing zones near Omodhus and captured George Matsis close to his hideout near Kannavia. Highly regarded by Colonel Grivas as a patriot, Radio Athens claimed that with Matsis' capture 'the Troodos are not singing; not even the birds are singing'. His main claim to fame was the raid on a British armoury in Famagusta. He was also half-brother to Kyriakos Matsis. The Battalion scored further success when a patrol led by Lieutenant D G Smith were searching the house of the village policeman, a known EOKA collaborator, and noted that in spite of the cold weather, the fire had only recently been lit. Smith kicked aside the embers and, stamping on the hearth, exposed a shaft and three anxious guerrillas gasping for air and surrounded by arms and explosive. The Battalion would claim

## THE DESTRUCTION OF THE MOUNTAIN GANGS 127

the elimination of twenty-one guerrillas and the capture of forty-six weapons, including two rocket launchers.

The attrition against the EOKA Mountain Groups again led to Grivas demanding that the Town and Village Groups divert the attention of the Army. The murders of three expatriates in the first ten days of the New Year in Nicosia led on 15 January to 50 Infantry Brigade District again sealing the city centre and confining all males aged between fourteen to forty years into holding cages so that the Cyprus Police could carry out a detailed investigation into the murder of Mr Herbert Pritchard, a Cable and Wireless executive who had been murdered on 9 January. When the information on several murders on Ledra Street were analyzed, the focus of suspicion centred on Nicos Sampson, largely because he often happened to be in the close vicinity of the murders soon afterwards. Tracked to a house at Dhali, at the end of the month, a Royal Horse Guards patrol and Special Branch officers arrested him in possession of a weapon. In Nicosia, two female EOKA suffered serious injuries when a grenade they intended to throw at a 1 Ox and Bucks officer prematurely exploded. At the beginning of February, acting on information that he was providing shelter to EOKA, Special Branch raided a bungalow owned by PC Andreas Houvardos and found in a cache beneath a bed, thirty-eight revolvers, fifty-three grenades, fuses for bombs and 2,000 rounds of ammunition. One .38-inch Webley had been used in fifteen murders and seven attempted murders. Since bomb disposal officers regarded the cache as too dangerous to move, Royal Engineers blew the house up. Houvardos and an accomplice, a police sergeant, received long sentences in May. Within days of the arrests, acting on information received, the Nicosia Group leader, Andreas Chartas, was arrested, as were Evangelos Evangelakis and several couriers. Evangelakis, a gunman, had escaped from Kyrenia Castle in September 1955 and was a close associate of Sampson. Their interrogations revealed more arms and explosive caches in Nicosia.

In one of the first moves to undermine the Church, in *The Church and Terrorism in Cyprus*, the Cyprus Government accused Archbishop Makarios of being the prime instigator of the violence on the island and implicated the Cyprus Orthodox Church as a conduit for terrorism. Several days later, seven priests with Troodos Mountain parishes were arrested on the instructions of Field Marshal Harding on suspicion of giving shelter to EOKA terrorists and forming EOKA groups. Since 1 April 1955, thirty-seven priests had been taken into custody. At a briefing for Operation *Kingfisher* that centred on Milikouri and Kykko Monastery, Major General Kendrew thanked Grivas for identifying weaknesses and criticizing the performance of his troops, not that he needed to, and told his brigade commanders to continue the attrition against EOKA. In his hideout in Limassol, Grivas became anxious as he saw EOKA crumble under the pressure. On 17 February in Operation *Mailbox* B Troop, 40 Commando surrounded Palendria and Potamitissas to smoke out the explosives expert Stylianos Lenas. Lieutenant Marshal, who commanded 9 Section and Lieutenant Michael Haynes, of 8 Section, dispensed with the usual long night approach and early morning cordon by storming the villages in vehicles at first light and trapped several guerrillas trying to break out. The Potamitissas Group leader, Christodoulou Demetrakis, firing an Italian rifle and throwing grenades, was killed, as were two other EOKA. Lenas was captured severely wounded. When three armed men were seen shortly before first light next day, Haynes challenged them in accordance with standing orders and was cut down by a terrorist opening fire with a Sten gun, who was in turn killed in a hail of bullets from angry Royal Marines. Lenas, who with Demetrakis had a £5,000 bounty on his head, died at the British Military Hospital at RAF Akrotiri six weeks later.

In 51 Infantry Brigade District operations, Private Raymond Young, of 1 Leicesters was part of a patrol commanded by Corporal T W James that surrounded a remote farmhouse near Lysi on 10 February. He was about to search an outhouse when he saw, in the shadows, two men aiming shotguns at him. He dived for cover just as they fired at him, then five other EOKA inside also opened up. As the gun battle developed, James, a Regular soldier, ordered his patrol to surround the outhouse. One of the trapped guerrillas then darted out of the building and was chased across a ploughed field by James repeatedly shouting instructions for him to surrender until the gunman turned and fired. James fired back and then watched as 300 yards away, the Cypriot collapsed and died from a bullet wound. The remaining guerrillas were trapped in the outhouse until their ammunition ran out twenty minutes later and they then surrendered with, 'All right, Johnny, you win!' Among them was the bomb-maker Dinos Michaelides who specialized in supplying devices to the Limassol and Larnaca Town Groups. The dead EOKA was identified as Andreas Kokkinos, a local farmer. Three weeks later, Corporal Moore was leading three Leicesters through an orange grove near Akhna when they saw an elderly man running towards a house. The patrol took cover and watched, intrigued, as four men tumbled out of the house and ran towards them. When they saw the soldiers, they changed direction and began running across a ploughed field until Moore challenged them to stop, which they did. A search of the house revealed four more terrorists, one hiding underneath a bed. All surrendered, once again without a fight. Operation *Black Mak*

26 January 1955. The crew of the *Ayios Georghias* under escort. In the background is the caique (*Cdr Michael Clapp*)

31 October 1955. A Staffords sergeant carries an injured civilian during Greek Independence Day riots. A Private wheels his bicycle (*Robert Egby*)

6 December 1955. A Royal Artillery sergeant questions a child from a bus after Lefkoniko post office had been burned *(Robert Egby)*

A Royal Scots patrol searches a Greek-Cypriot farmer and his family in Paphos District *(Robert Egby)*

24 May 1956. The burning Land Rover damaged by a grenade *(Robert Egby)*

24 May 1956, Nicosia. A badly wounded Stafford is supported by his colleague while a woman shouts for her help for her husband. A grenade had just been thrown at an Army Land Rover *(Robert Egby)*

Troops search a car on a lonely road in Paphos District
(*Robert Egby*)

7 June 1956. A Leicesters riot squad in Famagusta. Members of the 'snatch squad' are wearing plimsolls and hockey boots (*Robert Egby*)

A riot squad in a Bedford lorry *(David Carter)*

1957. Colonel Grivas and several EOKA pose in uniform *(From captured film)*

Gregoris Afxentiou and Markos Drakos pose with Sten guns *(From captured film)*

The Loizou EOKA Group in the Kykko area. The guerrilla top rear left seems to have a Royal Artillery cap badge (*From captured film*)

June 1956. Kykko Monastery (*Maj Gen Julian Thompson*)

Operation *Lucky Alphonse*. A Parachute Regiment Mortar Platoon on a road in the Troodos Mountains (*Robert Egby*)

18 June 1956. Operation *Lucky Alphonse*. Two burnt Bedford lorries used by the Gordon Highlander near Vroisia (*Robert Egby*)

16 July 1956. 1 Staffords line up civilians in Ledra St after it had been reported that Markos Drakos was in Nicosia (*Robert Egby*)

25 July 1956. Ledra St, Nicosia. Drosoula Demetriadou looks in shock at her murdered fiancé, Special Constable Bonici Mompalda. To the left of the Staffords major, holding the camera is the EOKA gunman Nicos Sampson (*Robert Egby*)

1 October 1956, Ledra St. UK Police Unit Sgts Thoroughgood and Webb have just been killed; while Sgt Webb fires at the group of gunmen that included Nicos Sampson (*Robert Egby*)

The 1 Norfolks Lt Col Brinkley and his Tactical HQ outside MILPOL Limassol *(Source unknown)*

31 October 1956, Nicosia. A Staffords patrol wearing respirators during riots marking the commemoration of Greece's entry into the Second World War *(Robert Egby)*

December 1956. Men of D Coy, 1 Suffolks brew tea during operations in the Troodos Mountains *(Robert Egby)*

February 1957. A 45 Commando ski patrol in the Troodos Mountains *(Robert Egby)*

February 1957. A 1 Berkshires mule supply train in the Troodos Mountains *(Robert Egby)*

February 1957. A 1 Berkshires section in the Troodos Mountains *(Robert Egby)*

Makhaeras Monastery. The arrow indicates the Afxentiou Group hideout that was attacked by 1 Duke of Wellington's
(*David Carter*)

7 March 1957. Field Marshal Harding visits 1 Duke of Wellington's after the Afxentiou attack
(*Robert Egby*)

A controversial photo that accompanied articles in British newspapers and *Paris-Match* criticising the arrest of a boy aged 10 for rioting (*Robert Egby*)

Kakopetria Company Base in the Troodos Mountains (*David Carter*)

Troops abseiling from a Sycamore helicopter (*David Carter*)

22 November 1958, Nicosia. Greek-Cypriot NAAFI staff protest at being dismissed as security risks *(Robert Egby)*

22 December 1958, Nicosia. British families selecting Christmas trees are guarded by a Royal Signals patrol *(Robert Egby)*

17 March 1959. The gaunt Col Grivas and his wife, Kiti, after he had returned to Athens (*David Carter*)

Independence Talks 1959. From left to right: a Greek delegate; Makarios; Governor Foot; Colonial Minister Amery; Dr Fazil Kuchuk; a Turkish delegate (*Robert Egby*)

20 July 1974. Turkish landing craft at Five Mile Beach (*David Carter*)

22 July 1974. A Turkish tank in Kyrenia (*David Carter*)

14 August 1974. Turkish infantry advance through the Kyrenia Mountains towards Nicosia (*Source unknown*)

August 1974. 3 RRF road block on the Dhekelia to Larnaca road in the ESBA (*Source unknown*)

# THE DESTRUCTION OF THE MOUNTAIN GANGS 129

finished at the end of February and was assessed by Major General Kendrew to be the most successful operation so far.

The pressure was kept up by 3 Infantry Brigade launching Operation *Whisky Mak* specifically to kill or capture Gregoris Afxentiou, Number 2 to Grivas with a £5,000 bounty on his head and known to be controlling EOKA operations in the Pitsilia, Famagusta and Makhearas area. After being wounded at Zoopiyi on New Year's Eve, Afxentiou and his twenty-five men found sanctuary in the twelfth century Makheras Monastery that dominated the countryside from the slopes of Mount Kionia. Its Abbot Ireneos, a former Second World War RAF Regiment clerk, was independent of Archbishop Makarios. He supported the EOKA while they built hideouts on Mount Kionia.

Although the planning of Operation *Whisky Mak* was on strict need-to-know, it was compromised by a trusted Special Branch inspector based at Police HQ, who was tape-recording the daily operational meetings between senior Army and police officers and relaying the details to Grivas. During the night of 27 February, Afxentiou and four EOKA moved into a hide a mile north of the monastery. With an entrance no more than eighteen inches square, it was expertly concealed in thick scrub in between a path that led to the summit and a lower track that also led from the monastery and skirted the hill. At the bottom of the hill was a stream bordered by terraced fields.

When two EOKA suspects were captured by a special operations group at Omodhus next day and were taken to the Platres interrogation centre, one turned out to be a member of Afxentiou Group. When he confirmed that Afxentiou often used the Forest Rest House complex about three miles from the monastery, two 1 Duke of Wellington's platoons deployed to the vicinity. The suspect also said that supplies for Afxentiou were delivered by mules led by a slow-witted shepherd employed at the monastery named Petros. With Afxentiou now confirmed to be in the area, Brigadier FitzGeorge-Balfour ordered Lieutenant Colonel Laing, the Duke of Wellington's Commanding Officer, to find him. On 1 March Petros was arrested by a patrol and under interrogation at HQ 3 Infantry Brigade said that two pistols were buried outside the monastery walls. Soon after Captain Newton had been ordered to assemble a patrol, Major Rodick and Petros arrived from Platres with the news that the shepherd had been tempted by a reward to guide the patrol to the EOKA hideout. However, as the plan developed, it soon became apparent the patrol was too small, and Laing instructed Major D M Harris, whose D Company was patrolling the area, to attack the hide on 3 March. During the late evening, a platoon raided the monastery and arrested Abbot Ireneos on suspicion that he was harbouring Afxentiou; in spite of his protestations and denials, the monks and novices were confined to a single room. Battalion HQ set up in the cloisters. Next day, soldiers thoroughly searched the monastery and the surrounding slopes but found nothing. Ireneos refused to answer any questions, but Petros was more forthcoming and indicated the general location of the hide.

Laing rejected a night attack and opted for a first-light assault next day, but Harris was anxious because his men would be advancing over broken terrain, potentially against a defended position, somewhere, on a dark, moonless night. After a difficult march in pouring rain, by 5 am D Company were high on the western slopes of Mount Kionia before dawn and divided into four elements. Party 'D' were 150 yards north of the suspected hideout astride an obvious escape route along the lower path and stream. Regimental Sergeant Major Randall and a small party were in a second cut-off position about 300 yards across the valley to the east in a position to view the hillside opposite. There were no cut-offs to the south and the monastery because B Company was in the vicinity. A Sycamore was ready to fly an officer and a signaller to track anyone escaping the net.

By about 5.30 am D Company had advanced through the soaking undergrowth until it was about 200 yards above the upper track, but there was no evidence of the hideout until Petros, in the increasing grey, rainy dawn, timidly pointed it out 300 yards down the slope in between the two tracks. Covered by Company HQ beefed up with two Bren guns of Party 'C', Snatch Party 'A' and a Bren gun commanded by Lieutenant Dasent swung to the north while Snatch Party 'B' commanded by Captain Newton moved south in a pincer movement; but by 6 am there was still no sign of the hideout. As Harris then moved down the slope with Party 'C', the decidedly anxious Petros refused to go any further and pointed where he thought the hideout was. The two Snatch Parties were quietly searching ground between the two paths when Corporal Trinder, from Party 'B', followed a trail up a slope from the lower path until, after about ten yards he spotted bootprints and then noticed that the branches of a bush on the right of the path had been tied down to form a canopy about 4 feet high. Investigating inside, he shifted some large stones and found a 40-gallon oil drum containing a 2-inch mortar wrapped in brown paper. It was a sure sign of an EOKA hideout. Captain Newton then joined Trinder and while they were following the track they both sensed that the ground below was hollow. Moving aside another large stone, they found the entrance and peering inside, saw some clothing but, hearing nothing, concluded the hideout was empty. More soldiers arrived, including Second Lieutenant Grant, the Battalion interpreter, and when voices were heard from underground, he

## THE DESTRUCTION OF THE MOUNTAIN GANGS     131

speculatively shouted to the guerrillas to surrender.

Inside the hideout, the five EOKA had been asleep and unaware of the search until dislodged stones tumbled down the slope. Knowing the game was up, Afxentiou said it was pointless everyone sacrificing their lives and ordered his four colleagues to leave, insisting that he alone would die for the cause. The four scrambled out and were captured without trouble. And then a sudden Sten gun burst from the hideout took everyone by surprise. Grant again invited Afxentiou to surrender and then Corporal Peter Brown, who was with Snatch Party 'A', leant over the entrance and shouted that it was all over, but Afxentiou fired again and Brown fell back mortally wounded. Newton managed to get close enough to throw the only hand grenade possessed by the attacking force into the hide. Meanwhile Second Lieutenant Middleton of the Royal Northumberland Fusiliers, who commanded a detachment of interpreters, persuaded one of the four prisoners, Augustis Efstathiou, to tell Afxentiou to surrender. A very reluctant Efstathiou returned to the hide and found his chief bleeding badly from grenade splinter wounds to his neck and knee. After a brief conversation, Afxentiou fired a single shot and shouted in English that there were now two in the hide and to 'Come and get us', citing the spirit of Leonidas of Sparta challenging the Persian surrender terms at the Battle of Thermopylae.

In between firing the occasional shot to keep the troops at bay, the pair discussed their part in EOKA, with Afxentiou convinced that they had contributed to lighting the flames of liberation. They plotted to escape by rushing out, guns blazing, under cover of a phosphorus grenade, and disappearing into the forest until night. But when Afxentiou threw the grenade, it was yellow smoke not phosphorus, and as Efstathiou stood up to give covering fire, he forgot to release the safety catch of his Sten. Both men slunk back into the hideout, trapped. Aided by lingering yellow smoke pinpointing the hideout, Major Rodick, Corporal Trinder and Lance Corporal Martin laced its entrance with fire while Lance Corporal Dowdall tried to recover the body of Corporal Brown, but he was driven back after dragging it a few yards. Harris then assembled the four Brens onto a spur overlooking the hide about forty yards to the south. Overhead, the Sycamore hovered.

At about 7.15 am Brigadier Hopwood and Lieutenant Colonel Laing arrived and, ordering that needless casualties were to be avoided, then instructed that the two EOKA should be burnt out or buried by a heavy charge. Fearing that Grivas would order a rescue, 10 Platoon, D Company supported by two Brens formed an inner cordon while four patrols from 3 Company, 3 Grenadier Guards reinforced the Duke of Wellington's. 1 Company was in reserve. Royal Engineers used a Second

World War tactic of bouncing powerful search light beams off low lying clouds to illuminate the hide. Meanwhile, Major Harris had learnt from the prisoners that Afxentiou and Efstathiou had two Thompsons, two pistols, several hundred rounds of ammunition and some grenades.

At about 9 am a donkey train laden with petrol jerry cans arrived, but when the fuel was poured around the hide entrance, rain and hailstones prevented the soaking bushes from catching fire. Captain Dennis Shuttleworth, a Royal Engineer and former English rugby international, then tried to collapse the roof with a 6lb Plastic Explosive satchel charge, but this only induced the two trapped EOKA to reply with more grenades. For the remainder of the morning, apart from occasional, short exchanges of harassing gunfire and explosion of grenades as vegetation around the entrance was pruned, it was eerily silent. Inside, Afxentiou was weakening from loss of blood. At midday, several jerry cans of highly inflammable aviation fuel arrived by Sycamore and were delivered to Captain Hoppe, another Royal Engineer officer. Located above the hideout, he slowly poured the fuel down the slope, allowed it to seep into nooks and crannies and then ignited it with a match. As the fuel exploded with a sizeable 'whump' and the four Brens opened fire, a figure burst through the flames and stumbled into some smouldering bushes. Shuttleworth and a small group of soldiers armed with Sten guns were then directed by Captain Newton to the entrance and Shuttleworth slid down the steep slope, placed a beehive charge over the hide and hauled himself back up the slope trailing a fuse behind him. At 1.30 pm the resulting explosion was heard several miles away. One of his men then threw a tear gas grenade into the wreckage while others sprayed the entrance with their Stens. There was no reply. It was 2 pm.

Meanwhile, a burnt, terrified Efstathiou, no longer the valiant guerrilla, had been hauled from the bushes, and, after being patched up, was driven to the military hospital at Akrotiri. The hide burned for most of the afternoon and it was not until the following day that a search party found the charred body of Afxentiou surrounded by two burnt-out Thompsons, two pistols and a revolver, three grenades, ammunition and a US bayonet. One leg was severed and underneath his body was a copy of *Christ Recrucified* signed by Abbot Ireneos and lent to Afxentiou. With the monastery now confirmed to have links with EOKA, it was taken over by the Army as a detention centre for priests. Journalists had been invited to the battle, in the hope that they would conclude that EOKA was finished; instead, they portrayed Afxentiou to be a hero. There was some civil unrest in Lysi.

Although a coroner concluded that Afxentiou had died when he was hit in the head by a bullet cooking off in the inferno, Greek-Cypriot nationalists claimed that he had been shot and have now commemorated him by restoring the hide. In front is a large statue of Afxentiou. His is also the image on a 2005 Greek-Cypriot medal commemorating the Emergency. Over 21,000 applied for the medal, although EOKA actually numbered only several hundred activists. So far as the British soldiers were concerned, the battle was short of the Greek epic claimed by nationalists. Although Grivas knew that Afxentiou would fight, his reaction was to ask, 'Why so sad? People get killed in a war, and that is what we are fighting for. We shall have as many more as brave as he'. But the fact remains that many guerrillas did not live up to the courage displayed by Afxentiou; however, in the absence of mysterious 'Digenes' in his bunker, the Greek-Cypriots badly needed a local hero, and a legend evolved around Afxentiou. In spite of assurances by Grivas that he would look after the welfare of families of EOKA casualties, Vasilia Afxentiou lived in poverty for several years, scratching a living in the fields until she remarried. When it emerged in 2000 that the sculptor of the Afxentiou monument planned to exhibit in Newark, Nottinghamshire, the local British Legion protested sufficiently for the project to be abandoned. Alan Meale, a Labour MP, then claimed the Turkish Embassy had engineered the row, until it emerged that he was associated with the nationalist Greek-Cypriot Brotherhood.

The pressure was maintained in early March by 3 Infantry Brigade launching Operation *Blackbird* with 40 Commando and the Suffolks reinforced by two 1st Battalion, The Lancashire Fusilier companies (1 Lancashire) sweeping through the broken ground in the Kakopetria area; although no EOKA were found, the troops were becoming more skilful at finding caches. The Battalion had landed at Limassol from HMT *Asturia* and had been absorbed into 1 AGRA battle group. As the winter snows melted and gave way to warmer days, spring flowers and green trees, it was clear that Operations *Black Mak* and *Whisky Mak* had badly damaged EOKA. During the nine-month offensive since June 1956, a significant number of guerrillas had been killed or arrested. Grivas was thought to be somewhere in the mountains, and although morale had risen with the successes, it was disappointing that he had not been found. Isolated in his Limassol bunker, Grivas reeled from the successive disasters of losing several reliable officers and was finding it increasingly difficult to motivate the Town Groups because they were under considerable pressure. Murders committed by EOKA had been reduced to twenty in January and February compared to forty-nine in the last two months of 1956. Grivas later wrote,

> If it was possible for one man, a man fatigued in body and mind by long years of harsh struggle, to make decisions which were so consistently right. Napoleon said that it was not God that inspired him at difficult moments, but prudence. I cannot believe that, in my case, it was solely my personal abilities which brought me success and supplied me always with correct decision; this I ascribe rather to divine providence. (*Memoirs of George Grivas*)

In spite of the damage, Grivas was determined to fight on but was warned by the Greek Government that if he did not declare a ceasefire, the British would seize the political high ground and that Turkey would inevitably be included in any negotiations. Although Greece regarded NATO as nothing more than 'a bunch of colonial powers', negotiations were underway within the alliance to change its terms of reference to allow for solutions to be negotiated in disputes between member states. Even though Evagorus Pallikarides and another EOKA were hanged on 12 March, Grivas heeded the warning and issued orders next day later that as soon as negotiations between London and Archbishop Makarios began, EOKA would suspend operations. Field Marshal Harding was sceptical because the offer did not refer to the cessation of hostilities and ordered that operations should continue.

In the middle of March, 3 Infantry Brigade launched Operation *Lucky Dip* with five infantry battalions to root out hideouts and caches reported to be in south-west Cyprus. When Aristidou Droushot was quickly captured without the expected struggle, Grivas lost another senior officer. Thought to be EOKA third-in-command, Grivas was sufficiently concerned that Droushot would compromise his bunker under interrogation that he asked Deacon Anthimos to circulate disinformation that he himself was hiding in the area between Milikouri and Kykko Monastery. The information inevitably reached 3 Infantry Brigade, and Brigadier Hopwood launched Operation *Lucky Mac* in which the area was systematically searched with the troops concentrating on looking for caches and hideouts in the unlikeliest places in houses, outbuildings and farmyards. Milikouri, with the brooding Kykko Monastery two miles to the north, had been strongly suspected of providing succour to EOKA for months and it was singled out for an indeterminate 24-hour curfew in which villagers were escorted by troops to and from the fields, vineyards, woods and grazing areas between 7 am and 7 pm. If there were not enough soldiers, the farmers had to wait until a patrol became available. Inevitably, there were complaints of lost business, particularly when the petals for rose water production had to be collected when the plants were in bloom and soaked by the early morning dew. Vines could not be pruned because the escorting soldiers would have been isolated some distance from the village. During the evenings, the bars lost business. Inevitably, ubiquitous journalists became frantic at being prevented from entering the village, and consequently the longer the block on information lasted, the greater the speculation. Wild reports from Greece claiming that the troops were torturing villagers and starving them and their animals led to food parcels being sent to the village, but when the curfew was lifted on 13 May, fifty-four days after it began, and eager journalists rushed to the village for a scoop, they found the claims unfounded. The reality was that the soldiers had bartered their bland Compo rations for fresh eggs, fruit and vegetables, medical officers had treated the sick and injured, Royal Engineers had carried out repairs and children scrounged chocolate and boiled sweets; the village economy was not significantly affected.

After being briefed at 1 am on 23 March, by 5 am a Middlesex company had silently surrounded Lysi, west of Larnaca, where an informant claimed that Michaelakis Rossides was hiding. After escaping from Kyrenia Castle in September 1955 and from the Trimithia Detention Centre in January 1956, Rossides was appointed by Grivas to be the Larnaca District Group Leader. As dawn broke, the first person who walked into the cordon was Rossides. Later in the day, the body of Private Ronnie Shilton was found in a shallow grave not far from Prastio, about six miles east of Lysi. At his trial, claims by Rossides that his two confessions to the Cyprus Police for the murder of Shilton were made under duress were rejected. He claimed that when he was told by the Larnaca Group Leader in May 1956 that Grivas had instructed that Shilton should be executed, Rossides appealed against the directive because he had grown to like the soldier. However, he had little choice, it was his life or Shilton's; nevertheless, it was with some regret, he said, that he hit the soldier with a shovel and then shot him three or four times with an automatic. He claimed remorse by claiming 'Be sure that as from that day I continually lost my sleep and I used to see Ronnie's ghost in front of me'. Rossides was sentenced to death, although this was later commuted to life.

In his final assessment before handing over his appointment as Chief of Staff to Brigadier Sir Victor FitzGeorge-Balfour, Brigadier Baker concluded that critical to the military success since January 1956 had been information from interrogations and informants. Since the commencement of Operation *Turkey Trot* and *Fox Hunter* in November 1955, at least seventeen major hideouts had being found, the sixteen Guerrilla Groups had been reduced to five, a substantial amount of equipment had been seized and several key EOKA had been killed or captured; the detention camps were full of men and women now out of circulation known to have been, or strongly suspected of being, EOKA. Grivas had been reduced to executing suspected traitors and attacking soft civilian targets in order to keep EOKA in the headlines. Educated at Eton and Cambridge, FitzGeorge-Balfour was commissioned into the Coldstream Guards in 1934. Five years later, he was awarded the Military Cross for gallantry in Palestine and then served in North Africa, Sicily and North West Europe mainly in key staff appointments, reaching Acting Brigadier in 1942. In 1948, he reverted to Major and had commanded 2 Coldstream Guards in Malaya.

CHAPTER TEN

# A Glimmer of Hope
(April to November 1957)

After a short period of procrastination, in mid-March Archbishop Makarios agreed to lead the Cypriot delegation on the future of Cyprus. Although the Greek Government regarded him as the principal negotiator for any settlement, the British regarded his return to be high-risk, particularly with Grivas still at large, and insisted that while he and his entourage could be released from exile, they would not be permitted to return to Cyprus. Turkey saw the move as inflammatory but was assured by London that Ankara would be included in any negotiations. The Greek-Cypriots, who had been largely unrepresented in the political and diplomatic search for a resolution to the violence, celebrated with considerable style by beeping car horns, ringing church bells and inviting armed British patrols to join in their rejoicing. As the Leicesters reported from Famagusta, 'No force on earth would have stopped the Cypriots celebrating on that night', except that some mobs had to be dispersed with batons next day. Although some Greek-Cypriots were beginning to turn against him because of the endless terrorism, Grivas claimed that it was EOKA that had forced the British into releasing Makarios. Although the celebrations may have eased the tense relationships between the Greek-Cypriots and soldiers, intelligence sources were suggesting that they had been engineered by EOKA as a rallying call.

On 30 March Field Marshal Harding returned from London determined to destroy EOKA, because he believed that it posed a serious threat to an eventual settlement. He ordered that Greek flags and pictures of Makarios be removed and internal security be tightened up with increased vigilance around the barracks and camps and internal security patrols maintaining the pressure on EOKA. So far as the troops and the Service families were concerned, the truce allowed welcome relaxation as they strolled through Old Nicosia, which had been out of bounds since mid-February 1956, bringing much-needed business to shops, coffee shops and ice cream parlours. Personal protection revolvers were no longer necessary. Except for the illegal possession of weapons, Harding relaxed internment for terrorist offences and released several prominent Greek-Cypriots from house arrest.

During his exile on the Seychelles, Archbishop Makarios and his entourage were guests of Captain Le Geyt and his wife at the Governor's Lodge at Sans Souci. Le Geyt had served in the Indian Army and Uganda Police. The regularity of EOKA escapes from prisons and detention camps in Cyprus, with Athens occasionally spreading mischievous rumours that escapes were being planned and the fear that the Greek community in East Africa might organize a rescue, led to the Lodge grounds being patrolled by armed police and two tracker-dogs sent from Kenya. Even though they were denied olive oil and bread sent from Cyprus, life for the exiles was not onerous. Walks outside the grounds and entertaining guests were permitted. Mrs Le Geyt taught Makarios English after a teacher baulked at doing so when the revelations in Grivas's diaries and his association with EOKA were made public. Makarios was generally courteous and cheerful, but, when the violence in Cyprus escalated in 1956 and EOKA reeled from the military operations, he displayed some anxiety that with Grivas nowhere to be seen, the Greek-Cypriots were essentially rudderless and he could not influence events.

When Athens agreed that Makarios could go to Greece, it took several days to find passage on Greek ships in the Indian Ocean to take him to Mombasa; but, such was British sensitivity about his departure, that when berths were found on the Greek-owned liner *World Harmony*, London objected because he had been exiled under conditions that were anything but harmonious. Since 1 April 1955, seventy-eight British soldiers, nine UK Unit police officers, twelve Cyprus Police officers, sixteen British civilians, one American diplomat, 130 Greek-Cypriot civilians, which included EOKA casualties, and five Turkish-Cypriots had been killed. Eventually berths were found on the Greek tanker *Olympic Thunderer* and on 5 April, after several receptions, including one on the last night for the Sans Souci staff, the tanker slipped from her anchorage at Port Victoria and headed towards Madagascar, where Makarios was met by the Labour MP, Francis Noel-Baker. A former Second World War Intelligence Corps captain fluent in Greek and with strong links to Greece, he had become a thorn in the side of Whitehall as the unofficial emissary of Greek-Cypriot leaders and had made repeated visits to Cyprus. The exiles then flew to Nairobi to find that, with the Mau Mau uprising still very fresh, the Kenyan colonial authorities were dismayed to be hosting a representative of a nationalist movement meeting African leaders in the best hotel in town, the Hotel Norfolk.

Makarios was then flown, courtesy of Air France, to Hellenikon Airport at Athens on 17 April, to be met by a guard of honour and a horde of journalists. During the chaotic drive to the city, he was welcomed in numerous villages and suburban districts by mayors keen to seal their place in history, until he eventually appeared in triumph on the balcony of the Hotel Grande Bretagne looking down on a huge crowd.

Under pressure from NATO to resolve the Cyprus question and restore her shattered relations with her eastern ally, Athens went some way to minimize the presence of Makarios in Greece and disapprove of his proven association with EOKA. Although Anglo-Greek relations slowly improved, there was substantial tension between Greece and Turkey; nevertheless, there was general agreement that as long as Grivas was in Cyprus, a settlement was unlikely. In early April, the Minister of Defence Duncan Sandys published a Defence White Paper detailing Great Britain's strategy to reduce its military commitment outside Europe and to concentrate on 'mutually assured (nuclear) destruction' in the event of a military confrontation with the Soviet Union and its Warsaw Pact allies in Europe. To compensate for proposed reductions in overseas commitments, a Strategic Reserve was to be formed from 3rd Division in Great Britain. National Service would end in 1960. The Army was to take the brunt of the reductions with a ceiling of 180,000 all ranks, and the seventy-seven infantry battalions would be cut to sixty. Far-sighted regiments began forging natural alliances, such as the Norfolks and Suffolks forming the East Anglia Regiment in 1958. In the event, the creation of the V-Bomber force and the development of the Thor intercontinental ballistic missile soaked up the resources available to the RAF. The Amphibious Warfare Squadron was upgraded to two Commando carriers with their embarked assault helicopter squadrons.

Harding predicted that British presence in Cyprus would eventually be confined to several small enclaves and the Emergency reduced to a holding operation until the Greeks, Turks and Cypriots resolved their differences. In July, reports emerged that HQ Middle East Command might be transferred to Kenya, although it was recognized that RAF Akrotiri and the signals intelligence facilities on the island were an important NATO asset. One organization that benefited from the professionalisation of the Army was the Intelligence Corps, which was permitted to raise a cadre of Regular officers.

As has so frequently happened to the British Army, it had arrived at a crisis with little or no intelligence – two recent examples being Northern Ireland in 1969 and the war against Argentina in 1982. Cyprus in 1955 was no different. A beautiful sleepy backwater in the Eastern Mediterranean, the island presented no apparent threat and consequently the intelligence and security apparatus of the colonial authorities and Cyprus Police had decayed. When the Army began arriving in 1955, it had nothing on EOKA. On the other hand, Colonel Grivas knew from his military experience that intelligence was crucial as:

> the pilot which guides one to the right course of action and brings one to one's objective; it is also a scout which spots traps and rocks which the enemy sets in one's path in the hope of tricking and finally crushing his opponent. No fight can be carried on without intelligence. *(Memoirs of George Grivas)*

He claimed, with some justification, that every EOKA operation was planned after an intelligence assessment of information gathered by his sources in the Greek-Cypriot community, sympathetic Cyprus Police and government officials, employees with the Armed Forces and Greek Intelligence Service officers attached to the Greek Consulate in Nicosia. He exploited the inquisitiveness of youth and femininity of women to report on the routines and off-duty habits of the soldiers and their families. Although Grivas enforced the need-to-know principle, he was ruthless with traitors and discouraged conversations on EOKA matters that could be overheard on the pavements and in the bars and cafés. However, as we have seen, he breached EOKA strategic and operational security by taking insufficient care of his diaries and compromised the organization, personalities, methods of operation and conversations with such characters as Makarios. Collectively, the diaries went some distance to EOKA's surrendering the initiative to military intelligence and Special Branch. A document seized in early February 1957 gave an interesting insight into EOKA finances and suggested that its campaign was cost effective, with twenty-nine per cent of the budget being spent on the Mountain Groups, nineteen per cent on supporting families of EOKA and ten per cent on legal fees of EOKA on trial, the courier services and incidental expenses. Interrogations of EOKA suspects proved crucial throughout the Emergency, but the lack of Greek linguists and the inability of British patrols to read names and some street signs meant that difficulties were experienced in reporting incidents. The linguistic difficulty was resolved by recruiting soldiers who had studied classics at school and university, not that the Greek spoken by Pericles was similar to that used by Greek-Cypriots in 1955.

The Intelligence Corps contribution consisted of four basic elements, the first of which was the provision of officers and NCOs to senior headquarters. Operational intelligence was controlled by the senior military intelligence officer, usually a lieutenant colonel from any Arm, reporting to the Director of Operations. Included in his structure was a military vetting and identification section attached to Special Branch, the Travel Control Security Group at ports and airports, a Field Security headquarters and an intelligence section collecting, collating, analyzing and disseminating the intelligence product in time for it to be of use – all manned by Intelligence Corps. Since the Intelligence Corps did not provide intelligence units until 1959, the Brigades formed their own intelligence platoons as did the battalions. At lower levels, the eight regional District Security Committees reported to the Command District Committee. Although they took time to bed in, the intelligence interface, operational organization and community relations improved as the MILPOLs gripped their operational areas. As the terrorism climaxed in 1958, a Chief of Intelligence at HQ Middle East Command was appointed to co-ordinate Special Branch, District Security Committees, the MI6 operations and a large central intelligence records registry. Communities that directly or indirectly supported EOKA and were intimidated by collective punishment of fines, curfews, detention without trial, expanded capital punishment, censorship, and restrictions on movement were frequently rich sources of intelligence.

Counter-intelligence and protective security were split between 147 Field Security Section in Nicosia with responsibility for Eastern Cyprus and 253 Field Security Section at Famagusta looking after the remainder of the island. A Postal Detachment of two NCOs established at the Post Office in Nicosia supporting Customs in examining packages sent to the island was enlarged to a detachment of about ten soldiers examining all mail for contraband and collecting information relating to EOKA and foreign embassies, in particular that of Greece. The Joint Air Reconnaissance Intelligence Centre carried out the vital role of interpreting air photographs.

Part of counter-intelligence was Travel Control Security. Developed during the Second World War as a function to monitor entry through ports and airports, it worked closely with MI5 to identify agents and importation of subversive documents. Those selected for Travel Control Security in Cyprus were trained by serving Territorial Army soldiers who had gained experience during the Second World War. HQ Travel Control Security Group at Police Headquarters worked closely with other intelligence and security agencies, Maritime Headquarters and RAF commanders. The 52 (Famagusta) Section was the first to arrive, followed by 53 (Limassol) Detachment, 54 (Larnaca) Detachment and 73 (Airport Nicosia) Detachment and small sections deployed at Karavostas, Kyrenia, Latchi, Paphos, Xeros and Zyyi. At RAF Nicosia 51 (Mobile) Detachment was based ready for immediate deployment.

Travel Control operations included searching aircraft and ships of all sizes in port and at anchor and checking crew, passenger and cargo manifest lists. Most nights, Intelligence Corps soldiers joined naval or police launches looking for gunrunners. A soldier with 54 Detachment described his role as part soldier, part customs official and part policeman, dividing his time between the Customs shed and searching ships. In addition, 54 Detachment used a high speed ocean launch crewed by two RASC Maritime NCOs that could catch virtually any craft, except that she had a slight problem – her keel had been damaged during the bombing of Malta and it was this that that led to her being retired from service when she grounded on rocks. She was replaced by a flat-bottomed harbour launch complete with a stern-to-stem white awning that pitched and rolled horribly in anything above a gentle swell. One lance corporal who provided ship-to-shore communications from a Travel Security Control launch when the tanker MV *Clyde Guardian* ran aground, years later received a £3 cheque from the Divorce Probate and Maritime Department as his share in the salvage. As he later wrote, 'There can't be many National Service soldiers who have received salvage money'. Yet ultimately all depended on the observation of individuals. One corporal ignored protests while checking some clay Madonnas listed as 'religious symbols' and found they contained pencil bombs. A Royal Artillery sergeant at a roadblock found two messages wrapped inside a cigarette lighter, one of them being an order for the execution of a supposed traitor.

It was largely a counter-intelligence operation that led to the arrest of a Limassol Customs official on 1 December, the smashing of the weapons smuggling ring in the town two weeks later and the arrests of forty-four suspects, including Customs officials, businessmen, drivers, storekeepers and two teachers prepared to cache weapons. The arrests worried Grivas because three of those arrested, namely Manolis Savvides and Andreas Papadopoulos who had built his hideout and Dafnis Panayides who had sheltered him during the summer, knew his location. The group had smuggled in an estimated forty-three sub machine guns, twelve pistols, grenades and explosive material mostly stolen or smuggled from Greek Army armouries and magazines with the knowledge of senior officers. Still needing weapons and supplies, Grivas contacted Socrates Eliades, a successful businessman, who combined with Deacon Kyriakides Anthimos to set up another smuggling network. A former soldier, Anthimos is often described as the 'soul of EOKA'. A highly intelligent man, in the absence of Makarios in exile Grivas used him as his conduit from his Limassol bunker. The new smuggling network remained undiscovered.

During the Kenya campaign, white settlers and Colonial Police officers fluent in Swahili daubed their skin black and met with Mau Mau leaders at night in jungle clearings. From this tactic arose the deployment of false gangs of de-oathed and turned ex-Mau Mau and allied Africans led by white officers infiltrating Mau Mau gangs on search and destroy missions. These intelligence operations proved to be so effective that they became a standard British tactic in post-1945 low intensity operations and were designed to destabilize insurgency with snatch squads and deception. Q-Patrol operations were part of the Special Operations Group of volunteers recruited from within the Armed Forces in Cyprus, 'turned' EOKA and loyal Greek-Cypriots. The term 'Q' originated during the First World War when apparently weakly defended Allied merchant ships lured U-Boats into making surface attacks. In fact, a Q-ship was heavily armed with guns concealed behind hinged plates which were dropped when the submarine was sufficiently exposed – essentially a wolf in sheep's clothing. The Group was supported by Emergency Special Constables with the appropriate experience and ability to arrest. The patrols lived apart from the conventional soldiers, sometimes in isolated houses or in camps in the mountains and relied heavily on credible intelligence. One of the first operations occurred on New Year's Night 1956 when patrol led by an intelligence officer, acting on information received, entered Zoopiyi in the Troodos Mountains intending to raid the house of Minas Constantinou where it had been reported that Gregoris Afxentiou and several men were visiting. However, the patrol knocked on the door of the house of Constantinou's father next door. In the ensuing doorstep hiatus, Afxentiou and Michael Georgallis rushed into the street and engaged the patrol; in the gun battle that followed, Georgallis was killed.

A naval group run by the Royal Marines used several caiques, fishing boats and motor boats manned by the volunteers masquerading as traders and fishermen, except that they were well armed with machine guns, rifles and grenades, to intercept suspicious vessels reported by 188 Search Light and Radar Battery and patrolling warships and aircraft; they then boarded them in the search for smuggled contraband and weapons. As opposed to sheltering in bays and inlets, they were supported from below the horizon by warships. Intercepted vessels were usually scuttled by the boarders.

After the death of Afxentiou, Grivas re-organized a weakened EOKA by appointing Lambros Kafkallides to lead the remnants of the Pitsillia Group. Kafkallides was his former bodyguard and had been with him when the Castle was evacuated in December 1955. Neophytes Sofocleos, who had put the bomb in Harding's bed, took over the Marathassa Group from Polycarpos Georghiades and was joined by the diminutive killer, Andreas Kokkinos. Elenitsa Seraphim he placed in command of the Larnaca Town Group after it had been decimated by arrests. She was a chemist who had been part of the team that developed improvised bombs at the Larnaca Pan Cyprian Gymnasium and had helped organize sabotage at Dhekelia until she was arrested, only to be released on medical grounds. In spite of the truce, military operations continued apace, with Operation *Bullfinch* in the north-west flushing out the group led by Georghios Demetriou, the Lefka Group Leader. On Good Friday, 19 April 1957, part of the 1 Suffolk's Machine Gun Platoon commanded by the National Service officer Second Lieutenant Marriott was patrolling through the northern foothills of the Troodos Mountains when they literally collided with a group of seven EOKA resting in the shade of some trees. Among the prisoners they took were Demetriou, Mikis Firillas, one of the Kyrenia Castle seventeen, and Neofytes Sofocleos. Their capture meant that just fifteen names remained in the Wanted List booklets carried by the soldiers. In early May, 45 Commando took over from 40 Commando in the Troodos Mountains and, using its Operation *Musketeer* helicopter assault experience, sent two Troops to the Internal Security Training School at Forest Park to develop tactics using the Sycamores, but one Sycamore crashed killing the E Troop Quartermaster Sergeant Graham Casey.

With EOKA largely in tatters, Colonel Grivas adopted a familiar line of attack by accusing the Army of misconduct on counts common with other terrorist groups facing defeat – needless damage to property during searches and torture and abuse by named interrogators and intelligence officers. For very many EOKA, being captured as a member of a proscribed organization in possession of a weapon and facing the death penalty was an entirely new experience, and those transferred to the interrogation centres faced interrogators who knew that most prisoners are willing to be debriefed but still need to ensure that the information extracted is of value and is timely. Interrogation for the average EOKA was a frightening experience, particularly if the investigators were Turkish-Cypriot policemen determined to maintain the equilibrium of Cyprus, and prisoners set out to ensure the experience was as short as possible by talking with little prompting and agreeing to identify people associated with EOKA or guide military patrols to caves, caches and hideouts. Prompted by newspapers such as the *Manchester Guardian* calling for an inquiry in July 1957, the interrogation centres became focuses of attention, particularly as many of the suspects captured in the winter and spring came up for trial in the summer. The fact was that most EOKA were not prepared to die for *enosis* and saved their skins by betraying the organization but then sought to justify their treachery by claiming that they had been tortured. Some were unearthed as liars, but mud sticks. Throughout the Emergency, the inability to present intelligence as evidence, difficulties in the legal process and witness intimidation often obliged the prosecution to rely on confessions. Defences were quick to deflect allegations by subjecting some Crown witnesses, in particular, junior soldiers, to accusations of torture and brutality. After one arrested bomber had made a voluntary statement about his association with EOKA, his lawyer, who frequently attempted to discredit prosecution evidence, claimed that he had been mistreated – until an inquiry proved that the suspect had made his statement within thirty minutes of being arrested, during which time he had always been in the custody of three police officers. The lawyer turned out to be an active member of EOKA. Since intelligence officers were rarely called as witnesses, the consequence was that the security forces were unable to defend their reputation.

Difficulties were also experienced with some judges. Mr Justice Bernard Shaw had been severely wounded by an EOKA gunman in June 1956 and was thought by the Army to be too lenient in order to avoid being accused of exacting personal retribution. For instance, during the trial of Nicos Sampson for the murder of the two UK Unit police officers, Carter and Thorogood, Shaw rejected allegations by Sampson that he had been tortured, but he censured the Cyprus Police for not ensuring that when Sampson was arrested, in heavy rain, he had not been given a change of dry clothes. Shaw concluded that since he could not be assured that the confession was made voluntarily, Sampson was acquitted, even though Sergeant Webb identified him to be a gunman. However, he was convicted of the possession of arms at Dhali and sentenced to death. This provoked further outbreaks of violence until the authorities commuted his sentence to life imprisonment in England. There was some feeling among observers in Cyprus that acquittals and the commutations of other death sentences led to the security forces believing that it was pointless arresting known and suspect EOKA, particularly as throughout the summer EOKA acquittals continued to hit the newspapers headlines. In 1961, Sampson admitted to a Greek-Cypriot newspaper that he and two other EOKA had shot the three police sergeants and Sergeant Demmon in Nicosia General Hospital.

In mid-June, Field Marshal Harding counter-attacked by publishing the Cyprus Government White Paper *Allegations of Brutality in Cyprus*, in which he accused EOKA of using the Church to subvert the public against the Security Forces; attacked Greece for using its publicity and propaganda machine to promote terrorism; criticized Greek-Cypriot lawyers for persuading witnesses to claim ill-treatment, only for those witnesses to become sufficiently concerned about perjury to retract their statements. Harding acknowledged that some soldiers had handled suspects roughly at the point of capture but then emphasized that apart from the cashiering of two captains, none of the allegations made by EOKA and the nationalists had been substantiated. The Armed Forces were full of National Servicemen from every region in Great Britain. All had survived the rigours of the Second World War, had been raised on traditions and history of the Armed Forces and had been educated in an era when atlases showed large areas of pink of the British Commonwealth. Many from tough estates in Glasgow, Liverpool, Newcastle and the East End of London were assembled into regiments, each with its different cultures. As would be evident twenty years later among the Regulars who fought in Northern Ireland, the English county battalions were noted for their humour and calm approach to life; the Royal Marines for the ability to get on with most people; and the Parachute Regiment for their no-nonsense culture. Few had met foreigners until they arrived in Cyprus where they were greeted with hostility and experienced friends killed and wounded and Service families attacked. With the capture of prisoners and extension of the battlefield, it was no wonder that some suspects were roughed up during arrests. That is the nature of the battlefield. The comment made by one soldier to a *Manchester Guardian* journalist of, 'What do you expect us to do with them. Sit down and have a cup of tea with them?' typified their attitude but not necessarily that of the interrogators, who found that a cup of tea to an anxious suspect was the ideal ice-breaker. Compare Harding's counter-attack to the meek surrender by the British Government to allegations of Army mistreatment in Northern Ireland. Recalling the murders of the two HLI at the Lefkoniko water fountain, Harding rejected allegations that the subsequent searches had been punitive and reminded the population that, 'The people of Lefkoniko had reason to be thankful that it was British troops with whom they had to deal that day.' Across the Mediterranean in Algeria at the same time was a French Army of National Servicemen and the Foreign Legion winning a reputation for excessive robustness. Apart from the liberal chattering classes, there was little public interest in the allegations in Great Britain where the families and friends of those serving in Cyprus showed them little sympathy.

The combination of the rejection of the White Paper by the Cyprus Bar, the refusal by the British Government to hold an independent inquiry and allegations of mistreatment of convicted EOKA prisoners sent to Wormwood Scrubs Prison led to the allegations being aired in Athens by Archbishop Makarios, by the House of Commons, the Human Rights Sub-Committee of Europe and finally at the United Nations. It is likely that had the British Government held an inquiry, it would have acknowledged that there had been some mistreatment and would have then have been forced into exposing the deceit of EOKA at a time when politically this was not desirable. As is common, little fuss was made about the execution of 'traitors' and the two Leicester soldiers by EOKA or that Grivas was prepared to let the innocent die for his cause. When the former Metropolitan Police officer Sergeant Tipple was shot dead in his car in Larnaca on 12 June 1957 by Andreas Kokkinos, a grocer named Nicos Tsardellis was arrested during the subsequent sweep and picked out as the killer in an identification parade, Kokkinos sought permission to give himself up. Grivas forbade it, even though Tsardellis was sentenced to death. Fortunately, such was the fragility of the conviction that three weeks later he was reprieved by Harding.

Grivas claimed that on 6 June soldiers came close to finding him when the Limassol suburb in which he was living was subjected to a major cordon-and-search operation. Seeing that the troops systematically searched each street and property, he concealed himself in the hideout and listened as the studded Army boots entered the house. When a soldier opened the cupboard door below the sink, he feared the worst and prepared to shoot his way out of trouble and escape across the fields, until he then heard Elli Christodoulides offer the soldiers a glass of whisky. Not unexpectedly, they accepted. He would later write how much he relied on EOKA women to support the movement, particularly in early September 1957 when informant information led to the arrest of Nikki Artemiou and EOKA activist Maroulla Economides in Nicosia. Artemiou's house was a key distribution point in the courier system and the police and military search teams seized a substantial quantity of EOKA documents. It took time for the code-breakers to crack the cipher used by Grivas. In the meantime, the informant, a driver who had once driven Economides to Limassol and knew how the courier system worked, had been executed.

When, in mid-June, Harding was instructed by London that since Grivas was adhering to the truce, offensive military operations should be scaled down, it was not something that he agreed with because intelligence was suggesting that EOKA was on the brink of defeat and any sort of breathing space would give Grivas time to regroup. Early on 24 July in Operation *Sherry Spinner*, a 45 Commando battle group that included elements from 1 KOYLI, 3 Grenadier Guards and 1st Battalion,

The Royal Ulster Rifles (1 RUR) who had arrived in May landed several patrols by Sycamores and established cordons around several villages nestling in the eastern extremities of the Troodos. Three days later shortly after nightfall, an X Troop patrol was about to leave Palendria when they saw a car stop and then reverse. A few minutes later, Marines Brian Thornton and Geoffrey Salisbury challenged two men in military uniforms they thought to be police officers until Thornton saw the leading one was carrying a Thompson and arrested them. One was Michael Costas, a prominent EOKA with a £5,000 bounty on his head and the satchel that one was carrying contained bomb components.

Throughout the summer, Grivas kept the EOKA pot boiling by maintaining the pressure for *enosis* with memorial services for dead EOKA at which excessive grieving was a regular feature. As part of the intimidation programme, Greek-Cypriot parents risked accusations of treachery if they sent their children to government schools as opposed to Greek schools. He demanded strikes, even though the truce had seen improved business for many traders, particularly from Service families. Tourism was non-existent. Then, several days after Stavros Stylianides had died in Nicosia General Hospital in September after being badly injured when a bomb that he was constructing detonated, intercepted pamphlets signed by 'Digenes' suggested that EOKA was using the truce, as had been expected, to re-organize and plot. After several months of relative tranquillity compared to the previous two years, considerable anxiety spread across the island that the security forces would recommence internal security operations, particularly at the end of the month when Central Police Headquarters was attacked by several EOKA gunmen and a cache of pipe bombs was found in the suburb of Strovolos.

Although Harding played the psychological warfare card by openly questioning the sincerity of Grivas about negotiating a solution, Grivas planned the next phase of the EOKA campaign on the perception that the British were encouraging the Turkish-Cypriots to attack Greek-Cypriot enclaves. He therefore directed Greek-Cypriot leaders to plan the defence of their communities and to collect intelligence on Turkish-Cypriot enclaves. The Valiant Youth of EOKA (*Alkimos Neolaia Tis EOKA*: ANE) was formed, with priests and teachers instructed to talent-spot youths and unmarried nationalists aged between fourteen and twenty-five who would replace EOKA casualties and be trained in weapons, surveillance, intimidation and in understanding the political glorification of *enosis* and the defence of Greece by the Greek Army in 1940. When the Turkish-Cypriots heard about the intelligence-gathering, they formed the Turkish Defence Organization (*Turk Mudafa*

*Teskilat*: TMT) and began to agitate for partition along the 35th Parallel, with the Greek-Cypriots confined to the south. An explosion in a Turkish-Cypriot house at the end of August and the find of explosives at the scene confirmed that they were forming local defence organizations. Sectarian violence was now inevitable.

As the long, hot summer gave way to autumn rainstorms, the first sign of a major escalation in sectarian violence emerged when the respected Mukhtar (headman) Loizas Pierou was shot dead in his village of Dhali by an EOKA gunman in mid-October and several other mukhtars were beaten up elsewhere. Nicos Sampson had been arrested in Dhali. It then emerged that Pierou had been on the list of suspect traitors seized in the hideout used by Michael Ashiotis.

Michael Ashiotis was a youth who had graduated into EOKA in 1955. After being lifted as a suspect, he had been interned in Camp K until in January 1956 he had escaped and joined the Kyperounda Guerrillas Group. However, his escape meant that he was suspected of being an informer, and when he learnt that his two companions had been ordered by Grivas to kill him, he shot them and surrendered to a 1 RUR sentry at Kakopetria on 10 October. Ashiotis was persuaded to guide a patrol to their hideout and next day a sergeant, a veteran of the Korean War, and a National Service signaller dragged the two dead terrorists from their hideout. The patrol also found several items of intelligence value, including the hit list of Cypriots to be eliminated and a radio set, which were handed over to Special Branch. The hideout was destroyed by a lieutenant with sufficient explosive to dislodge parts of the hillside. Several days later, Brigadier FitzGeorge-Balfour, who had earlier relinquished his appointment as Chief of Staff to Brigadier Paul Gleadell CB CBE DSO, and had returned to Cyprus from England in command of 1 Guards Brigade, announced, at a news conference, that several documents found in the hideout indicated that Grivas intended to break the truce if the UN talks on the future of Cyprus proved unsuccessful. The Brigade had taken over the 3 Commando Brigade sector. Ashiotis was considered to be a valuable intelligence source and although he was sent to live in England with a new identity, his guilt overcame him and, returning to his family in Cyprus, he appealed to Grivas for clemency, in vain. He was executed as a traitor.

Grivas also focused on the antipathy of the left wing AKEL to *enosis* by humiliating several trade unionists. Further deterioration in the internal security situation continued four days later when Radio Cyprus was silenced by one of several bombs that interrupted power supplies at RAF Nicosia. On 22 October handwritten orders from Grivas summoning the Youth of EOKA to display their allegiance to Greece by flying Greek flags and daubing *enosis* slogans in villages during the lead up to the Oxi Day celebrations were found by Trooper Murray of the Royal Horse Guards when a school bus was searched at a roadblock. In spite of the deterioration, Commissioner of Police White relaxed the legislation governing the display of Greek flags and insignia and, permitting the Greek-Cypriots to celebrate Oxi Day, then announced that the same rules would apply to Turkish Independence Day celebrations two days later. In spite of the relaxations, Oxi Day dissolved into several serious riots, the most serious being in Nicosia where D Company, 1 Suffolks broke up unrest in Metaxas Square.

By November, Field Marshal Harding had served two years as Governor and the time was right for him to resign. Athough he believed that the Army had crushed EOKA and the time was ripe to resolve the Emergency, progress was undermined by unhelpful comments from London apparently ignoring Greek murmurings that Turkey would never be recognized in Cyprus and that Ankara would not accept anything that did not protect Turkish-Cypriots and the important strategic value of the island to Turkey. He was particularly incensed by a clause in the opposition Labour Party manifesto that Cyprus should be given self-determination because this, he believed, would invite extremists on both sides, in particularly EOKA, to continue the violence and prejudice any sort of settlement. Instead, Harding envisaged a settlement in which the British had sovereignty for five years during which Greek-Cypriot and Turkish-Cypriot representatives would progressively advise on matters affecting their communities until independence. The British presence thereafter would be confined to two bases. On 3 November, after a farewell tour of parades and visits to units throughout Cyprus, Harding and his wife left RAF Nicosia in a 216 Squadron Transport Command Comet for London pursued by EOKA leaflets claiming that he left a broken man. In fact, he was deeply respected by all those who had dealt him in the search for a solution. Even Grivas would later write that he had high regard for him as a soldier but did wonder if he was constrained by the old hands in the Colonial Office. The facts are that Harding had restored law and order, had broken the back of EOKA and that negotiations with Makarios were imminent. This is reflected in the fact that 213 deaths in 1956 had been reduced to thirty-four in 1957, of which six were Servicemen, four were police and twenty-four were civilians, twenty of them Greek-Cypriots including EOKA and 'traitors'. Nevertheless, Harding commented that his two years in Cyprus were the worst than any colonial administrator had experienced since 1945.

## CHAPTER ELEVEN

# EOKA at Bay

(November 1957 to November 1958)

When the unpalatable suggestion emerged during 1957 that the *enosis* campaign was being led by a Greek Army officer strongly suspected of collaborating with the Germans in Occupied Greece, it was an embarrassment to the Greek-Cypriots and rejected as British and communist propaganda. The fact was that, aged fifty-nine years in 1957, fame had come late to Grivas as a resistance leader who had converted a bunch of unsoldierly and amateurish guerrillas into a compact and loyal terrorist organization tying down several thousand British troops on an island.

On 25 November EOKA achieved one of their most spectacular sabotage attacks when two electrician members of Limassol Town Group employed at RAF Akrotiri smuggled two small time-bombs into a maintenance hangar and then at lunchtime, while the work force was at lunch, placed the devices near the fuel tanks of two Canberra bombers and set them to explode at midnight. But there were no explosions, and thus it was with some anxiety that the electricians turned up for work next day in the knowledge that either the devices had been found or had not detonated. Although everyone was kept at work over lunch for a rush job, everything was normal until shortly after the whistle for the end of work, when the two bombs exploded, wrecking four bombers and a Venom and badly damaging the almost empty hangar. One of the electricians, Andreas Vassilou, aged seventeen years, was briefly arrested. Two months later, when he was named as EOKA on a list found by the security forces, Grivas sent him to join a group in the Troodos.

Sir Hugh Foot arrived as Governor fresh from Jamaica on 3 December. A urbane diplomat, he arrived with a stark warning from Under Secretary for the Colonies John Profumo that he must have no illusions about the seriousness of the situation in Cyprus, particularly as several Greek-Cypriot leaders had refused to negotiate until Archbishop Makarios was re-instated and the State of Emergency was rescinded.

Although Foot was Commander-in-Chief, Major General Kendrew, as Director of Operations, took over all military responsibilities. Brigadier Gleadell remained as Chief of Staff to Foot. In the first week of January 1958, Lieutenant General Sir Roger Bourne took over from Lieutenant General Keightley as Commander-in-Chief of the new Middle East Land Forces. At the same time, following the withdrawal of the RAF from Iraq and Jordan and the formation of HQ Arabian Peninsula in Aden, HQ Middle East Air Force merged with RAF Levant and moved Air HQ from Nicosia to Episkopi. Foot overhauled the intelligence apparatus by importing John Prendergast as Chief of Intelligence from Kenya where he had been the Director of Intelligence and Security during the Mau Mau rebellion.

Within three days of Foot's arrival, the Cyprus Police and two 1 Glosters companies ran into a serious riot by youths promoting solidarity outside a Nicosia church after an inaccurate report was circulated that the release of the UN report on the future of Cyprus was imminent. The outbreak was the worst since April and was followed two days later by further disturbances in Famagusta and Paphos. Next day, rioting by secondary students in Nicosia after rumours circulated that a Turkish-Cypriot police officer had been killed by Greek-Cypriot youths was the first sign of community tension. When Greek-Cypriots found themselves under attack in the Old City, the Royal Horse Guards erected barbed wire barricades to keep the communities apart. The two days of unrest left forty-one soldiers wounded by stones, bottles and broken furniture and 218 civilians arrested. Although Grivas had attempted to defuse the disorder, the Greek-Cypriots had again used violence to ensure the island remained in the global headlines. In a display of diplomatic conciliation, Foot visited the Old City, walked down the murderous Ledra Street and met the Mayor of Nicosia. He also toured rural areas, often on horseback. But the youths of EOKA had graduated to ambushing police cars and military convoys and there were still determined EOKA to be rounded up. A week before Christmas, an informant identified a house in Styllos that was being used by two brothers said to be EOKA officers. A Company, 1 Leicesters threw a cordon around the house and when District Leader Theodoros Georgiou attempted to break through the sector held by the platoons of Second Lieutenants Tom Hiney and Peter Graham, he was shot dead. His brother was not at home. During the search of the house, Sergeant Brown and Private Warnock found a cache of weapons, ammunition and explosive.

Two days before Christmas, Foot announced in a message of reconciliation the release of a hundred male and the eleven female detainees, lifted restrictions on several hundred EOKA sympathizers, permitted the Larnaca Pan Cypriot Gymnasium, which been closed because of student unrest for a year, to be opened and authorized that the father of Theodorus Georgiou be flown by helicopter from Pyla Detention Camp to attend the funeral of his son. Some senior Army officers regarded Foot's conciliatory approach as signs of weakness, and a rift developed with those who believed that EOKA should be crushed, once and for all. But, in spite of Foot's approach, on New Year's Eve Grivas threatened 'total war' and, placing EOKA on alert in mid-January, warned Foot that if he did not return from Christmas leave in Great Britain with firm proposals for *enosis*, the violence would continue.

By the end of January 1958, Makarios was confident that Athens would support Cypriot self-government but still refused to give any guarantees to the Turkish-Cypriots. This resulted in several days of serious sectarian unrest, with the minority clamouring for partition. On the 27th, a 43 Light Anti Aircraft Regiment RA patrol that stumbled on an illegal assembly in Nicosia was pelted with bricks, stones and bottles by a large crowd until the Turkish-Cypriot leader, Rauf Denktash, calmed the mob. However, a military Land Rover containing a 50 Infantry Brigade District staff officer and his driver then tried to drive through the mob and knocked over four civilians, fatally injuring a woman. The crowd went berserk and amid burning buildings and explosions from a burning petrol station, C Company, 1 Suffolks and the Royal Horse Guards fired live rounds into the air and made repeated baton charges. The next day, troops shot dead three Turkish-Cypriots trying to breach a military checkpoint and two youths scaling the Old City walls, in the belief that they were taking up positions to throw missiles at the troops. When the unrest diminished after a week, seven Turkish-Cypriots had been killed and fifty civilians, twelve soldiers, twenty-eight Police Mobile Reserves and five Fire Services had been injured.

Cyprus was again on the verge of a complete breakdown of law and order, except that there was now more of a hint of sectarianism. When rumours circulated that the Greek Government had been sidelined by a British and Turkish conspiracy, Foot placed Grivas on notice not to respond or face the weight of a full military response; he then met Makarios in Athens where he tabled the plan developed by Field Marshal Harding in the weeks before he departed. But the Greek-Cypriots were suspicious of the plan for unitary self-government. At the beginning of March, the Greek Government collapsed over internal disagreements, leading to further regional instability. Against a backdrop of threats to attack military and government buildings, on 6 March Grivas launched a campaign of passive resistence; British goods and services were boycotted, British employees in Greek-Cypriot businesses were dismissed, British airline and shipping booking offices and travel offices lost business, the government lottery was abandoned and Greek-Cypriot mayors were instructed to hand in their seals of office. Underpinning the boycott was intimidation, and although Grivas claimed that the boycott 'aroused patriotic sentiment', it impacted badly on shopkeepers and businesses trading under difficult conditions. After six weeks Makarios demanded that the restrictions be relaxed, a demand that appalled Grivas because he had been aiming to destabilize the Cyprus Government.

With persistent intelligence reports indicating a renewed EOKA offensive, in mid-March Foot again warned Colonel Grivas not to resort to violence and invited him to allow Great Britain, Greece and Turkey to find a solution; but Grivas took exception to the appeal as criticism of EOKA and Foot found himself heavily criticized by Greek-Cypriot organizations. Grivas' chronic fear of communism led to sectarian clashes between right and left and when three trade unionists were murdered and a cycle of accusation and counter-accusation developed, he could exert little influence as the differing social and political trends tore Cyprus apart. As his original philosophy veered from liberation and a fight for *enosis* to one of a religious crusade against communism, he instructed Greek-Cypriot teachers to foster nationalism and allow students to take part in political discussion.

In early February, 40 Commando returned to Cyprus from Malta. At the same time, the 1st Battalion, The Argyll and Sutherland Highlanders (1 Argyll and Sutherland Highlanders) arrived from the UK on the troopship *Devonshire* and were sent to Limni Camp on the small coastal plain between Polis and Paphos. Returning to England on the troopship were the Glosters; handing over to 1 Lancashires and destined for West Germany. Also on board were the Leicesters, who had lost twelve soldiers killed since 1955. In addition, 29 Field Regiment RA relieved 40 Field Regiment at Famagusta. In their third major move since arriving in Cyprus, the 1 Royal Ulster Rifles passed the Panhandle to $1^{st}$ Battalion, The Royal Welch Fusiliers (1 RWF) while 1 Middlesex moved into the new Alexander Barracks at Dhekelia.

One method employed by the Cyprus Government at a very early stage to reduce the effect of EOKA propaganda was to order the removal of slogans. Lieutenant Alistair Campbell of the Argylls, in an early patrol, convinced a village to remove EOKA slogans; however, when he returned to find that the inhabitants had simply added more, in particular to the Church walls, he gave the mayor a second opportunity to remove the offending phraseology. But when he returned again and windows and doors were slammed shut and slops thrown over the Jocks, he ordered his men to overwrite the slogans with a mix of paint, ink and creosote requisitioned from the shops; unfortunately, the Jocks painted 'Home Rule for Scotland' and 'Rangers for the Cup'. Inevitably, there were accusations of British soldiers desecrating the Greek Church.

The murders of Brian Dear, a linguist attached to Special Branch, in mid-April and two Royal Military Police lance corporals shot dead in Famagusta by gunmen on 5 May again showed the depths to which Cyprus had dived; nevertheless, the incidents prompted the Mayor of Famagusta to complain to the European Human Rights Commission about military aggression when suspects were being rounded up. In mid-March there were serious mutinies at Nicosia Prison and Camp K. The tension throughout the island resulted in off-duty troops being banned from walking out unarmed. Foot appreciated that his softly, softly approach was unproductive and had no alternative but to agree with his military commanders that EOKA needed to be defeated.

On 16 May, 3 Infantry Brigade launched Operation *Kingfisher* in the southern Troodos Mountains to search for Grivas and follow credible intelligence that several bomb attacks had originated from the same area. Since the strategy was to avoid warning EOKA, no recces were carried out and the long convoys of Bedford lorries full of troops from 1 Ox and Bucks from Limassol, the Argylls and Sutherland Highlanders and 40 Commando were covered by Auster and Pioneer aircraft, while Sycamores flew patrols on to high ground. On one night ambush laid by the Argyll's Pipes and Drums Platoon, two men were heard walking along a track, with the leader using a well-known EOKA ploy of throwing stones ahead in order to invite ambushes to open fire too early. In the beam of a searchlight bouncing reflections from the clouds, as the two men walked into the killing zone, a piper opened fire, but the ambush lost sight of them when the searchlight went out. A shot fired across the valley by A Company alerted the two EOKA and they took cover in a ravine and opened fire. The A Company Commander, Major Colin Mitchell, then realized that his platoon had overreacted and lobbed two grenades to where the two EOKA were thought to be and asked a Shackleton supporting the operation to drop flares. Next day, according to Mitchell, a blood-soaked bandage found in the ravine was sent to Scotland where a retired general who practised dowsing stood over a map of Cyprus and indicated an area where a hitherto unknown network of EOKA hideouts were later found. Otherwise, the cordons established around the ravines and ridges dividing the small fields of carob and groves of olives and grapes achieved little.

When the 1st Battalion, The Durham Light Infantry (1 DLI) arrived by sea and relieved 46 Heavy Anti Aircraft Regiment in the Paphos sector, it ended two years of gunner occupation in the town. A bomb damaging the Turkish Information Office in Nicosia during the morning of 7 June and the shooting by a Turkish-Cypriot policeman of two men induced the worst sectarian unrest since the British had arrived in the nineteenth century. Although HQ 50 Infantry Brigade District imposed a midnight curfew and deployed soldiers along the Mason-Dixon Line separating the communities, it was not until about 3 am that a semblance of order was achieved by 1 Middlesex; then for five days the young National Servicemen stood in between the warring communities, enforcing dusk-to-dawn curfews and escorting homeless families from wrecked homes to safety, but every time curfew was lifted for humanitarian reasons, there was violence. In the skies above, 653 Squadron Austers and RAF Wessex helicopters dropped leaflets and scouted for signs of trouble, but when more violence flared each time the curfew was lifted, on the 11th, 1 Lancashires were rushed to Nicosia to join the Middlesexes, 1st Battalion, The Royal Berkshire Regiment (1 Berkshires), Suffolks and 43 Light Anti Aircraft Regiment RA while 1 RWF rescued several homeless Greek-Cypriots families in Lefka. The bewilderment of the National Servicemen was epitomized in a British newspaper cartoon in which a soldier asks, 'Who are we fighting today, sarge?'

At about midnight on 11/12 June, UK Police Unit Sergeant Gill, the local police commander in the Greek-Cypriot village of Yerolakkos, received a report that the Turkish-Cypriots at Skylloura believed their village was about to be attacked and they intended to defend themselves. Yerolakkos Police Station was part of the Nicosia Rural Sub-Division. Gill maintained law and order for a sector of about forty-three square miles in which 5,000 people lived, mainly in six large villages. Skylloura is about twelve miles east of Nicosia on the road to Myrtou and, although mixed, favoured Greek-Cypriots. Three miles to the north-west lies the Greek-Cypriot village of Kondemenos. Since there had been recent sectarian tension, Gill and an Auxiliary Police constable drove to Skyroulla and found that both communities had mobilized to defend themselves. Gill then drove toward Philia and saw crouched in a dry stream bed about 250 yards from the outskirts of Skyroulla about 175 Greek-Cypriots armed with sticks, clubs and knives. Nearby were parked several buses and lorries with their lights switched off. Illuminating the group with his Land Rover headlights, Gill sent the Auxiliary to Skyroulla to fetch military support from 4 Troop, B

Squadron, The Royal Horse Guard, which was commanded by Cornet Legge-Bourke. The Regiment had been patrolling non-stop since 7 June. By the time that two Ferrets arrived, about fifty Greek-Cypriots had escaped, nevertheless the remainder were arrested, disarmed and driven to Nicosia Central Police Station where Gill recorded their names and then released them.

At about 5.30 am on 12 June Gill returned to Skyroulla intending to return to Yerolakkos but when two Turkish-Cypriots reported that their hamlet at Ayios Vasilios, two miles to the east, was about to be attacked, Legge-Bourke allocated three Ferrets to accompany Gill. On the way, the patrol intercepted about 250 armed Greek-Cypriots in five buses from the village of Mammari, but since there were too many to be taken to a rural police station, Gill disarmed them and invited them to walk back to their homes. At about 3.30 pm, Sergeant Gill was at Yerolakkis Police Station when some Turkish-Cypriots reported that their community in Skyroulla had been attacked. He immediately sent for military support and with his Greek-Cypriot police sergeant, drove to the village where he found that both communities were tense, with the Turkish-Cypriots fearing an attack from Philia or Kondemenos. After Legge-Bourke arrived with two Ferrets, Gill and his sergeant then headed for Kondemenos and about 350 yards outside the village saw thirty-five Greek-Cypriots crouched in a dry riverbed. They claimed that they were waiting to escort Kondemenos neighbours to their village from work in Nicosia. Gill noted that they were armed with farming implements, were aggressive and, believing that they probably intended to attack the Turkish-Cypriot quarter of Skyroulla, with the help of a Squadron Leader N F Smith, who happened to be passing, Gill and his sergeant ordered the men to climb into their two lorries, which were parked nearby. He intended to charge them at Yerolakkos Police Station with possession of offensive weapons. Legge-Bourke then instructed Sergeant Taylor and Corporal Straker, his Troop NCOs, to escort Gill and the prisoners to Yerolakkos.

At the Camp Elizabeth MILPOL Operations Room in Nicosia, Assistant Police Superintendent Trusler, who had responsibility for the Nicosia Rural Sub-Division, had noted the trouble brewing at Skyroulla and drove to the area with a Turkish-Cypriot police inspector and intercepted Sergeant Gill and his convoy en route to Yerolakkos. But hostile Greek-Cypriots had gathered in the village and since the police station was too small to hold thirty-five prisoners, Trusler instructed Gill to take them to Nicosia Central Police Station. Gill was then joined by an Auxiliary Police constable. By the time, the convoy had reached the suburbs of Nicosia, a serious riot had developed outside the Central Police Station and so Trusler instructed the Duty Officer to instruct Gill not to enter Nicosia. Meanwhile Sergeant Taylor had been instructed by Major Roy Redgrave, the B Squadron Leader, to drop the prisoners at Geunyeli and not where they had been arrested because an example needed to be made of 'bad boys' by inviting them to walk home. Geunyeli is about ten miles west of Skyroulla with a further three miles to Kondemenos. Redgrave's reasoning was that the road to Geunyeli was the first turning into countryside from the main road to Kyrenia and no trouble had been reported between Geunyeli and Skyroulla. As the convoy passed Wolseley Barracks, Taylor drove to the front of the convoy and relayed Redgrave's instructions to Gill, who assumed that the instruction had come from Trusler via military communications. Sergeant Gill turned the convoy around and headed toward Geunyeli. Meanwhile, Major Redgrave radioed Cornet C.P. Baring, who was not far from Geunyeli, to take his Troop and the two Grenadier Guards sections commanded by Lieutenant R S Corkran he had as mobile infantry and assist Sergeant Taylor and Corporal Straker secure the place where the prisoners were to be dropped. At about 4.15 pm and about 400 yards north-east of Geunyeli, Gill halted the convoy, instructed the thirty-five prisoners to line up in two rows on the side of the road and then invited them to walk home. Most were resigned to the fact and showed no concern even when a Turkish-Cypriot RAF Auxiliary Policemen and four Turkish-Cypriots wandered from Geunyeli to see what was happening. With the Royal Horse Guards watching the road from Geunyeli, the Grenadiers escorted the prisoners across a couple of fields for about 400 yards. Meanwhile, Trusler had received an inaccurate report that Sergeant Gill had reached Ayios Dhometios on the outskirts of the city and issued orders for the prisoners to be processed at the local police station.

It had not occurred to anyone that the Greek-Cypriots were walking across Turkish-Cypriot fields not far from a Turkish-Cypriot village and out of sight of security forces patrols using the road between Nicosia and Kyrenia at a time of high sectarian tension. The Greek-Cypriots decided to make for Yerolakkos and quickly made their way up a hill about a mile from the Kyrenia road, because it was quite late and they wanted to reach their homes before dark; they then crossed a field of bearded wheat at the top of the hill. As they descended, the field behind them went up in flames. It was about 5 pm. The Greek-Cypriots were then ambushed by two motor cyclists speeding from the direction of Geunyeli, one with a pillion rider, who unexpectedly opened fire on them. In a panic, they ran back up the hill but were surrounded by about seventy-five angry Turkish-Cypriots armed with sticks, axes and knives, who believed they had something to do with the burning crops. Some of the Greek-Cypriots scattered while others braved the blazing field.

The Grenadiers had returned to their lorries and joined Gill and the others soldiers watching the prisoners disappear over the crest of the hill. Seeing flames, Gill and the soldiers assumed that the Greek-Cypriots had set fire to the crops and then they saw a mob stream out of Geunyeli heading towards the fire. The Grenadiers acted quickly and intercepted them with a roadblock while Baring sped to a fork in the road in his Ferret where he arrested two Turkish-Cypriots on a motor-cycle and noted the pillion passenger was holding a blood-stained club. As his driver drove the Ferret up the hill toward the flames, Baring came across a body, several injured people and a small mob hustling the two Greek-Cypriots. The appearance of Baring stopped the slaughter, but four Greek-Cypriots were dead and nine had been badly injured, of whom four would die.

It was inevitable that the Greek-Cypriots would accuse the Army of deliberately exposing the prisoners to Turkish-Cypriot attack, with the *Cyprus Mail* one of several newspapers demanding an explanation. Chief Justice Sir Paget Bourke was tasked to investigate by Sir Hugh Foot and in his *The Findings of the Commission into the Incidents at Geunyeli, Cyprus on 12 June*, he focused on the inability of Sergeant Gill to deliver the prisoners to Nicosia Central Police Station and a communication breakdown in the MILPOL operation room during a period of intense public disturbances in Nicosia. Challenging the practice of making suspects walk home although not recommending against it, Bourke rejected Greek-Cypriot allegations against the security forces; indeed, he commented that the timely arrival of Cornet Baring on the hill had interrupted the massacre of all thirty-five Greek-Cypriots. The acquittal of eight Turkish-Cypriots for murder led to the Greek-Cypriots suggesting that British justice in Cyprus was corrupt.

By the end of June, another rift had developed between Makarios and Grivas over the hardships created by the British boycott. Isolated, confined to his bunker in Limassol, largely out of touch and feeding off reports from his commanders, Grivas believed that the British and Turks had combined in an offensive against the Greek-Cypriots and responded by mobilizing EOKA and waited for a suitable opportunity to take the offensive.

On 5 July, the Troop from A Squadron, the Royal Horse Guards commanded by Lieutenant Blake drove into the Greek-Cypriot village of Avgorou near Famagusta to follow up reports that the terrorist Andreas Karios had been seen in the area. On 1 April 1955, Karios had been involved in the attack on Famagusta Power Station during which Modestos Panelli had been electrocuted. He had been detained but had escaped from Pyla Detention Camp in March 1956 along with the former teacher Fotis Pittas, who was the Lysi Group deputy leader. When the soldiers noted several EOKA slogans daubed on a coffee shop and were taunted by several youths refusing to remove them, two troopers grabbed a youth with the intention of giving him a brush and bucket of water. But a mob of village women encouraged by mother-of-six, and expecting the seventh, Mrs Loukia Papagiorgiou attacked the soldiers, freed the boy and spirited him to a house. With the mood in the village ugly, Blake radioed for reinforcements from the Standby Troop commanded by Cornet Pilkington, but it was prevented from joining him by a storm of bottles, bricks and stones. Around Blake's Ferrets, the chaos was aggravated, with Mrs Papagiorgiou prominent among the rioters. Blake ordered his Troop to withdraw but as he was climbing into his Scout Car, a brick thrown at close range hit him in the face and stunned him. This incited the crowd to swarm on to the Ferrets and, with the situation becoming extremely dangerous, Blake elevated his Browning machine gun and fired a short bust of warning shots; however, some rounds ricocheted off a wall and an elderly man and Mrs Papagiorgiou were fatally wounded. As the mob took cover, the Troop drove out of the village and lurked in the area until a 1 RUR company arrived and imposed a punitive curfew. Such was the ferocity of the riot that thirteen civilians and twenty-two soldiers required medical treatment. The incident was the detonator that Grivas needed. Not only did he send a wreath to the funeral of Mrs Papagiorgiou promising revenge, he also ordered the Famagusta Town Group to mount immediate reprisals for 'the outrage of Avgorou' by 'British murderers'.

On 10 July, 3 Infantry Brigade launched Operation *Spring Time* in which 45 Commando, 3 Grenadier Guards and 1st Battalion, The Queen's Own Royal West Kent Regiment (1 RWK) searched for an EOKA hide reported to be near Akanthou in the Karpas Peninsula. Deployed from Malta on the cruiser HMS *Bermuda* were four Westland Whirlwind helicopters of 728 (Commando) Flight and a Tactical HQ and X and Z Troops, 45 Commando formed into Heliforce. After its success on Operation *Musketeer,* the Joint Helicopter Unit had returned to Middle Wallop to continue operational research and evaluation, but disagreement had emerged between the Army, who viewed helicopters as battlefield support weapons, and the RAF, who saw them as short range transports. Helicopter tactics in a terrorist environment were still in their infancy, particularly in night operations, nevertheless the Fleet Air Arm pilots were willing to experiment and ensure that troops were delivered on time. The shortage of helicopters resulted in a tactic of the first stick of troops being delivered to their landing site and then the pilots collecting more troops by meeting the road convoy at agreed rendezvous and continuing to leapfrog until all the troops had been delivered.

For three days the troops screened seven villages in the rugged terrain and then on the fourth day ten helicopters of a mix of Heliforce and RAF Sycamores flew Royal Marines and a Royal West Kent company to a suspected hideout south of Akanthou; however, the ground was too rugged for the helicopters to land and several men were injured abseiling down ropes. Lieutenant Colonel Richards was still on the rope when the Whirlwind pilot thought that his stick had all landed. Rather than wait until the helicopter landed, Richards dropped 30 feet and broke his ankle. On the same day, two Royal Marines were killed and three wounded by friendly fire when they strayed into a killing zone. Nevertheless, Heliforce had proved a success but it was disbanded shortly afterwards when the Royal Marines were withdrawn from the operation to rejoin 45 Commando on board HMS *Tenby* and returned to Malta.

On the 10 July the Famagusta Town Group avenged the Avgorou incident by killing a Royal Horse Guards subaltern and a trooper in a grocer's shop in Hermes Street; but when the Army followed up and found a large quantity of explosives in the Anorthosis Sports Club, bomb disposal officers believed it unsafe and blew it up causing substantial collateral damage. Grivas retaliated by instructing the Nicosia Town Group to blow up a teacher training college, but the bomber lost both hands when the device exploded prematurely. The swift retaliation gave Grivas confidence to mount an offensive against the Turkish-Cypriots; 13 July was an especially bad day with five Cypriots killed and substantial damage caused. When Governor Foot failed to convince Archbishop Makarios of the need for a partnership approach to negotiate a ceasefire, he imposed a month's curfew and authorized a further 300 British police officers to be seconded to UK Police Unit. For the troops, it was a tough period of patrolling and guarding sensitive installations, fighting forest fires and defusing disturbances, and always under frequent Greek-Cypriot accusations of deliberate negligence whenever a house or church went up in flames, while warning the Turkish-Cypriots of planned searches.

In the meantime, aggression by the newly formed, Soviet-funded United Arab Republic (Egypt and Syria) had led to Cyprus again becoming an aircraft-carrier for operations in the Mediterranean and Middle East and signalled the return of 16 Parachute Brigade minus 2 Para. When HQ 3rd Infantry Division then arrived to support regional operations, there were twenty-six major units in Cyprus. On 17 July the Brigade, minus 3 Para, deployed to Jordan to deter the United Arab

Republic from invading the pro-British kingdom. Then 19 Infantry Brigade arrived with the five infantry battalions and 20 Field and 34 Light Anti Aircraft Regiments RA to support regional operations and rotated its units between Nicosia, Famagusta and Limassol. In September, the tension in Jordan subsided sufficiently for the Brigade to return to England, except for 1st Battalion, The East Surrey Regiment who went to North Africa to bolster Libya against Egyptian intrigue. On 21 July the island-wide Operation *Matchbox* swept up suspect 1,200 EOKA and fifty TMT as a pre-emptive measure to de-escalate the descent into civil war. The Turkish Resistance Organization (*Turk Mukavernet Teskilati*: TMT) was formed in 1958 by Rauf Denktash and a Turkish Army officer as a pro-partition buffer defence organization to counter EOKA. By the end of July, fifty-six Greek-Cypriots and fifty-three Turkish-Cypriots had been killed. When there was another incident in which British troops opened fire at Akhyritou on 30 July, Grivas threatened to kill one Briton for every dead Greek-Cypriot and then, declaring that he had lost patience, he ordered his murder squads to kill British soldiers.

On 2 August a member of the reformed Nicosia killer group shot Sergeant Reginald Hammond of the RAOC while he was buying an ice cream for his two-year-old son in Ayios Dhometios market. Passers-by again callously ignored the bewildered child sat beside his dying father. Even though they had become familiar with Greek-Cypriot indifference, the murder angered the troops in a manner not seen so far. A 1 Berkshires patrol later captured the gunman, Andreas Yakoumis, and although he claimed that a confession had been beaten out of him, a psychiatrist assessed him to be a dangerous psychopath; nevertheless, he was acquitted when the presiding judge said there were 'lamentable gaps' in the prosecution case. In July 1960, the film *Exodus* was being filmed in Cyprus and when the well-known photo-journalist Robert Egby snapped several extras and one turned to be Yakoumis wearing a British Army uniform and the picture was published in London, the subsequent uproar brought filming to a halt. When it began again, it was without Yakoumis. The day after Sergeant Hammond was shot, the Famagusta Town group, seeking opportunity targets, shot Lieutenant Colonel Frederick Collier, an Assistant Director, Supply and Transport at HQ Cyprus District, while he was watering his Limassol married quarter garden. The same group had just seriously wounded a senior Special Branch officer. With the death toll and arson rising across Cyprus and the island again the subject of international diplomacy, Grivas suspended attacks on the British and Turkish-Cypriots and an uneasy calm fell across Cyprus, except for those Greek-Cypriots targeted by EOKA as traitors. The TMT reciprocated with a truce. Although Major General Kendrew was convinced that Grivas was reorganizing, Foot also suspended military operations and lifted the curfew on 7 August after sixty days, except in Lysi, Asha and Vatali where 3 Infantry Brigade had detained 300 EOKA suspects in Operation *Swan Lake*.

The escalation in sectarian violence had alarmed NATO, and Secretary-General Paul-Henri Spaak held talks with the Greek and Turkish delegations. Prime Minister Macmillan appealed to Greece and Turkey to help stop the violence but when he proposed that their representation on the Governor's Council be at ambassadorial level, it was rejected by Athens but considered worth discussing by Ankara. Grivas then chipped in that the appointment of a Turkish delegate would inevitably lead to violence, strikes and demonstrations. With little progress on the political front, on 22 August Grivas lifted the truce and announced that the British boycott would be rigorously enforced. Although the guerrillas had been reduced to twenty-two small groups in the west, Shotgun Commandos were active in Nicosia, Famagusta and the central plain and the offensive meant that the grim level of violence and intimidation was unlikely to decline. New types of mines, hand grenades and time pencils had also been developed, much of them designed in the laboratories of the Nicosia Pan Cyprian Gymnasium. The patrols and convoys of 1 RWF ran into twenty-seven ambushes in the Panhandle and although one soldier was killed and seven badly wounded, the Battalion reduced casualties by checking roads for mines, mortars and bombs every day.

In the first week of September, the Army Air Corps was formed from the RAF Observation and Liaison Flights. A 1 Suffolks search of Eylena acting on information received found the taxi used in the murder of RAF Warrant Officer Francis O'Heagan Sloane on his way to Mass in Nicosia. His wife had been wounded in the attack, the second attack on a Service family attending church. The ban on bicycles being used at night had helped to reduce terrorist activity and movement between communities, but in mid-August near Lysi, a Royal Ulster Rifles patrol ambushed four men pushing two bicycles laden with arms and killed three, one them a local commander. On the 13th, an Argyll football team returning from a match in an Army lorry was ambushed on the hilly, twisting road between Polemi and Limni and three soldiers were wounded, Private David Morrison later dying and thus becoming the Argylls' first fatality. Although the ambushers had disappeared, during a cordon-and-search of three villages, two Jocks were stabbed by a known gunman in Kathikas. Next day, a Greek-Cypriot was shot dead when he ignored a challenge at a marked Army roadblock. Two days later, an alert Royal Artillery bombardier in a lorry between Nicosia and Larnaca noted movement in roadside vegetation and, opening fire with his Sten, wounded two EOKA. They later guided a patrol to their hide in which a radio, arms and ammunition were found.

Four days after the Kathikas incident, Mrs Barbara Castle MP, the fiery senior member of the Labour Party, arrived in Cyprus to investigate allegations of military mistreatment and visited the village. In claiming that 128 villagers were being treated for injuries and inferring that the Jocks had been 'permitted and encouraged' by the authorities, she joined the Greek-Cypriot chorus accusing the soldiers of brutality. She later withdrew the word 'encouraged' but stood by the figure of 128 casualties. It was notable that Mrs Castle failed to obtain a balanced view by visiting the Battalion. The incident took place a week before the annual Labour conference and an imminent General Election in UK, and when she returned to London, Mrs Castle found herself isolated by Hugh Gaitskell, Leader of the Opposition, who expressed his appreciation of the open-minded behaviour of the troops under 'almost intolerable provocation'. When the Mayor of Kyrenia complained about the 'brutality' of the troops, he was reprimanded by Foot for not offering condolences to the family of Private Morrison, reminded that more than 100 Servicemen had been killed during the Emergency and told that, 'I am not surprised some damage was done in the searches. It is impossible to search for arms in cleverly concealed hides without doing damage, but I am satisfied from the report of the special investigation team that although there was extensive damage, injuries were minor.' An Office of Human Rights delegation visited the villages, but the brutality claims turned out to be a charade when several 'injured' villagers asked to remove the bandages revealed no injuries. Another resident was caught wrecking his own house.

On 26 September a mine exploded behind the Humber staff car of Major General Kendrew on his way to Government House. The escorting Royal Military Police Land Rover took the full force of the explosion and overturned, fatally wounding Lance Corporal William Bell. The assassination attempt failed because the EOKA lookout was late in identifying the Humber in the early morning rush hour. October began with EOKA again failing to conduct its operations within the customs and traditions of warfare by ambushing yet another medic, this time a marked RAF ambulance en route to RAF Akrotiri from Nicosia.

In many respects, Friday 3 October 1958 in Famagusta was the day when the troops reached the limit of their patience. Tension in the town had been increasing over several days after Service dependants were jostled and several empty prams set on fire. Although under instructions since April 1955 to be impartial, by now some troops regarded all the Greek-Cypriots as opponents; it was, after all, their community that supported EOKA and had killed, maimed and rioted. At least one soldier, a Royal Signals corporal, was convicted at a court martial for inciting violence against Greek-Cypriots.

Shortly before mid-afternoon, a Royal Military Police patrol commanded by Second Lieutenant Rosier was driving through the centre of Famagusta when they noted that shopkeepers and traders were shutting their shops and the street was emptying of pedestrians; yet Friday was usually a busy shopping day. Patrols regarded such activity with suspicion that something had happened or was about to happen. Sure enough, when the Land Rover turned into the largely deserted Hermes Street, the military police saw an hysterical English girl aged about eighteen years kneeling over two women lying on the pavement beside a car. She said that both women had been shot and one of them was her mother, Mrs Catherine Cutliffe, and the other was her mother's friend, Mrs Robinson. While Rosier reported the shooting, his patrol began searching for the killers.

Catherine Cutliffe, aged thirty-eight, was the mother of five children and married to a sergeant serving with 145 (Maiwand) Battery, 29 Field Regiment stationed at Karaolos Camp on the outskirts of Famagusta. Mrs Cutliffe met her friend, Mrs Elfriede Robinson, who was the German wife of another 29 Field Regiment sergeant, for lunch and then they went into Famagusta where they met Margaret, Mrs Cutliffe's daughter who was was engaged to another 29 Field Regiment sergeant. The trio bought some electrical goods and then went to a dressmaker to buy the wedding dress for Margaret. As the women left the shop, Mrs Cutliffe mentioned that the atmosphere seemed strange because the shops were closing, men were hanging around street corners and there were no women. Very soon after leaving the dressmaker, Margaret heard several bangs behind her and spun around to see her mother lying on the pavement and Mrs Robinson crumpling to the ground. Looking up, a young fair-headed Greek-Cypriot armed with a .45 Colt semi automatic fired a shot at her but missed. He and another gunman then fled. Mrs Cutliffe had been hit twice in the back by the gunman who then shot her twice more, killing her. Mrs Robinson was badly wounded by a gunman using a .38 Webley and shot again as she lay on the pavement.

Knowing there had been other incidents involving Service families, the young National Servicemen had had enough of 'Firmness with courtesy', and in less than two hours, 1,000 soldiers from 29 Field Regiment RA and 1 Royal Ulster Rifles had erected about forty checkpoints in and around Famagusta and were controlling people leaving and entering the town. During a rigorous search of businesses, shops and houses in the immediate area of the attack, Sergeant James Lane of the Ulsters was accidentally shot. *The Times* correspondent noted that the soldiers were 'in the grip of sheer cold rage. No pretence was made that kid-glove methods were used.' One shopkeeper was offered substantial compensation by Lieutenant Colonel Thomas Wheeler, the Ulster's Commanding Officer, to compensate for damage to his shop. When the report of the attack reached Government House, Sir Hugh Foot and Major General Kendrew predicted there might be trouble, but by the time they arrived in Famagusta by helicopter, at about 5 pm, to reinforce the principle that there must be no retaliation, about 600 Greek-Cypriots aged between fourteen and twenty-six years had been rounded up in a manner the *Cyprian Chronicle* (as cited in *Mayhem in the Med*) described 'less than civil', packed into lorries and driven to one of four screening centres, including a quarry at Karaolos Camp nicknamed The Snake Pit. Three people died, including a father of six and a boy aged twelve years. More than 250 required medical treatment and later filed claims of mistreatment. The *Daily Telegraph* correspondent reported, 'I was shocked when I saw rows of bloody and bandaged Greek-Cypriots lying on floors in Famagusta hospitals.' A Royal Military Police captain was accused of inflicting a head injury on one of the casualties. Inevitably, the inquiry into the reaction heavily criticized the soldiers and the degree of force as unjustified. The immediate relatives of two of the dead received compensation. Sergeant Cutliffe and his five motherless children returned to England within the week.

The denial by EOKA that it was involved in the murder of Mrs Cutliffe was ridiculed, and although the killers were never formally identified, two hardliners who continued their activities into the 1970s were suspected of the attack. The Greek Government disgraced itself by first claiming that the murder was carried out by the security forces to discredit EOKA and when this was rejected, claimed that the murderer was a rejected lover. Although Greek-Cypriot leaders condemned the murder and the Mayor of Nicosia offered a £5,000 reward, the attack damaged the credibility of the Greek-Cypriot cause throughout the world, in particular in West Germany. Sir Hugh Foot accused Archbishop Makarios of deceiving the Greek community in Cyprus into violence. HQ 51 Infantry Brigade District concluded that the attack was premeditated and probably in retaliation for the death of a Greek-Cypriot mother of six when a church was burnt by Turkish-Cypriots on 18 September, and that it was an attempt to goad the Army. Grivas was unrepentant, and yet another military ambulance was ambushed four days later, this time at Zyyi, killing Corporal Peters of 1 RWF and wounding two other soldiers.

When an informer reported that Colonel Grivas had sent five experienced EOKA led by Xanthos Samaras to train local activists near Liopetri, the 1 RUR and Minden Battery, 20 Field Regiment were tasked to root them out. By 3 am on 3 October, the same day as the murder of Mrs Cutliffe, the troops had surrounded Liopetri after a three-mile approach march. B Company were detaining all males aged between fourteen and sixteen years in a barbed wire cage at the school when a patrol intercepted a van leaving the village and exchanged fire with several gunmen. The driver was arrested as he tried to breach the cordon, but his colleagues disappeared into the darkness of the village. A dawn search of the van revealed a loaded M3 submachine gun magazine and an identity card in the name of Elias Samaras, a known local EOKA leader and brother to Xanthos. Special Branch had confirmed the arrested van driver to be Elias and when he was sent to Famagusta Police Station, shocked after being arrested in a gun battle, facing the death penalty and untrained in resisting interrogation, he did what most terrorists do, and provided information that led to extensive searches in Liopetri that lasted all day. He also agreed to guide troops to the EOKA hideout.

By mid-afternoon, Samaras had led the Ulsters to two hides three miles south-west of Liopetri, one in a deep shaft near a water tank and the other in a coffee shop opposite the cemetery in which he indicated a cache of boxes containing four improvised devices. Three more were found under the floor. During the night, he led troops to a chaff house in which he claimed three EOKA had been hiding since the previous morning. Early next day, A Company and Minden Battery surrounded the house with a cordon. When Second Lieutenant Kenneth Boyd's B Company platoon were clearing the chaff from the barn, they came under heavy fire from inside and Riflemen Bolger was wounded, Boyd withdrew his platoon under suppressive fire poured through its doorway. Using his Intelligence Corps linguist, Corporal Fleet of the Intelligence Corps and attached to the Battalion Intelligence Section, he invited the gunmen to surrender, in vain. After about half an hour, an alert rifleman wounded a terrorist attempting to leave the barn. Two platoon commanders then threw Mills 36 grenades into the barn which set the hay on fire. After Captain Lucy had suggested using a 3.5-inch Rocket Launcher, one sent from Famagusta was used to fire eleven projectiles, but still the guerrillas resisted. Lieutenant Boyd then charged the barn with sixteen men and, in spite of heavy fire, he and four men gained a foothold on the verandah of the adjacent house, but at the cost of three wounded. A terrorist then dashed into the open firing a Sten, wounding Boyd in the leg and shooting Rifleman Kinsella fatally in the head. In an act for which he would receive the Military Medal, Corporal Paddy Shaughnessy, who had run out of ammunition, ran into the open, threw a brick at the gunman and snatched his weapon just as Rifleman Moore shot him. Lieutenant Gallowey took over from the wounded Boyd, who had been dragged into cover. With two surviving EOKA now known to be in the barn. Lieutenant Colonel Thomas Wheeler, the Commanding Officer, the dog handler Lance Corporal Gill and Lance Corporal Dillan from the MT Section, climbed onto the barn roof, bore a hole through the tiles and ignited petrol poured through the hole with a match, setting the hay and wood inside alight. Forced into the open by the flames, the last two terrorists were shot – another EOKA cell destroyed. One was Christos Samaras, brother to Elias. Branded a traitor, Samaras agreed to be sent to England, but he was overcome by guilt and returned to Cyprus where he appealed to the mercy of Colonel Grivas and claimed that he had been tortured by the security forces. The reality was that they had no need to do so and his plea was pointless. Grivas had him executed.

When two airmen were killed and seven Servicemen wounded by a bomb hidden by a Greek-Cypriot employee in a jukebox at the RAF Nicosia NAAFI Club on 9 October, two days later, NAAFI Services, Cyprus dismissed its 3,000 Greek-Cypriot employees as security risks and then circulated advertisements in Great Britain to replace them. A total of 7,500 applications were received and the first batch departed from Blackbushe Airport within the week.

CHAPTER TWELVE

# The Defeat of EOKA
(November 1958 to March 1959)

On 14 October, Major General Kenneth Darling took over from Joe Kendrew as Director of Operations and introduced a refreshed determination to defeat EOKA. Commissioned into the Royal Fusiliers in 1929, he had commanded 11 (TA) Battalion during the Second World War before joining 12 Para as its second-in-command. Dropped into Normandy on D-Day, he was wounded and when the commanding officer was later killed he led the Battalion in the tough fighting en route to the Rhine crossing. In 1946, he commanded 5 Parachute Brigade in Java and used disarmed Japanese soldiers to control a nationalist uprising. In 1950 he had commanded 16 Parachute Brigade and as Chief of Staff, HQ II Corps, had been part of the planning team for Operation *Musketeer*.

By 1958, MI6 was taking much greater interest in Cyprus. Sir Hugh Foot was popular with MI5 and MI6 because he was liberal-minded. Among the new arrivals at HQ Middle East Land Forces was Geoffrey McDermott, the Foreign Office adviser to MI6. While acknowledging Kendrew to be a brave man, he accused him, and by implication Field Marshal Harding, of not adapting to terrorism and guerrilla warfare, suggesting that his men had presented 'a broad and vulnerable backside' for EOKA to pepper 'without first procuring adequate intelligence on where they should winkle out the insurgents.' While entitled to his opinion, he seems to have disregarded the ineffectiveness of the Cyprus Police before 1955, the untrustworthiness of some Greek-Cypriot officers and that the British Government had thrown the Armed Forces into a political morass without adequate intelligence. He also ignored the fact that both organizations had failed to identify the nationalist threat posed by EOKA in time because they were focused on the communist threat. Both organizations are rarely, if ever, presented with such a dilemma and when they are, military or police support is usually available. However, there was one skill that MI6 brought – technical intelligence gathering. Without the active participation of

Colonel Grivas there could no negotiation and so MI6 mounted Operation *Sunshine* to locate and isolate him.

In suggesting that the Army did not know where to search for terrorists, McDermott ignores that Operations *Turkey Trot* and *Fox Hunter* had both been launched literally within weeks of the Emergency being declared against a largely full strength EOKA, particularly in the Troodos Mountains, and had laid an intelligence platform for the future. The year 1956 had been a bad one, with an estimated sixty Servicemen killed in action, eighteen of them during the period of the Suez landings; however, by 1957 the fatalities had dropped to six but they rose to twenty-seven in 1958 with nine in October when EOKA was on the ropes. The reality was that Kendrew had done a good job and it was his use of 3 Infantry Brigade that had largely destroyed EOKA. A popular leader, he left Cyprus to become Governor of Australia for several years.

With 35,000 men under his command, 10,000 more than in Northern Ireland at the height of the troubles in 1972, and the full support of the British Government, Darling was determined to intimidate the terrorists and their sympathizers and disrupt their life with mass arrests and sudden curfews. A week after taking command, while watching an operation in the Kythrea area during which several suspect EOKA were captured, he remarked to correspondents that, 'The only EOKA terrorists I am interested in are dead ones.' Less interested in the few surviving EOKA cells, Darling wanted their leaders caught and introduced an intelligence strategy of constant surveillance that made it difficult for anything to happen without it being reported. He devised an elaborate system to control militant Greek-Cypriot youths by permitting them to attend schools, colleges and workplaces under curfew and then confining them to their homes when British civilians were shopping and circulating, all under curfew regulations. Curfew-breakers were reported by troops manning observation posts on roofs and balconies overlooking narrow streets and risked arrest. The posts also covered patrols. When A Company, the Argylls used the system in Paphos it resulted in Lieutenant Campbell's platoon arresting two suspects on a motorcycle at a snap checkpoint in possession of bomb components and eighteen sticks of dynamite concealed in a sack. Major Mitchell developed the tactic when he famously led the Battalion into the Crater district of Aden.

As political negotiations stumbled toward a solution largely without his contribution, Grivas escalated the violence. During the next six weeks, more damage was done than in any period since November 1956. Forty-five people were killed, including ten soldiers, and about 370 people injured. Mines and ambushes continued to plague convoys. In the Troodos Mountains, a Royal Horse Guards trooper was killed and an officer was severely wounded when an explosion blew their Ferret into a ravine. A Royal Marine from 45 Commando was killed and several others wounded when their convoy was ambushed, but during their counter-attack they killed a terrorist and later captured three others. In early November, an officer, who was the son of a Royal Marines general, died when a bomb exploded near a patrol in Ledra Street. In the Panhandle, 93 Battery, which was part of 25 Field Regiment RA and was attached to the Royal Welch Fusiliers, was camped about two miles from Yialousa Police Station on the edge of Akrades Forest. EOKA observers had noted that the Army sentries at the Police Station often withdrew into the building from about 3 am until dawn and saw an opportunity to attack it. At about 3 am on 23 October, Andreas Modestos, aged fifteen years, dragged two mines on a small trolley through a narrow storm drain that ran underneath the vehicle compound, but when he had to manhandle them over some pipes, one was damaged. Retracing his subterranean crawl with the damaged mine, the next morning he crawled back with the repaired mine and wriggled out dragging a cable that was attached to a detonator. During the early afternoon of 25 October, when two lorries full of gunners arrived at the Police Station on their way for a swim at a nearby beach, EOKA detonated the two mines, killing a member of the Royal Army Pay Corps and wounding eighteen gunners, three critically.

At the end of the month, Brian Preece, aged seventeen and the son of RASC sergeant, was reported by his employers to have failed to arrive for work at the Golden Sands Leave Camp at Famagusta. The camp was to be closed down next day. When a patrol retracing his route from his married quarter found his body in an orange grove, an investigation concluded that he had been murdered by gunmen using a car. Preece, shot in the body and head, had staggered into the grove where he died. Troops quickly disrupted normal life with snap searches and the detention of young men and women for screening. Following the murders of three British civilians, Darling encouraged the issue of revolvers to civilians and off-duty soldiers. Predictably, Athens described the soldiers as 'wild cannibals' and elevated Hitler to 'a saint' in comparison to Darling. Darling responded by jamming Radio Athens. The murders of a Church of Scotland mobile canteen work and an expatriate aged seventy-one years in Nicosia in the first week of November and the continued reluctance of expatriates and Service dependants to be intimidated by EOKA led to Sir Hugh Foot and senior Army officers discussing precautions to lessen the risk. One problem was the number of British expatriates living in the Old City, an area that had mostly been out of bounds to off-duty Service personnel and their families, refusing to be bullied by EOKA. When, at a Nicosia District Security Committee meeting a few days after two bank employees were murdered in Nicosia in early November, 400 British residents were warned by officials that, if they did not already know it, they were in the front line of terrorism and Major General Darling was offering to supply them with small arms for personal protection; EOKA reacted with a communiqué that it regarded anyone with a weapon to be a legitimate target, a largely pointless response because EOKA had been murdering unarmed people since 1955. Claims by Grivas that EOKA only shot British Servicemen and Greek-Cypriot traitors had a hollow ring. Very few expatriates took up the offer of weapons.

At the end of the month, after three years at Dhekelia and without losing anyone killed in action, 1 Middlesex handed the Larnaca sector to the Argylls. Then 1st Battalion, The Black Watch (1 Black Watch) arrived in December and took over the Limni area and in Episkopi, the newly amalgamated 1st Battalion, The Devonshire and Dorsetshire Regiment (1 Devon and Dorsets) relieved 39 Heavy Regiment RA. At the start of November, 3 Infantry Brigade began another operation with 1 Berkshires and 1 Wiltshires tasked to destroy the surviving EOKA groups in an area that ranged along the western and central Pentadactylos Mountains. Among about thirty EOKA captured were seven Cyprus police officers. By the 16th, when intelligence was suggesting that Kyriakos Matsis, the Kyrenia District commander, was in Kato Dhikomo, three days later the Wiltshires surrounded the village, imposed a curfew and searched homes, businesses, barns and outhouses for him. During the morning, information emerged that he had arrived the previous day and was now trapped in the basement of a four-room house owned by Kyriakos Diakos on the edge of the village. Soldiers tapped the tiled floors with bayonets until one, prodding the floor of a ground floor bedroom at the back, detected a space. When an intelligence officer instructed an interpreter to invite anyone inside to surrender, Matsis replied, 'There are two men down here with me. I'm sending them up first, unarmed. Don't shoot!' Soon after troops had withdrawn from the bedroom, a trapdoor was pushed open and Special Branch arrested the two low-level EOKA who emerged. When the interpreter invited Matsis to surrender and he answered, 'I'll come out shooting', a smoke grenade was lobbed into the cellar and a warning given that the next grenade would be high explosive. When he again threatened to come out firing, a second grenade was lobbed into the cellar followed by a third to detonate any explosives. An autopsy later concluded that he had committed suicide. The house later became a place of pilgrimage. Major General Darling acknowledged that the Battalion had been 'first class under conditions requiring great patience and endurance. It is a terrific show and only the beginning.' Eight days later, Savvas Rotsides, a former storeman at the Mitsero Mines, was shot dead when troops ambushed a spring used by EOKA near Kyperounda. A second guerrilla escaped. Meanwhile, the Royal Horse Guards, 1 Grenadier Guards, 1 DLI and Argylls carried out a nine-day operation in Paphos that yielded ninety EOKA, including several captured when a hideout at Emba was destroyed. Nineteen weapons and 1,500 rounds of ammunition were seized.

The Joint Helicopter Unit arrived with Westland Whirlwinds and Chipmunks from 114 Squadron in Cyprus to develop tactics and procedures to support operations. During the first week of December, the Queen's Own Royal West Kents arrested about ninety EOKA suspects in a major operation in the Kyrenia area, most of whom were again willing to share information with their interrogators. The next week, the Battalion joined the 3 Infantry Brigade Operation *Dove Tail* and searched Akanthou, while 3rd Grenadier Guards searched Lefkoniko. With the international situation in the Middle East calmer, the sectarian tension gradually subsiding and Grivas and EOKA driven on to the defensive, 1 Guards Brigade and 26 Field Regiment returned to Great Britain, leaving Darling with eleven battalions, one commando and three gunner regiments and the Royal Horse Guards providing armoured patrols. The strike force remained 3 Infantry Brigade, with 1 Para forming its third battalion.

The breakthrough to resolving the Emergency came on 18 December when NATO Secretary-General Spaak and the Foreign Ministers of Britain, Greece and Turkey met in Paris, where Foreign Secretary Selwyn Lloyd agreed that Cyprus should have independence in exchange for ground around Akrotiri and Episkopi in the east and Dhekelia in the west to be converted into British bases. Athens, happy to see an agreeable solution, applied pressure on Colonel Grivas to the extent that on 24 December he announced EOKA would cease operations provided that the security forces reciprocated – but this was not before SAC Alan Scaife and LAC Thomas Boaden were killed when their fuel tanker ran over a mine near Galinoporni in north-east Cyprus. Some doubted that it had been laid before Grivas declared his ceasefire, while others believed that a rogue EOKA group had ignored Grivas' instruction; nevertheless it was of some significance that Deacon Anthimos expressed his regret at their deaths. Grivas wriggled, first claiming that the attack was in retaliation for the ambush of Savvas Rotsides and then that his courier system had been slow to warn EOKA in the area that a truce was in force. Arguably, the two airmen were the last to be killed by enemy action during the Emergency. The news was received by the troops with stoicism because Grivas was still at large.

To show commitment to a solution, Foot released 350 Cypriots from detention and commuted eight death sentences to life imprisonment. In order to control events and in the expectation that he would be invited to the negotiations, in early February 1959, Grivas, accompanied by Elli Christodoulides and Maroulli Panayides and his personal assistant, Georghiades, were spirited in a van owned by Socrates Eliades to a field outside Limassol, where they transferred to a lorry and were guided by Kikkis Kyriakides, the wife of Deacon Anthimos, to a newly prepared bunker in a house in Nicosia. In the event, EOKA was not represented at the negotiations because it did not own a democratic mandate. By 11 February, London, Athens and Turkey had agreed a 'way forward' for Cypriot independence, with Great Britain insisting on safeguarding the rights of all communities and Turkey and Greece agreeing to intervene if attempts were made to alter the agreed state of affairs. Until independence, Cyprus would be governed by a Transition Council. Since the constitution was to follow the ethnic composition of Cyprus, the President was to be Greek-Cypriot, the Vice-President a Turkish-Cypriot with a veto, and they would be supported by a civil service with a ratio of 70:30 in favour of the Greek-Cypriots. The Supreme Court was to appoint an equal number of judges and there was to be an independent judge of a nationality other than Greek, Turkish or British. The Cyprus Armed Forces would be established at about 2,600 men, divided 60:40 in favour of the Greek-Cypriots, supported by Greek and Turkish Army military contingents to safeguard the security of the two communities. The Treaty of Establishment gave Britain two bases – the Western Sovereign Base Area (WSBA) at Akrotiri/Episkopi/Paramali and Eastern Sovereign Base Area (ESBA) at Dhekelia/Pergamos/Nikolaos Xylophagou – and several training areas and ranges. Eight days later, on 19 February in London, Archbishop Makarios and Dr Kutchuk signed the Zurich Agreement. A week later, Greek Army officers returned to the regional NATO HQ at Izmir and brought added stability to the region.

Meanwhile, the task of locating Grivas had acquired some urgency because he needed to be neutralized in case he retaliated against the Agreement. MI6 then had a breakthrough when a device planted in a consignment of radios purchased for EOKA by a Greek-Cypriot arms dealer in Egypt, in their pay, led to the triangulation of his location. The combination of an intercept device planted on telephone lines passing over a telegraph pole outside the Archbishop's Palace and surveillance of key EOKA supporters narrowed the location of his hideout. When Major General Darling was informed that Grivas had probably been found, he was delighted but, mindful that political agreement was so close, rejected arresting him pending authority from London. Prime Minister Macmillan was told as he was about to host a dinner with President Karamanlis of Greece at Downing Street and when he casually asked the Greek Foreign Minister Averoff what action would Athens take if Grivas was arrested and was told that the Greek delegation would leave London immediately as anti-British feeling in Greece would spread quickly, Macmillan replied that it was sad that relations between Greece and Great Britain should have reached such a low ebb. He consequently instructed that Grivas 'should stew in his own juice'.

Grivas firmly believed that knowledge of his hideout was restricted to those who needed to know, until on 19 February, the day the Zurich Agreement was signed, he was shocked to be advised by the Greek Consul that the British most probably knew where he was located and that unless he accepted the Agreement, he would be arrested. For Grivas, the news was devastating and over the next three weeks he lived in constant fear of arrest. Instead, Detective Sergeants Wilson and Dawson, from the Special Branch element of the UK Police Unit, interviewed Leonidas Markides, a businessman with EOKA links, at his house, ostensibly seeking information on Socrates Eliades. When one of the detectives opened a briefcase and some documents fell on to the floor, he hurriedly collected them. After they had departed, Markides chanced on two highly classified memos apparently not collected by the two officers, one suggesting that the surveillance on Deacon Anthimos had led to Grivas. Grivas, physically tired after two years of isolation and in poor health from lack of exercise and fresh air and an indifferent diet, still did not appreciate that EOKA was politically isolated and believed that the memos were a trap to force him to accept the Agreement or be arrested.

On 2 March Archbishop Makarios returned to Cyprus to a tumultuous welcome at Nicosia Airport. EOKA leaders were aggrieved because they were not invited. Next day, Makarios met Sir Hugh Foot and agreed that Grivas should be deported and not permitted to make any statements in Cyprus. His departure would also be low-key. Major General Darling, determined that the British would not be humiliated, instructed Lieutenant Colonel Bill Langton-Gore, a 6ft 5ins Coldstream Guards officer then serving as the senior Operations Officer at his HQ, to supervise the deportation. Langton-Gore had served in North Africa and was seriously wounded after landing with the 3rd Battalion at Salerno in Italy. Surgeons had no alternative but amputate his shattered right arm without anaesthetic because supplies had run out. His sensible judgment and wit, including answering the telephone with 'Hello. One-Arm here', and, crucially, his inability to salute became critical in preserving military pride. Also to be deported to Greece until they had served their sentences were EOKA prisoners convicted of serious terrorism and thirty-one prisoners serving sentences in British jails. Meanwhile, Grivas was resisting just about every suggestion to cease hostilities and considered rejecting the Agreement, thereby forcing civil war between EOKA and the British and Makarios, until on 9 March at a meeting with Makarios he agreed to be deported under safe conduct without ceremony. Grivas then negotiated with the Greek Consulate a triumphal return to Greece. Next day, the deportation was announced and instructions issued to EOKA from Grivas that weapons were to be handed in to police stations. British intelligence officers suspected that hardcore EOKA would continue the fight for *enosis* using the fanatical Bishop Kyriakides of Kyrenia as their figurehead until he was persuaded by Makarios that the cause was lost and he should retire from politics. The rapidity of the ceasefire led to disturbances, the most serious being a clash between Greek-Cypriot youths and about fifty off-duty Royal Ulster Rifles in Famagusta. Still fearing arrest, Grivas met his surviving EOKA leaders in two sessions at the houses of Socrates Eliades and Mr Gabrielides, a successful businessman. Most had never seen Grivas and yet, for three years, they had responded to orders from this diminutive man approaching retirement on the receipt of letters delivered through a chain of couriers signed by 'Digenes'. He wondered, as he prepared to leave for Athens, how they would address the fate of Cyprus.

On 13 March HQ Cyprus District began withdrawing units, with 25 Field Regiment, 188 Search Light and Radar Battery, the Suffolks and 1st Battalion, the Green Jackets flying back to England. This Battalion had been formed from 1 Ox and Bucks in 1958. In Malta 40 Commando rejoined 3 Commando Brigade. Next day, in Operation *Handover*, EOKA began handing in about 650 guns, 17,000 rounds of ammunition and 2,000lbs of explosive at eight collection points, the figures equalling the estimates calculated by the Director of Operations of EOKA stocks. The explosive was destroyed by 1 Ammunition Disposal Unit. Three days later, Grivas visited the Greek Consulate to finalize his deportation.

During the early morning of 17 March, Colonel Grivas, dressed in his beret, breeches and with a holstered pistol, was driven by the Greek Consul to the house of a former athlete with no political affiliations in Severis Street in the Strovolos suburb and was greeted in the parlour by Makarios, several senior EOKA and Charles Foley of the *Times of Cyprus*.

Escorted by a Greek Police captain, the Greek Consul and the Bishop of Kitium, he was then driven in a blue Mercedes to Nicosia Airport in a small convoy along streets and roads lined by small crowds and soldiers, with their backs to him, although no doubt some tried to sneak a peek. At the terminal, he was shown to a room where he chatted with Makarios and Andreas Azinas. Two Royal Hellenic Air Force C-47 Dakotas then landed and several senior Greek Army officers known to Grivas in his X Group days welcomed him. After the baggage was loaded and departure formalities concluded, at about 11 am, with Gore-Langton towering a foot above him and unable to salute him, as Grivas's rank demanded, Grivas boarded one of the Dakotas with Antonis Georghiades, Deacon Anthimos and Bishop Kyriakides of Kyrenia. The aircraft then took off and was escorted from Cypriot airspace by two RAF fighters. The Cyprus Emergency was over, 1,590 days after Grivas had landed.

As the two Dakotas passed over Rhodes, Grivas spoke to several EOKA released from British prisons. At about 2.30 pm, the aircraft landed at Hellenikon Airport and during the eight mile drive into the centre of Athens, Grivas was mobbed by large crowds. He then returned to his little flat in Thyssion and his long-suffering wife, Kiki. A dentist treated his badly decayed teeth, otherwise he was good condition, if thin. At an audience with King Paul I, he was promoted to lieutenant-general, awarded a pension and several Orders and was given the freedom of Athens. Although something of an embarassment to the Greek Government, Grivas took advantage of his fame and moved to a villa lent to him on the outskirts of Athens where he was provided with cars and a bodyguard of police and Greek security officials until he was quietly sidelined by the Greek Government, his forays into politics stonewalled. With the help of several EOKA, including Nicos Sampson, he began writing his autobiography.

In Cyprus, Sir Hugh Foot, Archbishop Makarios, Dr Fazil Kutchuk and Rauf Denktash, representing the Turkish-Cypriots, held the first meeting of the Transitional Council. Next day, several hundred uniformed EOKA were cheered by a huge crowd as they marched along Ledra Street to a special mass in Phaneromeni Church. Not all had been active.

## CHAPTER THIRTEEN

# Independence
## (1959 to 1974)

As a sense of pre-1955 normality returned to Cyprus, the consequences of the future of the island began to sink in. The Cyprus Government was expected to pay for the Emergency unless London could be persuaded to contribute; in the meantime, the Cypriots would have to bridge the gap. The departure of British troops and their families led to unemployment as barracks, tented camps and fortified outposts outside police stations and the mines were dismantled. A recession bit as fuel prices rose and harvest prices and revenue crashed. Some Cypriots emigrated, mostly to Great Britain and Australia. The island had yet to be discovered as a mass tourist destination.

Within days of the treaty being signed, the 950 men of the Hellenic Forces Regiment in Cyprus arrived, as did the 700 soldiers of the Turkish National Contingent, and they moved into separate camps about a mile north of Nicosia Airport. The Greeks were often known as ELDYK (Elleniki Dynami Kyprou) or sometimes the 1st Greek Battalion.The Turkish-Cypriots vetoed amalgamation into the joint Special Mixed Staff, Cyprus Headquarters and consequently both units reported to their national GHQs.

The Greek-Cypriot drive for *enosis* had irreversibly damaged community relationships with the Turkish-Cypriots, and while troops provided medical, agricultural and construction aid to ease their reconciliation, in the towns and villages that had supported EOKA patrols often encountered hostility. During the summer, there were several outbreaks of violence, including an alleged police informer burnt to death and off-duty British servicemen attacked, in one instance by Greek-Cypriot youths seeking small arms. A bomb exploded under a culvert between Lefka and Pedhoulas. Some former EOKA formed the United Democratic Party (EDMA) and although they professed support for Makarios, their allegiance was to Grivas, because it was he who had fought for *enosis* whereas the Archbishop had betrayed the cause.

Nevertheless, he was shrewd enough to invite several EOKA into his cabinet, including Polycarpos Georgadjis, whom he appointed to be responsible for employment and labour affairs. Several *enosis* hardliners formed the Cyprus Enosis Front (KEM), however the Cyprus Police were more adept than in 1955 and they effectively nullified the threat with arrests.

The Turkish-Cypriots seemed largely tranquil until on 18 October 1959 a Royal Navy boarding party from the minesweeper HMS *Burmaston* boarded the Turkish MV *Deniz* off Cape Plakotti and found its holds full of weapons and ammunitions destined for the TMT. As the crew then opened the seacocks and she began to sink, the boarding party grabbed two cases of ammunition as evidence and returned to the minesweeper. Two days later, the three crew were remanded in custody charged with importing ammunition without a valid permit. The seizure sparked community sectarian tension, particularly when reports emerged that 5,000 TMT were in Turkey for military training; however, three weeks later charges against the Turkish seamen were dropped because the evidence was sitting on the seabed.

Social and political instability led to concerns that Independence Day planned for 19 February 1960 might be delayed; indeed, such was the sectarian tension that some believed that if the British Army left Cyprus, there would be civil war. Talks between Makarios and Dr Kutchuk collapsed, however Athens and Ankara insisted they must negotiate and it was thus on 16 August that Cyprus was declared to be a Republic under the Treaty of Guarantee. The Honour Guard for the lowering of the Union Jack was provided by 1 Black Watch. It was now up to the Cyprus Government to govern, defend and police the island.

In spite of their differences, the Greek- and Turkish-Cypriots were proud of their respective origins and believed that they were better educated and less conservative that their mainlander cousins; however, as the colonialism that had bound the two communities into a single nation disappeared the underlying fractures that had emerged during the Emergency deepened. The communities retreated into separate and polarized cultural and social traditions and secularization fostered nationalism, with the Turkish-Cypriots focusing on the nationalist principles of the father of modern Turkey, Kemal Ataturk. The Greek-Cypriots feared that the separate Turkish-Cypriot municipalities agreed in 1960 would result in *takism* (Turkish-Cypriot partition). Some suspected that the minority had been assigned a larger share of governmental posts than the size of their population warranted and believed it would give their delegates opportunities to make government difficult.

By 1963, RAF Akrotiri was an important airport until the flying ban over Israel and her Arab neighbours quickly reduced the value of Cyprus as a military base. HQ Middle East Command was then split into two with HQ Middle East Command covering East Africa and the Persian Gulf based in Aden while Eastern Mediterranean operations were transferred to the new HQ Near East Command at Episkopi. Defence cuts and commitments in Aden and Borneo saw the one brigade still in Cyprus, 3 Infantry Brigade, providing battalions to defend the Sovereign Base Areas. Troops from England frequently used the training areas and ranges.

In November, tensions between the two communities began to escalate, in particular frequent vetoing on legislation and taxation. When Makarios forced the resignation of the independent West German judge and then informed Kutchuk that the President and Vice-President would lose their vetoes, that the separate municipalities would be abandoned and the Civil Service adjusted to reflect population ratios of 82:18 in favour of the Greek-Cypriots, thereby giving them more power, he essentially undermined the Treaty of Guarantee. While the Greek-Cypriots saw the proposals as necessary to prevent Turkish-Cypriots frustrating government, the Turkish-Cypriots saw them as a ploy to reduce their status as the minority and the first step towards *enosis*. Behind the proposals lurked the hardline Polycarpos Georghadjis, now Minister of the Interior with responsibility for law and order and the Cyprus Police. Earlier in the year, when he had said that 'There was no place in Cyprus for anyone who was not Greek', this was backed up by Makarios suggesting that until the Turkish community was expelled, the duty of EOKA was incomplete. For several months, Georghadjis and several hardline EOKA, such as Nicos Sampson, had been developing Plan Akritas to mobilize a secret army of mainly EOKA hardliners to rid Cyprus of undesirable elements and, in the event of Turkish intervention, to defeat it with a knock-out blow. By 'undesirable', was meant Turkish-Cypriots. Makarios rejected the concept. When he then began to expose the NATO Southern Flank by dallying with Eastern Bloc countries keen to invest in and trade with Cyprus and Communist intelligence services were also keen to establish a base in the Eastern Mediterranean, Washington and London discreetly encouraged Turkey to develop plans to land 10,000 troops and take over a bubble from Kyrenia to Lefka and south to the northern suburbs of Nicosia in order to prevent the Eastern Bloc gaining a foothold in Cyprus.

The simmering sectarian tensions burst into violence in December 1963 when several Greek-Cypriot 'special constables' investigating a quarrel in a Turkish-Cypriot quarter in Nicosia clashed with a crowd, leaving one man dead and a woman injured. And then early on 21st, a Turkish-Cypriot couple driving between Kyrenia and Nicosia were stopped at a roadblock by several Greek-Cypriots claiming to be police officers conducting searches for illegal weapons. A brief burst of automatic fire killed the driver and fatally wounded his pregnant passenger, but she was able to tell Turkish-Cypriots who came to her assistance what had happened. Escalating sectarian protests in Nicosia gave Georghadjis the opportunity to activate Plan Akritas and he instructed that Turkish-Cypriot police officers should be disarmed, on the pretext of defying Cypriot legislation, and that Turkish-Cypriot civil servants be dismissed from their posts. His close ally, Nicos Sampson, then used Radio Cyprus to encourage the Greek-Cypriots to storm the Turkish-Cypriot enclaves; however, the Turkish-Cypriots had secretly prepared for such an eventuality and up went the barricades. On Christmas Day, Greek soldiers from ELDYK joined Sampson and his mob of EOKA attacking the Turkish-Cypriots in the mixed suburb of Omorphita. Confrontations spread to Famagusta, Larnaca, Limassol and Paphos, eventually peaking when about 150 Turkish-Cypriots were taken hostage at Kumsal and the wife of a Turkish National Contingent Army major, another woman and three children were butchered, the children being left in a bloodstained bath. In three days of clashes in Nicosia, seventeen Turkish-Cypriots and eleven Greek-Cypriots were killed and about 700 taken hostage. With Cyprus slipping into civil war, for the first time Turkey placed its navy on standby, sent jets to buzz Nicosia at low level and ordered its contingent in Cyprus to take up strategic positions around Geunyeli and Ortakoy and dominate the road from Kyrenia to Nicosia.

Realizing that he could not rely on the impartiality of the Cyprus Army, Makarios sought British military muscle to restore order. Such were the concerns that the British Cabinet abandoned their Christmas Day lunches to hold an emergency meeting at which it was agreed that Cyprus District and the Cyprus Army would form a Truce Force to be commanded by Major General Peter Young, a former World War Two Army commando leader, late of the Ox and Bucks and now commanding Near East Command. The 3rd Green Jackets (The Rifle Brigade) immediately deployed from Dhekelia to protect Service families living in Larnaca. On Boxing Day, 1 Glosters in Episkopi and 3rd Wing, RAF Regiment based at RAF Akrotiri moved to Nicosia Airport. By the 27th the British had negotiated a ceasefire and stepped into the no-man's-land between the communities and arranged the release of hostages. Meanwhile, when the UN Security Council reviewed a complaint by Cyprus accusing Ankara of intervening in its internal affairs, Turkey retorted that for two years Makarios had been trying to reduce the rights of the minority community. By the end of the year, about 190 Turkish-Cypriots and 130 Greek-Cypriots had been killed and about 210 Turkish-Cypriots and forty Greek-Cypriots were missing. More significantly, the UN estimated that about 30,000 Turkish-Cypriots had abandoned 103 villages, with many of the inhabitants fleeing to the overcrowded suburbs of Nicosia.

Two days later, Young and several community leaders formalized the demarcation line that ran through the centre of Nicosia named the Green Line – from the British practice of using green pencils to mark obstacles on maps. Soldiers and the RAF Regiment erecting barriers were seen by Greek-Cypriots as interfering without authority but by the Turkish-Cypriots as protectors. Young divided Cyprus into three zones that paralleled the Brigade Districts during the Emergency, placing Eastern Zone under control of the Dhekelia Garrison with 1st Battalion, The Sherwood Foresters taking over from the Green Jackets. The Western Zone included 2 Light Regiment RA moving its guns to Episkopi. Two dismounted batteries were sent to Nicosia to join 1 Para and the Guards Independent Parachute Company with its Ferret Scouts Cars. It was replaced by a Royal Dragoons squadron. The Northern Zone was placed under command of HQ 16 Parachute Brigade and was reinforced by a 14/20th Hussars armoured car squadron until it was relieved by the Life Guards at the end of January. In mid-February 1964, when HQ 3rd Division, from the Strategic Command in UK, arrived ostensibly as a peacekeeping force but in reality as a public demonstration to counter Turkish murmurings of intervention, Major General Young handed over the Truce Force to Major General Mike Carver and returned to HQ Cyprus District. Then 1st Battalion The Duke of Edinburgh's Royal Regiment arrived from Malta and over took the Nicosia sector along with the armoured cars of Life Guards and a second Royals squadron and the 1 Royal Inniskilling Fusiliers and dismounted 26 Medium Regiment RA, all arriving from England.

At the end of February Makarios ignited regional international tension when he established links with the Soviet airline, Aeroflot. The combination of this bombshell and the sectarian violence led to London and Washington secretly agreeing that the long term solution to the impasse between the two communities, the instability of the Cyprus Government and the threat to the NATO Southern Flank was the geographical and sectarian partitioning of the island. The Turks supported the notion. The Greeks did not. Makarios attacked Turkish diplomacy at the UN by accusing Ankara, in spite of the considerable evidence to the contrary, of interfering with the sovereignty of an independent state. Under pressure from London, three weeks later, the UN Security Council adopted Resolution 186 in which the United Nations Peacekeeping Force in Cyprus (UNFICYP) was to be established on 27 March 1964 with a mandate to:

> ...in the interest of preserving international peace and security, to use its best efforts to prevent a recurrence of fighting and, as necessary, to contribute to the maintenance and restoration of law and order and a return to normal conditions.

But within ten days of the Resolution being passed and the news that UNFICYP would take over from the British on 2 March, communal violence broke out during an exchange of hostages and inquiries into missing people.

In the small town of Ktima near Paphos, the Turkish-Cypriot community had been planning to attack the Greek-Cypriots while they were celebrating a religious festival on 7 March. Advice from the local Turkish National Contingent commander against the plan was ignored, then tension escalated when a Greek-Cypriot shot a Turkish-Cypriot postman during a day of rioting. Several Greek-Cypriots were then taken hostage. Next day, the Greek-Cypriot militias and ELDYK soldiers used mortars, machine guns and bulldozers to drive the Turkish-Cypriots back into the Muttalo quarter and then seized a large number of hostages and killed several Turkish militia. Of the ninety-five British troops in the town, seventy gunners of 18 Battery, 26 Medium Regiment pinned down in Ktima Police Station used a .30-inch Browning machine gun to dissuade the Greek-Cypriots from using an armoured bulldozer to attack a minaret which they believed was a machine gun post. In another part of the town, a Royal Dragoons Troop was threatened by a police chief insisting on disarming the Turkish-Cypriots. When Major General Carver flew to Paphos by helicopter and was pinned against his car by 3,000 furious Greek-Cypriots, a Greek-Cypriot police inspector swinging his cane prevented further violence. Elsewhere, at Mia Milia, a Glosters platoon ignored threats of an attack on their base at a school. In the Kyrenian Mountains, a Life Guards Troop rescued schoolchildren under Turkish-Cypriot fire, only to be stoned by the same children when passing their school several days later. Two troopers were killed when their Ferret crashed as they were speeding to the scene of a Greek-Cypriot attack.

When Ankara again threatened intervention unless UNFICYP was established within the day, a Canadian journalist wondered if the force of peacekeepers from largely neutral countries would be any more successful in enforcing a UN Resolution drafted in distant New York than the British. The Browning was used as a last resort! A few minutes before the Turkish deadline, Australia, Austria, Canada, Denmark, Finland, Ireland and Sweden joined Great Britain in supplying military and police contingents to the UNFICYP force of 6,500 men. On 27 March, the British Contingent of the 2 Light Regiment RA, 1 Para with G Battery, 7 Royal Horse Artillery RA under command, 26 Medium Regiment, 1 Royal Inniskilling Fusiliers and 1 Sherwood Foresters exchanged their headgear for the distinctive light blue berets of UN troops and passed under command of the Indian Major General Prem Singh Gyani. However, he was on a fortnight's leave and command was delegated to Major General Carver, his deputy. When the Inniskillings hosted the Irish, the units discovered they had much in common, not the least of which was that several men had deserted from each and re-enlisted with the other. By the end of March, Finnish patrols in the Ktima area and the Swedes pacifying Famagusta allowed the British to return to the Sovereign Base Areas. In April the Canadians took over the Northern Zone from HQ 16 Parachute Brigade, but could not prevent the Greek-Cypriots attacking Kokkina, which had become a conduit of arms, ammunition and equipment from Turkey.

In an attempt to appease the minority, Makarios invited the UN to supervise the disbandment of the Cyprus Army, but the Turkish-Cypriots rejected this and appealed for the restoration of the 1960 Constitution. On 25 April, UNFICYP intervened when Greek-Cypriot paramilitaries attacked the Turkish-Cypriot stronghold at St Hilarion but did not interfere with a Turkish National Contingent force that had taken up strategic positions overlooking the Kyrenia Pass. In the second week of May, the murder of two Greek officers and the son of a senior Greek-Cypriot police officer in Famagusta induced further violence and more kidnapping. UNFICYP began taking casualties, including some deaths. The Turks raised the tension by landing a small force of military advisers at Kokkina and practising amphibious landings off their southern coast. Divisions between the two communities deepened when the Turkish-Cypriots created independent administrative functions in their enclaves in Famagusta, Larnaca, Limassol, Nicosia and Paphos and the Turkish Army created the Turkish Cypriot Fighters home defence battalions, each commanded by a Turkish officer.

Part of the UNFICYP role was to settle disputes. Major Edward Macey RAOC, a Greek and Turkish linguist who had served in Greece during the Second World War and had been awarded two medals for bravery by the Greeks during the civil war, was appointed the UN Special Liaison Officer to the Republic's Vice President Dr Kutchuk. Archbishop Makarios also had a liaison officer in a similar role. One of

Macey's assignments was to investigate the disappearance of thirty-two Turkish-Cypriots captured in Famagusta in mid-May. Sometimes regarded as a 'lone wolf', Macey was distrusted by the Greek-Cypriots who claimed that he was MI6 and was supplying the Turkish-Cypriots with the military information. Part of his role was to make regular visits to Turkish-Cypriot communities, and when he said that he intended to visit Galatia, a village on the Panhandle, to investigate concerns raised by the villagers, he was warned by the Cyprus Defence Ministry that he was being watched. On 7 June, Macey and his Land Rover driver, Driver Leonard Platt RASC, drove to Galatia. Platt was a short term replacement driver. Both wore UN insignia and were armed with personal weapons. As usual, Macey called in at the Police Station and was then entertained to cold drinks by Mr Hallil, the assistant Mukhtar. As they were walking around the village and Hallil asked for a lift to Nicosia, Macey mentioned the Greek-Cypriot allegations about him and commented that he was not sure if he was going to make it home. During the afternoon, Macey and Platt left Galatia. They were never seen again. On the 11th, the *Daily Mirror* reported that the UN was checking reports that their Land Rover had been seen overturned and Platt shot dead beside it. Of Macey there was no sign. The *Guardian* implied that if Makarios was involved, it 'will be an affront not so much to Britain as to the United Nations (whose help the Cypriots sought) and a matter of urgent concern.' In spite of appeals for information, offers of rewards and UN and British investigations, nothing was forthcoming, and five weeks later Major Macey and Driver Platt were declared 'missing presumed dead'. There was a belief that a former hardline EOKA in Famagusta was probably responsible for their murders and that it had been sanctioned by the Cyprus Government because it was rumoured that Macey was training and equipping Turkish-Cypriots. As a memorial, the Junior Rank's Club at the Ordnance Depot, Cyprus was named the Macey Club.

Operating in an altogether more tranquil way, Lieutenant Commander Martin Packard, a Greek-speaking naval intelligence officer despatched from Malta, was also working with the UN. Always accompanied by Greek and Turkish officers, he promoted reconciliation between the communities, much to the frustration of American politicians and diplomats working hard to force the partition of Cyprus. After successfully resolving the theft of sheep by Greek-Cypriots from a Turkish-Cypriot village, Packard was congratulated by the US Acting Secretary of State George Ball, but Ball suggested that his efforts were deluded because partition was inevitable. Packard was planning the return of Turkish-Cypriot communities to their abandoned villages when Major General Carver had him flown out of Cyprus for his own safety after the disappearance of Macey and Platt. At the time, Packard had been investigating the killing of twenty-five Turkish-Cypriots in Nicosia General Hospital when his efforts were complicated by the discovery of a mass grave at Vasilios in which it seemed that the victims had been buried after being brought from the hospital mortuary. Nicos Sampson was strongly suspected of involvement in the murders.

By mid-June, HQ 3rd Division had returned to Great Britain, and by August the British UNFICYP Contingent, the largest national contingent, had slimmed to a roulement infantry group at Wolseley Barracks on six-month tours manning the Green Line in Nicosia and a sector around Limassol. Faced with the usual tests of patience, particularly from the Greek-Cypriots, they manned sandbagged observation posts and visited communities in the knowledge that UN rules of engagement prevented them from returning fire at anything that was not aimed at them. Hours were spent parleying over cups of coffee and Turkish Delight.

In the early summer, the Cyprus House of Representatives disbanded the Cyprus Army and raised the Cyprus National Guard from Cypriot men aged between eighteen and fifty-nine years conscripted for one year. In mid-June, Makarios, with the indirect support of Washington intent on reducing Eastern Bloc influence in the region, invited Lieutenant General Grivas to command the new force. Next month, he forced the Turkish-Cypriot representatives to abandon the Articles in the 1960 Constitution stating that the minority should provide forty per cent of the strength. In effect, the National Guard became a Greek-Cypriot force. Grivas set up National Guard Command in Athalassa and over the next few months he divided Cyprus into the British division-sized East, Centre and Western Sectors and established brigade-sized Higher Military Commands (HMC) in Tactical Groups at Famagusta, Larnaca, Limassol, Paphos, Morphou and Kyrenia, each supported by several conscript and reserve infantry battalions with artillery and logistic support grouped into Tactical Groups. His best forces were four Raiding Force Units (RFU) of commandos. The Navy had two motor torpedo boats, three fast patrol boats and several smaller vessels from the Soviet Union. When Grivas invited Athens to send an infantry division to Cyprus, Ankara mobilized, until brusquely warned by Washington to relax. He developed Operation *Aphrodite* as a contingency plan to defeat a Turkish landing using the sandy beaches at Famagusta Bay and the flat Mesaoria Plain for a fast armoured thrust to Nicosia. He planned to neutralize Turkish-Cypriot Fighters, support for the landing by seizing key Turkish-Cypriot enclaves. His main problem was that while the Turks were well supplied with NATO equipment, the National Guard had a wide variety of Second World War, ex-Soviet and locally made equipment, which played havoc with his logistics.

Tension increased on 5 August in the Tyllira District when the National Guard disarmed the Swedish UNFICYP in the Kato Pygros, and the 12th Tactical Group, which was built around 206 Infantry Battalion and 31 RFU, attacked several villages and seized Mount Lorovoumu; however, their main objective of Kokkina held out. Four days later, Turkish aircraft retaliated by attacking the two fast patrol boats T1 and T2 lurking offshore but lost an F-100 Super Sabre shot down. Its pilot was captured and murdered. A Turkish naval task force then appeared off Kyrenia while British aircraft from RAF Akrotiri intercepted several Greek Air Force jets over Cyprus. After the UN had negotiated a ceasefire, UNFICYP troops entered Kokkina after its four-year siege and found the port wrecked and its 800 civilians emerging from the safety of surrounding caves. A political solution a distant dream, Cyprus was extremely tense. Although the Americans had dissuaded the Turks from launching interventions, the UN Secretary-General accusing the Turkish-Cypriot leaders of being:

> committed to physical and geographical separation of the communities as a political goal, it is not likely to encourage activities by Turkish Cypriots which may be interpreted as demonstrating the merits of an alternative policy. The result has been a seemingly deliberate policy of self-segregation by the Turkish Cypriots.

Nothing was mentioned of the Greek-Cypriot manipulation of the House of Representatives to remove Turkish-Cypriot influence in government or the determination of Makarios to break the will of the Turkish-Cypriots by restricting their goods reaching market and imposing a heavy tax on grain.

When a junta of Greek colonels seized power in Athens in April 1967, Makarios, not wishing Cyprus to be part of the dictatorship and wary of strong Turkish retaliation, distanced himself from the coup. Learning that Grivas was heavily implicated in the coup, Makarios, fearing his unpredictability and loyalty within the National Guard, strengthened the Cyprus Police with loyal paramilitary units of battalion strength. In July, London believed that the Colonels were planning a coup in Cyprus, however the British Government was somewhat taken aback when they offered Ankara a military base and ten per cent of the island in exchange for *enosis*. Ankara, backed up by Washington, suggested two bases, but this was rejected. Meanwhile, the crisis in the Middle

East, the 1967 Six Day War and the loss of oil supplies driving Great Britain into deep economic trouble led to London announcing substantial defence cuts. Although this infuriated Washington which was then increasing its involvement in South-East Asia, London had one resource important to NATO strategy – the signals intelligence listening post on Cyprus. UNFICYP despatched troops to intervene during the war.

Kophinou was a Turkish-Cypriot stronghold that overlooked the important road junction connecting Nicosia, Larnaca and Limassol. On 20 July, Turkish-Cypriots opened fire on some Greek-Cypriots in Ayios Theodhorous and warned 1 Duke of Wellington's, the Limassol UNFICYP sector force, that any encroachments into the village would be resisted. In November, 1st Battalion, The Royal Green Jackets (1 RGJ) took over the sector and the manning of several observation posts near Kophinou. For several months Turkish-Cypriot Fighters had been denying Cyprus Police patrols access to Ayios Theodhorous, but Grivas, frustrated by Makarios and angry at the temerity of the Turkish-Cypriots, on his own initiative escalated the tension in mid-November by sending a National Guard battalion to threaten the two villages. When he turned up accompanied by a battery of photographers and journalists, it was inevitable that the violence would escalate. The trigger was the Turkish-Cypriots in Kophinou firing on National Guardsmen removing a roadblock. This precipitated a ferocious four-hour battle in which National Guard infantry supported by artillery attacked the village, and led to about twenty-five Turkish-Cypriots being killed. ELDYK soldiers attached to the National Guard demanded that the Royal Green Jackets surrender their weapons, but the British soldiers replaced their UN berets with their light infantry green berets and resisted with fist, boot and rifle butt; nevertheless, one small post had no alternative but surrender. When the National Guard consolidated beyond the villages, Ankara warned the UN that if the National Guard did not withdraw immediately and was not disbanded as a force, the Turkish Armed Forces would restore the *status quo*. The Turks also insisted that Grivas return to Greece immediately and that compensation should be paid to the victims of Kophinou. To show its determination, Ankara mobilized its forces on the border with the northern Greek province of Thrace, sent aircraft to buzz Cyprus and assembled an amphibious task force in southern Turkey. Athens knew that its bluff had been called and in mid-November Grivas was recalled, ostensibly for consultation. Makarios ordered the National Guard to withdraw from Kophinou and Kokkina, which had been besieged for nearly four years, and arranged for the compensation to be paid, but he refused to disband the National Guard. Among those who were dismissed was Polycarpos Georghadjis, the Minister of the Interior. Since 1959 he had used his influence to infiltrate virtually every aspect of Cypriot life except for AKEL with his private army of EOKA thugs and cronies and he posed a threat to Makarios.

Two NATO members, who had fought as allies in Korea and were key to the defence of NATO's Southern Flank, had come close to war, and it was only agreements brokered by Washington that prevented hostilities. Realising that *enosis* with an unpredictable government in Athens was not achievable, in December Makarios thinned the Greek military presence to its 1960 force level of 950 men; nevertheless, a substantial number of Greek officers were still in command positions. National Guard Command revised its anti-invasion plans to Operation *Aphrodite Two,* still aimed against a landing in Famagusta Bay and offensives against the Turkish-Cypriot enclaves. Makarios reformed the Cyprus Police into a mixed constabulary and instructed that weapons held by militias and unauthorized civilians be surrendered. He also agreed that the UNFICYP mandate to keep the peace and protect the minority was to be enforced. US high-level U-2 recce flights over the Soviet Union used RAF Akrotiri, and the CIA was permitted to set up listening posts to complement the British assets. In 1968 the Turkish-Cypriots escalated the underlying sectarian tension by creating an administration that replicated the Greek-Cypriot one. But when President Nixon came to power and warmed to the Colonels' junta, he joined them in mistrusting Makarios as an Eastern Bloc lackey. In January 1970 Makarios survived assassination when his helicopter was shot down in Nicosia during a commemoration for Gregoris Afxentiou. The attempt was part of a National Guard coup organized by a Greek colonel and several former EOKA, including Polycarpos Georghadjis. He was murdered.

When a general election in Cyprus in July saw a slide toward AKEL, secret talks within NATO again examined the principle of the partition of the island. During a visit to Moscow, Makarios gained Soviet support for the removal of foreign troops on the island – that is to say, principally troops from Britain, a member of NATO. In 1971 Grivas escaped from house arrest in Athens and returned clandestinely to Cyprus where he formed EOKA-B with the specific aims of overthrowing Makarios and implementing *enosis,* encouraging the same terrorism that he had fostered during the Emergency – theft of weapons from police stations, intimidation and leaflet distribution. When Makarios organized the importation of a large quantity of Czech weapons for the Cyprus Police, this alarmed Washington and Ankara, who again saw yet more Eastern Bloc influence and the increased risk of sectarian attacks. Makarios rejected Greek demands to surrender the weapons but did agree to store them in a UN compound.

By 1972 the National Guard numbered 10,500 serving men and 29,500 reservists with at least one year's military service. Their structure was as follows:

### HQ National Guard Command
- Artillery Command of five field artillery regiments, two anti-air defence battalions, one anti-tank battalion and two light artillery batteries equipped with British and Soviet guns
- 23rd Tank Battalion equipped with modified Soviet T-34/85 tanks
- 21st Armoured Recce Battalion equipped with British World War Two armoured cars. Both battalions were at the former Kokkinotrimithia Detention Camp
- 286th Mechanized Infantry Battalion equipped Soviet BTR-152 wheeled armoured personnel carriers (APC) in addition to two infantry battalions
- An engineer battalion
- Raider Command of four Raiding Force Units of commandos
- Naval Command forces at Kyrenia, Boghaz, Famagusta, Larnaca and Paphos
- Air Wing with six coastal radars

### Eastern Sector Command
#### 1st (Famagusta) Higher Military Command
5th (Famagusta) and 15th (Trikomo) Tactical Groups of four infantry and four Reserve infantry battalions, two field artillery battalions and one anti-tank battalion

### Central Command
#### 3rd (Nicosia) Higher Military Command
3rd (Kyrenia) Tactical Group of two reserve infantry battalions.
9th and 11th Tactical Groups of two infantry and one reserve infantry battalions
12th (Kythrea) Tactical Group of two infantry and one Reserve battalions

#### 4th (Limassol) Higher Military Command
6th (Larnaca) Tactical Group of two infantry and two reserve

infantry battalions
**Western Command**
**2nd (Morphou) Higher Military Command**
4th and 6th (Morphou) Tactical Groups of three infantry and three reserve infantry battalions

**5th (Ktimi) Higher Military Command**
8th Tactical Group of one infantry and two reserve infantry battalions

In July the Cypriot intelligence services unearthed a third coup d'etat planned by Greek officers attached to the National Guard; nevertheless, in spite of the escalating destabilization from terrorism but with the near total support of AKEL, Makarios was elected for a third term as President during the spring of 1973. Although politically and diplomatically isolated, with very few allies in Cyprus and the international community outside the Eastern Bloc, he craftily used the newly-established Tactical Police Reserve to tackle the subversive EOKA-B. A fourth assassination attempt using a mine on a road failed in August, as did a fifth attempt using the same technique in October. In November a student uprising in Athens against the Colonels led to the *coup d'état* by the Chief of Military Police, Brigadier General Dimitrios Ioannides, which brought in General Phadedon Gizikis as President. Ioannides had served in Cyprus in the mid-1960s and, forming an alliance with Nicos Sampson, had been furious in 1964 when Makarios rejected Plan *Akritas*. The potential re-appearance of Sampson on the stage added further instability to an already simmering situation, particularly as the Greek-Cypriots were seeking a powerful character to succeed Lieutenant General Grivas who had died in Cyprus on 27 January 1974 from a heart attack. During Grivas' funeral in Nicosia, Sampson was noted for his extravagant show of grief.

Ioannides quickly assumed indirect control of EOKA-B, however in the spring, after a large consignment of weapons had been stolen from a National Guard armoury and inhabitants had been beaten up during raids on two Turkish-Cypriot villages, the Cypriot Intelligence Service discovered another plot to overthrow Makarios. Makarios reacted by proscribing the subversives. When the Tactical Police Reserve then seized documents implicating Athens, at the end of April, he protested to the Greek Ambassador about the subversion of his authority, demanded that the length of Greek Army officers' postings to Cyprus be reduced and stated that only 100 instructors were needed to train the National Guard. But the interference continued and at the beginning of July, after Makarios had become impatient with Athens, he wrote to

General Gizikis complaining about his support to EOKA-B, and leaked the letter to journalists and publicly accused Athens of challenging his authority. It was a risky initiative to a regime whose principal aspiration was single-minded Greek-speaking Hellenic nationalism. Meanwhile, the uncompromising attitude towards Ankara by Ioannides and the finding of oil raised regional tension. Washington believed that Athens was spoiling for a fight. The stance taken by Makarios encouraged the Greeks to protest at the excesses of the regime. Ioannides badly needed a diversion and encouraged EOKA-B to seize power in the knowledge that UNFICYP could not interfere in Greek-Cypriot affairs.

By 1974, the UN force had slimmed from 6,500 in 1964 to 2,500, with Austrians, British, Canadians, Danes, Finns and Swedes manning observation posts and patrolling throughout Cyprus, controlled from a HQ in Nicosia. During the 1973 Yom Kippur War between Israel and Egypt and Syria, Austrian, Finnish, Irish and Swedish elements of UNFICYP were sent to Egypt to form the United Nations Emergency Force 2. When the Irish 25th Infantry Brigade Group did not return to Cyprus, the Austrian Contingent took over the Irish sector at Larnaca and the British sector also took over, with 2 Coldstream Guards arriving in May, its companies deploying to Paphos and Limassol, each supported by a Troop of the Royal Armoured Corps Independent Parachute Squadron. The remaining two companies were in the Western Sovereign Base Area (WSBA).

During the early morning of 15 July, HQ UNFICYP started receiving reports of heavy fighting in Limassol. When news that the National Guard had attacked Police HQ, rumours circulated that Archbishop Makarios was dead and that Nicos Sampson had been appointed provisional President to head a 'Government of National Salvation'. There was widespread disbelief that the Greek Junta had selected him, in spite of his controversial history.

At about 5 pm, Major Richard Macfarlane, who commanded No. 1 Company in the Paphos Sector, was handed a note by the Paphos District officer allegedly sent from Makarios to say that he was alive and well and in the Paphos Bishopric. He wished to meet with the UN Representative in Cyprus and the UNFICYP commander in order to press for a meeting of the Security Council. Makarios had returned to the Presidential Palace from his Troodos Lodge early on the 15th, one of his first appointments being to meet a party of schoolchildren visiting from Egypt. But as soon as the National Guard knew that he was back in Nicosia, the conspirators had struck, and disloyal infantry and tanks in the city fought pitched battles with pro-Makarios police and National Guard. Makarios was meeting the schoolchildren and when he learnt that rebel forces were at the Palace gates, he ushered them into the shelter of a corridor. With a small escort he then escaped from the Palace and while flagging down cars met a loyal officer, who guided his party around roadblocks; they then headed for Kykko Monastery. There he broadcast that he was still alive and then set out for the Paphos Bishopric. Although doubting the authenticity of the note, Macfarlane agreed to meet Makarios and pass on his requests. When the BBC reported that an UNFICYP officer had met Makarios, and rebels in Paphos moved against the Bishopric, the Archbishop sent a note to Macfarlane asking for a helicopter to fly him to RAF Akrotiri. Amid a sharply deteriorating situation, Makarios pitched up at Battalion HQ at St Patrick's Camp and was shown to the Officers' Mess. At Episkopi, Air Chief Marshal Sir John Aiken, who commanded HQ Near East Command, discussed the situation with the Foreign and Commonwealth Office and the UN Representative in Cyprus and suggested sending a helicopter to Paphos to collect Makarios and that he then be flown to London. Not wishing to be involved in a local difficulty, when London was unenthusiastic and suggested that he been given sanctuary in RAF Akrotiri, Aiken protested that this would place the Service families living in married quarters outside the SBAs at risk from Greek-Cypriot retaliation. Agreement was eventually granted for a UNFICYP Whirlwind helicopter to take Makarios to RAF Akrotiri where within fifteen minutes he had boarded a RAF Argosy bound for London via Malta. He had no doubt that Turkey would invade.

As Cyprus slid into the chaos of bitter civil war, 3,000 British and their families in the SBAs were defended by 1 Royal Scots, two 2 Grenadier Guards companies, a 16/5 Lancers armoured car squadron and support units. Immediate reinforcements were HQ 19 Infantry Brigade and 12 Light Air Defence Battery, then both on exercise in Cyprus. Under Operation *Platypus*, several units quickly began arriving from UK, including 40 Commando, as the Spearhead Battalion, which usually meant training for rapid deployment to Northern Ireland, and 41 Commando en route to Malta from New York on board HMS Hermes. Other ships also converged on Cyprus including a US amphibious task force, a US carrier force and a Soviet Black Sea Fleet destroyer.

Such was the concern at HQ Near East Command of the implications of Sampson being declared President that Air Chief Marshal Aiken used the British Forces Broadcasting Service to warn dependants living in hirings that they were to be evacuated into the SBAs. At about 4 pm, as a convoy of Army and RAF lorries sent to collect the dependants in Limassol approached a road junction with the M1, Cyprus Police advised them that EOKA-B intended to ambush about 500 armed Greek-Cypriot Makarios loyalists en route to Limassol from Paphos at Kolossi Castle. Since the British soldiers were unarmed, the convoy returned to Episkopi. Next day at noon a large concentration of National Guard were cleared from the M1 by unarmed RAF Police, and the convoy, this time with an armed escort and displaying Union Jacks, collected the dependants, their baggage and private cars. Many had experienced an anxious night amid outbreaks of shooting. A National Guard contingent later drove through Episkopi, the picture of a disciplined force and keen to impress. The families moved into empty married quarters or stayed with friends. Those living in Larnaca were collected by the aircraft carrier HMS *Hermes* and landed at the Dhekelia.

Ankara had no doubt that Athens was behind the coup and, with Sampson declared President, assessed that there was an imminent threat against the Turkish-Cypriot minority. On 18 July, the Turkish government invoked its right under the Treaty of Guarantee to protect Turkish-Cypriots and guarantee the independence of Cyprus and instructed its VI Corps to activate Operation *Attila* and intervene in Cyprus. Commanded by Lieutenant General Nurettin Ersin, the landing force consisted of:

**The Special Strike Force Landing Brigade**
- 6th Marine Infantry Regiment
- 50th Infantry Regiment, 39th Infantry Division. One battalion was in Cyprus as the Turkish National Contingent
- Divisional battalions providing M-47 and M-48 tanks, M-113 APCs and twelve 105mm M-101s howitzers
- 1st Commando Brigade

**2nd Parachute Battalion** (Cyprus Turkish Forces Regiment)
- Geunyeli Group (2nd and 3rd Infantry and Heavy Weapons Companies)
- Ortakoy Group (Regimental HQ and 1st and 4th Companies)

**Air Force**
- 1st Tactical Air Force of five squadrons providing interdiction and air defence
- 2nd Tactical Air Force of three squadrons flying fast jets, including F-104 Starfighters and F-4 Phantoms
- 12 Transport Squadron

**Naval elements**

- Amphibious vessels
- Five former US Gearing class destroyers purchased by the Turkish Navy three years previously

The landing force numbered about 3,500 men and even though most were conscripts, the Turks had served with distinction in Korea and were trusted allies defending the NATO Southern Flank. There was no artillery support except for naval gunfire from the destroyers. Ashore were 20,000 Turkish-Cypriot Fighters divided into regiments with HQs in Nicosia, Chatos, Boghaz, Famagusta, Larnaca, Limassol, Paphos and Lefka, and commanded by Turkish officers. The follow-up force was the 28th Infantry Division.

Reports from Greek Intelligence Agency officers of the embarkation of the Brigade at Mersin Naval Base and the deployment of the Turkish Cypriot and Turkish National Contingent into defensive positions led to the Greek General Staff debating the implications of going to war with a NATO ally. Meanwhile Prime Minister Bülent Ecevit flew to London to solicit British aid, as agreed by the 1960 Treaty of Guarantee; but London, largely influenced by US Secretary of State Henry Kissinger, was unwilling to interfere in Cypriot affairs. Washington was quietly content that Makarios had been removed and the Cypriot links with Eastern Europe cut. But when Ankara indicated it could not watch the Turkish-Cypriots be placed at risk from a resurgent EOKA backed up by an unstable Greek Government, a US envoy was sent to Ankara to prevent Turkish intervention should her demand that Sampson be removed, the Greek Army officers leave and Cyprus remain independent be ignored. At least, that was the public perception. Ecevit returned to Ankara on 19 July and confirmed intervention for 6.30 am on Saturday 20 July.

On the same day, the Greek tank-landing ship *Lesbos* arrived at Famagusta for the regular rotation of ELDYK. The Swedish contingent had to intervene when Turkish-Cypriot dockers downed tools. When the *Lesbos* left during the early evening, the rotation had been reduced by twelve soldiers. The Greek Navy deployed its three Type-209 submarines to the Rhodes area. During the early evening, the BBC broadcast images of the Turkish task force leaving Mersin during the afternoon.

## CHAPTER FOURTEEN

# The Turkish Intervention
## (20 July to 15 August 1974)

At about 1.30 am on 20 July 1974, the Apostolos Andreas coastal radar at the tip of the Panhandle reported eleven ships thirty-five miles north of Kyrenia. The signatures were the landing ship *Ertugrul* carrying twenty infantry landing craft, two landing craft capable of carrying vehicles or 100 troops, five destroyers and three patrol boats. National Guard Command activated Operation *Aphrodite Two* in the expectation that the Turks would land in Famagusta Bay, but as the mobilization signal flashed its units, there was chaos because the operation had not been exercised and several key officers had been purged in the coup. Half an hour later, the radar's reporting six ships heading south led Command headquarters to believe that the landings would take place at Famagusta Bay.

At 4.45 am the Turkish Foreign Ministry informed the Greek Embassy in Ankara of its intention to intervene in Cyprus. Fifteen minutes later, National Guard naval operations at Kyrenia despatched two fast patrol boats to investigate the force of ships, but within fifteen minutes T1 had been sunk by aircraft while T3 was destroyed by ships and aircraft with the loss of all ten crew but one.

At 5.30 am, soon after dawn, Turkish aircraft began softening up military targets in Kyrenia; then half an hour later, nineteen C-47 Dakotas, six C-130 Hercules and eleven C-160 Transalls dropped the Cyprus Turkish Forces Regiment and their equipment near Geunyeli, Orta Keuy and Borghaz. Unfortunately for the Turks, the 120-strong Ortakeuy Group landed directly in the path of the 1st (ELDYK) Battalion as it advanced to attack the Turkish-Cypriot stronghold at Geunyeli and suffered ninety killed or wounded and one taken prisoner. One C-47 was badly damaged by ground fire and only just returned to its base.

The Commando Brigade was then delivered by about sixty-five UH-1H Iroquois of the 2nd Army Helicopter Regiment flying from Turkey to a landing zone near Aghirda. They quickly climbed the hills and seized the Kyrenia Pass through which the amphibious forces would advance to Geunyeli. Kyrenia was cut off. Another force climbed up Mount Hilarion to protect the Turkish signals station.

At about 7.30 am the Greeks and a National Guard infantry company supported by fifteen tanks and artillery attacked Geunyeli, but the gunners lost five guns destroyed when their position near Makedonitsas Abbey was bombed. A second Greek attack from the south resulted in two tanks destroyed and two trapped in the anti-tank ditch surrounding the village. A plan to attack the stronghold from the north and west by units from the Morphou and Nicosia Tactical Groups went awry when a battalion was ambushed by the Turkish-Cypriot Fighters. When it eventually arrived, it attacked Geunyeli piecemeal without success. Meanwhile, Turkish aircraft began raiding targets in Nicosia and Famagusta and refugees were streaming out of Kyrenia. With total air superiority, the aircraft generally operated in pairs by identifying targets and carrying out a bombing run followed by rocket and cannon attacks. Air raids cost four more tanks destroyed, a fifth abandoned and two Marmon-Harrington armoured cars and a Daimler Dingo scout car destroyed at Kokkinotrimithia Camp. National Guard Command abandoned its Athalassa headquarters after being raided three times.

The Turks had set H-Hour for 6.30 am and planned to make use of Kyrenia harbour by landing astride the town on a small beach at Ayios Yeoryios to the west and Six Mile Beach to the east. But when naval frogmen reported that Ayios Yeoryios was unsuitable, the amphibious force loitered offshore unhindered while the frogmen were transferred by gunboat to recce Five Mile Beach, four miles to the west of the town. When they reported no obstacles, at about 8 am, the first wave of two marine companies and amphibious engineers landed from seven landing craft and were followed by the 6th Marine Infantry Regiment from eleven landing craft. The landing caught National Guard Command by surprise because it did not conform to the principles of amphibious warfare. There were no wide open spaces for the breakout, indeed there were only two exits, both along narrow coastal strips to Kyrenia in the east and Karavas to the west. Tanks would be confined to roads and tracks over the Pentadactylos Mountains. On the other hand, the National Guard would have difficulty in mounting strong counter-attacks and could do little but pen the Turks in their beachhead pending a political solution.

Meanwhile, 3rd (Kyrenia) Tactical Group was caught totally unprepared. Of its two battalions, 326th Reserve Infantry failed to mobilize and 306th Infantry did so but slowly; thus in the crucial first hours the Turks established a beachhead without serious opposition. The first sign of an attack occurred at about 9.30 am when 251st Battalion from 2nd (Morphou) Tactical Group, supported by five T-34/85 tanks, overran two recoilless rifle positions on the western fringes of the beachhead but an immediate Turkish counter-attack cost them two M-113 APCs destroyed by a tank; nevertheless, the Turks extended their perimeter out 900 yards to the west. Artillery Command had no clear fire plan, nevertheless battery commanders using their initiative had considerable success in making the beachhead distinctly uncomfortable throughout the day. Near Kyrenia, 182nd Field Artillery Battalion with two 25-pounder batteries and the twelve 57mm guns of 190th Anti Tank Battalion forced some Turkish ships to withdraw out of range. Both units lacked sufficient lorries to tow all their guns.

With the Kyrenia Pass dominated by the Turkish commandos, National Guard Command decided to attack the beachhead using 2nd (Morphou) Tactical Group from the west and despatched the 286th Mechanised Infantry Battalion and three tanks to Morphou as reinforcements. But as the column motored along the road toward Panagra Pass in clear daylight without a cloud in the sky, it was pounced upon by Turkish aircraft near Kondemenos and lost six BTR-152s and the battalion commander, Lieutenant Colonel Georgios Boutos, who died of wounds. Morale collapsed and the column went firm at the Pass, except for a combat team consisting of BTR-152 company group, a jeep-mounted anti-tank platoon and the tanks that pressed on through Karavas towards the beachhead. At about midday, a second flight of sixty helicopters delivered a second parachute battalion to a landing zone near Aghirda. Meanwhile, 316th Reserve Infantry Battalion, from 2nd Tactical Group, had reached the western perimeter of the beachhead, but as its two leading companies advanced along the coast road to link up with the 3rd (Kyrenia) Tactical Group and encircle the Turks, at about 1 pm, it ran into a fortified roadblock. Three hours later, soon after the 286th Mechanised Infantry combat team arrived from Panagra Pass, 316th Reserve Infantry again tried to link up with the Kyrenia Tactical Group but ran into a Turkish roadblock and lost a tank destroyed.

Soon after National Command had activated Operation *Aphrodite Two*, bitter fighting broke out between the National Guard and Turkish Cypriot Fighters throughout Cyprus. The 4th (Limassol) Higher Military Command used the 450 EOKA-B assembled into the 203rd Reserve Infantry Battalion to attack Turkish-Cypriot enclaves in the town and in Avdimou, west of the town. By dawn next day the battalion was in control of Limassol, with 1,000 prisoners held in the football stadium. The commander had moved his HQ to a bar to escape the bombing. At around 5 pm the landing ship *Lesbos* shelled the Turkish-Cypriot enclave near Paphos harbour and then landed the 2nd (ELDYK) Battalion that had embarked at Borghaz on the 18th. Five hours later, the Turkish-Cypriots surrendered. When a Turkish destroyer was sent to investigate the activities of the landing ship, the *Lesbos* headed south into open sea. The Turkish-Cypriots in Famagusta prepared for a siege.

Major General Prem Chand, the UNFICYP commander, placed his force on full alert and increased observation posts and patrols to protect isolated enclaves and, where possible, to organize local ceasefires. His Chief of Staff was Brigadier Frank Henn, an experienced British soldier who had served throughout the Second World War. British Service families living in Platres and those living in Limassol who had assembled at the Unicorn House family centre and Youth Club assembly points were escorted to Episkopi. Military cooks, RAOC Barracks Services and the Supply Sub-Depot were soon busy issuing accommodation stores. Congestion in the WSBA gradually increased as tourists and Turkish-Cypriot refugees sought sanctuary. The Happy Valley sport fields below Episkopi became a tented camp. A 40 Commando and 16/5 Lancer patrol found a cache of TMT weapons inside the perimeter, and in the one contact with Greek-Cypriots, a Royal Marine killed a National Guardsman with a single shot. Thereafter, the National Guard co-operated with the British.

The Turkish invasion had stumped the Greek Government because Athens had assumed that Washington, through Secretary of State Henry Kissinger, would deter the Turks from intervening; thus the Greek Armed Forces had not been mobilized. The 20 July was a Saturday and, in spite of the crisis, politicians, diplomats and soldiers were taking advantage of a Mediterranean weekend. When the landings were confirmed, the politicians debated the implications of going to war with a NATO ally, until at about noon general mobilization was ordered. The Navy ordered two of its submarines off Rhodes to patrol between Turkey and Cyprus but they were not to attack Turkish naval forces. The Air Force flying from Crete and Rhodes sparred with Turkish aircraft over Cyprus but the distances meant that Greek time over target was limited. A pair of F-5 Fox pilots claimed a Turkish F-102 Delta Dart shot down, but this was not confirmed. Army chiefs claimed that it would take several days to demonstrate resilience along the mainland border with Turkey, but they agreed to fly a token force of the Thessalonika-based 2nd RFU to Cyprus from Crete using four Olympic Airways Boeing 707s. When one aircraft burst its tyres on landing in Crete, and the battalion commander then suggested that his unit would not reach Cyprus before dawn, the operation was cancelled.

In Cyprus at 5 pm helicopters delivered a third parachute battalion to the Aghirda landing zone and these were followed by about fifteen C-130 Hercules dropping heavy stores and light vehicles. An hour later, the UN Security Council unanimously adopted Resolution 353 for a cease-fire to become effective at 4 pm on 22 July. The Turkish landing craft then left for Mersin to collect the follow-up forces. Shortly before dusk, the National Guard made another attempt to overwhelm Geunyeli by ordering two battalions to divert the attention of the defenders by advancing from the north while the 1st Greek Battalion and tanks attacked from the south, but, once again, the National Guard's inefficient command and control led to the attack being piecemeal. At the same time, the four National Guard RFU battalions drove the Turkish commandos from the St Hilarion area, captured over 200 Turks and wrecked the signals antenna, thereby causing substantial disruption to Turkish communications. Not only could the beachhead now be observed, the Kyrenia Pass was also opened for reinforcements.

As darkness loomed across the battlefield, the daytime temperatures, which had reached 106F, eased. The Turkish hold on the beachhead had been tenuous throughout the day; but with the landings ships gone to collect the follow-up forces, no naval gunfire support because the destroyers were escorting the landing ships and with no tanks landed, the position of the Turks was extremely vulnerable. They had to hold on or be driven into the sea. It was going to be another long night for the troops, many of whom had not slept for thirty-six hours. National Guard Command saw an opportunity, while the defence of Kyrenia was strengthened by an infantry battalion and more artillery, its 241st Infantry and the Engineer Battalion erected obstacles and laid mines on Six Mile Beach, in anticipation of a second landing and a breakout across flat country

At about 8 pm Lieutenant Colonel Konstantinos Boufas, a senior National Guard Command Operations officer, arrived at HQ 2nd Tactical Group with orders to pressure the beachhead from the west using four infantry battalions plus 286th Mechanised Infantry and three tanks. While 306th Reserve Infantry and the irregular Pantazis Battalion (loyalists to President Makarios) were to divert Turkish attention from Kyrenia and the south respectively, the main attack would develop from the west without preliminary shelling. As 306th Reserve formed up at 2 am ready for H-Hour at 2.30 am, a mortar barrage wounded its commanding officer. The main attack began on time and the deeper the National Guard advanced, the stiffer the fighting became. A T34/85 tank was destroyed. At about 3 am Colonel Karaoglanoglu, the Turkish 50th Infantry Regimental commander, was killed when a Turkish M-20 Bazooka team loosed a rocket at the beach villa he was using as his HQ.

The fighting lasted until dawn and, although the National Guard had come close to defeating the beachhead, the rising sun also brought marauding Turkish aircraft. The Pantazis Battalion had taken such heavy casualties that it was disbanded. Geunyeli had also taken a hammering during the night from the two ELDYK battalions but had held out. The 2nd Greek Battalion had arrived from Paphos as reinforcements until it was withdrawn to strengthen the defence of Nicosia Airport, which was thought to be high on the list of Turkish objectives. In a move that would have the serious consequence for UNFICYP of isolating the UN buildings, the British abandoned RAF Nicosia. At 1 pm on 21 July, when Raider Command was ordered to abandon St Hilarion and to move west to secure Pavlos Pass, through which the Turks were expected to attack, the Turkish commandos quickly re-occupied the heights and were able to direct the fire of their destroyers. A company from 33rd RFU joined the defence of Kyrenia. During the afternoon the Turks intercepted radio transmissions indicating that the National Guard naval commander, Lieutenant Colonel Papayiannis, was driving to Karavas in order to assess the Turkish beachhead and review counter-attack options. In an audacious plan, at about 2.30 pm twelve Turkish paras dropped near Myrtou and ambushed his convoy, wounding Papayiannis before they were all killed by his escort. His assessment was cancelled. Meanwhile, UNFICYP had arranged a two-hour local ceasefire to permit the evacuation of foreign missions to Dhekelia.

The previous day, Greek Army Signals Intelligence sent signals suggesting that several Greek Army units had been warned to embark in an amphibious task force being assembled at Rhodes. That morning, Turkish air recce confirmed several ships apparently heading for Cyprus, however no attempt was made to identify them. Further aircraft sightings then reported several Gearing-class destroyers and a convoy heading for Paphos. Gearings were used by the US 6th Fleet and the Greek and Turkish navies. Convinced that the Greeks were sending reinforcements, the Turkish Air Force assembled a strong squadron of F-100 Super Sabres and F-104 Starfighters to attack the ships while the Turkish Navy detached the *Adatepe, Cakmuk* and *Kocatepe* from protecting the landings to intercept them. Off Cape Akamas, they clashed with three Greek motor torpedo boats. At about 2.30 pm Turkish aircraft saw two freighters on course for Cyprus, however reports from the destroyers' commander that their radio operators were speaking Italian did not reach Ankara; thus when the Turkish squadron saw the destroyers about ten miles north of Paphos, they attacked. 'Friend-or-foe' identification procedures failed, and in the ensuing chaos the warships were all hit by bombs, the Kocatepe sinking with the loss of fifty-four seamen. A Starfighter was shot down. It was classic example of deception and inefficient operational procedures leading to a friendly fire incident. A rescue operation involving the Royal Navy, Israeli ships and the RAF saw survivors being handed over to the Turks outside the twelve-mile limit.

The Greek GHQ next mounted Operation *Niki* (Victory) to reinforce the National Guard by planning to fly the 1st RFU to Nicosia Airport. By the evening of 21 July, 360 commandos from its squadrons in Macedonia, Crete and Rhodes and sixty naval divers assigned to the Aegean Sea sector had assembled at Suda Military Air Base in Rhodes, along with the twenty ageing Nord 2501 Noratlases and ten C-47 Dakotas of 345 (Pegasus) Transport Squadron. The troops divided into sticks of twenty-eight and, with their bergens crammed full of ammunition, then clambered into the aircraft, having been assured that the National Guard would provide rations. Noratlas 'Niki 15' was loaded with about 1,500 kilograms of equipment and ammunition. At 10.30 pm the first Noratlas took off, the plan being that the remaining aircraft would leave at five minute intervals; however, by the time that 'Niki 15' was rolling, delays had resulted in the last five Noratleses and all the C-47s, which contained all the heavy equipment, being unlikely to reach Cyprus before dawn, therefore their missions were aborted. To avoid Turkish radar interception, electronic navigation aids were shut down and radio transmissions kept to a minimum. The pilots climbed over the White Mountains of Crete and then dropped to between 300ft and 500ft over the sea, dipping very low was they approached Cyprus. The skill of the navigators was critical. At about 2 am, the leading 'Niki 1' followed the approaches to RAF Akrotiri and skimmed inland to Nicosia Airport, a tactic that drew a sharp rebuke from London, warning Athens that further incursions would be shot down. To the north, large fires blazed on Mount Troodos.

Artillery Command had been warned at 12.30 am to expect Greek military transport aircraft but it was not until an hour later that the orders reached the gun positions. For two days, 195th Anti-Aircraft Battalion defending Nicosia Airport had seen nothing but Turkish aircraft, including transports dropping paratroopers, and thus when the first Noratlas approached at about 2 am, the jittery and exhausted gunners opened fire. The first three Noratlas landed safely, if peppered, but 'Niki 4', was shot down two miles short of the runway and its four crew and twenty-eight commandos killed. Private Athanasios Zafiriou was the only survivor. Hit in both engines and with two commandos killed and eleven wounded, 'Niki 7' made an emergency landing. Just before dawn, 'Niki 15' was last to arrive. Two aircraft never made it to Cyprus, one reporting navigational difficulties. All bar three returned to Greece. 'Niki 3' with engine problems and 'Niki 7' and 'Niki 12' both short of fuel were destroyed in an attempt to conceal evidence of direct Greek involvement in the war. The Battalion, which had lost thirty men and had eleven wounded, was designated the 35th RFU and despatched to Archbishop School in Nicosia to reorganise.

At 10 am on the 22nd, with the ceasefire scheduled for 4 pm and the Turks determined to gain as much negotiable territory as possible, Task Force Bora, which consisted of a squadron of seventeen M-47 tanks and a mechanized infantry company from the 5th Armoured Brigade (Brigadier General Haki Boratas) landed on Five Mile Beach as an immediate reinforcement, having left Mersin Naval Base at 1.30 pm the previous day. Major General Bedrettin Demirel, commander of the 39th Tank Division, handed control of the beachhead to Boratus, and even though most of the Special Strike Landing Force had not slept since the 19th and had been under constant shelling, Demirel was determined to capture Kyrenia using 50th Infantry Regiment and Task Force Bora. This would give the Turks a decent harbour and also access to roads leading towards the paras at Geunyeli.

The failure of 3rd (Kyrenia) Tactical Group to eliminate the beachhead led to Colonel Kombokis, who commanded Raider Command, taking control of operations from his HQ near Ayios Pavlos. His principal aim being to defend Kyrenia, he was reinforced by a company of the 346th Reserve Infantry Battalion, from 4th (Limassol) Higher Military Command, mounted on modified tracked artillery tractors and an AT-1 'Snapper' Anti Tank Platoon. Soon after mid-morning, an attempt by Turkish landing craft to land troops in Kyrenia harbour failed and was followed by 50th Infantry Regiment breaking out of the beachhead and driving 306th Infantry from its positions at Ayios Yeoryios. This effectively exposed the flanks of the 251st Infantry and the 33rd RFU, and as they withdrew, the defence of Kyrenia began to crumble; nevertheless, the Turks lost five M-48 tanks and an M-113 destroyed in stiff fighting. However, the National Guard were unable to prevent Turkish infantry entering Kyrenia at midday. Meanwhile, armoured columns breached the Kyrenia Pass and, passing through Bellapais and Dikomo, relieved the embattled Geunyeli Group by 5.30 pm. Another column linked up with the paras dropped near Borghaz naval base. An advance west along the coast road to Karavas was held up by the 2nd (Morphou) Tactical Group. The Turks quickly consolidated their hold on Kyrenia and during the afternoon 28th Infantry Division began landing, but further exploitation from the beachhead into the foothills was hindered by forest fires ignited by Turkish bombing. The landing brought the number of Turkish forces ashore to about 25,000 men. Elsewhere in Cyprus, the National Guard had largely neutralized the Turkish-Cypriot Fighters.

Throughout the fighting in the north, appeals from desperate expatriates and tourists had been picked by the Finnish UNFICYP, however not much could be done until the ceasefire came into force. Nevertheless, by 22 July, a Royal Navy task force was lurking off Kyrenia, and when evacuation arrangements were announced on the British Forces Broadcasting Service next day, the ships closed inshore and with the help of the Finns, 814 Naval Air Squadron Sea Kings and 845 Naval Air Squadron Wessex helicopters from HMS Hermes began lifting about 1,700 civilians, mainly British expatriates and tourists but also a Ukrainian dance troupe, from Six Mile Beach. Some had been trapped, along with wounded National Guard and Greek-Cypriot refugees in the Dome Hotel. The kindness of the commando carrier's sailors became legendary. Even when the warships were within range of Turkish tanks, the evacuation continued. The hotel was later taken over

**MAP 4 - NICOSIA AIRPORT**

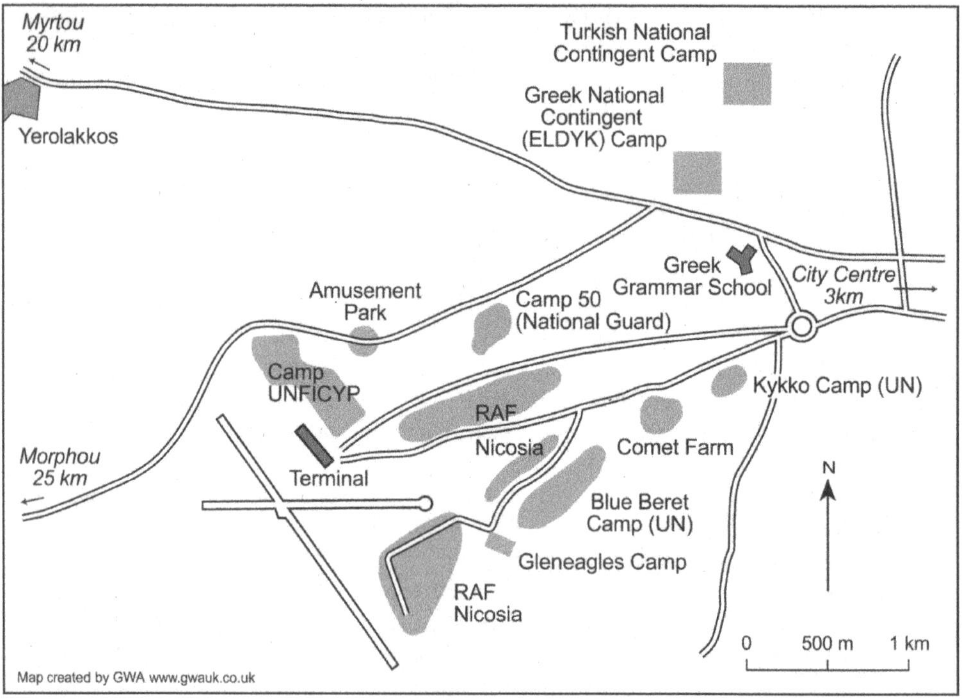

by A Troop, 7 (UNFICYP) Squadron RCT as a UN protected area. The dance troupe were handed over to a Soviet ship.

The British activated Operation *Fallacy* to evacuate Service dependants living in hirings and some of the several thousand tourists and foreign nationals collected by UNFICYP by flying them back to the UK as soon as possible. The Swedes and Americans also had evacuation plans. RAF transport aircraft converged on Cyprus, and while C-130 Hercules and Argosys hopped between Kingsway Airstrip, near Dhekelia, and RAF Akrotiri, VC-10s and Britannias flew to and from the UK. Over the next four days, about thirty flights flew 6,700 dependants and passengers from forty-six nationalities to RAF Brize Norton and Lyneham where RAF and Army reception teams, including Women's Royal Army Corps and the Royal Army Pay Corps organized cash advances and helped tired and frightened mothers and children. Throughout the evacuation, Air Chief Marshal Aiken openly broadcast that the British did not support the Turkish invasion. Meanwhile 518 Company, Royal Pioneer Corps, which had been flown out from Bicester, drove lorries through aggressive Turkish checkpoints into the deserted Famagusta to collect Service family property left in the 400 married quarters. A similar exercise took place in Limassol where a 40 Commando company in Operation *Snatch* helped pack belongings into 40,000 crates all of which were driven to Episkopi and later flown to the UK.

In Nicosia, 35th (Greek) RFU was instructed to reinforce the defence of the Airport against expected Turkish attacks. If the Turks captured it, it would be easier for them to fly in reinforcements. The airport also had symbolic value to the Greek-Cypriots. Several UNFICYP units were based in former Cyprus Emergency camps, such as Kykko Camp, that surrounded the abandoned RAF Nicosia. Camp UNFICYP to the north of the Terminal was occupied by a small REME Workshop and B Troop, 7 Squadron RCT. Its inmates witnesses to the fighting, the camp had been hit by bombs during a Turkish air raid. At about 10 am at Archbishop School the commandos discretely filed on to several old buses, away from inquisitive UNFICYP observers, and were driven by National Guard military police taking different roads to the Terminal, where they bolstered the existing defenders in the shape of a National Guard company, an ELDYK company, a field artillery battery, two tanks and an Airport Security company equipped with light anti-aircraft guns and five M-8 Greyhound armoured cars. One squadron was sent to National Guard Camp 50 while another one dug in around Air Traffic Control. Meanwhile, 41 Squadron joined a National Guard machine gun detachment on the Terminal roof.

By midday, it was again very hot. The Greeks were settling into their positions when a column of lorries carrying about 150 Turkish National Contingent stopped near Camp UNFICYP. Covered by an M-47 and an M-113, the infantry advanced towards the Terminal in extended line. The National Guard planned to ambush them in a killing zone of open, dry scrub in front of the Terminal and then finish them off with the Greyhounds. As the Turks passed the Terminal, the ambush was sprung, and to make matters worse for the attackers, M-79 phosphorus grenades set the scrub on fire. The survivors had no alternative but to withdraw to a small park near Camp UNFICYP with their wounded. The Camp was then caught in the exchanges of fire as Turkish 4.2-inch mortar bombs crept progressively closer to the Terminal in 200-yard bounds, one barrage destroying an airliner parked on the apron. Turkish infantry in the small park then provided covering fire for about a battalion to advance, however it was caught in the open by the Greyhounds. A National Guard sniper harassed a Turkish observation post using an abandoned house on a hill about 1,000 yards from the Terminal. A 90mm recoilless rifle crew on the roof also fired at the post, and when a shell dropped 200 yards short the Turks abandoned the house, apparently fearing they were about to be bracketed by a mortar.

During the early afternoon, Brigadier Henn instructed Colonel Beattie, the Canadian UNFICYP Deputy Chief of Staff, to negotiate a ceasefire at the Airport. Collecting two 1 Commando, Canadian Airborne Regiment jeeps and arriving at Camp UNFICYP, Beattie was briefed that it seemed the Turks were prepared to ignore the ceasefire until they were ready to negotiate. When Beattie arrived at the Airport, he was somewhat taken aback to find Greek commandos among the defenders. Major Herbert, who commanded 7 Squadron, then arrived at the Terminal to negotiate with the defenders and suggested, a little rashly, that UNFICYP would ensure the Airport would not fall into Turkish hands. When he realized he had made a gaffe and withdrew the statement, a Greek officer accused him of lying and a commando was restrained as he leapt forward to shoot him. Major General Prem Chand then declared the Airport to be a UN protected place, and within hours a UNFICYP force drawn from the British, Canadian and Finnish contingents arrived. The Greeks lost two men killed in this epic four-hour battle that became part of Greek-Cypriot military folklore. When the UN ceasefire came into force, the Turks held about seven per cent of Cyprus in a triangle stretching from a few hundred yards west of Five Mile Beach to Kyrenia and south to Geunyeli. They had lost an estimated fifty-seven killed, about 185 wounded and 242 missing. About 5,000 Greek-Cypriots had been displaced.

## THE TURKISH INTERVENTION

Nicos Sampson, now largely discredited, was forced from office by Glavkos Clerides, who complemented the terms of the 1960 Constitution. The British military authorities believed it safe enough for Service families sheltering in Episkopi to return to their married quarters in Limassol. The refugee camp at Happy Valley accommodated about 5,600 refugees, almost all Turkish-Cypriot. An *ad hoc* Turkish coffee shop had equipment that bore a remarkable similarity to parts used by the Bath Section of 10 Ordnance Support Battalion. 'Save the Children', 19 Field Ambulance and a medical centre established at St John's School provided medical care and welfare. Next day, under intense pressure after its damaging interference in Cypriot affairs, the Greek Junta collapsed and was replaced by Prime Minister Constantine Karamanlis, who returned from exile in Paris; this first step in the return to democratic government was welcomed by Turkey. However, discussions in Geneva between Greece, Turkey and Great Britain ran into trouble on 26 July when Ankara refused to consider any constitutional plan unless the Turkish National Contingent and intervention forces remained in Cyprus and the National Guard withdrew from Turkish-Cypriot enclaves. Athens insisted that both opposing forces must be withdrawn. The Greeks objected to any discussions they considered to be outside the 1960 Constitutional Agreement. Meanwhile, agreement reached at the end of July to re-establish the Green Line in Nicosia was fragile, but when the Turks tinkered with the territory that they had gained, UNFICYP doubled its strength to 4,100 men with reinforcements, in particular additional British anti-tank weapons, and withdrew isolated units and those likely to be exposed to the further fighting to safer areas.

Heavy fighting then broke out at Ayios Ermolaos and Sisklipos, with the ill-equipped National Guard driven out after three days, and then on 1 August, in the first stages of the Battle of Kornos, the 28th Infantry Division probed 2nd (Morphou) Tactical Group positions and seized Hill 1024 from 316th Infantry near Kyparissavoun and advanced toward Lapithos. During the night, B Company, 31st RFU recaptured the hill and defeated a Turkish commando counter-attack but was forced to abandon it next afternoon. 316th Infantry ambushed an armoured column, destroying an M-47 tank and M-113 APC and handing over a captured tank and an APC to 286th Mechanized Infantry Battalion. Although 2nd Tactical Group occupied strong positions at Karavas and had been reinforced by an ELDYK company, at dawn on the 6th, Turkish marines and tanks, their left flank protected by Turkish commandos and 61st Infantry Regiment on the high ground and supported by tactical air support, breached the block but were held up outside Lapithos for two days by the Greeks fighting a stiff rearguard action that allowed the National Guard to withdraw to positions along the road from Panaga Pass to Nicosia.

National Guard Command knew that although its forces had fought with tenacity and courage, there was little chance of holding the Turks anywhere. The only option was to fight a delaying action until diplomacy and a political solution prevailed, with indications that partition was likely. The strategy was based on holding the defensive Troodos Line that ran roughly from Morphou to Nicosia and south-east to Famagusta. The current situation was that the Turks were boxed into its enlarged beachhead. On the left flank, 2nd (Morphou) Higher Military Command defended the road that ran from the coast through Panagra Pass and south to Skylloura. In the centre were the two Greek battalions. On the right flank, where it was expected the Turkish assault would fall, was 3rd (Nicosia) Higher Military Command supported by the eleven remaining tanks and most of the artillery in depth. Defending Famagusta was 15th Tactical Group. Some battalions were still re-organizing after the ceasefire. Morale was low and desertions a problem, particularly by men with families trapped in Turkish-held territory.

On 10 August Glafkos Clerides and Rauf Denktash met in Geneva, but within two days the talks stalled when the Turks demanded that thirty per cent of Cyprus should be handed over. While Clerides rejected partition and the inevitable population displacement, the Turkish demand was largely supported by London. Ankara refused to allow the Greek-Cypriot delegation two days to consult, on the grounds that it would give them more time to procrastinate. Turkey was only too aware that Archbishop Makarios and hardline Greek-Cypriots had envisaged Cyprus as an Hellenic island free of its Turkish-Cypriot population. Shortly after 2 am on 14 August the talks collapsed, and in a move that would see general diplomatic support for the Turkish-Cypriots convert to immediate global disapproval, at about 6.30 am 6th Corps launched Operation *Attila Two*.

While the 28th Infantry Division advanced on two fronts east toward to Tymbou and west to Karavas, the 39th Tank Division tested 12th Tactical Group positions in the Mia Milia area and then, at mid-morning, tanks bypassed a minefield, sliced through 399th Infantry Battalion and headed through the eastern suburbs of Nicosia. The few National Guard anti-tank gunners were unable to prevent the tanks breaking out on the Mesaoria plain in a noticeably leisurely advance. Ahead, refugees clogged the roads. As the National Guard right wing collapsed, the shattered 9th and 12th Tactical Groups fell back through the city and retreated toward Famagusta and the Austrian UNFICYP

# THE TURKISH INTERVENTION

sector. Three Austrians were killed in a Turkish air strike. By the early evening, 341st Reserve Infantry had abandoned their positions defending Famagusta, leaving behind a battery of former British 6-Pounder anti-tank guns and three broken down T-34 tanks, and joined other dejected columns withdrawing to Larnaca, using a road through the ESBA, on the proviso that they loaded their arms into one vehicle in each convoy and were escorted by armed British soldiers.

The Greek sector saw the severest fighting of the war. When the ceasefire collapsed, the Turkish-Cypriot Fighters and National Guard along the Green Line began exchanging fire. Two 50th Infantry Regiment battalions overran Yerolakkos, west of Nicosia, but as they advanced up a shallow valley towards the ELDYK camp two miles north-east of the Airport and attempted to isolate it from Nicosia, they came under intense fire from the Greeks in strong defensive positions centred around a substantial three-storey school at the head of the valley. The problem for the Finnish UNFICYP based in Kykko Camp was that their camp overlooked the valley and the high ground was tactically important to the Greeks. When National Guard artillery and mortars were deployed adjacent to the British UNFICYP at Gleneagles Camp, several soldiers were wounded by Turkish retaliatory aircraft, artillery and mortars which soon pounded the area, sending shrapnel and rock splinters all over the place. During the morning, 28th Infantry Division attacked 2nd (Morphou) Higher Military Command and lost several tanks at Ayios Vasilios to 231st Infantry Battalion fighting an effective withdrawal toward Morphou. A captured M-47 was used against its former owners. During the night, 11th Tactical Group retired to the Troodos Line.

The British watched the fighting closing on the Sovereign Base Areas with increasing alarm. Although 40 Commando had left Cyprus after the 23 July ceasefire, Operation *Attila Two* led to its returning as part of a battle group that consisted of 7 (Sphinx) Commando Light Battery, 95 Commando Regiment naval gunfire support team, light helicopters from Dieppe Flight, 3 Commando Brigade Air Squadron and a forward air control section tasked to defend the Western Sovereign Base Area and minimize misunderstandings with the National Guard and the less predictable EOKA-B. Four 33 Squadron RAF Puma helicopters arrived to ease traffic between the two Sovereign Bases.

On the 15th, the National Guard right flank was largely quiet. The fighting around the school in the centre remained bitter, with every Turkish attack thrown back by the Greeks, and in the only tank action of the war, three T-34s destroyed an M-47. At about midday, 28th Division entered Morphou. The threat to the SBAs that the British had feared materialised during the late morning of the 15th when several Turkish tanks halted on a ridge overlooking Ayios Nikolaos. At about 2.45 pm, an A Squadron, 16/5 Lancer Ferret and a car carrying a BBC camera crew were shot up by a tank, and then an hour later a tank rumbled up the main gate. Lieutenant Colonel Ian Cartwright, who commanded 3rd Battalion, The Royal Regiment of Fusiliers, met its dusty, dirty commander and learnt, through an interpreter, that his fuel tanks were empty, he had no ammunition, his machine gun had jammed and he was lost. Observers of the leisurely Turkish advance from Nicosia had noted that Turkish tank crews seemed to have difficulty communicating with each other and navigation was not their strong point. Shown his position on a map and given several jerrycans of fuel, the Turkish tank commander was sent on his way. The threat increased significantly at 5 pm when Observation Point Charlie reported a tank battalion and M-113s formed up in battle formation in a shallow valley that led to the Base. Cartwright contacted the Turkish battle group and, with F-4 Phantoms patrolling overhead, had a tense fifteen-minute confrontation during which it appeared the Turks thought the ESBA was the National Guard camp at Milestone 3. The Turks wheeled left and overran the camp.

Most of Famagusta's 46,000 Greek-Cypriot inhabitants had fled the town, with about 10,000 making their way by foot, donkey, tractor, car, lorry and bus to the safety of Dhekelia where they were directed toward a camp 'complete with toilets' constructed by Royal Engineers in Athna Forest. A 19 Field Ambulance detachment set up a medical aid station and Army Catering Corps cooks supervised selected refugees preparing food, with 1,000 loaves needed daily, until the Red Cross and government organizations took over the welfare of the refugees.

At 6 pm a ceasefire brokered by the UN became effective. The Turks had reached their pre-determined Attila Line and occupied thirty-eight per cent of the island, more territory than had been agreed at Geneva but less than they expected. Casualty statistics are thought to be as follows:

|  | Killed | Wounded | Missing |
|---|---|---|---|
| Turkish Forces | 498 | 1,200 |  |
| Turkish Cypriots | 70 | Not known |  |
| Greek Forces National Guard | 88 | 148 | 83 |
| Greek-Cypriots | 309 | 1,179 | 909 |

(Source: Wikipedia: *Military operations during the Turkish invasion of Cyprus*)

Significantly, the Turkish territory produced about seventy per cent of the total gross product of Cyprus from the agriculture of the Mesaoria plain, the mining and quarrying, water and tourism. Some 200,000 Greek-Cypriots, who made up eighty-two per cent of the population, had abandoned their homes; by 1975, there were just 20,000 in the north, most living in the Karpas Peninsula. Faced with Turkish threats, the Cyprus Government and the UN organized the transfer to the north of 70,000 Turkish-Cypriots trapped in the south. In February, Turkey enraged the international community by declaring the occupied area to be a federated Turkish province and, in an apparent attempt to balance the demographics of Cyprus, moved in 37,000 Anatolians, most into houses once owned by Greek-Cypriots. This was contrary to Article 49 of the Geneva Convention stating that, *'The Occupying Power shall not deport or transfer parts of its own civilian population into the territory it occupies.'* Accusing this plantation of being a form of colonialism, the UN continues to demand the restoration of human rights across Cyprus, freedom of movement, freedom of settlement and the right to property. The UN-sponsored Committee on Missing Persons continues to demand that the remains of the missing be returned their families and investigates those who cannot be accounted for, including those who failed to return from prison camps. Mutual accusations of atrocities, destruction and plundering of cultural heritage and artefacts, such as mosques and churches, persist. In 1983, there was near universal condemnation of Turkey when Ankara converted the provincial administration in the north into the independent Turkish Republic of Northern Cyprus. Attempts to resolve the partition have been unsuccessful, with Turkey regarded as the obstruction. The Cyprus Government, in rejecting a UN-sponsored referendum for a United Cyprus Republic in which displaced Greek-Cypriot families would have had their properties returned or be offered compensation, have been equally difficult.

Meanwhile, UNFICYP continues to patrol the Green Line, now essentially dividing the two countries. British and Argentine troops serving alongside each several years after the Falklands War offered an example of the reconciliation so clearly missing on the island.

## CHAPTER FIFTEEN

# Conclusions

After nineteen years of violent tension on the beautiful island in the eastern Mediterranean, the Turkish-Cypriots had achieved *takism* (separation), a concept that had not been on their shopping list in 1955 when the Greeks-Cypriots raised EOKA. The Greek-Cypriots had achieved independence but little else, *enosis* now a very distant target from the objectives set by Makarios and Grivas in 1954. Their drive to rid Cyprus of the Turkish-Cypriots in their bid to join the Hellenic motherland by using force failed during the Cyprus Emergency, as it did after independence. Partition was inevitable as soon as UNFICYP stepped into the neutrality breach. For the next ten years, US and British diplomacy fended off Warsaw Pact aspirations for a base in NATO's southern backyard and dissuaded the Turks from going to the assistance of their cousins, except for the limited provision of arms and equipment and some posturing. The crunch came when Grivas died in January 1974, followed by the increasing militancy of Athens, the imposition of Nicos Sampson as President and implied threats to Turkish-Cypriot security. In many respects, the Turkish intervention was justified under the 1960 Treaty of Guarantee, however procrastination by the Greek-Cypriots in giving the Turkish-Cypriots guarantees of security led to Operation *Attila Two* and the wrath of the international community against Turkey. The Turkish-Cypriots, victims of aggression since 1955, very quickly found themselves isolated from the national community. But how many tourists relaxing on the beaches and sipping brandy sours know of the violent history of Cyprus or that between 1955 and 1959, British soldiers died here and Service families were attacked.

For the man who brought such chaos to Cyprus, George Grivas, the island proved to be ideal for his idea of managing a guerrilla campaign almost entirely on his own. A firm believer in his own capability but unwilling to delegate, his drive to succeed where he and Greece had failed during the Second World War alienated those closest to him, notably Archbishop Makarios, who soon regarded him as a liability, and Gregoris Afxentiou, arguably his most able guerrilla. Apart from his recces and the few months he spent with the Guerrilla Groups, Grivas had little contact with the average Cypriot but claimed that 'EOKA used methods that were based on mass psychology by persuasion and providing an example of endurance and stimulated the people's faith in *enosis*'. He firmly believed that proclamations issued from his dugouts were regarded as sacred documents and that his orders overrode the existing laws.

As had frequently been the case since 1945, British Armed Forces were initially committed to Cyprus to aid weak civil authorities at short notice and were faced with generally unreliable intelligence on EOKA. They were largely ignorant of the political setting, inadequately trained for the environment and lacked appropriate equipment; however, as soon as responsibility for tackling the insurgency was handed over to a soldier, Field Marshal Harding, matters changed. Harding knew the value of intelligence, and within weeks units began patrolling against EOKA hides. In spite of the headline-grabbing pressures of Murder Mile, the Troodos fire and some weaknesses in field discipline, he refused to give in over the vexed question of the military interrogation of armed insurgents. Human Intelligence is a critical information asset. Grivas frequently claimed that the Security Forces had alienated the population by employing harsh measures but was careful to deny that the conduct of EOKA in executing Greek-Cypriots or attacking the Red Cross insignia and Service dependants was unjustified. In his Memoirs, he advocated that civilized peoples can be won 'only through good treatment and a just and paternal administration', a principle that EOKA could not claim to promote as a feature of its political philosophy.

In many respects, the Cyprus Emergency established some fundamental principles of internal security and counter insurgency that the Armed Forces had first adopted in urban and rural settings in Palestine, Malaya, Indonesia and Indo-China (Vietnam) after 1945 and would use in Borneo, Aden and Northern Ireland. Comparisons between the Emergency and the Troubles in Northern Ireland, just ten years apart, should not be avoided. During the intervening ten years, several Regular officers and NCOs gained experience in middle and senior leadership appointments and applied the experience they had gained since 1955. In 1969, the Armed Forces were deployed to support the civil authorities in Northern Ireland and were also initially reliant upon selected intelligence provided by a sectarian police force. At the height of the Emergency in 1958, there were more troops in Cyprus, about 30,000, most of them National Servicemen of a larger army, than in Ulster in 1972 (25,000 Regulars). A critical factor in the intervening period was that society was less receptive to the robust military response to insurgency and terrorism, and while it took three years to defeat EOKA, it took thirty-seven years to neutralize armed rebellion a one-hour flight from London.

In terms of casualties, successive British governments since 1945 have played down numbers by selectively excluding non-battle casualties, such as training and road traffic accidents. This is not the case for those commemorated in Commonwealth War Graves Commission First and Second World War cemeteries, where all those who died at home and in theatres of operations are listed. This compares with the official figure for Cyprus of 105 Service personnel killed and 603 wounded. The British are buried in Wayne's Keep Cemetery. It has a history back to 1878 when the British first landed in Cyprus and houses the graves of Sergeant Samuel MacGaw VC and four members of the Black Watch who died during that year. However, it is now in the UN Buffer Zone, and this and the cost of travelling to Cyprus and the attendant bureaucracy has prevented most families and friends from visiting the graves of their sons and husbands. One woman recently visited her brother's grave fifty-one years after he was killed.

To compensate for the inaccessibility of Wayne's Keep, the British Cyprus Memorial Trust was formed to erect a memorial. It lists 371 Service personnel killed, including the non-battle fatalities most aged twenty-one years and under: thirteen Royal Navy, sixteen Royal Marines, 274 Army and sixty-nine RAF. The Patron is Brigadier Arthur Valerian Wellesley, the 8th Duke of Wellington, who commanded the Royal Horse Guards during the Emergency. Not mentioned are the two dependants murdered, which is a shame. Their sacrifice and support is a critical but frequently overlooked resource. Trustees include General Sir John Waters of the Glosters, and Lieutenant General Sir Henry Beverley of the Royal Marines. Also represented on the Trustees are the British Cyprus Veterans Association, which is open to anyone who has served with the British Armed Forces in Cyprus, the Cyprus Memorial Family Association, for relatives of those remembered on the memorial, and Friends of the Cyprus Memorial, which includes the Royal British Legion. The Memorial, at last, now offers still grieving families some closure, but as is so common with the post-1945 campaigns, few names of those who died in Cyprus appear on war memorials in cities, towns and villages across Great Britain. Examining 353 casualties listed in *Mayhem in the Med* between 1 April 1955 and 17 March 1959 gives a typical distribution of those who died:

- Ninety-one were killed in action during riots, patrol clashes, ambushes, and by landmines and grenades/bombs
- Forty-one murdered while off-duty by gunmen and bombs, including several involved in the Suez operations

- Forty-one non-battle fatalities such as friendly fire incidents, weapon accidental discharges and other causes, such the Troodos forest fire
- Fifty-six fatalities involving vehicles and aircraft and drownings and lost at sea
- One hundred and twenty-four causes not known bar five dying in hospital, including an airman in transit from Iraq

When the late David Carter came to believe that those who served in Cyprus deserve recognition, he became custodian of the Cyprus element of the Cyprus chapter of the British Small Wars website (www.britains-smallwars.com).

So far as the police are concerned, the Cyprus Police lost thirty-seven officers (twenty-two Turkish-Cypriots and fifteen Greek-Cypriots) killed and 185 wounded. The Colonial Police Service lost seven officers, of whom five were murdered. The UK Police Unit lost eleven of whom six were murdered and two had accidental discharges. Constabularies represented were Bristol, Cheshire, Durham, Herefordshire, Kent, Leicester and Rutland, as well as three from the Metropolitan Police. Twenty-six British civilians were killed, most during 1958. Of the 238 civilians killed, 263 were Greek-Cypriots, 1956 being the worst year with 109 fatalities. Estimated EOKA casualties are 102, with twelve executed on the orders of Grivas. Sixty-five Turkish-Cypriots were killed, fifty-three of them in the sectarian violence between June and August 1958.

Cyprus has long been a favourite posting for the British. It was used to rest troops after long tours in Northern Ireland and is now a decompression staging post for those returning from Afghanistan. However, its location on the fringes of the Near and Middle East tinderbox meant that it sometimes gets caught up in events. Egyptian commandos stormed a hijacked plane in 1978 and, in 1988 Larnaca Airport experienced the longest hijack in aviation history of a Kuwaiti aircraft by some Iranians. At the time, the island was on a war footing after the bombing of Tripoli. Not only did Israeli frogmen limpet mine a Palestinian ship in Limassol, a car containing several Arab activists mysteriously blew up, probably the result of a bomb remotely triggered from an Israeli aircraft. The British did not escape. One Sunday evening in August 1986, the Palestinian Abu Nidal Group mortared RAF Akrotiri, hitting several married quarters and raking a beach with automatic fire. EOKA-B periodically emerges from the shadows, not so much in the pursuit of *enosis* but aiming to eject the British from the Sovereign Base Areas. The organization does not receive much support because the

Bases are a significant employer and contributor to the Cypriot economy. Nevertheless, it took advantage of the Palestinian threat in 1985 to blow up a water filtration plant near RAF Akrotiri and distributed leaflets in Limassol. It was nothing but an opportunistic strike.

As the British Cyprus Memorial Trustees record, 'But out of sight is not out of mind, and the Memorial is its own testimony that they have not been forgotten by the country to which they never returned and in whose service they died. Fifty years on, they deserve nothing less.' So far as the Military Covenant is concerned, the Cyprus Emergency has been largely forgotten.

# Bibliography

Anderson, David and Killingray, David, *Policing and Decolonisation: Nationalism, Politics and the Police 1917-65/Policing and Communal Conflict: The Cyprus Emergency 1954-69* Manchester University Press, Manchester, 1992.

Barker, Dudley, *Grivas: Portrait of a Terrorist* The Cresset Press, London, 1959.

Beadle, Major J C, *The Light Blue Lanyard: 50 Years with 40 Commando Royal Marines* Square One Publications, Worcester, 1992.

Birchall, Peter, *The Longest Walk: The World of Bomb Disposal* Arms and Armour, 1997.

Byford-Jones, W, *Grivas and the Story of EOKA* Robert Hale, London, 1959.

Clayton, Anthony, *Forearmed: A History of the Intelligence Corps* Brassey's (UK), 1993.

Crawshaw, Nancy, *The Cyprus Revolt* George Allen & Unwin, London, 1978.

Cyprus Government, *The Findings of the Commission of Inquiry into the Incidents at Geunyeli, Cyprus on 12 June 1958* Cyprus Government Printing Office, Nicosia, 1958.

Dimitrakis, Panagiotis, *British Intelligence and the Cyprus Insurgency 1955-1959* International Journal of Intelligence and CounterIntelligence Volume 21 Number 2, p375-349 (2008).

Godfrey, Major F A,
*History of the Royal Norfolk Regiment 1951-1969 Volume IV* The Royal Norfolk Regiment Association, Norwich, 1993.
*The History of the Suffolk Regiment 1946-1959*, Leo Cooper, 1988

Hallows, Ian, *Regiments and Corps of the British Army*, Arms and Armour, London, 1991.

Grivas, George, *The Memoirs of General Grivas* Longmans, London, 1964. (Ed. by Charles Foley)

Haswell, Jock, *British Military Intelligence* Weidenfeld and Nicholson, London, 1973.

Holland, Robert, *Britain and the Revolt in Cyprus 1954-1959* Clarendon Press. Oxford, 1998.

Johnson, David, *War in Peace 28 – Greek, Turkey or Cypriot; EOKA, Colonel Grivas and the terrorist campaign; From Mountain to Market Place* Orbis Publishing Ltd, London, 1983.

Linklater, Eric and Andro, *The Black Watch* Barrie and Jenkins, London, 1977.
McDonald, P G, *Stopping the Clock* Robert Hale, London, 1977.
Mitchell, Lt Col Colin, *Having Been a Soldier* Mayflower, Hamish Hamilton, London, 1969.
Parker, John, *The Paras: The Inside Story of Britain's Toughest Regiment* Metro, London, 2000.
Phelps, Major General L T H, *A History of the Royal Army Ordnance Corps 1945-1982* Trustees of the History of the Royal Army Ordnance Corps.
Royle, Trevor, *The Royal Scots: A Concise History* Mainstream Publishing Company, Edinburgh, 2006.
Stiles, Richard, *Mayhem in the Med: A Chronicle of the Cyprus Emergency 1955-1960* Savannah Publications & Richard GM Stiles, London, 2005.
*Time Magazine*: *With Rod and Gun* New York, 19 December 1955.
*Times, The*, Obituary – *Air Chief Marshal Sir John Aiken* 7 June 2005
Thompson, Major General Julian,
   *The Royal Marines: From Sea Soldiers to a Special Force* Sidgewick and Jackson, London, 2000.
   *Ready for Anything: The Parachute Regiment at War* Fontana/Collins, George Weidenfeld and Nicholson Ltd, 1989.
Vale, Colonel W L, *History of the South Stafford Regiment* Gale and Polden, Aldershot, 1969.
Young, David, *Four Five: The Story of 45 Commando 1943-1971* Leo Cooper, London, 1972.
Warner, Philip, *The Vital Link: The Story of the Royal Signals* Leo Cooper, London, 1989.

**Websites**
Argyll and Sutherland Highlanders History – Cyprus 1958 to 1959: www.argylls1945to1971.co.uk
Britain's Small War – Cyprus www.britains-smallwars.com
Carter, David, *Death of a Terrorist – Birth of a Legend*
   *EOKA Members List A to Z*
   *The United Nations Force in Cyprus*
   *The Secret War at Sea*
   *The Tragedy of 'Lucky Alphonse'*
Cranston, David, *Death on the Kykko Track*.
Dunlop, Jim, *With the Highland Light Infantry in Cyprus*.
Haff, Joseph, *Sea Patrol Cuts Cypriot Arming*.
Hunter, Bryan, *EOKA Meets the Parachute Regiment*.
Rickards, John, *The Gun Battle at Liopetri*.
Riley, Alan, *The Ashiotis Incident*
Rose, Christopher, *The Black Watch in Cyprus (1958-1961)*
Tippen, Lt Col, *Farewell to 1915 Flight*
Walker, Adrian, *The Intelligent Way*

Cooper, Tom; *Cyprus 1955-1973; Europe and Cold War Database;* October 1974; www.acig.org

Aberdeen Camp, 68
Abu Nidal Organization, attack on RAF Akrotiri, 214
*Adatepe* (Turkish destroyer), bombed by Turkish Air Force, 200–201
Adelphi Forest
   the Castle hideout network, 65, 78–9; search for Grivas (1957), 124
*Aegean*, SS (Piraeus-Rhodes ferry), 25
*Aelia*, SS (Greek ship), Customs discover haul of weapons, 77
Aeroflot, links with Cyprus, 181
Afxentiou, Georghiou (EOKA), 107
Afxentiou, Gregoris
   arrest warrant, 51; coroner's verdict, 131–2; EOKA second-in-command, 32; Famagusta town sabotage group, 26 firearms amnesty, 82; Group ordered to bomb Hermes airliner, 88; last stand and 'legend', 130–32; Lefkoniko Police Station raid, 63; the most able guerrilla, 211; Operation *Whisky Mak*, 128–32; Pitsillia Guerrilla Group, 65, 84, 105; and the raid on 'the Castle', 78, 79; recruits divers for Italian sunken ships, 32; sacked by Grivas, 51; whereabouts known, 124; wounded in Q-Patrol operation, 128, 142
Afxentiou monument, 132
Afxentiou, Vasilia (wWife of Gregoris), 132
Aganthangeolou, Papa Stavros, 22
   deported with Makarios, 89–90; Grivas and, 26–7
Aghirda
   RM Commando HQ, 58; Turkish parachute battalions delivered, 197, 198–9
Aiken, Air Chief Marshal Sir John RAF broadcast messages about Turkish invasion, 203
   Makarios leaves Cyprus, 192
   orders for evacuation of Service families, 192–3
aircraft
   Austers, 67, 117; Boeing 707, 198; Canberra bombers, 150; Dakota C-47, 201
   F-4 Phantom, 209; F-5 Fox, 198; F-100 Super Sabre, 200; F-102 Delta Dart, 198;

F-104 Starfighter, 200; Gannet A/S aircraft (FAA), 43; Gannet anti-submarine aircraft, 66; Hastings, 85, 86, 89; Hawker Hunter, 66, 86; hijacking of civil aircraft, 214; Meteors (air photo-recce), 86; Nord 2501 Noratlas, 201; Pembrokes, 86; Shackleton Maritime Reconnaissance aircraft, 28, 29, 43, 66, 85; Valettas, 86; Venom fighter bombers, 66, 150; *see also* helicopters
Aiya Varvara Monastery, EOKA weapons cache, 77
Akanthou
   1 Royal West Kents, 172; suspected; EOKA hideout, 159, 160
AKEL (Communist Reform Party), 16
   antipathy to *enosis*, 148; cell uncovered near Kykko Camp, 85; election support for Makarios (1973), 190; general election (1970), 188; methods studied by Grivas, 19; not infiltrated by Georghiadjis, 187; proscribed by Harding (1955), 81; resurgent (1952), 22, 26; thought by police to be the main threat, 39, 168
Akhna, 1 Leicesters action, 127
Akhna Police Station, weapons and radios seized by EOKA, 60
Akhyritou, shots fired by British, threats by Grivas, 161
AKOE, anti-EOKA leaflets (unofficial), 117
Akrotiri, Western Sovereign Base Area, 173
Akrotiri (RAF Base), 23, 48, 86
   attacked by Abu Nidal Group (1986), 214; decreasing strategic importance (1963), 179; EOKA bombings (1956 & 1957), 109, 150; EOKA devices found (June 1956), 99; a NATO asset, 138
   Princess Mary's Hospital (RAF), 41, 42, 127, 131; US U2 flights over Soviet Union, 188; *see also* Royal Air Force
*Alamein*, HMS, 42–3
Alastos, Doros (historian), 125
Alexander Barracks (Dhekelia), 153
Allen, Sgt Ernest RAF, honeytrap murder, 107
Alma Camp (Dhekelia)
   'Lobster Pot' detention compound, 81; Middlesex Regt, 68

Amiandos mine, EOKA raid, 65
Amiandos Police Station,
  EOKA attack, 54; *see also* Pano Amiandos
Amphibious Warfare Squadron, 58, 138
ANE (Valiant Youth of EOKA), 147, 148–9
Anglo-Egyptian Treaty (1936), 22
Anorthosis Sports Club, blown up by bomb disposal unit, 160
anti-smuggling blockade, Royal Navy/Fleet Air Arm, 28–31, 42–3, 66, 82
*Appleton*, HMS, boarding of Italian liner *Enotria*, 42
April Fool's Day 1 April, potential for disturbance, 51
Argentina, UNFICYP troops, 210
1 Argyll and Sutherland Highlanders (1 A & SH), 153
  constant surveillance system; (Paphos), 169; football team ambushed (Sept 1958), 162; nine day operation in Paphos, 172; Operation *Kingfisher*, 154; removal of EOKA slogans, 153–4; take over Larnaca sector, 171
Aristotelous, A.S. Kyriakos (Cyprus Police), murdered by EOKA, 95
Armitage, Sir Robert (Governor of Cyprus), 28, 51, 53, 92; assassination attempt, 53; posted to Nyasaland (Malawi), 61; arms and weapons, *see* weapons and explosives
Army Air Corps, 67, 162
Army Catering Corps, feed refugees from Famagusta, 209
Army/RAF families
  allowed back to married quarters (July 1974), 206; EOKA target, 55, 56, 78, 82, 91, 180; married quarters and hirings, 23, 47, 68, 91, 111, 121; safety of in Civil War (1974), 192–3, 198; safety of during Turkish invasion (1974), 203, 206
Artemiou, Nikki (EOKA courier), 36, 146
Ashiotis, Michael (EOKA), turns informer, 148
Ashmore, Jack Haliburton (Commissioner of Police), 21, 24
*Asturia*, HM Troopship, 132
Ataturk, Kemal, 178
Athna Forest, refugee camp, 209
Attila Line, 209
Austers

leaflet distribution, 117, 155; reconnaissance aircraft, 67
Australia
  Governor General Kendrew, 169
  UNFICYP troops, 183
Austria, UNFICYP troops, 183, 191, 207–8
Averoff, Evangelos (Greek Foreign Minister), 174
Avgorou, incident with Royal Horse Guards, 158–9
Ayios Dhometios, Sgt Hammond (RAOC) shot, 161
*Ayios Eleftherios* (caique), smuggled arms, 24
Ayios Ermolaos, National Guard driven out, 206
*Ayios Georghias* (caique)
  arms smuggling, 25–6, 28–31; impounded by Cyprus Police, 31, 51 sentences for all involved, 52, 111–12
Ayios Nikolaos
  2 Wireless Regiment, 49; 264 Signals Unit (RAF), 56
*Ayios Nikolaos* (caique), smuggled weapons, 22
Ayios Pantes church, EOKA hideout, 35
Ayios Spiridou, monastery searched, 77
Ayios Theodhorous, Cyprus National Guard attack, 187
Ayios Vasilios
  231st Infantry Battalion (CNG) fighting withdrawal, 208; intercommunal trouble, 156; mass grave of Turkish victims, 185
Azinas, Andreas (PEK General Secretary), 21, 24, 25; attempt to abort *Ayios Georghias* arms drop, 28–9 at Grivas departure, 176; incriminating note, 31; smuggled weapons, 22, 28
Azinas, Nicolas, 25

Baker, Brig Geoffrey (RA) (Chief of Staff to Harding), 65–6, 78, 90, 123; 1 & 3 Para for Special Operations, 85; final assessment before handing over to FitzGeorge-Balfour, 134–5
  launches Operation *Lucky Alphonse*, 101; launches Operations *Mustard Pot* and *Pepper Pot*, 97–8; need to guard Suez invasion force camps, 112; operational control of Sycamore helicopters, 118
Balfour, Brig R G V, *see* FitzGeorge-

# INDEX

Balfour
Balkans, Slavic Christian uprisings (19th century), 14–15
Ball, Gdsman (Grenadier Gds), 93
Ball, George (US Acting Secretary of State), 184
Banks, Pte Raymond (1 South Staffords), 111
Baring, Cornet C P (Royal Horse Guards), intercommunal violence, 157–8
Basif, PC Nihat (Cyprus Police), 94, 107
*Bastion*, HMS (LCT), 58
BBC
    counters Grivas' propaganda, 37; *Two Way Family Favourites*, 48
Beattie, Col (Deputy Chief of Staff Canadian UNFICYP), 205
Beatty, Pte John (1 HLI), Lefkoniko bomb, 119
Bell, L/Cpl William RMP, fatally wounded in Kendrew assassination attempt, 163
Benbow, Cpl Robert RM, EOKA Group captured, 102–3
Benson, Maj Gen (Chief of Staff to Keightley), 66
Benyon, Major, the Revd, wife and child injured EOKA attack, 77–8
Berengaria Village (army married quarters), 23, 47
Beresford, SAC John RAF, wounded by EOKA, 86
Berlin, Congress of (1878), 15
*Bermuda*, HMS, 159
Bevan, Aneurin, on the location of Middle East Command, 23
Bevan, Dr Charles (General Practitioner), shot by EOKA, 120
Beverley, Lt Gen Sir Henry RM, 213
Birbeck, Provost Sgt (WRAC), 119–20
birch, punishment for juveniles, 76
Bird, Chief Inspector (Cyprus Police), ballistics expert, 54
*Birmingham*, HMS, 58
1 Black Watch, 48, 171
    Honour Guard lowers Union Flag for last time, 178
Blake, Lt (Royal Horse Gds), in Avgorou, 158–9
Blakeway, Mne Benet RM, 87
Bloody Christmas (1963), 179–80
Boaden, LAC Thomas RAF, killed by mine, 172–3

Bolger, Rifleman (1 RUR), action at Liopetri, 166–7
bomb disposal officers (RAOC), 54–5, 114–15, 116, 126
bombs (home-made) *see* IEDs
Boratas, Brig Haki (5th Armoured Bde, Turkish), 202
Botelor, William (US Vice-Consul), killed by EOKA bomb, 106
Boufas, Lt Col Konstantinos, pressures Turkish beachhead, 199–200
Boult, Grp Capt Norman de W RAF, 89
Bourke, Sir Paget (Chief Justice), *The Findings of the Commission into the Incidents at Geunyeli... on 12 June [1958]*, 158
Bourne, Lt Gen Sir Roger (Commander-in-Chief MELF), 151
Boutos, Lt Col Georgios (286th Mech Inf Battn CNG), 197
Bowman, Pte Ronald (1 Leicesters), 93
Boyd, 2/Lt Kenneth (1 RUR), action at Liopetri, 166–7
Bradford, Surg Lt Guy RN, 58
Bradshaw, Lt (1 Gordons), ambushed by EOKA, 120–21
Britannia Camp, 1 Norfolks (Island Reserve), 68
British Army
    alleged mistreatment of prisoners, 94, 143–6, 163, 165; anti-EOKA leaflets (unofficial), 117; anti-terrorist tactics, 91; arrests of leading AKEL members, 81; basic training, 44; bomb disposal unit, 54-5, 114–15, 116, 126; camp security, 47–8; camps (Scale 'A', 'B' and 'C'), 47–8; civil disturbances in Cyprus (1931), 16; court martials follow torture allegations, 94; Cyprus after 1974, 214; Cyprus Emergency lessons learned, 212; defence spending reductions, 68, 138, 179; desertion attempts, 46; EOKA infiltration, 48; fires on demonstration, 27; GHQ Middle East, 23, 27; Grivas chased from 'the Castle', 79–80; Harding's reorganizations, 66–9; hospitals *see* military hospitals hostility received after Zurich Agreement, 177–8; HQ 3rd Division arrives as Peacekeeping Force, 181; HQ 3rd Division returns to UK (June 1964), 185; HQ Cyprus District, 27, 40, 55, 123, 181; HQ

Middle East Command, 22, 179; HQ Near East Command and safety of Service families, 192; joint search activities with Police, 55, 57, 58; liberation of Athens, 18–19; living conditions, 47–8; local employees, 35, 64, 93, 109, 139; lorry drivers, 59–60; Middle East Strategic Reserve, 85; National Servicemen, 43–4, 48, 85, 145; new equipment, 118, 121-2; off-duty troops banned from walking-out unarmed, 154; officer training, 44; overseas postings (travel), 44–5; permanent garrison installed in Cyprus, 23, 40–42, 46–8; profile of typical troops, 145; rear area logistics, 40; reductions and mergers, 138; regiments leave for UK (1958-59), 172, 175; reinforcements (October 1955), 67–8; response to Catherine Cutliffe murder, 164–5; response to EOKA actions, 49; review of fatalities and successes (1956–1958), 169; riot at funeral of Kharalambus Mouskas, 80–81; Riot Platoons, 60; rules of engagement, 57, 75; search for Grivas (1957 & 1958), 124, 154;
Strategic Reserve formed, 138; strength of in Cyprus (January 1956), 86; Suez Canal Zone, 13, 15; trading in curfew areas, 134; Truce Force (with Cyprus Army), 180–81; UNFICYP troops, 183, 185, 187, 191–2, 203, 204, 208; uniform in the Mediterranean, 45; worldwide committments, 85

British Army, *major units*
III Corps, 18; 1st Infantry Division, 55 3rd Infantry Division, 55, 121, 160–61, 181; 1 Guards Bde, 148, 172; 3 Infantry Bde, 121–2, 123–4, 128–34, 154, 159–60, 169, 171–2, 179; 19 Infantry Bde, 160–61; 50th (Independent) Infantry Bde, 55, 57, 66, 67, 68, 86, 126, 152, 155–8; 51st (Independent - Lorried) Infantry Bde, 55, 57, 66, 68, 85–6, 127–8, 165; *see also* Royal Marines; *and under names of regiments and units*

British Cyprus Memorial Trust, 213–14, 215
British Cyprus Veterans Association, 213
British Institute, burnt, 60
British Legion, 132, 213
protest against Afxentiou statue in Newark, 132
British Sovereign Base Areas, 172, 173, 179, 191; tourists and Turkish-Cypriot refugees, 198, 206; used for training, 179
Brown, Cpl Peter (1 Duke of Wellington's), 130
Bruce, Maj Hugh RM, comment on Kyrenia Castle break-out, 61
Bruce-Lockhart, Lt-Cdr (HMS *Comet*), 31
Buckley, 2/Lt Michael MBE (1 Norfolks), Guard Commander Government House, 93
*Burmaston*, HMS, intercepts Turk carrying arms TMT, 178
Burton, Cdr Tom RN (HMS *Comet*), 29–31
Cable and Wireless, 40, 126
*Cakmuk* (Turkish destroyer), bombed by Turkish Air Force, 200–201
Camp Elizabeth, Milpol Operations Room, 156, 158
Camp K *see* Kokkinotrimithia Camp ('Camp K')
Camp UNFICYP, Nicosia Airport, 204–5
Campbell, Lt Alistair (1 A & SH) removal of EOKA slogans, 153–4; success due to surveillance in Paphos, 169
Canada, UNFICYP troops, 183, 191, 205
Carter, David, Britain's Small Wars website, Cyprus chapter, 214
Carter, Sgt Hugh (Herefordshire Police, UK Police Unit), shot by Sampson, 114, 144
Cartwright, Lt Col Ian (3 RRF), 209
Carver, Maj Gen Mike,
in command of Truce Force, 181, 182; deputy commander UNFICYP, 183, 185
Casey, QMS Graham RM, killed while training, 143
Castle, Mrs Barbara (Labour MP), visits Cyprus, 163
the Castle, network of hideouts, 65, 78–9
casualties
attitudes of British governments, 213
British between 1955–and 1958, 41, 60, 81–2, 110–111, 114–15, 123, 163, 165, 169, 212–13; British Cyprus Memorial Trust, 213–14, 215; Cypriots (Greek and Turk) murdered by EOKA, 54, 81, 94–5, 123; from the Turkish intervention (July–August 1974), 209 intercommunal violence (Nov–Dec 1963), 181; UNFICYP, 183, 207–8

# INDEX

Chand, Maj Gen Prem (UNFICYP Commander), 198; declares Nicosia Airport a UN protected place, 205
Charalanbous, Dinos, weapons seized from police station, 55
*Charity*, HMS, search for *Ayios Georghias*, 28–9
Charlesworth, Lt (1 KOYLI), 103
*Charlton Star*, HM Troopship, 68
Chartas, Andreas (Nicosia Group Leader), 126
Chartas, Christos (EOKA), 65, 78, 79
children, of forces personnel, 82, 88
Chittock, Cpl Richard (1 Norfolks), 120
Christodoulides, Elli, 113, 146, 173
Christodoulides, Marios, 113
Christofi, Fotis (EOKA), captured by 2 Para, 118
church bells, silenced in Emergency regulations, 75
Churchill, Sir Winston, 18–19
civilians *see* expatriate British,; tourists
Clapp, Lt Michael RN, (*Comet* boarding party), 29–31
Clerides, Glafkos, 62
replaces Sampson as President, 206, talks with Denktash in Geneva, 207
Clerides, Yannis, 62
coastal surveillance, 66
codenames, EOKA members, 36
Colditz Castle, 61
2 Coldstream Guards, UNFICYP duties, 191–2
Collier, Lt Col Frederick (Asst Director, Supply and Transport), shot while at home, 161
Colonial Police Service, casualties of the Emergency, 214
*Comet*, HMS, intercepts *Ayios Georghias*, 29–31
Commings, Lt Col John (1 South Staffords), 89
Commonwealth War Graves Commission, 213
communications
Brigade Signals Troops, 67; field telephone lines, 67; HF and VHF, 67 Marconi Relay System, 40–41
Communist Bloc *see* Eastern Bloc
condoms, military use of, 46
Congress of Berlin (1878), 15
Constantinides, Demitrakis (EOKA), 35 captured by Marines, 103

Constantinou, Minas, Q-Patrol action, 142
Cook, Pte (1 Norfolks), 120
Coombe, Maj Brian GM (RE), ambushed by Drakos Group, 80; attitude to his medal, 81
Coral Bay
Leave Camp, 58; NAAFI jukebox bomb, 121; radar detachment, 27, 30
cordon-and-search operations, 57, 58, 79
Corkran, Lt R S (3 Grenadier Gds), Greek-Cypriots at Geunyeli, 157–8
COSHEG, 'Wanted Men in Cyprus' (booklet), 117, 143
Costas, Michael (EOKA), 147
Cotsapas, Evghenios, (sabotage group leader), 26, 50
courier system, EOKA, 36–7, 85, 98, 101, 113, 172–3
Cremer, John (retired Civil Servant), EOKA hostage, 109
Crimean War (1854–56), 15
Crisell, CSM Roy (1 Leicesters), murdered, 97
Crisham, AVM Joseph RAF, 89
Cromwell, anti-EOKA leaflets, (unofficial), 117
Culkin, Staff/Sgt Joe (RAOC), bomb disposal casualty, 114–15
curfews
Darling's programme of, 169; in rural areas, 133–4, 159; in urban areas, 100, 114, 155
Customs officials, EOKA smuggling and, 37, 141
Cutliffe, Catherine, murdered by EOKA, 163–4
Cutliffe, Margaret, tragedy in Famagusta, 163-4
Cutliffe, Sgt (RA), returns to UK, 165
*Cyprian Chronicle* (as cited in *Mayhem in the Med*), 165
*see also Mayhem in the Med* (Stiles)
Cypriot Intelligence Service, uncover assassination plots, 190
*see also* Cyprus Police
Cyprus
annexed by Britain (1914), 15–16; attempt to undermine the Orthodox Church, 126; Attila Line, 209; bicycles banned at night, 162; boycott of UK businesses (1958), 153, 162; British

Crown Colony (1925), 16; British enclaves predicted, 138; British Sovereign Base Areas, 172, 173, 179, 198; Budget crisis (1931), 16; ceasefire negotiated between Greeks and Turks, 180–81; civil war (1974), 192–4; communists *see* AKEL constitutional discussions (guarantor powers), 206 contribution to allied effort in WWII, 16; declared a Republic (Aug 1960), 178; demarcation line between communities, 181, 185, 209; disturbances follow EOKA ceasefire, 175; divided into three control zones by British Army (Jan 1964), 181; early history, 14; economic consequences of Emergency, 177; Emergency regulations, 75-6; *enosis* and inter community relations, 177–8; EOKA ceasefire (1957), 136–7; general strike, 55; geography, 13–14; government intelligence structure, 66, 138–9; Greek-Turkish constitution fractures, 178; Harding's internal security organization, 65–9; intelligence apparatus overhauled by Foot, 151; inter-community tensions (1957–58 & 1960-63), 151, 178–9; intercommunal violence (1963–64), 179–84; judiciary and EOKA intimidation, 64; Lancaster Gate tripartite conference on security (1955), 56, 63; Lancaster House negotiations, 169, 172–3; Legislative Council proposed, and dropped, 23–4; Makarios deportation aftermath, 91–3; mass arrests and sudden curfews under Darling, 169; military build up to combat UAR, 160–61; offered to Greece (1915), 15; punitive measures to counter EOKA, 59; removal of slogans, 153–4; Republic of Cyprus Government rejects referendum on a United Republic, 210; review of fatalities and successes against EOKA (1956–1958), 169; secretly ceded to Britain (1878), 15; State of Emergency declared (November 1955), 75–6; suitability for guerrilla warfare, 20; Transitional Council, 173, 176; Turkish civil servants dismissed, 180; Turkish and Greek army contingents arrive (1959), 177; undercover counter-terrorist actions by Israelis, 214;

UNFICYP *see* UNFICYP *see also* Greek-Cypriots; Turkish-Cypriots
Cyprus Airways, DC-3 Dakota blown up, 88
Cyprus Armed Forces, 173
  Cyprus Army disbanded, 185; Makarios considers disarming, 183; Truce Force (Dec 1963), 180–81
Cyprus Bar, rejects Harding's White Paper on *Allegations of Brutality...*, 145–6
Cyprus Broadcasting Service, EOKA attacks, 49, 56
Cyprus Emergency, lessons learned by British Army, 212
*Cyprus Mail* (newspaper), demands explanation for Geunyeli deaths, 158
Cyprus Memorial Family Association, 213
Cyprus National Guard (CNG)
  Grivas in command, 185–7; abandons Athalassa HQ, 196; artillery force Turkish ships to withdraw, 197; attacks Turkish villages and strongpoints, 186, 187; battalion ambushed by Turkish- Cypriot Fighters, 196; Battle of Kornos (Aug 1974), 206–7; battle for Nicosia Airport, 203–5; casualties (July-August 1974), 209; counter-attack Geunyeli (July 1974), 196, 199; coup to oust Makarios, 191–2; defence of Kyrenia (July 1974), 200, 202; delaying action until political solution (Aug 1974), 207; disarms Swedish UNFICYP unit, 186; drive through Episkopi BSBA, 193; driven out of Ayios Ermolaos and Sisklipos, 206; engaged with Turkish-Cypriot Fighters, 197–8; fail to repel Turkish beachhead, 196–7; fighting along the Green Line (Nicosia), 208; friendly fire on Operation *Niki* transports, 201–2; learn to cooperate with British Army, 198; morale and desertions, 207; Morphou reinforce-ments bombed and strafed, 197; Operation *Aphrodite Two* activated, 188, 195–8; organizational structure, 185, 189–90; pass through ESBA as withdraw to Larnaca, 208; patrol boats sunk by Turkish forces, 195; RFU battalions take St Hilarion, 199; Turkey demands disbandment, 187–8; unable to hold advance of Turkish Army, 207–8; 195th Anti-Aircraft Battalion, 201-2; 2nd

# INDEX

(Morphou) Higher Military Command, 207, 208; 3rd (Nicosia) Higher Military Command, 207; 4th (Limassol) Higher Military Command, 197, 202; 231st Infantry Battalion, 208; 241st Infantry Battalion, 199; 251st Infantry Battalion, 202; 316th Infantry Battalion, 206; 399th Infantry Battalion, 207; 286th Mechanised Infantry Battn, 197, 199–200, 206; 306th Reserve Infantry, 199–200, 202; 341st Reserve Infantry, 208; 346th Reserve Infantry, 202; 31st RFU, 206; 33rd RFU, 200, 202; 2nd (Morphou) Tactical Group, 197, 199–200, 202, 206–7; 3rd (Kyrenia) Tactical Group, 196–7, 202; 9th Tactical Group, 207–8; 11th Tactical Group, 208; 12th Tactical Group, 207–8; 15th Tactical Group, 207

Cyprus Police
accusations of misconduct, 143–4; allegations of mistreatment of prisoners, 94; appeal for volunteers, 55; arrest KEM members (1958), 178; attacks on Central Police HQ, 56, 147; Auxiliary Police (mostly Turkish), 56, 99, 155–8; *Ayios Georghias* impounded, 31; casualties of the Emergency, 214; disturbances subdued, 27; Emergency Special Constables recruited, 56–7, 142; EOKA collaborators, 59, 88, 97, 100, 111, 125, 126, 139, 168, 171; EOKA disturbances (April 1955), 51–2; EOKA intimidation campaign, 53–5; expansion of (1954–58), 100; fail to connect EOKA, Athens and Makarios, 32; failing morale, 63–4; general inefficiency, 21, 24, 28, 39, 168; greater reliance on Turkish-Cypriots, 99, 100, 143; Greek-Cypriots not trusted, 99 holding cages for suspects (Nicosia), 126; ignorance of *enosis* movement, 24; inform for EOKA, 35, 54, 78; joint search activities with Army, 55, 57–8 loyal officers in July 1974 coup, 191–2; Operation *Lucky Alphonse*, 101; operational capability collapsing (late 1955), 55–7; Operations *Mustard Pot* and *Pepper Pot*, 97–8; police stations radio antennas, 67; provide EOKA hideouts, 125; recognised as a security risk, 78; reformed by Makarios, 188; report of Cyprus Police Commission, 99–100; riots (Dec 1957), 151; search for gunrunners, 141; senior Colonial Officer killed, 120; slow response to British Instute fire and riot, 60; strategy to restore morale and normality, 99–100; success of (1 April 1955), 49; Turkish-Cypriot Police disarmed (Dec 1963), 180; unprepared for an emergency, 138–9; *see also* Cypriot Intelligence Service; Police Mobile Reserve; Special Branch; Tactical Police Reserve; UK Police Unit

Cyprus Police Commission, 99–100
Cyprus Prison Service
mutinies by prisoners, 154; operation of detention camps, 59
Cyprus Regiment, 16
Signal Troop, 40–41
Cyprus Supreme Court, 173
independent judge (West German), 173, 179
Cyprus Turkish Forces Regiment, opposed by 1 (ELDYK) Battalion, 195

*Daily Mirror*, (newspaper), 184
*Daily Telegraph*, (newspaper), 165
Darling, Maj Gen Kenneth (Director of Operations)
background, 168; arrangements for deporting Grivas, 174–5; awaits on London for arrest of Grivas, 174; personal weapons offered to all expatriates, 170–71; praise for 1st Wiltshires, 172; tightens screw on EOKA, 169, 170–72
Dasent, Lt (1 Duke of Wellington's), 129
Davis, Pte John (1 Duke of Wellington's), uncovers EOKA hideout and cache, 125
Dawson, DS (Special Branch), subterfuge concerning Grivas' location, 174
de Klee, Captain (Scots Gds/GIPC), 113
Dear, Brian (Special Branch linguist), murdered, 154
Demetrakis, Christodoulou (Potamitissas Group Leader), 127
Demetrios, Nicolas, birched, 76
Demetriou, Andreas (EOKA gunman), 77, 95
Demetriou, Georghios (EOKA), Lefka Group leader, 143
Demirel, Maj Gen Bedrettin (39th Tank Div, Turkish), 202
Demmon, Sgt Leonard (Metropolitan

Police, UK Police Unit), decorated for attempt to prevent prisoner escape, 111–12, 125
Demosthenous, Station Sergeant Ioannis (Cyprus Police), 54
Dempster, CSM (Provost Group, 16 Ind Para Bde), 119–20
*Deniz*, MV, carrying arms for TMT, 178
Denktash, Rauf (Turkish-Cypriot Leader), 152; first meeting of Transitional Council, 176; talks with Clerides in Geneva, 207; TMT, 161
Denmark, UNFICYP troops, 183, 191
detention camps, for EOKA suspects, 59, 134–5
1 Devonshire and Dorsetshire Regiment (1 Devon and Dorsets), at Episkopi, 171
*Devonshire* HM Troopship, 153
Dhavlos Camp, 48
Dhekelia
 Alexander Barracks, 153; Alma Camp, 68, 81; BFPO 53, 48; British Military Hospital, 41; Eastern Sovereign Base AREA, 172–73; EOKA bombings, 109; EOKA Sabotage Group, 33, 84, 91; foreign missions evacuated to, 200; 40 Motor Transport Company, 41; regiments leave, 171
Dhekelia/Famagusta, failed attack on Power Station (1 April 1955), 49, 158
*Diamond*, HMS, Operation *Lucky Alphonse*, 101
Digenes Akritas, 17
Digenes (codename for Grivas), 25, 31, 51, 64, 97, 132; arrives in Cyprus (1954), 25; leaflets in Makarios's house, 77; leaves Cyprus (1959), 175; pamphlets reveal EOKA still plotting, 147; *see also* Grivas
Dillan, L/Cpl (1 RUR), action at Liopetri, 167
*Dilwara*, HM Troopship, 121, 123
Doherty, Pte Benjamin, Lefkoniko bomb, 119
Dome Hotel (Kyrenia), 203
donkeys, military pack transport, 60
Dow, Sgt Alexander (1 Gordons), EOKA ambush, 120
Dowdall, L/Cpl (1 Duke of Wellington's), 130
dowsing, indicates area of EOKA hideouts, 154
Drakos, Markos (Guerrilla leader), 36, 39 ambush Gordons convoy, 120–21;

ambush Maj Coombe RE, 80; assassination attempt on Armitage, 53; detained in Kyrenia Castle, 55, 61; killed near Nikitari, 124–5; Kykko Guerrilla Group, 65; Kyrenia Castle break-out, 61, 83; orders from Grivas (June 1956), 105; Sabotage Group action (1 April 1955), 49; Vassiliki hideout, 84; weapons cache found, 121
Droushiotis, Yannakis (Guerrilla leader), 84
Droushiotou, Nina (EOKA courier), 113
Droushot, Aristidou (EOKA), captured in Operation *Lucky Dip*, 133
1 Duke of Edinburgh's Royal Regiment, takes ove Nicosia control zone (Feb 1964), 181
1 Duke of Wellington's Regiment captures Matsis and senior EOKAs, 125–6; Operation *Black Mak*, 125–6; search for Afxentiou, 128–32; UNFICYP unit Limassol, 187
Dulson, Capt (RAMC/Wiltshires M.O.), injured in bomb attack, 95
Dunn, Lt Tony RN (HMS *Comet*), 29–30, 32
1 Durham Light Infantry (1 DLI), 155, nine day operation in Paphos, 172

East End Camp (Ktima), 68
1 East Surrey Regiment, to Libya, 161
Eastern Bloc, seek intelligence base in Cyprus, 179, 211
 *see also* Soviet Union
Ecevit, Bülent (Prime Minister of Turkey), solicits aid from Britain (1974), 194
Economides, Maroulla (EOKA activist), 146
Eden, Sir Anthony, self-government proposal for two communities, 56, sends Lord Radcliffe to Cyprus, 91
Eden, Sgt Tony (Metropolitan Police, UK Police Unit), decorated for attempt to prevent prisoner escape, 111–12
EDMA (United Democratic Party), 177
Efstathiou, Augustis (EOKA), 130–31
Efstathiou, Chief Inspector Costas (Cyprus Police), drives Grivas to Limassol, 105
Egby, Robert, (photo-journalist), 161
Egypt
 British forces redeployed to Cyprus, 22; Egyptian commandos storm

# INDEX

hijacked airliner in Cyprus, 214; King Farouk deposed, 22; Six-Day War (1967), 187; Suez Canal Zone, 13, 15; Suez Crisis (1956), 109, 120; tension with Israel, 85; United Nations Emergency Force 2, 191; Yom Kippur War with Israel (1973), 191; *see also* United Arab Republic

ELAS
Allied support, 17; gun battles with Royalists, 18–19; methods influence Grivas, 19, 33

ELDYK (Hellenic Forces Regiment) 2nd Battalion, 198, 200; arrive in Cyprus, 177; attacking Turks at Geunyeli, 195, 196, 199; at the Battle of Kornos, 206; battle with Turkish 50th Infantry, 208; casualties (July-August 1974), 209; coup d'etat planned by Greek officers, 190; defence of Nicosia Airport (1974), 203–5; with Greek-Cypriot militias in Ktima (1964), 182; incident with Royal Green Jackets at Kophinou (1967), 187; join Sampson and EOKA attacking Turkish Cypriots, 180; Makarios cuts the numbers, 188; officers murdered (1964), 183; Operation *Niki* friendly fire incident, 201–2; 35th RFU, 202–4; troop rotation, 194

Eleftheriou, Christakis (Guerrilla leader), 39, 49, 84
attack on Colonial Secretariat (1 April 1955), 49

Eliades, Socrates, 141, 173, 174
hosts meeting of Grivas and EOKA leaders, 175

Elizabeth II, Queen of Great Britain, coronation violence, 22

Elliott, L/Cpl Peter (1 Norfolks), 102

*Empire Clyde*, HM Troopship, 68

Empire Day (23rd May 1955),
assassination attempt on Armitage, 53

*Empire Ken*, HM Troopship, 45, 121

English School (Nicosia), EOKA bomb, 88

*enosis*, 15, 16, 211
Grivas and, 17, 19, 20, 91, 211–12; inter community relations and, 177, 211 Makarios and, 19–20, 22, 56; Makarios realises it is unachievable, 188; support from Greek Government, 22

*Enotria* (Italian liner), 42

entertainments, troopships, 46

EOKA, 28
accuse interrogators of misconduct, 143–4; allegations by prisoners in Wormwood Scrubs, 145–6; ambulances ambushed, 41, 163, 165; April 1st 1955 actions, 39, 49–51; attacks on army wives and children, 51, 53, 56, 78, 82, 88, 89, 97, 100, 111, 114, 120, 121, 164; attacks British commerce and Civil Service officials, 54, 58, 107; attacks on military personnel, 56, 77, 80, 93; attacks on Police Stations, 54, 55, 56, 60, 63, 67, 81; attempt to assassinate female hospital patient, 82; attempt to assassinate Kendrew, 163; aviation targets, 82, 88, 93, 99, 109, 150; benevolent fund, 36; bombings of military targets (August-Sept 1956), 109; bombs, fires and sabotage at end of ceasefire, 111; British civilians with weapons a target, 171; Catherine Cutliffe and Elfriede Robinson, 163–4, 165; cease operations (Dec 1958), 172–3; ceasefire to allow for Makarios' negotiations (Aug 1956), 110, 111; cell destroyed at Liopetri, 166–7 codenames, 36; couriers, 36-7, 85, 98, 101, 113, 172–3; crumbles under pressure (1957), 127; damaged by Operations *Black Mak* and *Whisky Mak*, 132–3; declared an illegal organization, 58–9; disciplinary matters, 38; Eastern Kyrenia Mountain Groups destroyed, 118; EOKA oath, 36, 53; executions of police informers, 35, 80, 85, 114, 146, 148; firearms amnesty opportunity, 82–3, 85; Grivas' diversionary campaigns, 97–9, 101–2, 103, 106–7, 113–14, 118–19, 126; Grivas' expectations, 38, 39; Grivas' strategic aims, 32–3; Guerrilla Groups destroyed in *Lucky Alphonse*, 105; hardliners influence Cyprus Government, 179; hideouts, 33-5, 65, 78–9, 82, 97, 98, 105, 117–18, 125, 134, 154, 160, 166; hostage taking, 94, 95–6, 107, 109–110; IEDs, grenades and mines, 115–16; incompetence, 49, 54; infiltration of British bases, 48; intelligence networks, 28, 29, 35–6, 111, 139, 147; intimidation campaign against police, 53–4, 55; kidnap Pte

Shilton (1 Leicesters), 94; last actions and defeat, 168–76; leaflets, 50-51; link with Orthodox Church, 34, 94, 126–7, 128–9, 131; Matsis cornered and killed, 171-2; mountain Guerrilla Groups, 26, 33–5, 36, 38–9, 49, 51, 53, 54, 55, 65, 80, 83–5, 93, 98, 105, 117–18, 120–21, 148; ninety captured in Paphos, 172; not represented at constitutional negotiations, 173; Operation *Forward to Victory*, 65, 91–2; Operation *Handover*, 175; Operation *Matchbox* nets 1200, 161; operational security, 35–6; outlawed, 75; parade along Ledra Street in uniform, 176; Police/Army arrest 200 suspects, 58; prisoners in Cyprus and UK to be removed to Greece, 175; profile of recruits, 38; propaganda campaign, 37, 87; RAF (Akrotiri) bombs (Nov 1957), 99, 109, 150; reorganized after Afxentiou death, 142–3; retaliations for judicial executions, 95–6, 97, 109–110; revolutionary proclamation, 39; Sabotage Groups, 26, 27, 33, 35–7, 38, 39, 49–50, 50, 63, 64, 76, 84, 91, 94, 95, 103, 112, 113, 159, 160, 161; shootings (Aug 1958), 161; Shotgun Commandos, 83, 162; Suez Crisis gives opportunity for more activity, 112–13, 119–21, 169; suspects held without trial, 59; suspends operations while Makarios negotiates (1957), 133, 136–7; truce (1956 & 1958), 88, 161–2; violence during constitutional negotiations (1958), 169–72; women, 36, 37, 107, 111, 112, 113, 122, 126, 139, 146, 173

EOKA-B, 188, 190
203rd Reserve Infantry Battn, 197; actions post-1974, 214–15; attack Turkish enclaves in Limassol and Avdimou, 197; encouraged to sieze power by Ioannides, 191; plan to ambush Makarios loyalists, 192–3

Episkopi, Western Sovereign Base Area, 172, 173, 191, 198

Episkopi (British GHQ base), 23, 27
1 Devon and Dorsets, 171; EOKA bombings (August-Sept 1956), 109; EOKA devices found (June 1956), 99; EOKA Sabotage Group, 33, 84, 91; HQ MEAF, 151; 45 (Independent) Transport Company, 41; water supply from Kissousa, 23, 87; Ersin, Lt Gen Nurettin (Turkish Army), landing force commander, 193

*Ertugrul* (Turkish landing ship), 195

Ethnarchy
clashes with colonial authorities, 16; negotiations with Harding, 62–3, 88

European Committee/Commission on Human Rights complaint by Mayor of Famagusta, 154
EOKA Wormwood Scrubs allegations, 146; inadequate evidence of Army brutality, 163

Evangelakis, Evangelos (EOKA gunman), 126

Evrykhou, 124

*Exodus*, filmed in Cyprus with EOKA extras, 161

expatriate British, 66, 121
evacuated by Royal Navy (July 1974), 203; murders, 126, 170–71; personal weapons offered to all, 170–71

Famagusta, 23, 151
51st Infantry Bde, 57, 66, 68; abandoned by National Guard units, 208; Catherine Cutliffe murder and aftermath, 163–5; EOKA bombings (August-Sept 1956), 109; Greek-Cypriot population flee to Dhekelia, 209; intercommunal violence (1963-64), 180, 183; Mayor complains of aggressive military, 154; Mayor declares support for *enosis* struggle, 59; Sabotage and Shotgun Groups, 26, 38, 63–4, 84, 112, 159, 160–2; Turkish-Cypriot independent admin functions, 183;
Turkish-Cypriots prepare for siege (July 1974), 198

Famagusta Police Station, interrogation of Elias Samaras, 166

Famagusta/Dhekelia, failed attack on Power Station (1 April 1955), 49, 158

Farley, Cpl Paul (RAOC), bomb disposal casualty, 114–15

Finland, UNFICYP troops, 183, 191, 203, 208

firearms amnesty, opportunity for EOKA, 82–3, 85

Firillas, Mikis (EOKA), 143

FitzGeorge-Balfour, Brig Sir R G V, 128, 134

# INDEX

background, 135; takes over from Brig Baker as Chief of Staff, 128, 134
Fleet Air Arm
  728 (Commando) Flight, 159–60; 814 Squadron (Sea Kings), 203; 845; Squadron (Wessex helicopters), 203 847 Squadron (Gannet A/S aircraft), 43, 66; evacuation of tourists and expats from Kyrenia area (July 1974), 203; *see also* Royal Navy
Fleet, Cpl (Intelligence Corps linguist), action at Liopetri, 166
Foley, Charles (*Times of Cyprus* editor), 111
  at Grivas' departure, 175; prosecuted for breach of censorship laws, 121
Foot, Sir Hugh
  in post as Governor, 150–51, 168; arrangements for deporting Grivas, 174–5; Catherine Cutliffe murder, 165; curfew imposed (July 1958), 160; EOKA prisoners released and restrictions lifted, 151–2, 173; first meeting of Transitional Council, 176; lifts curfew (Aug 1958), 162; Makarios accused of fomenting violence, 165; partnership approach to ceasefire with Makarios, 160; reprimands Kyrenia Mayor for complaints of Army brutality, 163; softly softly approach to EOKA, 151–4
Forces Broadcasting Service, 48, 49
Forest Park, Internal Security Training School, 143
Forestry Telephone system, 40
Foster, Sgt Jimmy (1 Para), 102
Four Mile Point (Famagusta), 23, 40; 625 Ordnance Depot warehouse raided by EOKA, 64, 95; 2 Field Ambulance (RAMC), 41
Fowler, L/Cpl Henry (1 Suffolks), ambush Drakos, 124–5
Freeland, Lt Col Ian (2 Royal Inniskilling Fuslrs), 49
French army
  8th Infantry Division, 17; 10th Airborne Division, 112; Grivas, 17; invasion of Egypt (1956), 112
French Indo-China, 19
friendly fire
  Cyprus National Guard on Operation *Niki* transports, 201–2; Operation *Lucky Alphonse*, 102, 106; Operation *Spring Time*, 160; Turkish Air Force on Turkish navy, 200–1; Turkish army, Kyrenia beachhead (1974), 199
Friends of the Cyprus Memorial, 213

Gabrielides, Mr, hosts meeting of Grivas and EOKA leaders, 175
Gage, Cornet (Royal Horse Guards), 113
Gaitskell, Hugh (Labour Leader), counters Barbara Castle's allegations, 163
Galatia, disappearance of Maj Macey, 183–4
Gallowey, Lt (1 RUR), action at Liopetri, 167
Gandhi, Mahatma, passive resistance, 52
Garrett, Pte George (RAOC), shot and tortured, 99
Geneva, Cyprus constitutional discussions stalled, 206
Geneva Conventions, EOKA and, 37
Georgadjis, Polycarpos, 54, 111–12, 125
  anti-Turkish rhetoric, 179; appointed to cabinet post, 178, 179; dismissed from cabinet, 188; murdered after Makarios assassination attempt, 188; Plan *Akritas*, 179, 180
Georgallis, Michael, killed in Zoopiyi, 142
Georghiades, Antonis (Milikouri Group), 84, 98, 101, 103, 105, 173, 176
Georghiou, Michael (EOKA), shot by 40 Commando, 91
Georgiou, Theodoros (EOKA District Leader), 151, 152
Germany, occupation of Greece (WWII), 16–19
Geunyeli
  fierce fighting, ELDYK & National Guard against Turkish paratroops (July 1974), 195, 196, 199, 200; intercommunal violence, 157–8; Turkish armour relieves defending Group, 202
Gill, L/Cpl (1 RUR dog handler), action at Liopetri, 167
Gill, Sgt (UK Police Unit), intercommunal trouble Yerolakkos/Skylloura/Kondemenos, 155–8
Gizikis, Gen Phadedon (President of Greece), 190; alliance with Sampson, 190
Gleadell, Brig P (Chief of Staff to Governor Foot), 151
Gleneagles Camp, British UNFICYP base, 208

Glider Pilot Regiment, 66–7
1 Gloucestershire Regiment (1 Glosters), 123–4
  Nicosia riots (Dec 1957), 151; return to UK (1958), 153; temporary control deployment (Mia Milia), 182; to Nicosia Airport (Dec 1963), 180
Golden Sands Leave Camp (Famagusta) 1 Leicesters, 68, 99; Transport Companies (1 & 65), 41
1 Gordon Highlanders, 80, 81
  in action near Morphou, 107–8; allegations of mistreatment, 94; capture of Renos Kyriakides, 78–9; 3 Commando Bde district, 68; home in *Empire Ken*, 121; Operation *Golden Eagle*, 108; Operation *Lucky Alphonse*, 101, 104–6; Operation *Mangel Wurzel*, 82; Operations *Mustard Pot* and *Pepper Pot*, 97–8; Orderly Room bomb, 120; Paphos Forest fire (June 1956), 104–6; Paphos Forest patrols, 97; vehicles ambushed, 59–60, 120–21
Graham, 2/Lt Peter (1 Leicesters), 151
Grant, 2/Lt (1 Duke of Wellington's), battalion interpreter, 129–30
Great Britain
  additional judges sent to Cyprus, 64; annexation of Cyprus, 15–6; British police volunteers sent to Cyprus, 64; conditions for Cyprus self-determination, 63; Cyprus gains strategic value, 16; defence cuts (1967), 187; encourages Turkish invasion (1963), 179; evacuation plans for British and foreign nationals in Cyprus (1974), 203; Greek offer of bases for Cyprus not accepted, 20; ignores Greek and Turkish tensions; (1957), 149; MI6 interest in Grivas, 22; National Service to end, 138; negotiations with Makarios (1957, and 1958–59), 133, 136, 159, 172–3; prepares to invade Egypt (July 1956), 109, 112
  reduced commitment outside Europe, 138; refusal to hold independent inquiry into mistreatment allegations, 145–6; representation at London/Paris/Zurich negotiations, 172-3; response to Northern Ireland mistreatment allegations, 145; support for partition, 181, 207; tough measures implemented in Cyprus, 59, 75–6
UNFICYP troops, 183, 185, 187, 191–2, 203, 204, 208
Greece
  anti-British broadcasts, 24; bows to NATO pressure over Cyprus, 138 brings Cyprus before the UN (Oct 1956), 120; collapse of Government (1958), 152; Colonels seize power in 'Junta' (1967), 186–7; Colonels 'Junta' collapsed (1974), 206; comment on British reinforcements, 55; Communist Party, 17–19, 51; Consulates abuse diplomatic status, 37, 53, 91, 139; *coup d'etat* by Ioannides (1973), 190; Cyprus constitutional discussions stalled, 206; demands that Makarios surrender Czech weapons, 189; incites more disturbance in Cyprus, 24; main source of weapons and explosives, 37; Makarios in Athens (1957), 138; mobilization in reponse to Turkish invasion (July 1974), 198; no government support for Grivas, 22; no support for second boatload of arms, 24; objection to Turkey's presence at talks, 162; occupied by Germany (WWII), 16–19; offered Cyprus with conditions, 15; offers Britain military bases for Cyprus, 20; offers Turkey a military base in Cyprus in return for *enosis*, 186; official response to Catherine Cutliffe murder, 165; provisional government (1945), 18; recalls Grivas from Cyprus, 187; representation at London/Paris/Zurich negotiations, 172–3; resistance groups (WWII), 17-19; stability of doubted by Britain and Turkey, 56; support for *enosis*, 22, 28, 56, 87; tensions with Turkey (1957), 138; war with Turkey (1919–21), 16; warns Grivas to declare a ceasefire; (1957), 133; the White Terror, 19; *see also* Greek Government in exile
Greek air force
  345 (Pegasus) Transport Squadron, 201 sparring with Turkish aircraft (July 1974), 198
Greek army
  2nd (Athens) Division, 17; General Staff consider war with Turkey (1974), 194; Greek Mountain Brigade, 18;

# INDEX

Grivas, 17; Grivas departure from Cyprus, 175, 176; takes it place at Izmir NATO HQ, 173; training in guerrilla warfare, 53–4
Greek Government in exile, rejects offers from Grivas, 18; *see also* Greece
Greek Intelligence Agency, reporting Turkish invasion build up, 194
Greek Navy
  deploys submarines to Rhodes area, 194; shipment of X Group weapons to Khlorakas, 22; submarines patrol between Turkey and Cyprus, 198
Greek-Cypriot Brotherhood, Alan Meale and, 132
Greek-Cypriots, 14, 15
  agitation increased (1954), 23; ambushed outside Geunyeli, 157–8; attacks on Kokkina (1964), 183, 186; celebrate release of Makarios from Seychelles, 136; challenges to Grivas' orders, 110; condemn the murder of Mrs Cutliffe, 165; deaths from EOKA campaigns, 107, 109, 113, 118, 120; deportations to Greece (1931), 16; *enosis*, 15, 16, 17, 52, 91, 177, 211; fear of *taksim* (partition), 178, 207; Government House staff dismissed, 93; Grivas' expectations of, 38, 39, 52; intercommunal violence, 83, 92, 94, 98–9, 148, 152, 155–8, 179–84; lawyers discredit prosecution evidence, 144–5; liable to be accused of treachery by Grivas, 147; loyalists murdered (Aug 1956), 109; majority prefer a quiet life, 52; mass arrests, sudden curfews and constant surveillance, 169; middle classes, 91; most disapprove the murder of L/Cpl Hill and Pte Shilton, 96; no cooperation with army at Morphou, 107; no longer trusted in Police, 99; numbers displaced by Turkish Intervention, 205; population swollen by Anatolian refugees, 16; recruited in Greece for EOKA, 22; resentment at security restrictions, 91; resentment at (Turkish) Police Mobile Reserve, 59; resentment at Turkish Tribute tax, 15–6; role of religion in society, 26–7; security risks, 93; son of police officer murdered, 183; treatment of after Catherine Cutliffe murder, 165; walk past EOKA victims in street, 111,
114, 161
2 Green Howards, 27, 46, 49, 58, 68, 86
April Fool's Day (1955), 49
Greenwood, Capt J W (RAOC), 1
Ammunition Disposal Unit, 116
3 Grenadier Guards (3 Grenadier Gds), 121
  defence of Service families in Civil War (1974), 192; intercommunal trouble Yerolakkos/Geunyeli, 157–8; nine-day operation in Paphos, 172; Operation *Dove Tail*, 172; Operation *Sherry Spinner*, 146–7; Operation *Spring Time*, 159–60; siege of Afxentiou's hide, 130–31
Grivas, Col (*later* Lt Gen) George Theodhorous, 16, 18, 20
  abandons 'the Castle', 79–80; accuses Army of misconduct, 143; achievements and unpalatable suggestions, 150; agrees to be deported, 175–6; almost caught by 3 Para, 102; attempt on Harding's life, 92 attention turns to Turkish-Cypriots, 147; and the *Ayios Georghias* arms drop, 29, 32; at Ayios Theodhorous, 187; blitz on Operation *Musketeer* forces in Cyprus, 120; ceasefire wanted by Greece, 133; comment on British reinforcements, 55; comment on Operations *Pepper Pot* and *Lucky Alphonse*, 105; conditions for temporary truce (February 1956), 88; crusade against communism, 153; Cyprus National Guard commander, 185–7; death of Afxentiou, 132; death of, 190, 211; demands strikes, 147; denies EOKA ever attacked women and children, 78, 212; deportation of Makarios and, 91–2; diaries found in jar near Lysi, 110; diaries lost and sold by HMSO, 98, 102; disbands X, 19; diversionary campaigns, 97–9, 101–3, 106–7, 113–14, 118–19, 126; ecstatic welcome in Athens (1959), 176; and ELAS, 18, 19, 33; *enosis*, 17, 19, 20, 91, 211–12; EOKA to cease operations (Dec 1958), 172–3; escalates violence during constitutional negotiations (1958), 169–72; expectations of Greek-Cypriots, 38, 39, 52; firearms amnesty, 82; on Greek Army Reserve list, 19; and Greek Colonels' coup, 186; guided

by 'divine providence' (*Memoirs*), 133;
hideouts in Limassol, 105, 113, 132–3;
humiliates trade unionists, 148;
importance of good intelligence, 139;
inhibits settlement of crisis, 138; later
assessment of Harding, 149; located by
technical intelligence devices, 168–9,
173–4; Makarios refuses to meet (1952),
20; Matsis and, 125; meetings with
Makarios, 24, 32, 38, 53;
memorial services for dead EOKA,
147; moved to a new hide in Nicosia
(Feb 1959), 173; moves HQ to Vassiliki,
83; moves to the Castle hideout, 65; no
regret for deaths of Boaden and Scaife,
172–3; objection to Turkey's presence
at talks, 162; operational plan, 38–9;
orders execution of Hill and Shilton,
95–6; orders hostage taking against
lives of Zakos, Michael and Patsatsos,
107, 109–110; orders the murder of
British soldiers, 161; ostracises Nitsa
Hadjigeorghiou, 107; passive
resistance campaign (March 1958), 153;
police informed of his presence, 27;
pre-war and wartime career, 17–9;
promoted to Lt General, 176; reaches
Limassol (June 1956), 105; ready to let
innocent die, 146; receives ultimatum
to accept Zurich agreement, 174;
reconnaissance visit as 'Nicos Petrou',
20–21; recruits Cypriots in Greece, 22;
refused visa to visit Cyprus (1954), 24;
refuses Harding's 'Surprise' offer, 110;
release of Makarios (1957), 136;
reorganized EOKA after Afxentiou
death, 142–3; resistance groups set up,
25–7; response to US Vice-Consuls
killing, 106; retains allegience of
residual EOKA members, 177–80;
retaliates monastery searches, 77–8;
return to Cyprus (1954), 24–8
returns to set up EOKA-B, 188,
revenge for Avgorou promised, 159–60;
revolutionary committee established,
20; rift with Makarios (June 1958), 158,
211; ruthless towards opposition from
Greek-Cypriots, 94–6, 147; sabotage
groups organization, 35–8; sacks
Afxentiou, 51; saved by British in
Athens (1945), 18; saved by Elli
Christodoulides, 146; second Cyprus
offensive, 63, 65, 70, 74; sidelined by
Greek Government, 22; single-minded
drive caused chaos, 211–12; strategic
aims, 32–3, 65; takes advantage of Suez
situation, 109–112; toothache leads to
attack on 'the Castle', 78–9; total war
threatened (Jan 1958), 152; training of
resistance fighters, 26–7; with Troodos
Guerrilla Groups, 55, 83–4; use of
children and students, 53, 65, 76, 83,
139, 147–9; weapons caches, 26–7;
widens his targets, 82; writes
autobiography, 176; young women
and, 113, 122, 139, 146, 173; *see also*
Digenes (codename for Grivas)
Grivas, Kiki (wife), 25, 176
Grivas, Dr Michael (brother), 110
*The Guardian* (newspaper), 184
Gyani, Maj Gen Prem Singh (UNFICYP
Commander), 183

Hadjigeorghiou, Nitsa, EOKA honeytrap,
107,
in Nicosia prison, 111
Hadjimiltis, Demos (EOKA), Limassol
Town Group, 103
*Halcyon Med* (store ship), 64
Hale, Cpl Patrick RAF, murdered by
EOKA, 96
Hammond, Sgt Reginald (RAOC), shot
buying ice-cream, 161
Happy Valley (Episkopi), 23, 198, 206
Harding, FM Sir John, 22, 23, 40
background, 62; abortive negotiations
with Makarios, 62–3; agrees
reinforcement for Cyprus District, 55;
arrest of Orthodox priests instructed,
126; assassination attempt, 92–3;
attitude to UK-Makarios negotiations
(1957), 136–7; departure from Cyprus
(1957), 149; deportation of Makarios,
88–90; firearms amnesty and EOKA,
82–3; further negotiations prove
abortive, 87–8; future solution for
Cyprus, 91; hopes for Cyprus' future,
149; imposes strict curfew on Greek
suburbs, 114; internal security
organization, 65–9, 212; loses
confidence in Commissioner of Police
Robbins, 99; proscription of AKEL
(Communist party), 81; replaces
Armitage as Governor, 61–2; replies to
Lefkoniko compensation demand, 119,
145; sceptical of EOKA offers, 133;

# INDEX

search of monasteries ordered, 77; stiffens police with volunteers from Britain, 64; Suez Crisis and drive against EOKA, 112; surprise offer to EOKA, 110; value of good intelligence understood, 212; vilified by Radio Athens, 92, 94; White Paper on *Allegations of Brutality...*, 144–6

Harris, Maj D M (1 Duke of Wellington's), 128–31

Harrison, Flt-Sgt Tony RAF, capture of EOKA attackers, 96

Harrison, Maj William GM (RAOC), Government Explosives Officer, 116

Harvey, Pilot Officer Norman RAF, 56

Haynes, Lt Michael RM, shot by EOKA, 127

hearts and minds picnic lunch for residents in search operation, 57; surgeries and repairs during search operations, 97

helicopters, 42
    2nd Army Helicopter Regiment (Turkish), 203; 45 Commando assault tactics, 143; 728 (Commando) Flight, 59–60; assist ground search, 118, 124, 125, 147; evacuation of tourists and expats from Kyrenia area (July 1974), 203; Joint Helicopter Unit (Whirlwinds and Chipmunks), 172; leaflet drops, 155; Operation *Musketeer*, 120; Sea Kings (FAA), 203; Wessex (FAA), 203
    *see also* aircraft

Heliforce, 159–60

Hellenic Forces Regiment *see* ELDYK

Hellenic Mining Company, 36

Hellenism, 15

Henderson, 2nd/Lt (1 Gordons), 97

Henn, Brig Frank (Chief of Staff to UNFICYP commander), 198, 205

Herbert, Maj John (Canadian UNFICYP), 205

*Hermes*, HMS, 192, 193,
    evacuation of tourists and expats from Kyrenia area (July 1974), 203

1 Highland Light Infantry (1HLI), 48, 85
    bomb attack in Yialousa, 107; Operation *Lucky Alphonse*, 101; Operation *Sparrow Hawk One*, 117; retaliation for Lefkoniko bomb deaths, 119; return to Scotland, 123; waterfountain bomb at Lefkoniko, 118–19

Hill, L/Cpl Gordon (1 Leicesters), taken hostage and murdered, 95–6; grave discovered, 118

Hiney, 2/Lt Tom (1 Leicesters), 151

Hiropoulis, Paraskevas (EOKA), 96–7

Hjmiltis, Demos (Limassol Town Group), 113

Ho Chi Minh, 19

Hobley, Fuslr (2 Royal Inniskilling Fuslrs), 77

Hollis, LAC John RAF, EOKA attack, 96

Holton, Mrs Mary (WRVS), killed in ambush, 117, 118

Hopkinson, Henry (Minister of Colonial Affairs), 23

Hoppe, Capt RE, siege of Afxentiou, 131

Hopwood, Brigadier J A (3 Infantry Bde), 121, 130–31,
    launches Operation *Lucky Mac*, 133–4

House of Commons, EOKA Wormwood Scrubs allegations discussed, 146

Houvardos, PC Andreas (Cyprus Police), 126

How, Lt John (2 Para), capture of Tassos Sofocleus, 117–18

14/20th Hussars, sergeant murdered, 114; temporary control deployment (Jan 1964), 181

IEDs (Improvised Explosive Devices), EOKA made, 115–16, 166
    *see also* pipe bombs

Indonesia
    Confrontation with Malaysia, 19; independence movement, 19

informers, 27, 78
    Army search operations, 57, 77–9, 98, 101, 110, 166; executions by EOKA, 35, 80, 85, 114, 146, 148, 167, 177; and Grivas' diaries, 110

insurgency
    definition and aims of, 33
    EOKA launch April 1 (1955), 39, 49–51

Intelligence Corps
    allegations of mistreatment, 94; cadre of Regular officers, 138; contribution and organization, 139–40; interrogation, 100-101, 122, 126, 128, 139, 143–4, 166; search for gunrunners, 141

Internal Security Training School, 66

Ioannides, Brig Gen Dimitrios (Chief of [Greek] Military Police), 190–1 attitude towards Ankara, 191; indirect control of

EOKA-B, 190, 191
Ioannides, Polycarpos, deported with Makarios, 90
Ionnides, Andreas (bookshop owner), 77
Iouannou, Asst Superintendent Alexis, *Ayios Georghias* intercept, 30
Ireland, UNFICYP troops, 183, 191
Ireneos, Abbot of Makheras Monastery, 128–9, 131
Isbell, Pte George (RAOC), mine fatality, 99
Israel
 ban on RAF over-flying, 179; Six-Day War (1967), 187; tensions with Egypt, 85; undercover actions in Cyprus, 214; Yom Kippur War (1973), 191
Israeli navy, picks up survivors of Turkish
 navy *Kocatepe*, 201
Italy
 attack on Greece (1940), 17; complains of *Enotria* incident, 42

James, Cpl T W (1 Leicesters), Lysi and Akhna EOKA captured, 127
Jay, L/Cpl (1 Norfolks), offered cash by EOKA fugitives, 87
Jones, Maj Jos (1 South Staffords), 89
Jordan, 85, 160–61
jukebox bombs, 121, 167

Kafkallides, Lambros (EOKA), 103, Pitsillia Group leader, 142
Kakopetria, 32, 55, 79,
 EOKA hideouts, 82
Karadymas, Argyrious (*Ayios Georghiou* engineer)
 capture by 1 Duke of Wellington's, 111–2, 125; escape from Nicosia hospital, 111-12
Karamanlis, Constantine (President and Prime Minister of Greece), 174, 206
Karaoglanoglu, Col (Turkish 50th Infantry), killed by 'friendly fire', 199
Karaolos Camp (Famagusta), 27
 the Snake Pit, 165
Karberry, Garth (and wife), murdered by EOKA, 107
Karios, Andreas (EOKA), 49,
 believed in Avgorou, 158–9
  failed attack on Dhekelia Power Station, 49, 158
Katelaris, Theodoulou (EOKA bomb maker), 92
Kathikas, two Argylls stabbed by EOKA gunman, 162
Katsoullis, Ioannis, 55
 shelters Grivas, 79
 weapons and explosives training, 26
Keightley, Gen Sir Charles, 51–2, 66, 85, 94
 EOKA target, 54–5; GHQ Middle East transferred to Cyprus, 27; prepares for invasion of Egypt (1956), 109, 112; relieved by Lt Gen Bourne, 151
Kelly, Lt John (RA), 81
KEM (Cyprus Enosis Front), 16, 178
Kendrew, Maj Gen Douglas (Joe) (Commander Cyprus District), 123
 Director of Operations, 123, 150–1; achievement in Cyprus, 169; assassination attempt, 163; assessment of Operation *Black Mak*, 128; believes Grivas reorganizing during truce, 162 Catherine Cutliffe murder, 165; criticised by McDermott, 168–9; Operations *Kingfisher* and *Mailbox*, 126–7
Kenya
 Greek community, 90, 137; Makarios meets African leaders (1957), 137–8; Mau Mau rebellion, 142, 151
Kermia Camp (Nicosia), 121
Khato Khivides Camp, attacked by EOKA, 86
Khlorakas
 Grivas comes ashore, 25; smuggled weapons landed and hidden, 22, 28–9, 30; support for Pan Agrarian Union of Cyprus, 21
King, Cpl Brian (1 Suffolks), ambush Drakos, 124–5
1 King's Own Yorkshire Light Infantry (1 KOYLI), 68
 enforces strict curfew, 114; Operation *Lucky Alphonse*, 101, 103, 107; Operation *Sherry Spinner*, 146–7; Operation *Sparrow Hawk One*, 117; Operations *Mustard Pot* and *Pepper Pot*, 97–8
King's Royal Rifle Corps (KRRC), 93
Kinsella, Rifleman (1 RUR), action at Liopetri, 166-7
Kissinger, Henry (US SeEcretary of State), 194, 198
Kissousa Reservoir, pipeline to Episkopi, 23, 87

Kitchener, Maj (*later* FM) Herbert, 47
Kitium (Orthodox Bishopric)
  militant Hellenism, 15–6; Makarios III, Bishop, 19; Grivas meets the bishop, 21, 28; bishop at Grivas' departure, 175–6
Knobbs, Lt Jimmy RE, 80
*Kocatepe* (Turkish destroyer), lost to friendly fire, 200–201
Kokkina
  resists National Guard attacks (1964), 183, 186; Turkish military advisers landed, 183; Turkish-Cypriot arms conduit, 183
Kokkinos, Andreas (EOKA), 127, 143, 146
Kokkinotrimithia Camp ('Camp K'), 59, 82, 83, 148
  1 Norfolks, 68; Cyprus National Guard vehicles and tanks destroyed, 196; mutiny, 154
Kokkinou, Louella (EOKA courier), 113
Kombokis, Col (Raider Command), defence of Kyrenia, 202
Kondemenos, 155–6, 197
  Cyprus National Guard bombed and strafed, 197; intercommunal trouble, 155–6
Kophinou, ELDYK incident with Royal Green Jackets, 187
Korea
  1 Glosters, 123-4
  29 Infantry Bde, 40
Kornos, battle of (Aug 1974), 206–7
Kostopulous, Special Constable (Cyprus Police), murdered, 55
Koutalianos, Evanghelos (caique skipper)
  arms smuggling, 28–31; jettisons cargo of weapons, 26, 30; not aware of Grivas in Cyprus, 32
Koutsoftas, Michael (EOKA), 96
Ktima (Paphos), intercommunal violence, 182, 183
Kumsal (Nicosia), 180
  150 Turkish-Cypriots taken hostage, women and children butchered, 180; hostages released (Dec 1963), 180
Kutchuk, Fazil (Turkish-Cypriot Leader), 54, 83
  collapse of talks with Makarios (1960), 178; Cyprus a republic – Kutchuk the Vice-President, 178, 183; first meeting of Transitional Council, 176; Makarios

informs of changes to Zurich constitution, 179; signs Zurich Agreement (February 1959), 173
Kykko Camp
  1 & 3 Para (Island Reserve), 85; preparations for Suez assault, 119; UNFICYP base, 204, 208
Kykko Monastery, 21
  24- hour curfews, 133–4; EOKA evidence found (Operation *Pepper Pot*), 98; EOKA hideouts, 34, 98; explosives and subversive literature found, 94; Guerrilla Groups, 65, 83–4; Makarios - Grivas meetings, 38, 53; Makarios' escape from Cyprus, 192; Operation *Kingfisher*, 126–7; Operation *Lucky Mac*, 133
Kynoch, 2/Lt Bruce (1 Gordons), death in fire, 104
Kyperounda Guerrilla Group, 53, 148
Kyprianou, Petrakis (EOKA gunman), 114
Kyrenia
  Greek-Cypriot refugees, 196; Mayor reprimanded for complaints of Army brutality, 163; Sabotage Groups, 84; taken by Turkish Army, 202; town defences reinforced by National Guard, 199; Turkish beachhead (July-August 1974), 196–7, 199–200, 202
Kyrenia, Bishop of, 22, 53, 63, 89–90
Kyrenia Castle
  detention of EOKA suspects, 55, 60–1; prisoner break-out, 61
Kyrenia Pass
  seized and dominated by Turkish commandos, 195–7; taken by National Guard RFU battalions, 199
Kyrenia Police Station
  raid by Tassos Sofocleus Group, 113; weapons seized by EOKA, 55
Kyrenia Range, 13
Kyriakides, Anthimos, Deacon
  disinformation about Grivas, 133; leaves Cyprus with Grivas, 176; regret for deaths of Boaden and Scaife, 172; weapons smuggling, 141
Kyriakides, Kikkis (wife of Deacon Anthimos), 173
Kyriakides, Kyprianos, Bishop of Kyrenia, 22, 53, 63
  deported with Makarios, 89–90; leaves Cyprus with Grivas, 176; retires from

politics, 175
Kyriakides, Renos (Guerrilla leader), 53–4, 63, 78–9
Kyriakides Guerrilla Group, 65
Kythrea, Manoli Pierides shot in church by EOKA, 95

Labour Party (UK)
  Labour politicians, 132, 137, 163; Manifesto (1957) promises self-etermination, 149
Lagoudontis, George (Special Branch Inspector), 54
Laing, Lt Col G (1 Duke of Wellington's), 128–31
Lakatamia (former RAF station)
  310 Ammunition Depot, 64, 116; 651 Air Observation Post Squadron (1910 Flight – Austers), 67, 162; Independent Light Liaison Flight (Austers), 67, 162
Lakin, Mr (British Middle East Office), *Ayios Georghias* intercept, 28–31
Lambou, Christos, shooting of Sgt Maj Middleton, 121
Lambrou, Andreas (dentist), 78
1 Lancashire Fusiliers, 67, 153
  intercommunal violence in Nicosia, 155; Operation *Blackbird*, 132
*Lancashire*, HM Troopship, 85
Lancaster Gate Conference (1955), 56, 63
Lancaster House (London), negotiations towards Cyprus constitution, 169, 172–3
16/5 Lancers armoured squadron
  defence of Service families in Civil War (1974), 192; Ferret shot up by Turkish tanks (1974), 209
Lane, Sgt James (1 RUR), accidentally shot, 165
Langton-Gore, Lt Col Bill (Coldstream Gds), deportation of Grivas, 174–5, 176
Lapithos, 206–7
Larnaca
  51st Infantry Bde, 57, 68; army stores sheds, 40; EOKA actions (1 April 1955) 49–50; hijacked civil airliner, 214; intercommunal violence (1963–64), 180; Mayor declares support for *enosis* struggle, 59; murder of Police Sgt Tipple, 106–7, 146; rioters and army families, 68; Sabotage Groups, 38, 63, 84, 94–5; Turkish-Cypriot independent admin functions, 183
Larnaca Pan Cyprian Gymnasium, permitted to reopen, 152
Lausanne, Treaty of (1923), 16
Laventure, Pte Douglas (RASC), 111
Le Geyt, Capt P S, with Makarios in Seychelles, 137
leave, Forces personnel, 48
Ledra Palace Hotel, Caledonian Society's ball, 76
Ledra Street (Nicosia), reputation as 'Murder Mile', 110–111, 212
Lee, Lt Peter (1 South Staffords), 89
Lefka, Greek-Cypriots driven out by Turks, 155
Lefka Group, 143
Lefkoniko
  Grenadier Guards Operation *Dove Tail*, 172; waterfountain bomb outrage, 118–19
Lefkoniko Police Station, EOKA seize weapons and a radio, 63
Legge-Bourke, Cornet William (Royal Horse Guards), 155–6
Lenas, Stylianos
  attack on Wolseley Barracks (1 April 1955), 49; Caledonian Society ball attack, 76; captured, 127
Leonidas, compared to Grivas, 39
*Lesbos* (Greek tank landing ship), 194
shells Turkish enclave in Paphos, 197–8
Libya, threatened by Egypt, 161
Life Guards, 82
  temporary control deployment (Jan 1964), 181
Limassol
  3 Commando Bde (RM), 66, 68; 40 Commando quells disturbances, 58, 60; army married quarters, 23; collective fine of £35,000, 106; coup to oust Makarios, 191; EOKA bombings (August–Sept 1956), 109; EOKA victims (Nov 1956), 120; Grivas' hideouts, 105, 113, 132–3; intercommunal violence (1963–64), 180; Israelis limpet mine Palestinian ship, 214; 41 Motor Transport Company, 41; Norfolks replace Marines, 85; police station attacked, 54; riots (1955), 27; Sabotage Groups, 38, 50, 63, 84, 103, 113; Turkish intervention fighting (1974), 197; Turkish-Cypriot independent admin functions, 183; weapons smuggling smashed, 141

# INDEX

Limni Camp
  1 A & SH, 153; 1 Black Watch, 171; C Coy Royal Scots, 58; D Coy 1 KOYLI, 68
Limni Sulphur Mine (Polis), 58
Liopetri, search for Xanthos Samaras, 166–7
*Loch Fada*, HMS, 90
Loizides, Savvas, 19
Loizides, Socrates, 19, 25, 51
  incriminating note, 31; marital problems, 27; recruits Sabotage Groups in Limmasol, 27; sent to meet *Ayios Georghias*, 29–30; sentenced to 12 years, 52
Lucy, Capt (1 RUR), action at Liopetri, 166
Lysi
  1 Leicesters action, 127; 1 Middlesex Regiment capture Rossides, 134; Grivas diaries found, 110
Lyso Group, 34–5
  attacked by Royal Marines, 103; leaders captured, 122

Macdonald, Capt Peter (RAOC), 76
Macey, Maj Edward (RAOC) (UN Special Liaison Officer), disappearance of, 183–4
Macfarlane, Maj Richard (1 Coldstream Gds), Makarios and, 191–2
Macmillan, Harold
  proposes Malta style government for Cyprus, 57–8; calls on Greece and Turkey to halt Cyprus violence, 162; learns of imminent arrest of Grivas, 174
mail, BFPO 53, 48
Makarios III, Archbishop (*later* President) of Cyprus, 20
  accused of betraying *enosis* cause, 169–70; accuses Athens of undermining his authority, 190–1; agrees that Grivas be deported, 174; anti-Turkish restrictions and taxes, 186; anti-Turkish rhetoric, 179, 181–2; asks for more arms, 24; assassination attempts, 188, 190; British reactions to EOKA causes concern, 59; calls on Britain to restore order (Christmas 1963), 180; changes undermine the Zurich Treaty of Guarantee, 179; confident of Athens' support but no guarantees for Turks, 152; considers disarming Cyprus Army, 183; critical of Grivas, 88; Cyprus a republic – Makarios the first President, 178; deported to the Seychelles, 88–90, 137; diplomacy with Eastern Bloc, 179, 181, 188–9, 190; elected for third term as President, 190; EOKA and, 98, 110, 126;
  EOKA Wormwood Scrubs allegations aired, 146; favours 25 March for start of insurgency, 28 favours attacks on married quarters, 55; finances arms deliveries, 28, 32; first meeting of Transitional Council, 176; forces resignation of independent (West German) judge, 179; funeral of Kharalambus Mouskas, 80–1, gains Soviet support for removal of British troops, 188; Greek Colonels' coup and, 186; Grivas' departure, 175–6 imports Czech weapons for Cyprus Police, 188–9; invites former EOKA into his cabinet, 178; July 1974 coup, 191–2; Lancaster House (London) negotiations, 169, 172–3; meetings with Grivas, 28, 32, 38, 53; negotiating 'a free Cyprus', 110; negotiations with FM Harding, 62–3, 87–8; negotiations with London (1957), 133, 136; OHEN and, 22; predicts hostile reception for Middle; East Command, 23; protests at searches of monasteries, 77; refuses to cooperate with Foot on ceasefire, 160; refuses to disband the National Guard, 187–8; removes Turkish-Cypriots from House of Representatives, 185; return to Cyprus (March 1959), 174; rift with Grivas (June 1958), 158, 211; shocked by April 1955 bombings, 52; signs Zurich Agreement (February 1959), 173; strengthens Police to face the National Guard, 186; support for *enosis*, 19–20, 22, 55–6; talks with Kutchuk collapse (1960), 178
  *see also* Mouskos, Michael Christodolou
Makheras, Afxentiou Group, 84
Makheras Monastery,
  Afxentiou's last hide, 128–9, 131; detention centre for priests, 131
Malta, 45, 112
  preparations for Suez assault, 112; stopover for trooping flights and troopships, 45

*Manchester Guardian*, (newspaper), 143, 145
Mandras, Operation *Storm Sail*, 58
Marathassa Guerrilla Group, 93
Markides, Leonidas, interviewed by Special Branch, 174
Markos Drakos Group, 84, 105
Marriott, 2/Lt (1 Suffolks), capture of Lefka Group, 143
Marshal, Lt RM, capture of Lenas and Demetrakis, 127
Martin, CSM (1 South Staffords), 89
Martin, L/Cpl (1 Duke of Wellington's), 130
Martin, WO (6 RTR), killed by EOKA mine, 120
Mason-Dixon line (Nicosia), 98–9, 155
Matsis, George (EOKA), 64, 125
Matsis, Kyriakos (EOKA courier), 78, 82, 107, 125
    trapped at Kato Dhikomo, 171–2
Mau Mau rebellion (Kenya), 142, 151
Mavromatis, Stelios (EOKA), 96–7, captured after two shootings, 100
Mavron Kremas, 98
*Mayhem in the Med* (Stiles), 213–14
    see also *Cyprian Chronicle*
McClelland, Capt Horace (3 Para Chaplain), 106
McCorkle, Master Pilot Jim, capture of EOKA attackers, 96
McDermott, Geoffrey (Foreign Office adviser to MI6), criticisms of Kendrew and Harding, 168, 169
McGaw, Sgt Samuel VC (Black Watch), 213
McLean, AB RN (*Comet* boarding party), 31
Meale, Alan (Labour MP), Afxentiou monument and, 132
medals and awards
    attitude of British Government, 75;
    Cyprus General Service Medal, 75;
    Greek-Cypriot commemorative of Emergency, 132; 2/Lt Buckley MBE (1 Norfolks), 93; Maj Coombe GM (RE), 81; Sgt Demmon (Metropolitan Police), Queen's Police Medal for Gallantry, 112; Sgt Eden GM (Metropolitan Police), 112; L/Cpl Fowler (1 Suffolks), mentioned in despatches, 125; Maj Harrison GM (RAOC), 116; Cpl King (1 Suffolks), mentioned in despatches, 125; Mrs Middleton, Queen's Commendation for Brave Conduct, 121; Cpl Shaughnessy MM (1 RUR), 167; 1 Somersets miss Cyprus GSM, 123; Lt Sutton MBE (RAMC/Norfolks), 104; Mne Walker RM BEM, 81; Pte Woods (1 Suffolks), mentioned in despatches, 125
Melos, Anargyros, (*Ayios Georghias* owner), 31
*Meon*, HMS (HQ Amphibious Warfare Sqdrn), 58
Mersin Naval Base (Turkey), embarcation port for Cyprus invasion, 194
Messaoria plain, 13
Metaxas Square (Nicosia), student demonstrations and riots, 53, 60, 61, 94
Metropolitan Police, dog handlers, 64, 78, 79
MI5, Travel Control Security and, 140–41
MI6 (British Secret Intelligence Service) attempt to link EOKA with AKEL, 87 ignores influence of Greek Government, 87; interaction with Military intelligence and Special Branch, 140; interest in Grivas, 22; mounts counter propaganda campaign, 87; reports weapons smuggling, 24; signals intelligence listening post, 187; technical intelligence gathering, 168–9, 173–4
Mia Milia, intercommunal violence, 182, Turkish Army advance to Nicosia, 207
Michael, Charilaos (EOKA), 80
    killing of L/Cpl Morun, 88; murder of PC Poullis, 55, 95
Michaelides, Dinos (EOKA bomb-maker), 127
Middle East
    Arab-Israeli Six-Day War (1967), 186–7; ban on RAF over-flying, 179; politics and hijackings, 214
1 Middlesex Regiment, 68, 82, 153, 155, 171
    Nicosia sectarian riots, 155
Middleton, 2/Lt (Royal Northumberland Fuslrs) (interpreter), 130
Middleton, Sgt Maj (RASC), wounded by gunman, 121
Middleton, Mrs Muriel, chases gunmen, 121
Milikouri, Operation *Lucky Mac*, 133

# INDEX

Milikouri Group, 84, 98, 105, 124, 126
military chaplains
    Capt Horace McClelland (3 Para Chaplain), 106; mediators in monastery searches, 77; The Revd Major Benyon in EOKA; attack, 77–8
military hospitals, 41–2, 127, 131
military intelligence
    allegations of misconduct, 143–4; Brigade and battalion platoons, 140; counter-intelligence and protected security, 140–41; EOKA penetration problems, 36; false sense of security, 51
    Grivas' diaries, 98, 102, 110, 139; initial inadequacy of, 212; interrogation centres, 82, 97, 107, 128; Joint Air Reconnaissance Intelligence Centre, 140; lack of Greek linguists, 139; meshed with police intelligence, 100–101, 140; MILPOLs, 66, 140, 156, 158; operations in Prelates and Kykko Monastery, 93–4; Q-Patrol operations, 142; torture allegations, 94; unpreparedness in Cyprus, 138-9, 212; use of interrogation, 100–101, 122, 126, 128, 139, 143–4, 166; *see also* EOKA, intelligence network; Intelligence Corps; MI5; MI6; Special Branch
MILPOLS, 66, 140, 156, 158
Mitchell, Maj (*later* Lt Col) Colin (1 A & SH), 154, 169
    Operation *Kingfisher*, 154; Aden (Crater), 169
Mitsero mine, raided for explosives, 64
Moore, Rifleman (1 RUR), action at Liopetri, 167
Morphou, 107-8, 124, 197
Morrison, Maj Gen (Command Signals Officer), 40-41, 92
Morrison, Pte David (1 A & SH), killed in ambush, 162, 163
Morun, L/Cpl Brian RE, ambushed by Drakos Group, 80, 107, 109
Mount Hilarion/St Hilarion
    EOKA ambush, 117–18; reoccupied by Turks, 200; taken and abandoned by National Guard Raider (RFU), 199, 200; Turkish signals station, 196, 199; UNFICYP intervention, 183
Mount Kionia, EOKA hideouts, 128
Mount Olympus, 13
    Cyprus Signal Regiment communications centre, 40–41
Guerilla groups, 34
Mount Proferti, Lyso group, 34–5
Mouskas, Kharalambus (EOKA), death of and funeral riot, 80–81
Mouskos, Michael Christodolou
    elected Bishop Makarios III of Kitium (1948), 19; invites Grivas to present *enosis* ideas, 19; study in Athens and USA, 16–17, 19; support for *enosis*, 19–20; *see also* Makarios III, Archbishop of Cyprus
Mulady, Capt Terence (Army Air Corps), 67
Murder Mile, Ledra Street (Nicosia), 110–111, 212
Murphy, Seamus (IRA), 79
Murray, Tpr (Royal Horse Guards), finds Grivas' Oxi day instructions, 149
mutinies, in prisons and holding camps, 154
Myers, Rear Adm Anthony VC ('Gamp'), 42

NAAFI, 48
    all Greek-Cypriot employees dismissed and replaced from UK, 167; attacked by EOKA, 58; EOKA employees, 111, 121, 167; jukebox bomb (RAF Nicosia), 167
Nasser, Gamal Abdel, 22, 85,
Suez Canal blockaded, 109
Nasution, Col Abdul Haris, 19
National Guard *see* Cyprus National Guard
National Servicemen, 43–4, 48, 85
    face violence from Turks and Greeks, 155; reactions to hostility, 145; response to Catherine Cutliffe murder, 164–5
    shortcomings in Cyprus situation, 105
NATO
    concerned as sectarian violence escalates, 162; Greece and, 133, 138, 198; importance of Cyprus, 58, 138; reconsiders partition to thwart communist takeover, 188; Southern Flank threatened by Makarios' diplomacy, 179, 181, 188–9, 211
Neely, Pte Matthew (1 HLI), Lefkoniko bomb, 119
Newton, Capt (1 Duke of Wellington's), 128, 129, 130, 131

Nicosia
  50 Infantry Bde, 66, 155; British Military Hospital, 41; demonstration/parade, 23; EOKA attempt to blow up teacher training college, 160; EOKA bombings (August–Sept 1956), 109; Greek Consulate, 37, 53, 91, 139; Greek-Cypriot refugees, 207; Green Line fixed (1964), 181, 185; Green Line re-established (1974), 206; holding cages for suspects, 126; HQ Air Levant, 66; inter-community tensions (1957–58), 151
  intercommunal violence, 83, 94, 98–9, 155, 156–7, 180; Mason-Dixon line, 98–9, 155; Mayor says all Greek-Cypriots are EOKA, 59; Metaxas Square riots and demonstrations, 53, 60–1; Murder Mile (Ledra Street), 110–111, 212; riots, 27, 53, 60, 61, 151; Royal Air Force, 42, 96
  Sabotage and Shotgun Groups, 38–9, 49, 63, 76, 84, 103, 160, 161, 162; strict curfew imposed on Greek suburbs, 114; Turkish 39th Tank Division, 207; Turkish Information Office bombed, 155; Turkish-Cypriot independent admin functions, 183 UNFICYP HQ, 191; United States Consulate attacked by EOKA, 88
Nicosia Airport (abandoned), 42
  2nd Greek Battalion, 200, 34th (Greek) RFU, 203–4; 35th (Greek) RFU, 203–4 battle for, 204–5
Nicosia General Hospital
  25 Turkish-Cypriots killed (1964), 185 EOKA attacks, 82; Police Sgts Demmon killed and Eden shot, 111–12
Nicosia Pan Cyprian Gymnasium
  EOKA bomb makers, 143, 162
  student demonstrations, 53, 83
Nicosia Prison, mutiny, by prisoners, 154
Nikitari, 1 Suffolks ambushed, 124
Nikitas, Pavlos (EOKA), 103
Nixon, Richard, sees Makarios as Eastern Bloc lackey, 188
Noble, Lt Col F (1 HLI), replies to Lefkoniko compensation demand, 119
Noel-Baker, Francis (Labour MP), 137
Normandy Camp, 86
Northern Ireland
  British response to mistreatment allegations, 145; lessons from Cyprus, 212–13; Operation *Banner*, 101

*Ocean*, HMS, 121
O'Connor, A/Cpl Myles BEM RAF, 54
O'Donnell, Pte (2 Para), capture of Tassos Sofocleus, 117–18
OHEN, 22,
  members recruited by Grivas, 26; oil, tension between Greece and Turkey, 191
*Olympic Thunderer* (oil tanker), carries Makarios to Madagascar, 137
Omodhus Group, 105
  hideouts found, 124–5,
  suspects captured, 128
Omorphita, Sampson and EOKA attack Turkish Cypriots, 180
Omorphita Interrogation Centre, 82, 107, 180
Operation *Airborne* (deportation of Makarios), 89
Operation *Aphrodite*, to repel Turkish invasion, 185–6
Operation *Aphrodite Two*, to repel Turkish invasion, 188, 195–8
Operation *Apollo* (deportation of Makarios), 89
Operation *Attila*, Turkish landing force elements, 193-4
Operation *Attila Two*, 207–9, 211
Operation *Black Beard* (British forces), 77
Operation *Black Mak*, 121–2, 124–8, 132
Operation *Blackbird*, 132
Operation *Bullfinch*, 143
Operation *Cordon Bleu* (1 Ox and Bucks), 124
Operation *Dove Tail* (3rd Infantry Bde), 172
Operation *Fallacy*, evacuation of Service dependents, 203
Operation *Forward to Victory* - phase 1 (EOKA), 65
Operation *Forward to Victory* - phase 2 (EOKA), 91–2
Operation *Fox Hunter* (Marines, Gordons and Paras), 78–9, 84, 112, 119, 134, 169
Operation *Golden Eagle*, 108
Operation *Handover*, EOKA weapons handed in, 175
Operation *Kingfisher*, 126–7, 154
Operation *Little Chicago* (1 Norfolks), 87
Operation *Lucky Alphonse*, 101–5,
  assessment, 105-6; presumed cause of

# INDEX

fire, 106
Operation *Lucky Dip*, 133–4
Operation *Mailbox*, 127
Operation *Mangel Wurzel* (Marines and Gordons), 82
Operation *Matchbox*, 1200 EOKA and 50 TMT detained, 161
Operation *Musketeer* (Suez), 120
Operation *Mustard Pot*, 97–8
  intelligence gained, 101
Operation *Niki*, Greek forces (July 1974), 201–2
Operation *Pepper Pot*, 97–8
  intelligence gained, 101, 122
Operation *Platypus*, defence of Service families in Civil War (1974), 192
Operation *Purse Net* (Cyprus Police), 28–31
Operation *Sherry Spinner* (45 Commando battle group), 146–7
Operation *Snatch*, collection of Service family property (Limassol), 203
Operation *Sparrow Hawk One* (British Forces), 117–18
Operation *Spring Time* (3 Infantry Bde), 159–60
Operation *Storm Sail* (Royal Marines), cordon-and-search, 58
Operation *Sunshine* (MI6), 169
Operation *Swan Lake*, 200 EOKA suspects detained, 162
Operation *Tea Party* (MI6), 87
Operation *Turkey Trot* (British forces), 84, 134
Operation *Whisky Mak*
  damage to EOKA, 132; search for Afxentiou, 128–32
Orthodox Church
  active support for *enosis*, 19–20, 26–7, 34, 83; fosters concept of Hellenism, 15; linked with EOKA, 34, 94, 126–7, 128, 131; monasteries used as EOKA bases, 34, 126-7, 128–9
  referendum on *enosis*, 19–20
Ottoman Empire
  unrest in the Balkans (19th century), 14–15; *see also* Turkey
Ottoman Turks, capture of Cyprus, 14
Otway-Ruthven, Lt Robert (Gordons), 78–9
1 Oxfordshire and Buckinghamshire Light Infantry (1 Ox and Bucks), 121
  ambush in Nikitari, 124; leave for UK (1959), 175; Operation *Cordon Bleu*, 124; Operation *Kingfisher*, 154
Oxi Day, celebrations encouraged by Grivas, 148–9

Packard, Lt Cdr Martin RN, promoting reconciliation in Cyprus, 184–5
Pafitis, Yannis, Caledonian Society ball attack, 76
Pakhna
  EOKAs captured by 1 Ox and Bucks, 124; Guerrilla Group, 105; Operation *Little Chicago*, 87
Pakhna Police Station, attacked by EOKA, 87
Palendria, 127, 147
Pallikarides, Evagoras (EOKA), executed for murders, 122, 133
Palouriotissa, 32
Pan Agrarian Union of Cyprus *see* PEK
Pan Cyprian Federation of Labour, assassination attempt on general secretary, 56
Panaghides, Andreas (EOKA), 96
Panagra Pass, 197, 207
Panayides, Dafnis, 105, 113, 141
  arrested, 141
  refuge for Grivas, 105, 113
Panayides, Maroulla (EOKA courier), 113, 173
Panelli, Modestos, electrocuted in power station attack, 49, 158
Panhandle, 58, 81, 153
  EOKA activity, 81, 162, 170
Pano Amiandos
  raids by 45 Commando, 82, 86–7; riot control by 40 Commando, 58;
  *see also* Amiandos
Pantelis, Christofis, 49
Pantelis, Modestos, 49
Papadopoulos, Andreas (Limassol EOKA Group), 113, 141
Papadopoulos, Antonios, escape from Pyla Detention Camp, 112
Papagiorgiou, Loukia, fatally wounded in Avgorou riot, 159
Papagos, Field Marshal Alexandros, support for Cyprus, 22, 28, 62
Papayiannis, Lt Col, survives ambush by Turkish paras, 200
Paphos
  90 EOKA captured and cache of weapons (1958), 172; army and Royal

Marines deployments, 68, 112, 155
Coldstream Guards (UNFICYP), 191–2
earthquake, 42; EOKA bombings
(August–Sept 1956), 109; Guerrilla
Groups, 84; intercommunal violence
(1963–64), 180, 182; riots (Dec 1957),
151; strict curfew imposed on Greek
suburbs, 114; success of curfew and
surveillance system, 169; Turkish-
Cypriot enclave shelled by *Lesbos*,
197–8; Turkish-Cypriot independent
admin functions, 183
Paphos Forest, forest fire (June 1956),
103–6
Paphos Palace Hotel, 35
16 Parachute Brigade, 85
1 Para, 85, 102, 113, 121, 172, 181, 183;
2 Para, 108, 112, 117–18, 125; 3 Para,
85, 89, 90, 100, 102, 113, 120–1; Guards
Independent Parachute; Company
(plus support units), 108, 113, 181;
capture of Matsis, 125; communist cell
unearthed, 85; El Gamil airfield seized
(Egypt), 120; friendly fire incidents,
102; Grivas sighted, 102; house
searches with police, 100; Operation
*Black Mak*, 125; Operation *Golden Eagle*,
108; Operation *Lucky Alphonse*, 101–3,
106; Operation *Musketeer*, 120;
Operation *Sparrow Hawk One*, 117–8;
operations in Jordan (1958), 160–61;
Paphos Forest fire deaths, 106;
1 & 3 Para return to Aldershot, 121;
preparation for Suez, 119; return to
Cyprus (Nov 1956), 121; temporary
control deployments (Jan 1964), 181;
UNFICYP duties, 183; withdrawn from
operations near Kambos, 112–13
Paralimni Police Station, weapons seized
by EOKA, 56
Parker, Flt Lt William (RAF Regt), 99
partition
consequences of, 210–211; de facto
following Turkish Intervention,
209–210; NATO Powers (US and UK)
support for, 181, 188, 207; population
displacement, 210; Turkish-Cypriot
agitation, 147–8, 152, 207
passive resistance, Grivas and, 52
Patazis Battalion (Makarios loyalist), at
Kyrenia, 199-200
Patsatsos, Iakovos
captured, 94; Harding assassination
plot, 92; murder of Turkish-Cypriot
policeman, 94, 107
Paul I, King of Greece, meets Grivas, 176
Pavlakis, Pavlos (EOKA second-in-
command), 51, 64,
escape from Pyla Detention Camp, 112
Pearce, Pte (2 Para), capture of Tassos
Sofocleus, 117–18
PEK, 21, 53
unloads smuggled arms, 28, 29
penalties and punishments
the birch, 76; collective fines, 75, 106
death sentences trigger violence, 88;
Emergency regulations, 75–6
Pentadactylos Mountains, 13
45 Commando, 58, 81; Berkshires and
Wiltshires clean up EOKA, 171–2
EOKA Guerrilla group, 33, 34, 51, 84;
forest fires from Turkish bombing, 203
Pentadactylos/Karpas, EOKA Groups, 84
PEON, 21–2, 89
banned after coronation violence, 22
Drakos and, 36; members recruited by
Grivas, 26–7; rallies, 55
People's Liberation Army (China), 63rd
Army, 123–4
Peters, Cpl (1 RWF), killed in ambushed
ambulance, 165
Petropouleas, Notis, 19, 25, 26, 27, 52
Petros (shepherd), hunt for Afxentiou,
128, 129
Petrou, Nicos (Grivas alias), 20–21
Philia, intercommunal trouble, 155–6
Phrenaros, Leicesters patrol ambushed,
arms cache revealed, 93
Pierides, Manoli, shot in Kythrea church,
95
Pierou, Loizas (Mukhtar), shot by EOKA,
148
Pilkington, Cornet (Royal Horse Gds), in
Avgorou, 159
Pink, Squadron Ldr Wilfred RAF, 89
pipe bombs, 115, 147; *see also* IEDs
Pitsillia Guerrilla Group, 65, 84, 105
Pittarides, Solon (Guerrilla Group), 84
murders of informers, 95; surrenders
to Royal Marines patrol, 98
Pittas, Fotis (Lysi Group deputy leader),
159
Plan *Akritas*, 179, 180
rejected by Makarios, 190
Platres, 121
interrogation centre, 97, 128

Platt, Dvr Leonard (RASC), disappearance with Maj Macey, 184
Police Mobile Reserve, 59, 99, 152
  *see also* Cyprus Police
Polymedhia Camp, 47, 120
Poskottis, Stavros (sabotage group leader), 49–50
Potamitissas Group, 127
Poullis, Special Constable (Cyprus Police), murdered, 55
Preece, Brian (civilian victim), murdered near Famagusta, 170
Prendergast, John, Chief of Intelligence, 151
press
  at Afxentiou's last stand, 131; coverage of disappearance of Maj; Macey, 184 frustrated by curfews, 134; furore over Geunyeli deaths, 158; *Manchester Guardian* calls for inquiry into interrogation centres, 143; *Times of Cyprus*, 111, 121
Pritchard, Herbert (Cable & Wireless), murdered, 126
Profumo, John, warning to Governor Foot, 150
propaganda
  EOKA, 37, 87, 120; MI6 counter propaganda, 87; value of understood by Grivas, 37; *see also* psychological warfare
psychological warfare
  British and EOKA, 116–17; *see also* propaganda
Pyla Detention Camp, 107, 112
Pyrgos, EOKA hideout, 98

Q-Patrol operations, 142
Queen Alexandra's Royal Army Nursing Corps (QARANC), 41–2
1 Queen's Own Royal West Kent Regiment (1 RWK)
  arrests in Kyrenia area (late 1958), 172 Operation *Dove Tail*, 172; Operation *Spring Time*, 159–60

Radcliffe, Cyril John, 1st Viscount (Commissioner for Constitutional Reform), 91
  *Proposals for Cyprus*, 122
Radio Athens
  anti-British broadcasts, 31, 52, 83, 92, 94, 125; British attempts to jam broadcasts, 92, 94; on capture of Matsis, 125; 'Voice of the Fatherland' – passive resistance, 52
Raftis, George (Guerrilla leader), 34, 122
Randall, RSM (1 Duke of Wellington's), 129
Ray, P B (Cyprus Special Branch), 24
Read, Pte Colin (1 Wiltshires), killed in ambush, 117, 118
Redgrave, Maj Roy (Royal Horse Guards), intercommunal violence, 157
*Redoubt*, HMS (LCT), 58
*Reggio*, HMS (LST), 58
Richards, Lt Col RM, 160
Richardson, Pte (1 KOYLI), 103
Ricketts, Brig (*later* Maj Gen) Abdy (Commander Cyprus District), 40, 55, 66
Riza, Police Sergeant Abdullah Ali, murdered by EOKA, 83
Robbins, Ldg Seaman, RN (*Comet* boarding party), 31
Robbins, George (Commissioner of Police), 24, 66
  EOKA disturbances (April 1955), 51–2 Greek-Cypriot resignations, 56; Harding loses confidence in, 99; wife injured by EOKA grenade, 76
Roberts, Mne Terrance RM, 81
Robertson, Brig JAR (51st Infantry Bde), 57
Robinson, Elfriede, shot by EOKA gunman, 163–4
Robinson, Sgt Arthur RM, wounded in ambush, 92
Rodick, Maj (1 Duke of Wellington's), 128, 130
Rooney, Sgt Gerald (Kent Constabulary, UK Police Unit), 99–100
*Rosalind* (East African Naval Vessel), 90
Rosier, 2/Lt RMP, Catherine Cutliffe shooting, 164
Ross, Pte (RAMC/Gordons), 105
Rossides, Michaelakis (Larnaca District Leader), 51, 95, 134; captured at Lysi, 134
Rotsides, Savvas (EOKA), killed near Kyperounda, 172
Royal Air Force
  Aden - operational area, 66; 651 Air Observation Post Squadron (1910 Flight - Austers), 67, 162; aircraft

intercept Greek jets, 186; airmen murdered by EOKA, 86; Akrotiri *see* Akrotiri (RAF Base) attack on radar operators, 96; base security (RAF Regt), 86; escorts Grivas' Dakota from Cyprus airspace, 176; HQ Air Levant (Nicosia), 66; HQ MEAF merged with HQ Air Levant and moves to Episkopi, 151; HQ MEAF to deploy to Cyprus, 22, 66; Independent Light Liaison Flight (Austers), 67, 162; Levant Communications Flight, 118; Makarios flies out of Cyprus (July 1974), 192; Nicosia, 42, 96; Princess Mary's Royal Air Force Nursing Service, 42; RAF Police clear M1 road of National Guard elements, 193; RAF Police and dog handlers, 64; search for survivors of Turkish navy *Kocatepe*, 201; Shackleton Maritime Reconnaissance aircraft, 28–9, 43, 66, 85; 264 Signals Unit (Aiyos Nikolaos), 56; Transport Command - trooping, 44–5, 85, 86; V-Bombers and ICBMs, 138; withdrawal from Iraq and Jordan, 151; *see also* aircraft; Akrotiri (RAF Base)

Royal Air Force Regiment cordon-and-search operation with Army and Cyprus Police, 57; 3 Light Anti-Aircraft Wing, 86, 180; move to Nicosia Airport (Dec 1963), 180; Operation *Lucky Alphonse*, 101; 751 Signals Unit, 86

Royal Air Force, squadrons 6 Squadron Venoms, 66; 13 Squadron air photo-recce (Meteors), 86 208 Squadron Hawker Hunter fighters, 66, 86; 284 Squadron Sycamores, 118; 653 Squadron, 155

Royal Armoured Corps Independent Parachute Squadron, UNFICYP duties, 191

Royal Army Medical Corps (RAMC), 41–2 19 Field Ambulance, 206, 209; 23 Parachute Field Ambulance, 104–5; medical care for refugees, 206; Operations *Mustard Pot* and *Pepper Pot*, 97–8; Paphos Forest fire (June 1956), 104–5

Royal Army Ordnance Corps (RAOC), 40, 63–4
   1 Ammunition Disposal Unit (Internal Security), 114–15, 116, 175; 17 Mobile Ammunition Inspection Unit, 116; 625 Ordnance Depot, 64, 95, 109, 116; bomb disposal officers/Ammunition Examiners, 54-5, 114–15, 116, 126; Printing Unit, 117

Royal Army Pay Corps, EOKA victim, 170

Royal Army Service Corps (RASC), 40 1 Transport Column, 85, 109; 21 Army Fire Brigade, 94; 749 (Air Despatch) Coy, 86; fire death, 106; Maritime Service, 141; Motor Transport Companies, 41, 59; murder mile casualties, 111; off-duty soldiers wounded by EOKA, 77; RASC Cyprus East and Cyprus West, 109; supply drops to snow-bound communities, 86

Royal Artillery 1st Artillery (Battle) Group (1 AGRA), 112, 132; 2 Light Regt, 181, 183; 12 Light Air Defence Battery, 192; 16 Light Anti Aircraft Regt, 112; 20 Field Regt, 161; 21 Medium Regt, 112, 121–2; 25; Field Regt, 170; 26 Field Regt, 172 ; 26 Medium Regt, 181–3; 27 Light Anti Aircraft Regt, 152; 29 Field Regt, 153, 164–6; 34 Light Anti Aircraft Regt, 161; 39 Heavy Anti Aircraft Regt, 171; 40 Field Regt, 27, 30, 52, 68, 81, 117, 153; 43 Light Anti Aircraft Regt, 112, 152, 155; 46 Heavy Anti Aircraft Regt, 155; 50 Medium Regt, 112, 122; 52 Heavy Anti Aircraft Regt, 112; 188 Search Light and Radar Battery, 43, 142, 175; defence of anchorages and airfields (Suez Crisis), 112; defence of Service families in Civil War (1974), 192 EOKA ambush intercepted, 162–3; face-down Greek-Cypriot militia in Ktima, 182; NAAFI jukebox bomb, 121; Operation *Sparrow Hawk One*, 117; patrol attacked by Turkish-Cypriots, 152; response to Catherine Cutliffe murder, 164–5; search for Xanthos Samaras, 166–7; successes against EOKA, 122; temporary control deployments (Jan 1964), 181–2; UNFICYP duties, 183; Yialousa Police Station bomb, 170

1 Royal Berkshire Regiment (1 Berkshires), 155, 161, 171

Royal Corps of Transport (RCT)

# INDEX

7 (UNFICYP) Squadron, 203–4;
Kyrenia evacuations (July 1974), 203
Royal Dragoon Guards, temporary
control deployment (1964), 181, 182
Royal Electrical and Mechanical
Engineers (REME), 41, 67
at Nicosia Airport (July 1974), 204
Royal Engineers (RE)
1 Radar Air Survey Liaison Section, 47;
19 Command Postal Depot, 48; 32
Fortress Squadron (Tunnelling Troop),
23; 35 Engineer Regt (30 Sqdn, RE), 23,
27, 47, 58; 37 Field Sqdrn, 80; 42 Survey
Regt, 47; 51 Port Squadron, 46; EOKA
arms cache, 126; erect Mason-Dixon
line, 99; mine fatalities, 99; Operation
*Little Chicago*, 87; Operations *Mustard
Pot* and *Pepper Pot*, 97–8; refugee camp
construction, 209; repairs for villagers,
134; siege of Afxentiou's hide, 130–31
Royal Green Jackets
incident with ELDYK in Kophinou
(1967), 187; leave for UK (1959), 175;
protect Service families in Larnaca
(1963), 180
Royal Horse Artillery, UNFICYP duties,
183
Royal Horse Guards, 67, 113
arrest of Sampson, 126; casualties to
EOKA (Sept 1956), 114; erect barriers
in Nicosia Old City, 151;
intercommunal trouble
Yerolakkos/Skylloura/ Kondemenos,
155–8; issued with Ferret Scout Cars,
86; killings by Famagusta Town
Group, 160; mine ambush (Troodos),
170; nine day operation in Paphos, 172
; Operation *Lucky Alphonse*, 101;
sectarian riots (Nicosia), 94; trouble at
Avgorou, 158–9; Turkish-Cypriot riots
(Nicosia), 152
1 Royal Inniskilling Fuslrs
arrive to maintain ceasefire (Feb 1964),
181; UNFICYP duties, 183
2 Royal Inniskilling Fuslrs, 4, 40, 58
intercept and shoot gunman in
Famagusta, 77; patrol ambushed near
Famgusta, 56; popular ceremonial
parade, 27; return to UK, 85–6;
Wolseley Barracks, 49, 52
1 Royal Leicestershire Regt, 68, 99
combined army and navy search, 82;
hostage and murder of L/Cpl Hill and

Pte Shilton, 94, 95–6, 134; murder of
CSM Crisell, 97; one EOKA shot and
weapons cache found, 151; patrol
ambushed in Prelates, 93; return to
UK, 153; riot ring-leader shot, 83
Royal Marines (3 Commando Bde), 55, 58,
66, 68, 103, 145
40 Commando, 58, 85, 102–3, 108, 112,
127, 132, 153, 175, 192, 208; 41
Commando, 192; 45 Commando, 58,
61, 79, 81, 82, 86–7, 98, 101, 106, 120,
143, 146–7, 159–60, 170; Amphibious
Warfare Troop, 58; battle group facing
all sides (Aug 1974), 208–9; casualties
(1958), 170; concerns about lack of
amphibious exercise, 112; cross-
country ski-ing, 82; Cyprus National
Guard and, 198; defend Western
Sovereign Base Area, 208; EOKA
Groups captured, 102–3, 127; friendly
fire, 106; Heliforce, 159–60; Land Rover
patrol ambushed, 91–2; Light Air
Detachment recovery lorry fatalities,
87; maritime Q-Patrols, 142; Operation
*Blackbird*, 132; Operation *Golden Eagle*,
108; Operation *Kingfisher*, 154;
Operation *Lucky Alphonse*, 101–4;
Operation *Mailbox*, 127; Operation
*Musketeer* (Suez), 120; Operation *Pepper
Pot*, 97–8; Operation *Sherry Spinner*,
146–7; Operation *Snatch* (Limassol),
203; Operation *Spring Time*, 159–60;
Operation *Storm Sail*, 58; Paphos Forest
fire (June 1956), 104
Royal Military Police (RMP), 40, 60, 67
allegations of mistreatment after
Catherine Cutliffe murder, 165;
Brigade Provost Coys, 67, 119-20; lance
corporals murdered (April 1958), 154;
Operation *Lucky Alphonse*, 101, 105;
Operations *Mustard Pot* and *Pepper Pot*,
97–8; Paphos Forest fire, 105; WRAC
attached, 87
Royal Navy
1st Destroyer Squadron, 43; 6th
Destroyer Squadron, 28–31, 43, 82;
Amphibious Warfare Squadron, 58,
138
anti-smuggling blockade, 28–31, 42–3,
66, 82; divers find *Ayios Georghias* arms
cargo, 31–2; evacuation of tourists and
expats from Kyrenia area (July 1974),
203; exchanges with army personnel,

43; Inshore Flotilla minesweepers, 43; Maritime HQ, 42; Operation *Sparrow Hawk One*, 117; Operations *Mustard Pot* and *Pepper Pot*, 97–8; patrol boat squadron (Famagusta), 43; picks up survivors of Turkish navy *Kocatepe*, 201; preparation for assault on Egypt, 112; search for gunrunners, 141; *see also* Fleet Air Arm; individual ships by name; Royal Marines
1 Royal Norfolk Regiment
  Camp 'K', 68, 121; EOKA District Group destroyed, 102; face schoolgirls' demonstration, 83; friendly fire incident, 102; guard platoons in Government House, Wolseley Barracks, Camp K and and Britannia Camp, 68, 93; lorry wrecked near Polymedhia, 120; move to Paphos, 86; Operation *Golden Eagle*, 108; Operation *Little Chicago*, 87; Operation *Lucky Alphonse*, 101–2, 104; Operations *Mustard Pot* and *Pepper Pot*, 97–8; Paphos Forest fire (June 1956), 104, 106; replace Marines in Limassol, 85
Royal Pioneer Corps, collection of Service family property (Famagusta), 203
3 Royal Regiment of Fusiliers, defence of Eastern Sovereign Base Area, 209
1 Royal Scots, 86
  AKEL leaders arrested, 81; defence of Service families (1974), 192; at Limni Sulphur Mine (Polis), 58; at Paphos, 68
Royal Signals
  2 Wireless Regiment, 49, 92; 3 Signals Regiment, 120; Brigade Signals Troops, 67
Royal Ulster Constabulary (RUC), 99
1 Royal Ulster Rifles (1 RUR), 153
  ambush EOKA with bicycles, 162; in Avgorou (July 1958), 159; intelligence items found, 148; off-duty men clash with Greek youths, 175; Operation *Sherry Spinner*, 146–7; response to Catherine Cutliffe murder, 164–5 search for Xanthos Samaras, 166–7
Royal Warwickshire Regiment (1 Warwicks), 86, 92, 94; curfew control (Nicosia), 100; murder mile ambush, 111
1 Royal Welch Fusiliers (1 RWF), 153
  ambushes in the Panhandle, 162; rescue homeless Greek-Cypriots in Lefka, 155; Yialousa Police Station, 170

Russia
  Crimean War (1854–56), 15; Russo-Turkish War (1877–78), 15; *see also* Eastern Bloc; Soviet Union

Salisbury, Mne Geoffrey RM, arrests Costas and others, 147
Salisbury, Robert Cecil, 3rd Marquess, 15
Samaras, Christos (EOKA), shot at Liopetri, 167
Samaras, Elias (EOKA), turns informer, 166–7
Samaras, Xanthos (EOKA), searched for by 1 RUR, and Minden Battery (RA), 166–7
Sampson, Nicos (Nicos Georghiades) journalist and gunman, 111–12, 114; admits murders of police sergeants, 144; alliance with Gizikis, 190; arrested in Dhali, 126, 148; Greek-Cypriots to storm Turkish enclaves, 180, 211; helps Grivas write his autobiography, 176; Plan *Akritas*, 179; possibly connected with Vasilios mass graves, 185; provisional President after July 1974 coup, 191, 192–3, 211; removed from Presidency, 206 trial, 144
San Stefano, Treaty of (1878), 15
Sandys, Duncan (UK Defence Minister), Defence White Paper, 138
'Save the Children', care provision for refugees, 206
Savvides, Manolis, 113, 141 arrested, 141; Grivas and, 113
Scaife, SAC Alan RAF, killed by mine, 172–3
School-teachers Union, 83
schools, EOKA activity, 53, 83
search operations, types used, 57, 58
Selwyn Lloyd, John (UK Foreign Secretary), 172
Seraphim, Elenitsa (EOKA), 106, 143 Larnaca Town Group leader, 143 Paphos Forest fire claims, 106
Sèvres, Treaty (1920), 16
Seychelles Islands, Makarios exiled to, 88–90, 137
Shardlow, Lt (RAMC), 104–5
Shaughnessy, Cpl Paddy MM (1 RUR), action at Liopetri, 167
Shaw, Mr Justice Bernard
  acquits Sampson of murder of Carter

and Thorogood, 144; trial of EOKA murderers, 96–7, 106–7, 143; wounded by gunmen, 106
1 Sherwood Foresters
control of Eastern Zone (Jan 1964), 181
UNFICYP duties, 183
Shilton, Pte Ronnie (1 Leicesters), taken hostage and murdered, 94, 95–6, 134
Shuttleworth, Capt Dennis RE, siege of Afxentiou, 131
Sinclair, Sir George (Deputy Governor), 65
*Siren* (caique), takes Grivas to Khlorakas, 25
Sisklipos, National Guard driven out, 206
ski-ing, X Troop 45 Cdo, 82
Skylloura, 155–7, 207
intercommunal trouble, 155–7; strategic location on road south to Nicosia, 207
Skyways, Hermes airliner attacked, 88, 93
Sloane, WO Francis O'Heagan RAF, murdered on the way to church, 162
Smith, Cpl (2 Royal Inniskilling Fuslrs), 77
Smith, Sgt Alan (1 Gordons), mortally wounded near Morphou, 107–8
Smith, Lt D G (1 Duke of Wellington's), uncovers EOKA hideout, 125–6
Smith, Sqdn Ldr N F RAF, aids Police Sgt Gill, 156
Sofocleos, Neophytes (EOKA)
captured, 143; Harding assassination attempt, 92–3; Marathassa Group leader, 142–3
Sofocleus, Tassos (Guerrilla leader), 84, 107
ambush below St Hilarion Castle, 117–8; attempt to raid Kyrenia Police Station, 113
captured by 2 Para, 117–18
*Soldier* (magazine), 48
1 Somersetshire Light Infantry (1 Somersets), 121, 123
1 South Staffordshire Regiment, 57
arrest of US Consulate bombers, 88; combined army and navy search, 82; curfew control (Nicosia), 100; Mouskas funeral, 80–1; murder mile casualties, 111; Nicosia riots, 60, 83; Operation *Lucky Alphonse*, 101
Soviet Black Sea Fleet, stands by, 192
Soviet Union
supplies arms to Cyprus National Guard, 185–6; *see also* Eastern Bloc
Spaak, Paul-Henri (NATO Secretary-General), 162,
breakthrough in Paris, 172–3
Special Branch (Cyprus Police), 24, 148
arrest of Elias Samaras, 166; arrest of Sampson, 126; arrests in Kato Dhikomo, 171; *Ayios Georghias* intercept, 28–31; EOKA collaborators, 28, 29, 35, 54, 78, 128, 139, 168; fail to connect EOKA, Athens and Makarios, 32; false sense of security, 51; Grivas diaries and EOKA documents found, 98; Head to report to Military Intelligence Chief, 100; informant information, 87; interaction with military intelligence, 100–1, 140; Limassol arms cache uncovered, 51; murder of Brian Dear, 154; recruitment, 24; UK Police Unit and, 100; unprepared for an emergency, 138–9, 212; *see also* Cyprus Police
Special Operations Executive (SOE), in Athens, 18, 28
Spilia, Operation *Fox Hunter*, 78–9
Spyridon, Archbishop of Athens, Cyprus support group, 20
St Hilarion/Mount Hilarion
EOKA ambush, 117–18; reoccupied by Turks, 200; taken and abandoned by National Guard Raider (RFU), 199, 200; Turkish signals station, 196, 199; UNFICYP intervention, 183
St Patrick's Camp (WBSBA), 192
Staff, L/Cpl (2 Para), capture of Tassos Sofocleus, 117–18
Stavros Posokas, Christakis Eleftheriou Group, 84
Stokkos, PC Pavlos, 24
Storrs, Col Sir Ronald (Governor of Cyprus), 16
Straker, Cpl (Royal Horse Guards), intercommunal trouble near Geunyeli, 156, 157–8
*Striker*, HMS (LST), 58
strikes, demanded by Grivas, 147
Strovolos, 57, 147
joint Army/Police cordon-and-search, 57; pipe bomb cace uncovered, 147
students
Grivas encourages Oxi day celebrations/demonstrations, 148–9; pro-*enosis* demonstrations, 53, 83;

provocation of security forces, 65, 83, 139
Stylianides, Stavros (EOKA), 147
Suez Crisis (1956), Cyprus Emergency and, 109, 112, 119, 120–21, 169
1 Suffolk Regiment (1 Suffolks), 121
    capture of Lefka Group, 143; find taxi with murder evidence, 162; leave for UK (1959), 175; Operation *Black Mak*, 124–5; Operation *Blackbird*, 132; Oxi Day riots, 149; sectarian riots, 155; Turkish-Cypriot riots, 152
sunburn and sunstroke, a disciplinary offence, 45
Sutton, Lt Stanley MBE (RAMC/Norfolks M.O.), in Paphos Forest fire, 104
Sweden
    evacuation plans for Swedish nationals in Cyprus (1974), 203; UNFICYP troops, 183, 186, 191, 194
Symon, Pte (1 Gordons), EOKA ambush, 120–21
Syria,
    Yom Kippur War with Israel (1973), 191; *see also* United Arab Republic

Tactical Police Reserve, loyal to Makarios, 190
Tailyour, Lt Col Norman RM, 79
*takism, see* partition
target lists, Sabotage Groups, 35
Task Force Bora, 202
Taylor, Sgt (Royal Horse Guards), intercommunal violence, 156–7
Taylor, Pte Robert (2 Para), capture of Tassos Sofocleus, 117–18
Taylor, Sydney, fired on by EOKA gunman, 77, 95
Templar, Gen Sir Gerald, recommendations, 52
Temple, Maj Guy (1 Glosters), 123–4
*Tenby*, HMS, 160
terrorism
    a definition, 75; White Terror (Greece, 1945), 19
Thoma, Mr (EOKA), 120
Thomas, Pte (Provost Group, 16 Ind Para Bde), 119–20
Thompson, AB Alexander RN, injured in EOKA attack, 54
Thornton, Mne Brian RM, arrests Costas and others, 147

Thorogood, Sgt Cyril (Leicester & Rutland Police), shot by Sampson, 114, 144
*Times of Cyprus* (newspaper), 111, 121
*The Times*, of London, 165
Tipple, Sgt Reginald (Metropolitan Police, UK Police Unit), murdered, 106–7, 146
TMT (Turkish Defence Organization), 147–8, 161
    50 captured by Operation *Matchbox*, 161; importing arms from Turkey, 178; military training in Turkey, 178; truce (Aug 1958), 161–2; weapons cache found in BSB Episkopi, 198; tourists, 198, 203; evacuated by Royal Navy (July 1974), 203; refuge in British Sovereign Base Areas, 198; transport vehicles (army), 41; extra vehicle depots (late 1955), 63; lorries and Cyprus roads, 59–60 vehicle recovery (REME), 41
Travel Control Security Group, 140–41
Treaty of Guarantee for Cyprus Communities (1960), 178, 193, 194
*Trias*, SS (Greek ship), impounded, 77
Trinder, Cpl (1 Duke of Wellington's), 129, 130
Trollope, Lt (1 Suffolks), 124
Troodos Mountains, 13, 14
    EOKA guerrilla groups, 33, 55, 84, 98; military ski-ing, 82; Operation *Black Mak*, 121–2; Operation *Lucky Alphonse*, 101–5; Paphos Forest fire (June 1956), 103–6; search for Grivas (1958), 154; supply drops to snow-bound communities, 86
trooping
    air charters, 88; debarking at Cyprus, 46; RAF Transport Command, 44–5, 68, 85; Shackletons, 85; troopships, 45–6, 85, 121, 132
Trowbridge, Staff Sgt Donald (RS), ambushed by EOKA, 120
Trusler, Asst Police Supt, intercommunal violence, 156–7
Tsardelis, Nicos, death sentence (reprieved) for murder of Sgt Tipple, 146
Turkey
    alarmed by Makarios' Eastern Bloc connections, 188–9; allied with Germany (1914), 15; bargains for two military bases in Cyprus, 186;

# INDEX 249

conditions for constitutional settlement, 206; Cyprus of strategic importance, 56; declares North Cyprus a federated Turkish province, 210; informs Greek Embassy of intention to intervene, 195; international incident over Cyprus National Guard in Kophinou, 187–8; landing force elements (July 1974), 193–4; military advisers landed at Kokkina, 183; representation at London/Paris/Zurich negotiations, 172–3; riots against Greek [commercial] interests, 56; seeks partition in Geneva negotiations (1974), 207; settles 37,000 Anatolian Turks in North Cyprus, 210 surrenders claim to Cyprus at Lausanne (1923), 16; tensions with Greece (1957), 138; Treaty of Sèvres (1920), 16; war with Anatolian Greeks (1919–21), 16; *see also* Ottoman Empire

Turkish Air Force
in action against Cyprus National Guard, 186, 197; friendly fire causes loss of *Kocatepe*, 200–1

Turkish Army
6th Corps launch Operation *Attila Two*, 207–9, 211; 2nd Army Helicopter Regiment, 195; 5th Armoured Brigade, 202; 28th Infantry Division, 202–3, 206–8; 39th Tank Division, 202, 207; 50th Infantry, 199, 202, 208; 61st Infantry Regiment, 206–7; Battle of Kornos (Aug 1974), 206–7; battle for Nicosia Airport, 205; casualties (July–August 1974), 209; Commando Bde, 195–6, 206–7; create Turkish Cypriot Fighters battalions, 183

Turkish Cypriot Fighters
casualties (July–August 1974), 209; fighting along the Green Line (Nicosia), 208; home defence battalions, 183, 185–7; neutralised by National Guard, 203; support for Turkish invasion (July 1974), 194, 197–8

Turkish Intervention (July 1974)
plans for invasion of Cyprus, 193–4; the invasion (July 1974), 195–205; air superiority, 196; justified under Treaty of Guarantee, 211; landings and beachhead near Kyrenia, 196–7, 202–3; Task Force Bora, 202; Turkish casualties, 205

Turkish Intervention, round 2
(July–August 1974), 206–210; Battle of Kornos, 206–7; Operation *Attila Two*, 206–9, 211; UN ceasefire (Aug 1974), 209

Turkish National Contingent
arrive in Cyprus, 177; officer's wife butchered in Kumsal (1963), 180; takes up strategic positions, 180, 183

Turkish Navy
6th Marine Infantry Regiment (July 1974), 196; ship lost to friendly fire, 200–1; on standby (1963), 180; task force off Kyrenia (1964), 186; Turkish Republic of North Cyprus, 210

Turkish-Cypriots, 14
abandon villages as a result of intercommunal violence, 181; appeal for restoration of 1960; Constitution, 183; Auxiliary Police, 56, 99, 155–8; boycott referendum on *enosis*, 19; casualties (July-August 1974), 209; church burnt (Sept 1958), 165; civilian prisoners in Waynes Keep Camp, 47; in Cyprus Police, 21, 56–7, 83, 94, 99, 100, 143, 155; dislike of collective fines, 75; enclaves, 178, 180; EOKA offensive against (July 1958), 160; Harding-Makarios negotiations and, 63, 88; independent admin functions in enclaves, 183; intercommunal violence, 83, 92, 94, 98-9, 148, 152, 155–8, 179–84; murdered by EOKA, 94, 107, 120; no part in Grivas' strategic aims, 32; over-use of veto in Republic legislature, 179; Paphos Forest Fire (June 1956), 103–4, 106; partition (*takism*) of Cyprus called for, 147–8, 152, 207, 211; Police disarmed (Dec 1963), 180; Police Mobile Reserve, 59, 99, 152; Radcliffe's *Proposals for Cyprus*, 122; respond to EOKA intelligence gathering, 147–8; rioting crowds, 152; set up admin system like Repubic of Cyprus, 188; shot by police, 94

Tyllira
National Guard disarm Swedish UNFICYP, 186; Solon Pittarides Group, 84

UK Police Unit, 64, 99–100, 123
casualties of the Emergency, 114, 143,

214; Foot authorises 300 additional police, 160; Special Branch section, 174 *see also* Cyprus Police

UNFICYP
Austrians killed in Turkish air strike, 207–8; Britain abandons RAF Nicosia (July 1974), 200; casualties, 183; ceasefire arranged to permit evacuation of foreign missions, 200; doubles strength to 4,100 men, 206; Finns assist in evacuation of tourists and expats from Kyrenia, 203; help Makarios escape July 1974 coup, 192; initial make up, 182–3; mandate affirmed by Makarios, 188; Nicosia Airport bases, 204–5; patrols Green Line still (2010), 210; rules of engagement, 183, 185, 191; settlement of disputes, 183–5; slimmed down force (1974), 191; troops enter Kokkina, 186; troops sent to intervene between Israel and Arab powers, 187, 191

United Arab Republic, aggressive posture causes military build up in Cyprus, 160–61; *see also* Egypt

United Nations
ceasefire between Greeks and Turks (Aug 1974), 209; ceasefire between Greeks and Turks (July 1974), 205 concerns about Cyprus, 87; decolonization programme, 19; disagreements between Greece and Turkey over Cyprus, 61; EOKA Wormwood Scrubs allegations, 146 Greece brings the Cyprus situation forward (Oct 1956), 120; human rights demands and Cyprus, 210; self-determination for Cyprus debated, 20, 24, 32, 61, 63; United States objects to self-determination, 27, 32

United Nations , Committee on Missing Persons, 210

United Nations Secretary-General, accuses Turkish Cypriots of policy of self-segregation, 186

United Nations Security Council
Cyprus ceasefire (Resolution 353), 199; Cyprus and Turkey argue over grievances, 180–1; UNFICYP established (Resolution 186), 182–3

United States of America
alarmed by Makarios' Eastern Bloc connections, 188–9; attempt to prevent Turkish intervention in Cyprus, 194 concerns about Cyprus, 87; encourages Makarios to recall Grivas, 185; encourages Turkish invasion, 179; evacuation plans for US nationals in Cyprus (1974), 203; Nicosia Consulate attacked by EOKA, 88; objects to self-determination at the UN, 27, 32; prevents full scale war between Greece and Turkey, 188; removal of Makarios and, 194; support for partition, 18; U2 flights over Soviet Union, 188; vetos transfer of Cyprus to Greece, 20; United States Central Intelligence Agency (CIA), 22, 188; interest in Grivas, 22; listening posts in Cyprus, 188

United States Navy, amphibious task force stands by, 192

Vassiliki, 83
Vassilou, Andreas (EOKA), RAF (Akrotiri) bombs, 150
Vietnam, *see* French Indo-China
Visalia, sectarian violence, 92
*Volkan* (Turkish-Cypriot group), 61
Vroisia district, Paphos Forest fire (June 1956), 103–6

Walker, Lt Jim (1 Leicesters), 93
Walker, Mne David RM BEM, 81
Wallace, Capt A.W.C. RM, Paphos Forest fire, 104
Warsaw Pact *see* Eastern Bloc
Waters, Gen Sir John (Glosters), 213
Watkins, Pte Ray (1 Warwicks), 111
Wayne's Keep Camp, 27, 40
19 Command Postal Depot (RE), 48; military cemetery, 46, 213; 52 Military Corrective Training Centre, 46–7;
weapons and explosives
ammunition transferred from Egypt, 64; British adopt 7.62mm SLR, 118; caches, 26–7, 51, 77, 93, 102, 121, 125–6, 132, 147, 151, 166, 172, 198; Cyprus National Guard firepower, 189–90; guerrilla groups, 34; IEDs, 115–6; improvised mortars, 115–6, 117; Makarios orders that unauthorised weapons be handed in, 188; mines, 60, 115–16; naval boarding parties, 30–1;

new types of explosives, 162; Operation *Handover*, EOKA weapons handed in, 175; personal weapons (British expats), 170–1; personal weapons (Service personnel), 48, 75; problems of quality, 27; recovered from Italian sunken ships, 32, 115; sabotage groups, 35; smuggled into Cyprus, 21, 22, 24–6, 38, 85, 141; sources of dynamite and detonators, 37, 115; supply and distribution (EOKA), 37; thefts from Police Stations, 55–6, 60, 63, 82–3, 85; training, 26

Webb, Sgt William (Worcestershire Police, UK Police Unit),
shot by Sampson, 114, 144; witness at Sampson trial, 144; websites, Britain's Small Wars, 214

Welch, L/Cpl Peter (KRRC) (Harding's orderly), 93

Wellesley, Brig Arthur Valerian, 8th Duke of Wellington, 213

West Germany, reaction to Mrs Cutliffe's murder, 165

Wheeler, Lt Col Thomas (1 RUR) 165, 167
action at Liopetri, 167; compensation offered to shopkeeper, 165

Wheeler, WO1 Mark RM, 87

White, Lt Col Geoffrey (Chief Constable, Warwickshire Police)
advice on policing, 66; becomes Commissioner of Police, 99; Oxi Day restrictions relaxed, 149

White, Provost L/Cpl (WRAC), 119–20

Willis, A.S. (Cyprus Police), faces Turkish-Cypriot mob, 94

Wilson, DS (Special Branch), subterfuge concerning Grivas' location, 174

Wilson, Surg Capt Gordon (Royal Horse Guards M.O.), shot by Sampson, 114

Wiltshire Regiment (1 Wilts), 85–6, 90
in action near Morphou, 107–8; corners Matsis at Kato Dhikomo, 171–2

Wingate, Maj Gen Orde, Chindits, 40

Wintle, Capt Arthur (Royals), at the French Staff College, 17

Wolseley, General Sir Garnet, 15

Wolseley Barracks (Nicosia), 27, 40, 52, 57, 68

women
accomplices to EOKA gunmen, 111, 112, 126, 139; army/Service wives, 51, 53, 56, 78, 82, 88–9, 97, 100, 111, 114, 120–1, 164, 192–3, 198, 203; in British forces, 43, 57, 87, 119–20; Kumsal massacre, 180; used by EOKA, 36–7, 107, 111–3, 122, 126, 139, 146, 173

Women's Royal Army Corps (WRAC), 57
attached to RMP, 87, 119–20

Woods, Pte Sydney (1 Suffolks), ambush Drakos, 124–5

World War II
Cyprus and, 16, 42; RAF Nicosia, 42; sunken Italian ships, 32

Xapolitos, Mr (EOKA), 120

Xapolitos, Mrs (EOKA suspect), 119–20

Xenophontos, Nicos (EOKA), death sentence commuted, 107

Xeros Camp, 47

Xhi (X right-wing resistance group), Grivas and, 17–19

Xylophagen, amphibious raid (joint RM and RE), 58

Yakoumis, Andreas (EOKA), Sgt Hammond and the film *Exodus*, 161

Yerolakkos,
intercommunal trouble, 155–8; overrun by Turkish 50th Infantry, 208

Yerolakkos Police Station, Sgt Gill (UK Police Unit), 155

Yialousa Police Station, EOKA attacks, 81, 170

Yiangou, Andreas (EOKA courier), 36–7

Young, Maj Gen Peter (1/c Truce Force), 180–81

Young, Pte Raymond (1 Leicesters), capture of Lysi EOKA, 127

Zafiriou, Pte Athanasios, survivor of

We hope you have enjoyed reading this Pen and Sword Book. We have over 2000 other titles available, which can be obtained from most good bookshops or via our website: pen-and-sword.co.uk.

We also value your feedback and would encourage you to leave this on relevant forums related to this book, retailer websites or our own website. We check these regularly and encourage authors to check forums to respond to any questions.

\* \* \* \*

*Other titles from Nick van der Bijl and Pen & Sword*

## 5th Infantry Brigade in the Falklands War

9781783462636, RRP £12.99

No-one can complain that the Falklands' War has been neglected by authors and publishers. Countless books have been published, covering this mercifully brief and successful campaign over the intervening 30 years.

It is all the more remarkable that Nicholas van der Bijl and David Aldea should at this late stage unearth a central subject that has been overlooked, namely the role played by the British 5th Infantry Brigade.

The decision to send 5 Brigade was taken some time after 3 Commando Brigade had been despatched with, as bad luck would have it, many of 5 Brigade's own units. This in itself caused tensions within and without the Brigade and these were exacerbated by its hasty reconstitution and all too brief training prior to the long voyage south on the Cunard Liner Queen Elizabeth II and other vessels.

With the military and media spotlight firmly fixed on 3 Commando Brigade, the 'other brigade' made up principally of two Guards battalions, fresh from ceremonial duties, and a battalion of Gurkhas inevitably felt neglected. Yet their moment was to come in both glorious and tragic circumstances and, by the close of the hostilities, the Brigade had certainly made its mark, despite the many handicaps under which it had to operate.

Yet the drama and controversy were not over. For reasons that have long mystified many observers, the Brigade Commander was conspicuously overlooked in the post-war distribution of medals and awards.

This book is mandatory reading for all those who wish to understand a fascinating aspect of one of the most extraordinary military ventures in Britain's long martial history.

# Confrontation - The War With Indonesia 1962 – 1966

9781783030187, RRP £14.99

For over four years in the 'Swinging Sixties' the armed forces of the UK were engaged in a little publicised but crucial jungle war on the vast island of Borneo.

At any one time up to 15,000 Commonwealth troops were deployed along a 1,000 mile front. Their enemy were the communist-led Indonesians whose leaders were determined to seize the fledgling states of Sarawak, Sabah and the oil rich Brunei, all of whom for their part wished to maintain their Commonwealth links.

The catalyst for the war was the 1962 uprising in Brunei which was quickly crushed by the bold intervention of British army units.

The arrival of Major General Walter Walker, himself a controversial figure, gave the subsequent campaign a clear direction. Indonesian incursions were rigorously defended and ruthlessly pursued. Top Secret 'Claret' operations took the fight to the enemy with cross-border operations initially using Special Forces and later with Chindit-style long range jungle patrols. The outcome was a text book military victory thus avoiding a British 'Vietnam' debacle.

*Confrontation – The War with Indonesia 1962 – 1966* is a long overdue account of this major British-led campaign which has been inexplicably neglected by historians. The author, himself a former soldier, provides a thorough analysis of the politics involved as well as the military strategy and tactics employed. Thanks to extensive research and interviews with veterans, there are fascinating accounts of actions and the conditions endured.

'The 280-page book recounts the major British-led campaign which until now has been neglected from history...The book tells of the war and the offences, defences and skirmishes buts its skill is in detailing the history and politics with interviews and accounts of actions from veterans. There is also a black-and-white photograph section which gives the reader a better feel of the conditions soldiers endured and the weapons and vehicles used.' (*The Burnham and Highbridge Times*)

'This is the first full length book that I know of which covers the war with Indonesia between 1962 and 1966...Nicholas Van der Bijl has...used his wide knowledge of military security and intelligence from his time in the British Army to produce this book on the little known war...The book is clearly well researched and comprehensive in its scope...this is a serious book for serious military enthusiasts...Confrontation is the story of a war at a time when few people in this country knew they were at war. Until this book, it had been almost entirely forgotten.' (KJF, *War Books Out Now*)

# Operation Banner

9781844159567, RRP £19.99

Operation BANNER, as the military involvement in Northern Ireland was officially called, dominated life for generations of officers and other ranks for almost 40 years. Yet, until this book, there has been no accessible account of the British Army's controversial campaign in support of the civil power.

After setting the historic backdrop, the author describes the course of the campaign. In summer 1969 the annual Loyalist marching season sparked violence in Londonderry which spread rapidly. After three days of violence the British Government deployed troops in support of the Royal Ulster Constabulary. Initially the Catholic community welcomed the Army's presence but this was not to last. The first soldier was killed in 1971 and a further 48 died that year. The events of Bloody Sunday, 30 January, 1972, galvanised IRA recruitment and the British Embassy was burnt in Dublin. The Official IRA bombed the Aldershot HQ of the Parachute Regiment and, in August 1972, the Army launched Operation MOTOR-MAN to clear 'No Go' areas in Londenderry. Internment followed and by now the Province was firmly in a spiral of sectarian violence. The next 30 years saw a remorseless counter-terrorist campaign which deeply affected not just the lives of Northern Irish people but the image of Britain in the eyes of the world.

After ten years of the Peace Process, the campaign formerly ended in 2007 with the establishment of power-sharing. Hopefully this sad chapter of British history is now closed for good. The time is right for an account of the British Army's contribution to peace. No claim is made that this is a definitive study but it provides a valuable overview as well as an informed insight into intelligence and SF operations.


'This book takes a chronological approach to the 'Troubles'...[and] records almost on a day-to-day basis all the important incidents of conflict throughout the province...The 16 pages of monochrome photographs are very revealing, with detailed captioning...this book puts the the military events of Operation Banner into an historical perspective. As such, it is well worth the cover price.' (*Medal News*)

'For anyone wanting a sharp account of when and where things happened, this is like cut glass. Facts are noted with all the attention to detail of a parade inspection.' (*Defence Focus Magazine*)

'After setting the historic backdrop to Banner, the author details the course of the campaign, from the start during the marching season of 1969 through the events of Bloody Sunday and up to the peace enjoyed today.' (*Great War Magazine*)

# Victory in the Falklands
## 1962 – 1966

9781844154944, RRP £19.99

The hundred days of Spring 1982 that witnessed the robust British response to General Galtiere of Argentina's invasion of the Falkland Islands are for many the most remarkable of their lives. The anger of seeing foreign troops on British soil; the anxious waiting as the Task Force headed South; the shock of the loss of ships, aircraft and life; and, finally, elation over a stunning and complete victory. All these emotions and more were experienced by a nation unfamiliar with war.

Almost 30 years on, it is important to remember with pride the achievements of our Armed Forces so far from home. While there are many books on the War, Victory in the Falklands stands out as a superb overview of the conflict, covering all the military phases, be they land, sea or air, as well as the political context and manoeuvrings. The copious use of first-hand accounts brings an immediacy to the story and we gain a real impression of what it felt to be part of the tri-service team that won so great a prize.

Written by one who was there, this is the book to read for a clear understanding of what was achieved and how. What becomes abundantly clear is the narrow margin between victory and defeat. Without the determination and resilience of all involved from Prime Minister Margaret Thatcher down to the soldier on the ground, the outcome could so easily have been very different. *Victory in the Falklands* is a stirring story, which will revive many a memory for some and give a greater understanding for others.

'*Victory in the Falklands* stands out as a superb overview of conflict, covering all the military phases, by land, sea or air, as well as the political context and manoeuvrings. The copious use of first-hand accounts brings an immediacy to the story and we gain a real impression of what it felt to be part of the tri-service team that won so great a prize. Written by one who was there, this is the book to read for a clear understanding of what was achieved and how.' (*The Officer*)

'As an Army officer, the author took part in the liberation of the Falklands in 1982 and his stirring account is another important story of that momentous enterprise.' (*Pennant*)

'Nick van der Bijl's book recounts the whole story, from the political incidents leading up to the Argentinean invasion of the Falkland Islands and South Georgia to the final surrender in Port Stanley one hundred days later. He manages to encompass the achievements of all three British services and their role in the victory as well as those of the enemy...I found the book to be an easy and informative read; a good description of a fascinating conflict.' (KJF, *Wot's Out now?*)

## Commandos in Exile:
## The Story of 10 (Inter-Allied) Commando
## 1942-1945

9781844157907, RRP £19.99

*Commandos in Exile* is the story of one of the least known and most unusual units in the Second World War.

This Commando comprised members of French, Dutch, Belgian, Norwegian, Polish and Yugoslav Free Forces who had escaped from German occupation. All members of this multi-national Commando had to pass the Green Beret commando course at Achnacarry in Scotland and the book begins by describing this training. In addition to the six national contingents, the author reveals that there was a secret additional troop, drawn mainly from East European Jews who had either been exiled or had escaped Nazi occupation and persecution.

10 Commando never fought as an entity but loaned troops for specific operations relevant to their origins. For example One Troop (French) took part in the Dieppe Raid, 2 Troop (Dutch) fought at Arnhem and 5 Troop (Norwegian) raided the Lofoten Islands. At other times members played key intelligence roles questioning POWs, translating captured documents, conducting reconnaissance patrols and gathering intelligence on the D-Day beaches.

National troops became the nucleus for their nations' post-war Commando forces and the book reviews the evolution of national Commando forces post-war.

With its full accounts of 10 (Inter-Allied) Commando's action and intelligence operations, *Commandos in Exile* is a fascinating and revealing read.

---

For more information or to order any of the above titles, please contact:

PEN & SWORD BOOKS LTD
Freepost
47 Church Street, Barnsley
South Yorkshire, S70 2AS

Email: enquiries@pen-and-sword.co.uk
Tel: 01226 734555
Or visit our website at:
www.pen-and-sword.co.uk

## OVER 2000 TITLES AVAILABLE